# A COMPANION TO JULIAN OF NORWICH

St Julian's Church, Norwich, showing the reconstructed anchorhold on the south side of the church.

# A COMPANION TO
# JULIAN OF NORWICH

Edited by
Liz Herbert McAvoy

D. S. BREWER

First published 2008
D. S. Brewer, Cambridge
Paperback edition 2015


ISBN 978 1 84384 172 2 hardback
ISBN 978 1 84384 404 4 paperback


D. S. Brewer is an imprint of Boydell & Brewer Ltd
PO Box 9, Woodbridge, Suffolk IP12 3DF, UK
and of Boydell & Brewer Inc.
668 Mt Hope Avenue, Rochester, NY 14620–2731, USA
website: www.boydellandbrewer.com


A CIP catalogue record for this book is available
from the British Library


This publication is printed on acid-free paper

# Contents

# List of Illustrations

Frontispiece: St Julian's Church, Norwich. The Churches of East Anglia: Norfolk Churches Site. http://www.norfolkchurches.co.uk/

# List of Contributors

**Denise N. Baker** a Professor of English at the University of North Carolina at Greensboro, is author of *Julian of Norwich's* Showings: *From Vision to Book* and editor of *Inscribing the Hundred Years' War in French and English Cultures* and *The Showings of Julian of Norwich: A Norton Critical Edition*. She has published widely on the Middle English mystics, Gower, Langland and Chaucer.

**Alexandra Barratt** is Professor in the Department of Humanities, University of Waikato, New Zealand. She has published widely on Middle English women writers, in particular Julian of Norwich and Dame Eleanor Hull, and on anchoritic writing. She is currently working on a study of MS Harley 494, to be published by Brepols as *Anne Bulkeley and Her Book: Fashioning Female Piety in Early Tudor England*.

**Marleen Cré** is an associated researcher at the Ruusbroechenootschap, University of Antwerpen. She has published on the two fifteenth-century manuscripts containing Julian of Norwich material: Westminster Cathedral Treasury MS 4 and London, British Library, MS Additional 37790 (Amherst). Her monograph on the latter, *Vernacular Mysticism in the Charterhouse*, was published by Brepols in 2006. She is currently researching a study of Benet of Canfield, Augustine Baker and Gertrude More.

**Elisabeth Dutton** is Senior Research Fellow at Worcester College, Oxford. She has published on the medieval mystical writers Hadewijch and Julian of Norwich, and on the late-medieval compilation *Book to a Mother*. She has also published an edition of Julian's *Revelation of Love* (Plymouth, 2008) and her monograph on Julian, *The Influence of Late-Medieval Devotional Compilations* is forthcoming (Cambridge: D.S. Brewer, 2008).

**Vincent Gillespie** is J. R. R. Tolkien Professor of English Literature and Language at the University of Oxford and a Fellow of Lady Margaret Hall. He publishes on medieval mystical writing (especially Julian of Norwich), the circulation and transmission of religious, devotional and para-mystical texts, and the history of the Carthusians and Birgittines in England. His annotated edition of the *registrum* of the library of the brethren at Syon Abbey was published in 2002, and a selection of his papers will soon be published by the University of Wales Press as *Looking in Holy Books: Essays on Late Medieval Religious Texts*.

**Cate Gunn**'s Ph.D. thesis on the rhetoric of *Ancrene Wisse* has recently been revised as a book entitled *Vernacular Spirituality in the Thirteenth Century: The Pastoral Context of* Ancrene Wisse (Cardiff: University of Wales Press, 2008). She has published several articles and essays on vernacular spirituality and has taught medieval literature and religion for the Continuing Education departments of Essex and Cambridge Universities and for the WEA.

**Ena Jenkins** has recently been awarded an M.Phil. for her thesis on the poetics of Julian of Norwich from the University of Wales, Lampeter. A retired schoolteacher, she has been an active researcher in the area of Julian Studies for many years and has also written and lectured extensively on female mystics, both medieval and modern. She has presented on the links between Julian and Annie Dillard and also has a teaching and research interest in the area of Evelyn Underhill.

**E. A. Jones** is Senior Lecturer in Medieval English Literature and Culture at the University of Exeter. He works on the devotional and contemplative literature of the late Middle Ages, and the history and literature of the solitary vocations in medieval England. He is, in succession to Marion Glasscoe, the organiser and editor of the Exeter Symposium on the Medieval Mystical Tradition; volume VII was published in 2004. He has also assumed responsibility for completing the revision of Rotha Clay's *Hermits and Anchorites of England*.

**Liz Herbert McAvoy** is Senior Lecturer in Gender in English Studies and Medieval literature at Swansea University. She has published widely in the area of medieval women's literature and anchoritism, including *Authority and the Female Body in the Writings of Julian of Norwich and Margery Kempe* (Cambridge: D. S. Brewer, 2004). She has also edited a number of volumes, including (with Mari Hughes-Edwards) *Anchorites, Wombs and Tombs: Intersections of Gender and Enclosure in the Middle Ages* (Cardiff: University of Wales Press, 2005) and *Rhetoric of the Anchorhold* (Cardiff: University of Wales Press, 2008) and is currently working on a book focusing on issues of gender, space and enclosure in texts by, for and about anchorites.

**Laura Saetveit Miles** is a doctoral candidate in English at Yale University, with an M.Phil in Medieval Studies from Yale and an M.Phil in Medieval English Literature from Cambridge University. She is working on a study of the Annunciation scene in Middle English literature. Her research interests include the Bridgettine Order, texts and scribes at Syon Abbey, mystical texts and translation, and Carthusian spirituality.

**Kim M. Phillips** is Senior Lecturer in History at the University of Auckland. She has published widely on women in medieval Europe, especially in England *c.*1100–1550. Her research interests include women's and gender history, youth, life cycle, family, sexuality and the body, and her publications include *Medieval Maidens: Young Women and Gender in England, 1270–1540* (Manchester: Manchester University Press, 2003), (as editor with Katherine J. Lewis and Noel James Menuge), *Young Medieval Women* (Stroud: Sutton, 1999), and (as editor with Barry Reay), *Sexualities in History: A Reader* (New York: Routledge, 2002). She is currently working on a book on representations of the Far East in later medieval travel writing.

**Elizabeth Robertson** is Professor of English at the University of Colorado at Boulder. Co-founder of the Medieval Feminist Newsletter (now Medieval Feminist Forum) and the Society for Medieval Feminist Scholarship, she has published widely on the topic of women and religion in medieval English literature in collections of essays, and in *Speculum* and *Studies in the Age of Chaucer*. She is the author of a book on anchoritic literature, *Early English Devotional Prose and the Female Audience* and, forthcoming, a book entitled *Chaucerian Consent: Women, Religion and Subjection in late Medieval England*. She is co-editor of the Norton Critical Edition of Piers Plowman, the TEAMS edition of Bodley 34, Chaucer's Religious Tales, and *Representing Rape in Medieval English Literature*.

**Sarah Salih** is Senior Lecturer in Medieval Literature at King's College London. Her research interests include gender, subjectivity and sexuality; East Anglian culture; interactions between literature and the visual arts; and medievalisms. She is the author of *Versions of Virginity in Late Medieval England* (Cambridge: D. S. Brewer, 2001), co-editor of *Gender and Holiness* (London: Routledge, 2002) and *Medieval Virginities* (Cardiff: University of Wales Press, 2003) and editor of *A Companion to Middle English Hagiography* (Cambridge: D. S. Brewer, 2006). She is currently researching a study of paganity in medieval East Anglian writing, and co-editing with Denise Baker a collection of essays on the post-medieval reception of Julian of Norwich.

**Annie Sutherland** is a fellow of Somerville College, Oxford and a University lecturer in Old and Middle English. She has published various articles on medieval devotional literature, and is currently working on Middle English translations of the psalms.

**Diane Watt** is Professor of English at Aberystwyth University. She is the author of *Secretaries of God: Women Prophets in Late Medieval and Early Modern England* (Cambridge: D. S. Brewer, 1997), *Amoral Gower: Language, Sex, and Politics in Confessio Amantis* (Minneapolis: University of Minnesota Press, 2003) and *Medieval Women's Writing: Works By and For Women in England, 1100–1500* (Cambridge: Polity Press, 2007). She has also edited several volumes and has published widely on women's literature and spirituality in the Middle Ages and on Gower.

**Barry Windeatt** is Professor of English in the University of Cambridge and a Fellow of Emmanuel College. He has translated *The Book of Margery Kempe* (Harmondsworth: Penguin, 1985), edited the original (London: Longman, 2000; reprinted D.S. Brewer, 2004), edited an anthology, *English Mystics of the Middle Ages* (Cambridge: Cambridge University Press, 1994), and has published a number of articles on Julian of Norwich, on Margery Kempe and on Westminster Cathedral Treasury MS 4. His edition of Julian of Norwich is forthcoming from Oxford University Press.

# *Acknowledgements*

This volume has been several years in the making and my thanks are due first and foremost to all of its contributors, whose readiness to become involved with the project created a vibrant and cohesive group dynamic from the outset. I am particularly grateful for the enthusiasm with which they agreed to contribute and which they continued to generate throughout the lengthy editing process. Thanks too for their patient cooperation in the face of my requests for revision, elision and reduction, cutting, pruning and redaction. Special thanks go to Laura Saetveit Miles and Elizabeth Robertson for stepping into the breach at very short notice following the withdrawal of two of the original contributors. They produced two very fine essays in an unreasonably short space of time, and with great professionalism and aplomb. I am also indebted to Caroline Palmer at Boydell and Brewer for first mooting the project to me over coffee some years ago – and then for having faith that it would come to timely fruition, in spite of the various delays and setbacks it has incurred since then. Finally, my gratitude, as ever, goes to my family, who have spent yet another summer plying me with coffee as I edit out commas and add semi-colons. Their continued interest in and support of my academic endeavours have made all the difference.

# *Abbreviations*

CCCM      Corpus Christianorum Continuatio Mediaevalis
EETS      Early English Text Society
e.s.      Extra Series
MED       Middle English Dictionary
n.s.      New Series
o.s.      Original Series
PG        *Patrologia Graeca*, ed. J.-P. Migne (Paris, 1887)
PL        *Patrologia Latina*, ed. J.-P. Migne (Paris, 1841–64)
PL and P  *Paston Letters and Papers of the Fifteenth Century*, ed. Norman Davis,
          2 vols (Oxford: Clarendon, 1971–6)
PUS       Presses Universitaires de Strasbourg
TEAMS     Consortium for the Teaching of the Middle Ages
VCH       *Victoria County History*

# Introduction: 'God forbede … that I am a techere': Who, or what, was Julian?

> The curtain against which Wanton Kate's face was pressing suddenly ceased to yield. There was a face on the other side and the anchoress was kissing her through the white linen cross.[1]

The above quotation, taken from a 1934 novel by Enid Dinnis, the main character of which is based loosely on the figure of Julian of Norwich, speaks volumes for the 'industry' of imaginative projection which Julian has become during the course of the last century or so. The very fact that this now obscure novel reached its sixth imprint in 1934 attests to its contemporary popularity and to a burgeoning fascination with Julian and the anchoritic life which she embraced. Since that time, Julian has become an increasingly familiar figure within both literary and non-literary circles, and both religious and non-religious milieux. Interpreted famously as 'a woman of our day',[2] and as being of particular comfort to the more worldly woman (such as 'Wanton Kate' in Dinnis' novel), Julian's spirituality has spanned the centuries since her revelatory experiences of May 1373, which she proceeded to document and rework into two texts over the course of her long life.[3] Moreover, these texts appear to speak just as cogently, relevantly and urgently to a modern (and, indeed, postmodern) audience as they must have done to those of her late-medieval contemporaries who had access to them. Julian's importance as a religious figure, if not a writer, seems to have been constant since the time of her own enclosure as an anchoress in 1393, surviving into the Reformation among the recusant nuns of northern France, enduring well into the Victorian era and reaching its present crescendo during the course of the twentieth century and beyond.

But what is it about the figure of Julian which has brought about such an extraordinary longevity of attraction and interest – even amongst readers who otherwise have little familiarity with the writers of the later Middle Ages? Is it,

---

[1]   Enid Dinnis, *The Anchorhold: A Divine Comedy* (London, 1934). I am most grateful to Ena Jenkins for alerting me to this novel, and to the nuns of the Anglican convent of Ty Mawr in Monmouthshire for their generous loan of the book.

[2]   Michael McLean, 'Introduction', in *Julian: Woman of our Day*, ed. Robert Llewelyn (London, 1985), pp. 1–10 (2).

[3]   Although, as several of the contributors point out in this present volume, there could have been various interim versions of Julian's texts which simply have not survived.

perhaps, that her writing embodies an almost unique female voice emerging
from the conglomeration of male-authored texts which proliferated during the
period and continued to dominate into modern times? Or is it that her writing
intersected with a particular moment within English literary history which saw
an inexorable spread of theological vernacularity and the haemorrhaging of
widespread literacy into the laity? Does it merely reflect on the part of increasingly frenetic societies a perennial fascination with the solitary, reclusive vocation upon which Julian embarked mid-way through her life? Or is it the result
of a deeply embedded desire on the part of humanity for a comforting universal
mother-figure, a perennial archetype who has been defined more recently by
Julia Kristeva as 'the reassuring wrapping … the proverbial mirage … the more
or less discreet cult of the Mother',[4] and within which fetishistic desire-cycle the
female martyrs, saints and the Virgin herself also play a major part? Conversely,
perhaps Julian's current popularity is merely evidence of a 'quick-fix' confessional culture which demands the type of instant pleasure and constant grati-
fication so widely analysed by contemporary cultural theorists. The answer in
each case is probably 'yes – and no', since Julian of Norwich, as much in her
own day as now, seems to evade both definitive categorization and knowing.
The more widespread her renown, the more we try to pin her down, the more
of an enigma she seems to remain.

    The concrete 'facts' of Julian's life are scant: evidence internal to the texts she
produced point towards her having been born in 1342–3 but we are unsure as to
where that event took place, although her most recent editors, Nicholas Watson
and Jacqueline Jenkins, hazard that she grew up in or around Norwich and
that she was from a privileged and affluent background.[5] Both texts corroborate that she was in her thirty-first year when a dangerous illness overcame her
– one that she appears to have longed for in her youth – precipitating a series
of sixteen 'showings' or visions which gave her a range of mystical insights into
God's love for humankind and the reciprocity of that bond. Internal evidence
also corroborates that these visions precipitated an initial written text, which
Watson and Jenkins entitle *A Vision Showed to a Devout Woman* (based on the
incipit to the only surviving version of this text in London, British Library MS
Additional 37790),[6] in which Julian records her remarkable experiences and her
initial responses to them. Moreover, these initial responses reveal a tentativeness
and anxiety about her sex and gender, the purpose and meaning of her showings and, in particular, what she was supposed to do with them – and how:

> Botte God forbede that ye shulde saye or take it so that I am a techere. For I meene
> nought so, no I mente nevere so. For I am a woman, lewed febille, and freylle.
> Botte I wate wele, this that I saye I hafe it of the shewinge of him that es soverayne

4   Julia Kristeva, 'Stabat Mater', in *The Kristeva Reader*, ed. Toril Moi (New York, 1986, various
repr.), pp. 160–86 (76–7).
5   *The Writings of Julian of Norwich: A Vision Showed to a Devout Woman and A Revelation
of Love*, ed. Nicholas Watson and Jacqueline Jenkins (Turnhout, 2006), p. 4. Unless otherwise
stated, all quotations will be from this edition, both in this introduction and elsewhere.
6   'Here es a vision, shewed be the goodenes of God to a devoute woman. And hir name
es Julian, that is recluse atte Norwich and yit is on life, anno domini 1413'. See *Writings*, ed.
Watson and Jenkins, p. 63.

techare. Botte sotherlye charite stirres me to tell yowe it. For I wolde God ware knawen and min evencristene spede, as I wolde be myselfe, to the mare hatinge of sinne and lovinge of God. Botte for I am a woman shulde I therefore leve that I shulde nought telle yowe the goodenes of God, sine that I sawe in that same time that it is his wille that it be knawen? (*Vision*, 6.35–42)

This defensive *apologia*, however, with its overly assertive tone and protective rhetorical questioning, was wholly excised by Julian from the later version of her experiences, pointing towards various stages, perhaps even perpetual stages, of revision and reworking as the writer, her confidence and her exegetical abilities matured. In any case, towards the end of *A Vision*, following what seems to be a false peroration of 'Amen par charite' (*Vision*, 23.31),[7] Julian appears to have returned to her conclusion to add a series of questions to be addressed in the redraft which was to become the Long Text, *A Revelation of Love*: 'Whate er we', she demands, 'Whate is alle in erthe that twines us?' (*Vision*, 23.36, 39). More explicitly, perhaps, this added-on section states:

For the bodely sight, I haffe saide as I sawe, als trewlye as I can. And for the wordes fourmed, I hafe saide tham right as oure lorde shewed me thame. And for the gastely sight, I hafe saide somdele, bot I maye never fully telle it. And therefore of this gastely sight I am stirred to say more, as God wille gife me grace.
(*Vision*, 23.51–5)

Thus, on completion of the first text, Julian seems to have immediately embarked upon a new version ('I am stirred to say more') based on new insights and understanding which were clearly advanced by two further visionary insights, one in 1388 and the other in 1393, which she recalls in Chapters 51 and 86 of this new version.[8] Both of these secondary visions seem also to have illuminated for her the meaning of the entire series of original visions and the mystical knowledge to which they had rendered her privy; ultimately, Julian was led to conclude that 'love was [God's] mening' (*Revelation*, 86.14). For Julian, this becomes a universal truism which clarifies the extraordinary complexity of God's assurance to her during her initial experiences that 'alle shalle be wele, and alle maner of thing shalle be wele' (*Revelation*, 27.28–9), especially in the face of the ubiquitous evidence to the contrary which she finds within human sinfulness. This edict, of course, forms the core of the reassuring theology for which, perhaps, Julian is still best known and radiates out to form the primary exegetical structure of both texts.

The setting in which Julian experienced all her visionary encounters, both primary and subsidiary, is, again, indeterminate and the facts tantalizingly few. According to her first account, her mystical experiences began whilst she lay desperately ill and suffering in some kind of room – a 'chamber' – which was also populated by a number of other people, including a priest, a child and Julian's own mother. Whether this priest was Julian's confessor or another ecclesiastic,

---

[7]   This is a commonly used peroration appearing at the end of many medieval texts and suggests that Julian had initially intended to end *A Vision* at this point.
[8]   '[F]ifteen yere after [the first experience] and mor' (*Revelation*, 86.12); 'twenty yere after the time of the shewing, save thre monthes' (*Revelation*, 51.73).

whether this child was an acolyte or a family member, whether Julian's mother
was her natural mother or a mother superior, all remain unclear and open to
surmise. This indeterminacy has led to intense speculation by both scholars and
readers as to whether Julian was a nun or a laywoman at the time of her illness,
whether she was unmarried, a widow, or a wife and mother – and the arguments for and against her status as professed religious are cyclical. In the 1970s,
for example, her editors, Edmund Colledge and James Walsh presumed upon
her having been a nun, stating 'the most probable [conjecture] (at which she
seems herself in several places to hint) is that when young – that is, in her teens
– she entered a religious house, and that she was still there after February 1393,
when she was in her fiftieth year'.[9] Marion Glasscoe, however, editing Julian's
Long Text in 1976, remained unconvinced on this issue, stating 'there are no
grounds for supposing that she was herself a Benedictine nun'.[10] Subsequent to
Glasscoe's edition, a pivotal essay by Benedicta Ward added considerably to the
growing debate, precipitating a protracted re-appraisal of Julian's background,
her writing and her theology.[11] Ward's 'Julian the Solitary' drew seductively upon
overt and covert evidence, both internal and external (and, perhaps on occasion,
circumstantial), to postulate that Julian had been both wife and mother at the
time of her visionary experiences, possibly even widowed and deprived of a
child during the Black Death of the mid century.[12] Whilst Glasscoe's response to
this suggestion was that it was 'not very fruitful',[13] the possibilities of this alternative environment as prompt for re-examination of Julian's writing inspired a
number of commentators, myself included, to read her texts from a variety of
new perspectives, not least in an attempt to demythologize Julian and reinstate
her both as writer and as highly gendered subject.[14] Such a reappraisal was also
fuelled by Nicholas Watson's 1993 revision of the accepted dates of composition of both texts.[15] Prior to Watson's reassessment, it had been assumed that
Julian's Short Text, *A Vision Showed to a Devout Woman*, was an early and relatively unformed response to her experiences; the Long Text, *A Revelation of Love*,

[9]   *A Book of Showings to the Anchoress Julian of Norwich*, ed. Edmund Colledge and James Walsh,
2 vols (Toronto, 1978), vol. 1, p. 43. For a fuller appraisal by these editors of Julian's likely status
as a nun see Edmund Colledge and James Walsh, 'Editing Julian of Norwich's *Revelations*: A
Progress Report', *Medieval Studies* 39 (1976), pp. 404–27.
[10]  Marion Glasscoe, 'Introduction', in *Julian of Norwich: A Revelation of Love*, ed. Marion Glasscoe
(Exeter, 1976; various repr.), pp. vii–xvii (vii).
[11]  Benedicta Ward, 'Julian the Solitary', in Ken Leech and Benedicta Ward, *Julian the Solitary*
(Oxford, 1988), pp. 11–35.
[12]  Ibid., pp. 24–5.
[13]  Marion Glasscoe, *English Medieval Mystics: Games of Faith* (London, 1993), p. 24.
[14]  See, in particular, Elizabeth Robertson, 'Medieval Medical Views of Women and Female
Spirituality in the *Ancrene Wisse* and Julian of Norwich's *Showings*', in *Feminist Approaches to
the Body in Medieval Literature*, ed. Linda Lomperis and Sarah Stanbury (Philadelphia, 1993),
pp. 142–67; Alexandra Barratt, ' "In the Lowest Part of Our Need": Julian and Medieval Gynecological Writing', in *Julian of Norwich: A Book of Essays*, ed. Sandra J. McEntire (New York and
London, 1998), pp. 239–56; Liz Herbert McAvoy, *Authority and the Female Body in the Writing of
Julian of Norwich and The Book of Margery Kempe* (Cambridge, 2004). And, more recently, Diane
Watt, 'Julian of Norwich', in Diane Watt, *Medieval Women's Writing: Works By and For Women in
England, 1100–1500* (Cambridge, 2007). Here, Watt posits the possibility that Julian may have
been in service in another family.
[15]  Nicholas Watson, 'The Composition of Julian of Norwich's *Revelation of Love*', *Speculum* 68
(1993), pp. 637–83.

was understood as the result of a reworking of this text twenty or so years later.
Watson, however, argued for a much later date for the Short Text, and for the
Long Text as being a work which occupied Julian for much of the rest of her life
up until her death sometime after 1416, a text which was begun as soon as the
Short Text was completed. As a result of Watson's reassessment, then, Julian's
writing took on a new impetus within late twentieth-century scholarship as the
likely life-work of a lay-woman-turned-anchoress spanning the end of the fourteenth century and the first decade (at least) of the fifteenth.[16] A more recently
articulated innovation on this position has been made by Vincent Gillespie (and
is reiterated in his essay included in this present volume): that Julian's first
account – the Short Text – constitutes a likely *probatio* text of the type required
of some aspirant anchorites, particularly female applicants, in order to justify
to the bishop their vocational drive and the orthodoxy of their spirituality.[17] It
may well be that increased activity within the field of contemporary anchoritic
studies will uncover more evidence in support of this supposition but there is
no doubt that there *are* elements of this type of justification or *apologia* in Julian's
Short Text which are missing from the Long, as we have seen.

Additional contributions to this debate have also been made by the aforementioned editors of the 2006 synoptic edition of Julian's writing (which has
been utilized by the contributors to this present volume). Nicholas Watson's
and Jacqueline Jenkins' intimate knowledge of both texts and the manuscripts
which house them has led them to conclude that 'there is a strong possibility
that [Julian] was a nun at the Benedictine convent at Carrow, a mile from the
church of St Julian's, Conesford [sic] in Norwich where she was later enclosed
as anchoress'.[18] Foremost amongst the evidence cited by Watson and Jenkins
in support of this stance is the fact that Julian's anchorhold, attached to the
church of St Julian's, was in the gift of the nuns at Carrow nunnery, a mile from
her abode. This cloistered environment would not only have provided her with
the educational background which is everywhere displayed in her writing but
would also account, so they argue, for Julian's somewhat garbled version in
the Short Text of the monastic greeting *Benedicite* and the traditional response,
*Dominus te benedicat*. On recounting the onset of her visionary experiences, Julian
recalls that her own words were 'Benedicite dominus!' (*Vision*, 3.15), leading
one to wonder why a nun familiar with this interchange on a daily basis would
make such a basic grammatical error, even if she were not entirely Latinate.
Similarly, Watson and Jenkins also cite Christ's words to Julian thanking her
for 'thy service and [...] thy travaile and namly in thy youth' (*Vision*, 8.53–4),
as possible evidence of her service to God as a young novice, but it is equally
likely, of course, that here Christ is referring to the exceptional piety which,
as Julian has already self-confessedly informed her readers, she possessed as
a young woman ('This sekenes desirede I in my youth': *Vision*, 1.34). Whilst

16  Watson himself has always remained equivocal on this issue but takes up a contrary stance
in the introduction to his co-edited edition, considering it most likely that Julian was a nun: for
a discussion of this, see p. 6 below.
17  I am grateful to Vincent Gillespie for sharing his thoughts on this in his private correspondence of 2 July 2007.
18  *Writings*, ed. Watson and Jenkins, p. 4.

acknowledging that 'the religiosity of nuns and devout laywomen may not have differed a great deal', nevertheless, Watson and Jenkins firmly conclude that 'a straightforward reading of this passage in light of other fragments of evidence makes it likely she was a nun'.[19] So, what we have, of course, is fragmentary and contradictory evidence on both sides of the argument and, moreover, evidence which can be read in a number of different ways – a debate and a dilemma which is probably best summed up by the shrewdly formulated words of Kim M. Phillips at the start of this volume: 'I am content to let the pre-reclusive Julian go, to admire the choices she evidently made to become a anchoress, mystic, author and thinker, and ultimately to let the focus of scholarship rest on her work, not her life.'[20]

Of Julian's choice to embrace the anchoritic life there is, however, considerably more consistent and solid evidence than is attached to her way of life prior to enclosure. Not only, as stated, does the scribal incipit to the only extant version of her Short Text inform us 'Here es a vision, shewed be the goodenes of God to a devoute woman. And hir name es Julian, that is recluse atte Norwiche and yit is on life, anno domini 1413',[21] but the writing of contemporary holy woman Margery Kempe in the autohagiographical account of her own life, *The Book of Margery Kempe*, corroborates Julian's status as respected anchoress of Norwich whose particular skill seems to have been in *discretio spirituum* – the discernment of spirits.[22] As both Rosalynn Voaden and Naoë Kukita Yoshikawa have demonstrated,[23] the doctrine of *discretio spirituum* was a highly important one at this point in the Middle Ages, more so for women, who were much more likely to be relegated to the grey area between orthodox thinking and heterodox subversion and who, therefore, were particularly in need of authoritative endorsement of any prophetic or visionary activity. Margery's written account of a protracted meeting with Julian, datable also to 1413, certainly corroborates the fact that Julian, now in her seventies, was 'yit [...] on life' in the spring of 1413 and still offering advice to passing visitors from her anchorhold. In addition to this, the evidence of local wills points towards Julian's enclosure as having been enacted in 1393–4: a series of bequests made between 1393 and 1414 – all helpfully reproduced by Watson and Jenkins in Appendix B to their new edition – confirm for us that Julian spent more than twenty years as a recluse, during which time she was evidently held in high esteem locally by a wide and influential network of people. Julian's posthumous benefactors for whom evidence remains include, for example, a local rector, Roger Reed; a Norfolk chantry priest, Thomas Emund; a local merchant, John Plumpton, who also left money to Julian's current servant and a former maid; and Isabel Ufford, daughter of the Earl of Warwick, at that time a nun at the famous house at Campsea Ashe in

19  Ibid., p. 4.
20  See p. 31 below.
21  *Writings*, ed. Watson and Jenkins, p. 63.
22  Margery Kempe, *The Book of Margery Kempe*, ed. Sanford Brown Meech and Hope Emily Allen, EETS o.s. 212 (Oxford, 1940; repr. 1997), pp. 42–3.
23  Rosalynn Voaden, *God's Words, Women's Voices: The Discernment of Spirits in the Writing of Later-Medieval Women Visionaries* (York, 1999); Naoë Kukita Yoshikawa, *Margery Kempe's Meditations: The Context of Medieval Devotional Literatures, Liturgy and Iconography* (Cardiff, 2007).

Suffolk. Far from constructing a solitary Julian, then, in the same spatial vacuum frequently implied by the paradigmatic anchoritic guidance text, *Ancrene Wisse* ('[I]n the same way as all the openings of all your windows have been kept closed from the view of everyone, so let them remain closed from now on – and the more tightly they can be closed, the more tightly they should be'),[24] all these long-distance glimpses at Julian point towards a woman who, whilst spanning the ideological solitude of the desert upon which the anchoritic vocation was firmly built, nevertheless also occupied a position at the heart of the Christian community within late-medieval East Anglia. Indeed, as Watson and Jenkins also point out, such an ambiguous positionality is also constitutive of Julian's writing: both *A Vision* and *A Revelation* 'traverse a conceptual version of the ground Julian occupied herself in her years as an anchorite: between self and community, God, church, and world'.[25]

Further problems arise, however, in any attempt to discuss 'Julian's texts' as a concept. We do not, for example, have any autograph version of her writing, nor do we even have a single medieval copy of the longer version, *A Revelation of Love*. The only truly medieval witness to her writing is that of the Short Text, *A Vision Shown to a Devout Woman*, extant in the aforementioned London, British Library MS Additional 37790, a mid fifteenth-century manuscript which is, in Watson's and Jenkins' assessment, 'a copy of a copy' of Julian's autograph Short Text,[26] a text which, of course, may never have been released for circulation amongst the general populace at all during its author's lifetime. Its appearance in this manuscript forms part of a compilation which also includes Richard Misyn's Middle English translations of Richard Rolle's *Emendatio vitae* and *Incendium amoris*, the Middle English translation of Ruusbroec's *Vanden blinkenden steen* and M. N.'s Middle English translation of Marguerite Porète's *Mirouer des Simples Âmes*, thus forming part of an anthology of mystical works compiled for devotional purposes. The fact that it is included in such an anthology, and the means by which the longer *A Revelation of Love* makes use of it as a source text, lead Watson and Jenkins to conclude that 'Julian and her scribes shared a common respect for *A Vision*, as in some sense an unsuperseded account of an act of divine revelation'.[27]

The so-called Long Text, *A Revelation of Love*, however, survives in its entirety in three versions, each containing some readings which are at variance with the others: Paris, Bibliothèque Nationale MS Fonds Anglais 40, produced somewhere in northern France in the seventeenth century (and the version upon which both

---

[24] *Ancrene Wisse*, in *Anchoritic Spirituality: 'Ancrene Wisse' and Associated Works*, ed. and trans. Anne Savage and Nicholas Watson (New York, 1991), pp. 41–207 (71). The original, which is extant only in the Anglo-French version, reads: 'toutes les ouertures de toutes voz fenestres, ausi come ci-deuant a la vewe de touz hommes vnt esté closes, ausi soient ça enaprés'. See *Ancrene Wisse : A Corrected Edition of the Text in Cambridge, Corpus Christi College MS 402 with Variants from Other Manuscripts*, ed. Bella Millett, EETS o.s. 325 (Oxford, 2005), Part Two, lines 208–10.

[25] *Writings*, ed. Watson and Jenkins, p. 6.

[26] Ibid., p. 33. For a full-length study of this manuscript, see Marleen Cré, *Vernacular Mysticism in the Charterhouse: A Study of London, British Library, MS Additional 37790*, The Medieval Translator 9 (Turnhout, 2006).

[27] Ibid., p. 35.

the Colledge and Walsh and Watson and Jenkins editions are based);[28] London, British Library MS Sloane 2499 and London, British Library MS Sloane 3705, both probably produced in the same house from the same copy in or around 1650 in northern France and, like the Paris manuscript, a product of the recusant nuns who had settled there following the Reformation; and London, Westminster Cathedral Treasury MS 4, a manuscript of unknown provenance which is datable to around 1500 and contains a single text made up of fragments from existing texts: *Qui habitat* and *Bonum est*, probably by Walter Hilton; Books I and II of Hilton's *Scale of Perfection*; and, of course, extracts from Julian's *A Revelation of Love*. In addition to these significantly different versions of Julian's Long Text, there also exists a series of fragments from *A Revelation* appearing alongside others taken from other medieval and post-Reformation spiritual writings in MS St Joseph's College, Upholland. Until recently, this seventeenth-century witness to the Long Text was thought to be part of the 'Englishings' of Augustine Baker, and produced for the benefit of the nuns at Cambrai in northern France to whom he was at one time spiritual director, although that view has been brought into some doubt by recent scholarship.[29] What is clear, therefore, is that we do not have any definitive version of what Julian wrote, either in the short or the long version, and that it becomes very problematic to talk definitively about her 'texts', and how – or even *if* – they were circulated or disseminated during the medieval period. Thus, as many of the contributors to this volume will also suggest, it may be more helpful to consider Julian and her writing in less teleological terms: as plural, as multiple, as variable, as unstable, metamorphosing between the centuries and becoming different things for different audiences, and, yet, containing at the core the stability and consistency of God's message to humankind, common to all manuscript versions, that 'love was his mening' (*Revelation*, 86.14). Such a remarkable *mouvance* has been, perhaps, effectively articulated in more modern times by T. S. Eliot's kaleidescopic conception that '[e]very phrase and every sentence is an end and a beginning … / for history is a pattern / Of timeless moments.'[30]

So, which and how many 'Julians', conceived of and produced over the countless 'timeless moments' since she came to writing, does this present volume aim to uncover? Firstly, its approach to Julian is self-evidently – and self-consciously – literary and historical. It is her status as a writer and historical recluse with which most of the essays concern themselves, since these are the aspects of Julian's work which are most widely scrutinized within the academic context. However, this is not in any way to downplay the importance of Julian's exceptional contribution to theological exegesis, which is of concern to a large proportion of her readership today: indeed, this aspect of her work would seem to call for a separate volume in order to build upon those highly insightful theological examinations already undertaken by scholars such as Denise Nowakowski Baker,

---

[28]  *A Book of Showings to the Anchoress Julian of Norwich*, ed. Edmund Colledge and James Walsh, 2 vols (Toronto, 1978). For the Watson and Jenkins edition, see n. 5 above.
[29]  Elisabeth Dutton considers this point in her essay, p. 135. Siobhan Condron also debates this issue in her recently completed Ph.D. thesis from University College, Dublin. I am grateful to her for allowing me access to some of her unpublished work.
[30]  T. S. Eliot, 'Little Gidding', part 5, ll. 11–12, 20–1.

Christopher Abbott, Barbara Newman,[31] and the contributors to a special issue of the journal *Spiritus* in 2005, which focused specifically on Julian's theology.[32] In this present volume, however, except for the essays of Denise N. Baker and Diane Watt, which are more directly concerned with aspects of Julian's theology, Julian's exceptional contribution to medieval theological exegesis is regarded as a given, implicit rather than explicit to the arguments presented by the contributors, who prefer instead to concentrate on Julian's place within the traditions of women's writing and its reception, and medieval anchoritism.

Certainly all of the original essays included here, which are gathered into two sections, will dispel the myth of Julian as an introverted and isolated solitary, a mystic-theologian separated off from the world by the stone walls which surrounded her and left alone in singular communion with God. Instead, they locate her deep within the heart of a range of communities, of which the present-day reader is no less a part.

To this end, Part I, 'Julian in Context', aims primarily to place the writer firmly within a variety of her own contemporary contexts: social, religious, artistic, cultural and mystical, to name but a few. Opening with Kim M. Phillips' astute and sensitive appraisal of the probable social background from which Julian emerged, this essay rises to the challenge laid down by an earlier suggestion made by Alexandra Barratt that Julian's preoccupation with issues of service, worship and lordship in her writing allows us to locate her within a gentry or lower aristocratic milieu.[33] Whilst avoiding unhelpful speculative assertion regarding Julian, however, Phillips' essay presents evidence for forms of femininity experienced by women of gentry status in late-medieval East Anglia and suggests ways in which such experiences may be contextualized within Julian's vocation and writing as belonging to a specific historical era. Similarly, Cate Gunn, in her contribution here, focuses on the artistic and cultural specificities of late-medieval Norwich: its architecture, images, noise, its social hustle-and-bustle. Such visual, auditory and olfactory immersion in the day-to-day life of the busy city would, she argues, have fed into an allegorical pattern of articulation within Julian's writings which helped transcend the mundane and offered expression for the mystical. In short, for Gunn the richly sensual culture of the world surrounding Julian in medieval Norwich gave her access to a tradition of allegory which surpassed the limitations of language.

The visual culture of medieval Norwich is also of interest to Alexandra Barratt, whose essay concentrates on visual images of the Trinity which, she argues, may well have had an influence upon how Julian filters out and reinvents prevalent

---

31 Denise Nowakowski Baker, *Julian of Norwich's* Showings: *From Vision to Book* (Princeton, 1994); Christopher Abbott, *Julian of Norwich: Autobiography and Theology* (Cambridge, 1999); Barbara Newman, *God and the Goddesses: Vision, Poetry, and Belief in the Middle Ages* (Philadelphia, 2003).
32 See *Spiritus: A Journal of Christian Spirituality* 5, 1 (2005). In addition, Denys Turner is currently working on a monograph for SCM Press focusing on Julian's doctrines of sin and providence.
33 Alexandra Barratt, 'Julian of Norwich and the Holy Spirit, "Our Good Lord"', *Mystics Quarterly* 28 (2002), pp. 78–84; and 'Lordship, Service and Worship in Julian of Norwich', in *The Medieval Mystical Tradition in England: Exeter Symposium VII*, ed. E. A. Jones (Cambridge, 2004), pp. 177–88.

Trinitarian theology in her writing. Of particular concern to Barratt's analysis are
the physical and visual experiences Julian may have undergone and their likely
influences on Julian's verbal imagery in her texts. Most arrestingly, Barratt posits
an acquaintance by Julian with the *Dixit Dominus* image of the Father and Son
which appears in the Ormesby Psalter (see Illustration 1), which lay open in the
choir of Norwich Cathedral during the latter part of the fourteenth century. She
argues that it is not out of the question that Julian had access to this displayed
psalter during her early life and that it may have had a long-lasting effect upon
her. A particularly vibrant example of the *Dixit Dominus* image, which depicts
both Father and Son sitting alongside each other in parity rather than hierarchi-
cally as in other images of the Trinity, appears at the opening to Psalm 109 in
this psalter and, as Barratt points out, its figures appear of relatively indeterminate gender. Could this, she queries, have inspired Julian, perhaps even subcon-
sciously, for her reconfiguration of an intensely masculine and patriarchal God
in familial terms as both mother and father, male and female, two equal parts
of the same equation?

In contrast – and moving away from the specific location of medieval Norwich
– Denise N. Baker's essay examines Julian as a mystical writer within the
context of the wider community of the English mystical tradition of which she
has long been considered an integral part. Such a tradition includes, of course,
Richard Rolle, Walter Hilton, the anonymous author of the *Cloud of Unknowing*
and Margery Kempe, all of whom have long been read alongside each other as
constituting some type of homogeneous 'group'. Following Nicholas Watson's
1999 appeal for caution in considering the English mystics as forming any type
of 'group',[34] Baker argues for Julian's occupation of a position wholly outside
this 'community' of English mystics. As she points out, on no occasion is Julian
ever alluded to by either Hilton or the *Cloud* author, both of whom were her
contemporaries; and even though Margery Kempe documents a protracted
meeting with the anchoress, as we have seen, at no point does she mention
or even allude to Julian's having produced any writing. And given Margery's
own preoccupation with the question of whether to write or not to write her
own experiences, we can safely presume that she was unaware of Julian's textu-
ality when she came to write her own *Book* in the mid 1430s. Baker comes to
the conclusion, therefore, that any similarities detected by scholars between
Julian's mystical theology and those of the other English mystics must have
arisen because of their common participation within a much *wider* framework
of mystical activity, rather than through Julian's having been familiar with their
writing – or they hers.

If not part of the 'community' of English mystics as such, Julian certainly
appears to have had some affinity with the writings of other female mystics
of the fourteenth century – Bridget of Sweden, for example, and Elizabeth of
Hungary, both of whom could well have been known either to Julian herself
or, at least, to members of her intellectual community.[35] Bridget, of course, had

---

[34]  Nicholas Watson, 'The Middle English Mystics', in *The Cambridge History of Medieval English
Literature*, ed. David Wallace (Cambridge, 1999), pp. 539–65.
[35]  See *Writings*, ed. Watson and Jenkins, p. 3.

been recently canonized amidst some controversy and, if Margery Kempe's own affinity with this visionary precursor is anything to go by, she was certainly known and admired by at least one East Anglian holy woman in the first decades of the fifteenth century prior to the founding of the Brigittine Syon Abbey in 1413. Whilst, however, there is again a strand within contemporary scholarship which places Julian outside such a specifically feminine mystical and prophetic tradition,[36] and which therefore claims Julian's theology and writing for a tran-scension of sex and gender, Diane Watt takes up a somewhat different stance on Julian's mysticism in her essay, which follows on from Baker's. Watt reads Julian firmly within the context of the twelfth-century English recluse, nun and prioress Christina of Markyate and Julian's younger contemporary Margery Kempe. Building on the exhortations of Felicity Riddy to read Julian as 'rela-tional' rather than solitary,[37] Watt asserts that, in her role as holy woman and intercessory, Julian was always part of a larger spiritual – and visionary – female community which both pre-dates and succeeds her. For Watt, however, in the visionary Julian's attempts at self-effacement she necessarily distances herself from the expectations presented by such a community, developing instead her own far more theologically daring and innovative brand of universalist apoca-lypticism.

Julian's relational and communal positions are further argued for by Annie Sutherland in her painstaking examination of the ways in which contemporary liturgical and quasi-liturgical practices have a bearing upon Julian's writing. In the same way that she places herself both firmly within and simultaneously extraneous to traditional mystical and prophetic discourse (as demonstrated by Baker and Watt), so Julian makes full use of communal liturgical practices and conventions to articulate her insights. As Sutherland demonstrates, whilst Julian is keen to assert the appropriateness of liturgical tradition as meditative device and methodological practice for the faithful, she is also aware of its limitations. Within the context of her own mystical understanding of the fundamental, yet overarching, 'goodnes' of God, such insights clearly surpass the 'comene course of prayers' (*Vision*, 1, 30–1) inherent to the Christian communion. The liturgy, therefore, and Julian's argued-for familiarity with aspects of it, is incorporated into Julian's texts as reiterative mainstay of orthodox performativity, whilst at the same time forming a spring-board for more radical and heterodox investiga-tion on the part of the author.

The final essay in Part I focuses on Julian's position within the English anchoritic tradition. E. A. Jones's appraisal of Julian as an anchorite draws upon and anatomizes a wealth of extant information available to us about the lives and activities of late-medieval anchorites. Not only does he make use of the

---

[36] Watson and Jenkins, for example, assert that 'the references to mothering and pregnancy in *A Revelation* are theological, not autobiographical', *Writings*, ed. Watson and Jenkins, p. 4. Christopher Abbott shows equal caution in his appraisal of Julian's depiction of the mother-hood of God, reading it as a concerted metaphor. See Christopher Abbott, *Julian of Norwich: Autobiography and Theology* (Cambridge, 1999), especially p. 2.

[37] See Felicity Riddy, ' "Women Talking About The Things of God": A Late Medieval Sub-Culture', in *Women and Literature in Britain, 1150–1500*, ed. Carol M. Meale (Cambridge, 1993), pp. 104–27 (115).

more obvious sources – anchoritic guidance texts such as the fifteenth-century *Speculum Inclusorum*, for example, but he also painstakingly sifts through evidence from sources such as wills and legacies which help to illuminate the lived experience of other female anchorites of the same period. In this context, Jones identifies the female anchorite as frequently occupying a conglomeration of subject positions in the late fourteenth and the early fifteenth century, some or all of which were almost certainly relevant to Julian's own experiences of reclusion. An anchorite, for example, was frequently a legatee of the local community, often of the wider community, sometimes even of the king. She might also be a householder, organizing servants, perhaps even maintaining a garden. Some anchorites appeared to be dynasts too. In this capacity Jones examines how, as in many cases, there were continued bequests to an unnamed female recluse at St Julian's throughout the 1420s, long after Julian is thought to have died, with a final bequest being made as late as the 1440s, pointing towards a practice whereby an anchorite could inherit the cell of a known predecessor who may also have been his/her acquaintance or employer. Thus, it is quite feasible that one of Julian's servants, who is named by two of her benefactors in their wills, went on to inhabit the anchorhold at St Julian's after Julian's death.[38]

Part II, 'Manuscript Tradition and Interpretation', seeks to build upon such contextual approaches, focusing on manuscript traditions, dissemination and new methodological approaches in order to prise open further the treasure-house of Julian's writing. It begins with an essay by Barry Windeatt, a contribution which is intensely textual in its focus, concentrating as it does on a close comparison between the initial Short Text and the highly wrought and complex Long Text into which it metamorphoses. Such a close and tightly wrought comparison allows for the tracing of Julian's development, both as a mystic and as a writer, and for the charting of the multiplicity of ways in which she learns to interpret the meanings of her original visionary experiences. For Windeatt, even *A Revelation* retains an aura of the original commentary it was established to be and in it he recognizes 'something of the layered, interleaved structure of a private working draft, perhaps never widely circulated'. This, of course, is in line with the claims of other contributors to this volume, many of whom surmise on the evidence suggesting lack of circulation in Julian's own lifetime.

In contrast to Windeatt's approach, the essays contributed by Marleen Cré and Elisabeth Dutton which follow Windeatt's are more concerned with mechanistic analyses of manuscript traditions and culture, choosing to scrutinize individual manuscripts containing Julian's work and the concomitant traditions. Placing the works firmly within their manuscript contexts, both contributors examine the complex issues of audience and dissemination – in the case of Cré in the context of London, Westminster Cathedral Treasury MS 4 which, as I have

---

[38] One of Julian's former servants, named as Alice in the 1415 will of John Plumpton (for which see *Writings*, ed. Watson and Jenkins, p. 433), could well be the 'Alicie hermyte' who later donated a chalice to the church of St Giles in Norwich and who quite feasibly could have taken up occupancy of Julian's cell after her death. This is a point first mooted by Aelred Watkin in his edition of the *Inventory of Church Goods, temp. Edward III* (Archdeaconry of Norwich), 2 vols (Norfolk Record Society, 1947), I, 18; II, 161, as cited in *A Book of Showings*, ed. Colledge and Walsh, p. 34 n. 70.

pointed out earlier, contains a single text consisting of extracts from a number of contemporary works of contemplation, Julian's *A Revelation* amongst them. By examining the Julian extracts wholly in manuscript context and assessing the ways in which they are aligned with the other textual fragments, Cré is able to offer valuable insights into the intentions of the anthologist, the medieval reception of Julian's writing and the positioning of her likely audience. Arguing for a strong cohesive unity to this text, with each textual fragment harking backwards or pointing forwards to other textual extracts, Cré's essay insists upon a determined and deliberate intentionality within the Westminster manuscript, claiming Julian's *A Revelation* as an important component of its rich, experiential impact.

Elisabeth Dutton's essay comprises an intricate examination of the variances between the surviving seventeenth-century Long Text manuscripts – Paris, Bibliothèque Nationale MS Fonds Anglais 40, British Library Sloane MS 2499 (Sloane 1) and British Library Sloane MS 3705 (Sloane 2) – in order to extrapolate valuable clues as to the ways in which the text has been read and interpreted since its origins in the first decade of the fifteenth century. Similarly, she turns her attention to the less frequently examined MS St Joseph's College, Upholland, which again contains short fragments of Julian's Long Text copied by recusant nuns at Cambrai in northern France at some stage during the latter half of the seventeenth century. Dutton concludes by focusing her attention on what she considers to be the extensive influence exercised by Augustine Baker, spiritual advisor to the Cambrai nuns, upon the preservation of Julian's works, adding to what is becoming a contentious contemporary debate on this particular issue, as I suggested earlier.

Reception and audience is an aspect of Julian's writing which is taken up by Elizabeth Robertson in a more discursively investigative approach which concerns itself in part with Julian's own construction of an audience, both internal and external to her texts. Here, Robertson traverses between the audiences Julian herself envisages within her texts and those who most probably constituted them in practice (and these two positions are by no means synonymous). She examines what Julian's likely audience became, from the inception of her work to its later dissemination, and the movement between 'audience' in the auditory sense, and 'audience' in the sense of 'readership'. Such multiple audiences are, so Robertson argues, both inscribed stylistically within Julian's texts and directed verbally as to how they should engage with her visions. These visions, moreover, as some of the remaining essays included in Part II will demonstrate, are presented from a plethora of dizzying perspectives and platforms, coming into focus and fading out again in ways which, for Robertson, 'shatter the distance between Julian as writer and her reader, whether the reader is of the past or the present'. And it is such a shattering of the distance between authorial and readerly perspectives that causes Robertson to make her most interesting claim: that Julian's style constitutes a forerunner to the modernist enterprise, specifically that of Virginia Woolf. Like Woolf, Julian's preoccupation is with an 'omnitemporality' and 'multipersonal consciousness', giving rise to a style which is 'fundamentally dilatory'. Repetition, contradiction and verbal spiralling disrupt readerly expectation at every turn, shattering any type of linear logic which can lay claim to finality, completion or closure and effacing the distance between author and audience. For both herself and her multiple audiences, Julian collapses all mediation – which, in innumerable ways, includes the mediational presumptiveness of her texts themselves.

Julian's use of space and imagery based on her own surroundings both before and after her anchoritic enclosure forms the focus of the next essay in this collection by Laura Saetveit Miles, who also alerts the reader to resonances between the styles of writing of Julian and Virginia Woolf. Miles' main concern, however, is the ways in which Julian experienced both the physical and conceptual spaces of the medieval anchorhold and how these were translated into her writing. Her particular interest is the relationship between physical space, mystical space and authorship as a methodology for opening up a window on a writer about whom, on the surface of things, we know so very little. For Miles, Julian's Long Text negotiates 'a tripartite system of enclosures': that of her anchorhold, that of her revelations and that of her text. By offering a Foucaultian, heterotopic reading of Julian's configuration of such spaces within the Long Text alongside an analysis of the treatment of space by two other visionary women of the period – Bridget of Sweden and Margery Kempe – Miles convincingly argues for the centrality of the anchorhold to Julian's expression of a mystical theology of *communitas* and the individual Christian's union with the Godhead.

Such issues regarding Julian's use and (re)configuration of gender binaries and space are also central to my own essay, which follows on from Miles'. Concentrating primarily on *A Vision Shown to a Devout Woman*, this essay offers a Kristevan reading of Julian's writing in order to illuminate her protracted search for an appropriate idiom with which to express her mystical insights into the 'oning' of 'kinde […] to the maker, which is substantial kinde unmade' (*Revelation*, 53.38–9), a linguistic search which, I argue, characterizes both texts but which is never fully realized. Faced with the ontological and teleological inadequacy of a phallogocentric language (that is, the privileging of the masculine in the construction of meaning) to express the inexpressibility of the mystical, it is to the poetic semiotics or sign-system of primary unity with the mother to which Julian increasingly resorts as her text takes shape and moves inexorably towards the explosive outbursting of its God-as-Mother, God-as Father conclusion. Beginning with and then moving beyond the corporeal body, Julian unearths its semiotic traces to produce an anti-phallic language and poetics constructed specifically to approximate upon a vision of ultimately ungendered wholeness.

And it is with Julian's language and its poeticity which the two essays which follow my own, those by Ena Jenkins and Vincent Gillespie, also concern themselves. Both commentators here offer close, sensitive, intensely aware and insightful readings of Julian not only as mystical theologian but also as a poet who uses a wide range of textual voices and who, in the words of Gillespie, employs 'subtle and strategically shifting nuances of style and register [which] demand a different way of listening'. Ena Jenkins' essay concurs with such a reading of Julian's poetics but prefers to focus specifically on the poeticity of her texts and, in particular, the role that metaphor plays within that framework. For Jenkins, there is an inherent simplicity within Julian's use of imagery which, she argues, develops into imagistic clusters which move on to form patterns and grow into the complex metaphorical system which pervades the Long Text in particular. Particularly useful, too, is Jenkins' insightful analysis of the parable of the Lord and Servant in this context (and she is one of the few contributors to concentrate significantly on this episode), a visionary encounter which Julian avoided discussing in her initial response to her experiences simply because of a complete failure to understand its import ('full understanding of this mervelouse example was not geven me in that time': *Revelation*, 51.59–60). The parable, then, is ideally placed to demonstrate the development of Julian's poetic sensibilities and modes of expression, which Jenkins reads as 'both functional and elegant and … the way in which seeing and seeking proceed'. Here, as elsewhere in Julian's text, Jenkins identifies iconic imagery which distills out into metaphoric complexity and the production of what can only be described as 'lyric fragments' of closely wrought poetic sensibility. Moreover, for Jenkins, such lyric fragments embody the essence of Julian's theological insight, expressing 'both intellectual grasp and emotional response', and uncovering, in a term adapted from William Wordsworth, the author's own 'feeling intellect'.[39]

For Gillespie, meanwhile, Julian's visions demand of her a new form of interpretation which suspends all preconceived hermeneutic formulations, resulting in her writing necessarily demanding from its readers similar qualities. Gillespie proceeds to demonstrate the extent to which Julian adopts and adapts both multiple discourses and textual voices to create a type of pastiche of contemporary styles of writing. He alerts the reader to the complex multivalence of Julian's intertextuality, its Bakhtinian heteroglossic resonances or multiple 'voices', claiming her text as 'a vast echo chamber' within which allusion, imitation, ventriloquism and parody endlessly resound but without its ever relinquishing its own originality and specificity.

In the final essay of this collection Sarah Salih takes the reader on a breathless helter-skelter tour of the myriad of 'contemporary Julians' who have surfaced during the course of the twentieth and twenty-first centuries in poetry, novels, film and other media, including a strong 'virtual' presence online. As Salih argues, such a proliferation of 'Julians' has contributed in no small measure to what can only be termed a 'Julian cult' which now centres on her reconstructed cell in present-day Norwich. Such a mélange of contemporary Julians makes its appearance on items of memorabilia: cards, pens, pencils – even fridge magnets. She is consulted by her followers, from evangelical Christians to new-age goddess-seekers, for what is recognized as her 'feminine' wisdom and comforting aphorisms in the face of a 'degenerating' world.

In appraising this extraordinary appropriation and reappropriation of Julian – the solitary, the writer, the mystic – Salih, perhaps, posits an answer to the question raised at the beginning of this Introduction: what is it about the figure of Julian which has brought about such extraordinary longevity of attraction and interest even amongst readers who otherwise have little familiarity with the writers of the later Middle Ages? In Salih's estimation (and quoting Carolyn

---

[39] William Wordsworth, *The Prelude* (1805), Book XIII, 1. 205. Cited by Jenkins, p. 181.

Dinshaw), for those coming to Julian from a non-academic perspective, 'Julian offers a life possibility for the present',[40] perhaps, even, in her multiplicity of aspects, belonging more to the fragmented postmodern view of the present than to the historical *telos* of the medieval past. Which leads me to return to the question which heads this Introduction: can we ever aim to 'know' who or what Julian 'really' was? The answer is probably 'no', but it is hoped that the multiple scholarly perspectives gathered together in this collection of essays, and the new ways of unpicking the Julian tapestry which they facilitate, will allow the twenty-first-century reader of Julian's texts to get as close to answering this question as can ever be possible, given Julian's own concerted resistance to ever being 'known' by anybody other than God.

---

[40]  See p. 218 below.

# PART I
# JULIAN IN CONTEXT

# 1

## Femininities and the Gentry in Late Medieval East Anglia: Ways of Being

KIM M. PHILLIPS

In present-day Norwich one can visit a version of the church where the recluse who called herself Julian spent perhaps forty years of her life. I say 'version' because although St Julian's Church, off Rouen Road in the south-east corner of the city, looks medieval it was largely reconstructed following severe damage suffered during bombing raids in 1942.[1] 'Mother Julian's Cell' is an entirely modern structure built from scratch in the early 1950s. It adjoins the south wall of the church and is accessible via a Norman doorway moved to the site from the bombed-out church of St Michael at Thorn. Despite the cell's recent construction, Norwich tourist literature confidently asserts that it is 'on the site of her original cell' or that the present structure is 'Julian's cell … now enlarged and furnished as a chapel'.[2] Like so much about modern reconstructions of Julian's life, this is a fiction. The cell is no more medieval than the post-war housing estates in modern Conisford. The site of Julian's anchorhold is not known for certain, but Roberta Gilchrist and Marilyn Oliva comment that it would be unusual for an anchoress's cell to be placed against the south wall of a church, given that most surviving examples are on the north side.[3] Compelling counter-evidence is also offered by the eighteenth-century antiquarian Francis Blomefield, describing the church he visited: 'In the East Part of this Church-yard stood an Anchorage, in which Ankeress or Recluse dwelt 'till the Dissolution, when the House was demolished, tho' the Foundations may still be seen: In 1393, Lady Julian the Ankeress here, was a strict Recluse, and had 2 Servants to attend her in her old Age.'[4] If we are to believe Blomefield the cell was never attached to either the north or south wall of the church, but was a freestanding structure. On a brief visit to St Julian's in January 2007 I peered over the churchyard wall towards

---

[1]  Drawings and photographs of the church at different stages from the nineteenth century to the present day may be found at http://www.norfolkchurches.co.uk/norwichjulian/norwichjulian.htm (accessed 20 February 2008).
[2]  'Norwich Mini Guide', produced by the Norwich City Council, current in January 2007; Robert Llewelyn, 'Julian of Norwich', pamphlet available in St Julian's Church, Norwich, current in January 2007.
[3]  Roberta Gilchrist and Marilyn Oliva, *Religious Women in Medieval East Anglia: History and Archaeology c.1100–1540*, Studies in East Anglian History 1 (Norwich, 1993), pp. 76–7.
[4]  Francis Blomefield, continued by Charles Parkin, *An Essay Towards a Topographical History of the County of Norfolk*, 5 vols (Norwich, 1739–75), vol. 2, p. 546.

the place where Julian's cell may once have stood and felt the futility of over-
enthusiastic attempts to reconstruct details of Julian's life.

The two versions of Julian's revelations – especially the later Long Text, *A
Revelation of Love* – deliberately omit autobiographical narrative, unlike Margery
Kempe's account or those of many other contemporary mystical writers. The
few biographical details that one can be reasonably sure about are summarised
by Liz Herbert McAvoy in the Introduction to this volume.[5] Julian's personal
identity has been almost emptied out. Although we cannot know whether Julian
or later scribes were responsible for this drastic editing of the authorial self,
the point remains: for a woman who left readers so much of her thought, she
left little else of herself. Yet many modern readers, because they admire Julian
and her message, have spun webs of fantasy around her. She was a nun before
becoming a recluse, *or* she had been a wife and mother; she was learned in Latin
and theology, *or* she had no more formal or Latin learning than other women
of her era; she was intensely orthodox and her ideas were steeped in patristic
authorities, *or* she was original and radical in her construction of a distinctively
feminine theology.[6] The level of speculation sometimes becomes painful, even
in the writings of the most reputable scholars. 'Had her young husband died
either of plague or in war?' asks Benedicta Ward, contending that Julian had
been a mother and widow before entering the anchorhold.[7] What a cruel fate for
her husband – so recently invented, to suffer such a death! Some build teetering
contextual structures on ill-founded premises: 'It is also possible that if [Carrow
Abbey] was the source of Julian's education and she had thereby come to the
notice of the cathedral priory, she might have been eligible for a special arrangement which made books from their library of theology and spirituality available
to her,' ponders Grace M. Janzten. Alternatively, '[i]f Julian had had a brother
who went to such a [grammar] school … she could have learned from him.'[8]

---

[5]  See also the remarks of Julian's most recent editors, Nicholas Watson and Jacqueline Jenkins
(eds), *The Writings of Julian of Norwich: A Vision Showed to a Devout Woman and A Revelation
of Love* (Turnhout, 2006), pp. 4–6.
[6]  For example, Fathers Edmund Colledge and James Walsh contended that Julian had been
a nun before becoming an anchoress, that she was highly learned and literate in Latin theological works, and that her theology was highly orthodox: *A Book of Showings to the Anchoress
Julian of Norwich*, 2 vols (Toronto, 1978), Introduction, p. 43; Sister Benedicta Ward made the
case for Julian having been a wife and mother before entering the anchorhold, 'Julian the Solitary', in *Julian Reconsidered*, ed. Kenneth Leech and Benedicta Ward (Oxford, 1988), pp. 11–35.
Annie Sutherland is among those who have recently argued that Julian's learning was derived
not from Latin literature but vernacular sources and oral devotional culture: '"Oure feyth is
groundyd in goddes worde": Julian of Norwich and the Bible', in *The Medieval Mystical Tradition in England: Exeter Symposium VII*, ed. E. A. Jones (Cambridge, 2004), pp. 1–20; and Joan M.
Nuth, though she goes along with Colledge and Walsh's arguments for Latin learning, argues
that Julian offered a distinctly feminine theology: *Wisdom's Daughter: The Theology of Julian of
Norwich* (New York, 1991). This is just a sample of a wide literature.
[7]  Ward, 'Julian the Solitary', p. 25.
[8]  Grace M. Janzten, *Julian of Norwich: Mystic and Theologian* (New York, 1987), p. 19. A number
of more recent scholars have argued that we should steer clear of speculation: for example,
Christopher Abbott, *Julian of Norwich: Autobiography and Theology* (Cambridge, 1999), p. 2; Liz
Herbert McAvoy, '"And Thou, to Whom This Booke Shall Come": Julian of Norwich and Her
Audience, Past, Present and Future', in *Approaching Medieval English Anchoritic and Mystical
Texts*, ed. Dee Dyas, Valerie Edden and Roger Ellis (Cambridge, 2005), pp. 101–13, esp.
pp. 101–2.

It is perhaps too easy to mock, and it is understandable that an author who has moved and stimulated so many readers will inspire curiosity about her life. Moreover, historicist practitioners argue that we gain better understanding of creative works if we are able to place their production in a secure biographical and historical context. Alexandra Barratt has, however, issued a slightly different historicist challenge: not for the reconstruction of a biography as such but a more developed context: 'We already celebrate [Julian] as a visionary and as a citizen of heaven: let us now start to recuperate and reconstruct a "social" Julian.'[9] This in some respects echoes remarks made earlier by Felicity Riddy, who argued that we must relinquish the 'gothic' mental picture of Julian as isolated recluse, walled up alive and alone in her cell, and recognise the social aspects of her authorship – her urban location, contact with her bishop and other officials of the Church, her contemporary audience, possible collaborators and so on.[10] Barratt undertakes a clever rereading of Julian's vocabulary, suggesting that her demonstrable familiarity with the language of service, worship and lordship indicates that Julian's social background was of the gentry or minor aristocracy. Rather than undertake a speculative exploration of Julian's pre-anchorhold experiences, then, we could take Barratt's suggestion about her probable social status as a starting point and attempt to flesh out her context by considering the forms of femininity experienced by women of gentry status in late medieval East Anglia. Linguistic experts have suggested that Julian may have grown up in northern England, noting certain northern forms present in her writing;[11] however, East Anglia was the region she lived in for the majority of her adult life, and therefore offers the most relevant setting. This essay, therefore, is in part a response to Barratt's challenge, although the results are probably quite different from what she had in mind.

East Anglia was a prosperous and populous region during the later Middle Ages due to its role in wool production and its ports, which provided a gateway to continental Europe. The area was home to numerous families whom one might label members of the 'gentry': the Boleyns, Brewses, Calthorpes, Castells, Cleres, Hoptons, Knyvets, Townshends and Woodhouses, to name a few, as well as the more famous Pastons. Gentry society is not particularly easy to define, as a 'gentleman' or 'gentlewoman' did not occupy a legally recognised category in the way a 'peer', 'knight', 'esquire' or 'serf' did, yet we can identify activities and preoccupations common to the group: possession of landed estates and control over the villagers who worked them, concern with lineage and future family prospects, the holding of local offices such as Justice of the Peace or Member

9   Alexandra Barratt, 'Lordship, Service and Worship in Julian of Norwich', in *The Medieval Mystical Tradition in England: Exeter Symposium VII*, ed. E. A. Jones (Cambridge, 2004), pp. 177–88 (188).
10  Felicity Riddy, 'Julian of Norwich and Self-Textualization', in *Editing Women*, ed. Ann M. Hutchinson (Cardiff, 1998), pp. 101–24, especially pp. 105–6.
11  *Book of Showings* I, ed. Colledge and Walsh, pp. 28–32; *The Shewings of Julian of Norwich*, ed. Georgia Ronan Crampton, TEAMS (Kalamazoo, 1993), p. 20. Christopher Abbott says that 'the dialectical characteristics of the manuscripts of both Long Text and Short Text are little help, since they possibly employ the preferred and native dialectical forms of the early copyists rather than Julian's own', *Julian of Norwich: Autobiography and Theology* (Cambridge, 1999), p. 2, but see Riddy, 'Julian of Norwich and Self-Textualization', pp. 111–12.

of Parliament, service to royalty or members of the great nobility, prudence in financial matters and preoccupation with courtesy and conduct.[12] Moreover, as Philippa Maddern observes, gentility was performative: 'To be a member of the gentry was to be constantly undertaking a performance: behaving like a gentleman/woman in the eyes of the world, and particularly for the benefit of the "gentry" society whose recognition alone could establish who was gentle and who was not'.[13]

As members of a self-conscious group, gentlewomen shared the values and ambitions of men of their status. However, I am keen to find a way of talking about a gentry femininity not entirely constrained by 'class' concerns; rather I wish to find terms that can work both within and across divisions of rank, and in this capacity I have been influenced by R. W. Connell and his now classic *Masculinities*. Connell's framework for thinking about masculinities derives from a desire to understand the ways men compete for supremacy or negotiate their position in the masculine hierarchy:

> To recognize diversity in masculinities is not enough. We must also recognize the *relations* between the different kinds of masculinity: relations of alliance, dominance and subordination. These relationships are constructed through practices that exclude and include, that intimidate, exploit, and so on. There is a gender politics within masculinity.[14]

Connell identifies four main varieties of masculinity in modern western societies.[15] 'Hegemonic' masculinity is 'the masculinity that occupies the hegemonic position in a given pattern of gender relations'. It is the form of masculinity 'culturally exalted' above all others in a given time and place – that is (like the other forms of masculinity discussed here), its expression changes according to social context. 'Subordinated' masculinity is hegemony's opposite: any male behaviour or attributes seeming to fall short of the hegemonic ideal. For example, gay, effeminate or physically non-robust men fit the category in the modern West. 'Complicit' masculinity marks the mass of men who do not fit the elite hegemonic group, yet support – or do nothing to oppose – its aims. Such men 'realize the patriarchal dividend, without the tensions or risks of being the frontline troops of patriarchy.' 'Marginalised' masculinities are affected by social subjugation through class or race. We could refine this definition by contrasting subordinated with marginalised masculinities: where the former are the subject for derision, antipathy or contempt they are nonetheless permitted to exist; the latter are met with more forceful modes of exclusion and suppression by legal or violent means.

It is fruitful to think about femininities in a similar way – thinking about femininities as they relate to women, that is, as Connell's discussion of masculinities focuses only on men – but not simply by imposing Connell's terms.

---

[12]  Philippa Maddern, 'Gentility', in *Gentry Culture in Late Medieval England*, ed. Raluca Radulescu and Alison Truelove (Manchester, 2005), pp. 18–34.
[13]  Ibid., p. 28.
[14]  R. W. Connell, *Masculinities* (Berkeley, 1995), p. 37.
[15]  Ibid., pp. 76–81.

Hierarchical relations within femininity, though they exist, are not as socially or politically significant as in masculinity because in most cultural contexts women are the already subordinated sex. Connell's categories are all structured around his hegemonic archetype. Masculinity is about being hegemonic, failing to match the hegemonic type, complying with hegemony or occupying a space of dangerous marginality in relation to it. Given that social dominance is not generally open to women the exercise of jostling for position is of limited importance.

I therefore offer the following categories of femininity. Like Connell's headings, these are meant to be broad and flexible enough to fit a range of historical contexts and to be applicable either in conjunction with categories of class or independently of them, though here the emphasis is on their applicability to late medieval society:

1. *Consort femininity.* Consort status applies to women who have gained the benefit of the 'patriarchal bargain'; that is, they have entered into inegalitarian marriages but in return receive benefits such as financial security, social prestige, marital companionship, the chance to bear children in a socially sanctioned environment, and household authority or dominance in widowhood.[16] Wives of men in 'hegemonic' or 'complicit' positions in late medieval society, whether of aristocratic, gentle, mercantile, or yeoman status, could be counted as consorts. Their reward for maintaining or furthering family status was a comfortable position within the status quo.

2. *Vocational femininity.* This applies to women who have avoided consort status (although, in some societies, they may actually be married or in partnerships) and built their lives around other pursuits, for example higher learning, religious life, literary or artistic activities, organisational or charitable work, profession, or political activity. Some succeed highly in spheres usually associated with masculinity. They possess a degree of independence or self-determination but this can only ever be limited. Although individually successful and even personally fulfilled, they operate within prefabricated structures of government, religion and profession.

3. *Deprived femininity.* This applies to women whose gender subordination is compounded by further negative factors: poverty, illness, disability, religious oppression or infirm old age. That is not to say that all old, ill or disabled women were entirely deprived, just that these factors would commonly have a negative impact. Deprivation can fall on women even of privileged social status, for example through sexual scandal which diminishes their worth in the eyes of the world or their own families, forced and unhappy marriages, or other misfortunes.

---

[16]  Deniz Kandiyoti developed the concept of 'patriarchal bargains' in her work on sub-Saharan Africa and the Muslim Middle East: 'Bargaining with Patriarchy', *Gender and Society* 2, 3 (1988), pp. 274–90. It has been applied to medieval society with excellent effect by Judith M. Bennett, most recently in 'Patriarchal Equilibrium', in Judith M. Bennett, *History Matters: Patriarchy and the Challenges of Feminism* (Philadelphia, 2006), pp. 54–81, at pp. 59–60.

4. *Alternative femininity*. This refers to women who have given up the attributes of feminine gender regarded as conventional within their society, so far as it is ever possible to do so. They have female physiology and biological life-cycle markers but in other ways have stepped aside from normal femininity, perhaps by rejecting motherhood, sexual relationships with men, 'women's work' and so on. Their divergence from established gender structures will be compromised to a degree – for example, women in all eras must find a material basis for living, even if through marriage. The nature of their alterity will depend on the society they spring from; what they have in common is that in some fundamental way they break the rules of gender.

These categories are offered as a set of lenses for looking differently at femininities in history, and for working around and within social rank or religious status. While they might seem unreasonably negative, Connell's categories for masculinity are not necessarily positive. 'Complicit', 'Subordinate' and 'Marginalised' are all negative terms.

Late-medieval East Anglia offers no shortage of impressive gentlewomen occupying the status of 'consorts'. We should understand these consorts as akin to senior business partners in a small or medium-sized firm. From the moment she got up in the morning to when she lay down at night, a consort devoted her energies to the betterment of the family she had married into. Her work could be quite hands-on: in addition to directing servants and overseeing general management she provisioned the household with foodstuffs,[17] ordered cloth and items of clothing from town,[18] made medicines and treated the sick.[19] Her maternal cares centred on bringing up the children to the greater benefit of the family, thus boarding girls in greater households, seeing to it that the boys received formal education and taking charge of finding suitable marriage partners.[20] Commenting on the harsh upbringing of the Paston daughters, Ann Haskell wonders how 'medieval girls became adult women of such self-assurance'. Like soldiers first taught to obey so that they might later command, gentry daughters learned discipline and the values of strict hierarchy. '[T]hose who could survive such subjection in early life, earned the right to command it later'.[21] The lessons in demure, quiet and submissive femininity taught in

---

[17]  *Paston Letters and Papers of the Fifteenth Century [PL and P]*, ed. Norman Davis, 2 vols (Oxford, 1971–6), I, nos 130, 148, 149, 211 [from Margaret].
[18]  *PL and P* I, no. 28 [from Agnes]; nos 125, 127, 130, 135, 140, 149, 156, 192 [from Margaret].
[19]  *PL and P* I nos 141, 218, 219 [from Margaret]; Elaine E. Whitaker, 'Reading the Paston Letters Medically', *English Language Notes* 31 (1993), pp. 19–27.
[20]  *PL and P* I, nos 13, 19, 27, 28 [from Agnes]; 150, 174, 186, 201, 203, 206, 216, 226 [from Margaret]. Also note the active role of Thomasine Hopton, second wife of Sir John Hopton, who made a secret deal with Roger Townshend to let him have more in the way of dowry for her daughter, Eleanor Lunsford, than Sir John had been prepared to give: C. E. Moreton, *The Townshends and their World: Gentry, Law, and Land in Norfolk c.1450–1551* (Oxford, 1992), p. 20; Colin Richmond, *John Hopton: A Fifteenth-Century Suffolk Gentleman* (Cambridge, 1981), pp. 126–7.
[21]  Ann S. Haskell, 'The Paston Women on Marriage in Fifteenth-Century England', *Viator* 4 (1973), pp. 459–71, at p. 470; also Colin Richmond, 'The Pastons Revisited: Marriage and the Family in Fifteenth-Century England', *Bulletin of the Institute of Historical Research* 58 (1985), pp. 25–36; Candace Gregory, 'Raising the Good Wife: Mothers and Daughters in Fifteenth-Century England', in *Reputation and Representation in Fifteenth-Century Europe*, ed. Douglas L. Biggs, Sharon D. Michalove and A. Compton Reeves (Leiden, 2004), pp. 145–67; Anna Dronzek,

various media, from conduct books to devotional literature, would have had little real-life application for gentlewomen once they were married.[22]

Both Agnes and Margaret Paston were left in charge of home estates while their husbands were away in London, having to take care of legal disputes, rent and debt payment, and dealings with tenant farmers, overseeing building repairs and the condition of stock and crops.[23] Most notoriously, Margaret commanded the armed defence of Gresham Manor on 28 January 1449 when Lord Moleyne's men came with swords, knives, bows and arrows, battering rams and pans of fire to take the estate by force.[24] This is an exceptional event, but in other respects there was nothing obviously 'East Anglian' about the activity of gentlewomen. The women of the Yorkshire Plumptons and Oxfordshire and Berkshire Stonors similarly demonstrate the practical capabilities of keeping home and manors functioning effectively in their husbands' absence.[25]

To be a consort does not require a living husband. Some widowed gentlewomen remarried, but those who chose not to do so remained preoccupied with their marital families and with protecting their own financial interests. Agnes Paston battled for possession of her dower land and Margaret joined her sons in quarrels over Sir John Fastolf's estate.[26] Looking to other East Anglian families of the fifteenth century, the sheep-farming Townshends possessed a determined matriarch in the shape of Eleanor Townshend, née Lunsford, who in her widowhood emerged as a forceful negotiator. She assumed control of the considerable Townshend interests, trading wool, buying land, building a mill, selling produce, leasing holdings and pursuing numerous debtors through the Court of Common Pleas even in the last year of her life. It is telling that accounts of household documents were written in English for her benefit rather than the usual Latin during this period of matriarchy.[27] Elisabeth Brews, second wife of Sir Thomas Brews, is best remembered for her role in helping to secure the marriage of her daughter Margery to John Paston III in 1477, but the charm displayed in her letters hides a steely and determined character. When Sir Thomas died in 1482 Elizabeth embarked on a lengthy legal battle with her step-son William, Sir Thomas's heir by his first wife Margaret Calthorpe. The dispute was not settled

---

'Gender Roles and the Marriage Market in Fifteenth-Century England: Ideals and Practices', in *Love, Marriage and Family Ties in the Later Middle Ages*, ed. Isabel Davis, Miriam Müller and Sarah Rees Jones (Turnhout, 2003), pp. 63–76.

[22] Normative and alternative models of femininity are examined in Kim M. Phillips, *Medieval Maidens: Young Women and Gender in England, 1270–1540* (Manchester, 2003), pp. 77–97.

[23] Haskell, 'Paston Women on Marriage', p. 460. See *PL and P* I, nos 128, 132, 136, 146, 149, 154, 164, 178, 179, 180, 182, 189 [from Margaret].

[24] *PL and P* I, nos 36, 129–131.

[25] Joan W. Kirby, 'Women in the Plumpton Correspondence: Fiction and Reality', in *Church and Chronicle in the Middle Ages: Essays Presented to John Taylor*, ed. Ian Wood and G. A. Loud (London, 1991), pp. 219–32.

[26] *PL and P* I, nos 12, 18, 32 [on Oxnede]; nos 199, 200, 201, 202, 204, 205 [from Margaret regarding Caistor].

[27] Moreton, *Townshends and their World*, pp. 107, 144, 173; Richmond, *John Hopton*, p. 127. On varieties of literacy among gentlewomen see Alison Truelove, 'Literacy', in *Gentry Culture*, ed. Radulescu and Truelove pp. 84–99, especially 87, 91–2, and Philippa Maddern, 'A Woman and Her Letters: The Documentary World of Elizabeth Clere', in *Maitresse of My Wit: Medieval Women, Modern Scholars*, ed. Louise D'Arcens and Juanita Feros Ruys (Turnhout, 2004), pp. 29–45.

until twenty years later, a matter of months before Elizabeth's death.[28] Elizabeth Clere, née Uvedale, was also widowed young and enjoyed a calm prosperous widowhood of forty-seven years in which she managed her affairs with great skill and competence.[29]

It would be misleading to imply that these women were solely concerned with social status. There is plenty of evidence for their religious devotion, and gentlewomen and their husbands gave valuable financial support to the Church through the patronage of devotional art, local priories and recluses.[30] An intriguing, though indirect, connection between Margaret Paston and Julian of Norwich is indicated in Margaret's bequest of three shillings and fourpence each to the anchoresses at Conisford, Friars Preachers and White Friars in Norwich on her death in 1484.[31] Julian was of course long dead by then. Lay gentlewomen had an eye to the next world, certainly, and seem to have been genuinely devout, yet their primary energies were reserved for the affairs of this world. It would also be inaccurate to suggest that lay gentlewomen were always happy or successful in the consort role. Sometimes marriage could go badly wrong, as it did for Alice Wodehouse when she married Sir Thomas Tuddenham around 1418. It seems that their marriage was never consummated, and Alice had an affair with her father's chamberlain and bore him a child. Consequently she became a nun at Crabhouse, possibly under pressure from her father, yet the bishop of Norwich called the parties to court and the marriage was annulled on the grounds of adultery in 1436.[32] Alice may have made a superficially 'good' marriage, but sexual scandal and failed marriage take her out of the 'consort' category: she better fits the 'deprived' category. Young women married against their will were also victims of misfortune. Gentlewomen were not immune from ravishment (abduction, sometimes combined with forced intercourse), as is illustrated by the experience of Joan Boys, daughter of a Norfolk lawyer, who was abducted by Robert Langstrother in 1451.[33] She cried out her protest against 'the knave' as she was carried off and in each village they passed, vowing that she would never consent to him, yet married Langstrother a few days later at Wiggenhall St Mary. Following the marriage she seems in some respect to fit the

---

[28]  Moreton, *Townshends and their World*, pp. 95–9.
[29]  Colin Richmond, 'Elizabeth Clere, Friend of the Pastons', in *Medieval Women: Texts and Contexts in Late Medieval Britain: Essays for Felicity Riddy*, ed. Jocelyn Wogan-Browne *et al.* (Turnhout, 2000), pp. 251–73; Maddern, 'A Woman and Her Letters', pp. 29–45.
[30]  Gillian Pritchard, 'Religion and the Paston Family', in *Daily Life in the Late Middle Ages*, ed. Richard Britnell (Stroud, 1998), pp. 65–82; Eamon Duffy, 'Holy Maydens, Holy Wyfes: The Cult of Women Saints in Fifteenth- and Sixteenth-Century England', in *Women in the Church*, ed. W. J. Sheils and Diana Wood (Oxford, 1990), pp. 175–96; Gail McMurray Gibson, *The Theater of Devotion: East Anglian Drama and Society in the Late Middle Ages* (Chicago, 1989), pp. 19–46; Joel T. Rosenthal, 'Local Girls do it Better: Women and Religion in Late Medieval East Anglia', in *Traditions and Transformations in Late Medieval England*, ed. Douglas Biggs, Sharon D. Michalove, and A. Compton Reeves (Leiden, 2002), pp. 1–20, here at pp. 14–18.
[31]  *PL and P* I, no. 230.
[32]  Roger Virgoe, 'The Divorce of Sir Thomas Tuddenham', *Norfolk Archaeology* 34 (1969), pp. 406–18. Virgoe supplies an abbreviated translation of the annulment case brought before the Norwich Consistory Court in 1436 in his article.
[33]  *PL and P* I, no. 45; Roger Virgoe, 'The Ravishment of Joan Boys', in *East Anglian Studies: Essays Presented to J. C. Barringer on his Retirement*, ed. Adam Longcroft and Richard Joby (Norwich, 1995), pp. 276–81.

'consort' model – bringing joint law suits with her husband, moving with him to London, and being named co-executor in Robert's will of 1463 – but they had no children together. The true nature of their marriage and Joan's feelings about it are lost to us.

Lay gentlewomen could experience deprivation, but the consort role was the standard model of femininity for women of this status. Consort femininity required dedication and a commitment to the worldly goals of advancing familial status. To maintain gentility required constant energies on the part of family members and the role of the consort was crucial. Such women, having married into prominent even if not truly elite families, reaped the rewards of the 'patriarchal bargain' for their tremendous efforts: financial security, social respectability, and authority in mid and later life, especially in widowhood.

Even if she had been a wife and mother before entering anchoritic life, the consort category does not appear to fit the fragmentary 'Julian' we can claim to know. There is no strong indication in her writings of the concerns of the consort gentlewoman. She writes of the motherhood of God but, as Christopher Abbott points out, her metaphor refers to *having* a mother, not *being* a mother.[34] Although she uses the languages of service and 'worship' she turns them to quite different purposes from their uses in lay contexts. 'Service' for the lay gentry was something others performed for them or which they performed for social superiors in order to improve their own prospects; 'worship' was a quality which gentlemen and women sought for themselves as they worked to enhance their position in the social structure. Julian's metaphorical uses of such language hold none of the self-interest of their meanings for the laity. The 'deprived' category does not seem suitable either, despite the illness which Julian describes as the prelude to her first visions. The 'vocational' category, however, looks more promising.

Gentility is usually defined in lay terms, but a good number of gentlewomen stepped sideways to enter the religious life. Was becoming a 'bride of Christ' simply to be another type of consort? Not really; for gentry daughters or widows, monastic life offered a future fundamentally different from matrimony. It was the chief 'vocational' form of femininity available to medieval English gentlewomen, and in a family with a number of daughters it would not have been unusual for at least one to take the veil. Dorothy Calthorpe, daughter of Sir Philip Calthorpe, was a nun at Bruisyard Abbey.[35] Roger Townshend I's daughter Agnes entered Barking Abbey in Essex in the late fifteenth century when her elder sisters Thomasine, Elizabeth and Anne had already been placed in good matches with sons of the Woodhouse, Cressener and Castell families respectively, while Cecily Fastolf became prioress of Bungay Priory in the early sixteenth century.[36] An estimated 64 per cent of East Anglian nuns derived from the lower or 'parish' gentry, with another 10 per cent from the more elite gentry

---

[34] Abbott, *Julian of Norwich*, p. 2.
[35] Marilyn Oliva, *The Convent and the Community in Late Medieval England: Female Monasteries in the Diocese of Norwich, 1350–1540* (Woodbridge, 1998), pp. 54 and 201.
[36] Moreton, *Townshends and their World*, pp. 21–2.

families.[37] There were eleven female monasteries in the diocese, none of which
were very large or wealthy, but monastic life may have had certain attractions for
women who aspired to a degree of authority.[38] Oliva has argued for meritocracy
over aristocracy in the office-holding patterns within these nunneries, noting
numerous instances of parish-gentry nuns in positions from second chambress
to prioress.[39] Prioresses and abbesses possessed seigneurial rights over their
lands and tenants – collecting rents and fines, controlling mills, holding manor
and leet courts, keeping gallows, possessing rights to the view of frankpledge
and assizes of bread and ale – rather like lay consorts with charge over familial
estates, although prioresses' authority extended beyond that of consorts. They
possessed spiritual rights over churches, chapels and rectories, with the power
to appoint parish priests and collect tithes from these institutions, in return
having the responsibility for their upkeep.[40] Lesser office-holders naturally had
more narrow responsibilities, yet undertook important roles, such as those of
cellaress, sacrist and almoner. To receive any kind of office presumed a level
of maturity and seriousness – usually a woman had to have been professed for
several years before attaining even a lowly post such as doorkeeper.[41]

Yet to enter the monastic life, even for those women who took on positions
of authority within the nunnery, was never to become 'like a man'. Medieval
monasticism was sharply gendered, and monks and nuns did not occupy
equivalent social or spiritual positions. Nunneries had to answer to higher male
ecclesiastical authorities – the bishop of the diocese, or male superiors of their
order.[42] Enclosure was *in theory* much more vigorously enforced on nuns than
monks in the wake of Boniface VIII's bull *Periculoso* of 1298 (although in practice
the order was regularly breached),[43] and of course no nun could be a priest as
a monk could.

The theory that Julian had lived as a nun, probably at Carrow Priory, before
entering her anchorhold was first posited by her editors Colledge and Walsh and
is supported too by her recent editors, Jenkins and Watson.[44] My preference is to
leave such questions aside; what we can say is that she assuredly fits the category

[37] Oliva, *Convent and Community*, pp. 52–61; see also her 'Aristocracy or Meritocracy? Office-Holding Patterns in Late Medieval English Nunneries', in *Women in the Church*, ed. Sheils and Wood, pp. 197–208.
[38] Oliva, *Convent and Community*, pp. 9–10, 22–7, 41; Gilchrist and Oliva, *Religious Women*, pp. 24–5. The average population of East Anglian nunneries over the period 1350–1540 was twelve and a half nuns. This would seem comparable with the average population of male monasteries of around fourteen. However, the latter figure veils much wider variation in population, from over fifty to only one or two. Derived from Oliva, *Convent and Community*, pp. 41 and 42, tables 7 and 8.
[39] Oliva, 'Aristocracy or Meritocracy', pp. 204–8.
[40] Oliva, *Convent and Community*, pp. 27–30.
[41] Gilchrist and Oliva, *Religious Women*, pp. 54–5; Oliva, *Convent and Community*, pp. 75–99.
[42] Oliva, *Convent and Community*, p. 32, where she also notes some exceptions.
[43] James A. Brundage and Elizabeth Makowski, 'Enclosure of Nuns: The Decretal *Periculoso* and its Commentators', *Journal of Medieval History* 20 (1994), pp. 143–55; Oliva, *Convent and Community*, pp. 35–6; John Tillotson, 'Visitation and Reform of the Yorkshire Nunneries in the Fourteenth Century', *Northern History* 30 (1994), pp. 1–21.
[44] See above, n. 6; *Writings*, ed. Watson and Jenkins, p. 4. On Carrow see Christopher Harper-Bill and Carole Rawcliffe, 'The Religious Houses', in *Medieval Norwich*, ed. Carole Rawcliffe and Richard Wilson (London, 2004), pp. 73–90, at pp. 88–91.

of vocational femininity, if not through the monastery then certainly through her life as a recluse. Anchoresses were women who avoided the consort role (or left it behind in widowhood) to enter a form of living which sits in comfortable parallel to matrimony: offering a degree of authority or limited autonomy, but in a manner quite unthreatening to broader cultural structures. Anchoresses, like nuns, lived and worshipped within institutional and ideological formations well-established within the society and culture of the late-medieval West, and received status and validation by contemporaries. Although their life choice might appear extraordinary, even radical or outlandish to modern eyes, it was certainly not extremist in their own historical context. Our society does not look benignly on individuals who seek out a solitary life but the 'desert' – real or symbolic – had an ancient and esteemed lineage in medieval Christianity. As Ann K. Warren says, these women should not be seen as 'exotics, deviants, or as individuals peripheral to medieval religious history', but rather 'at the apex' of the perfect Christian life.[45] Anchoresses remained tethered to the world, as they required a licence from their bishop and the support of the institution to which they were attached (parish church, cathedral or monastic house), and also of local communities who might be called upon to help maintain anchoresses. There are six surviving 'rules' for English anchoritic women, all authored by men, suggesting strong masculine intervention in shaping their experiences and spiritual selves.[46] Anchoresses were valued for their prayer, their intercessory function and as counsellors.[47] It was not normal for them to become authors in their own right, much less to compose complex and highly original theological tracts as Julian did.

Women recluses rarely lived in the wilderness. Their 'desert' was a state of mind and their cell was most probably attached to a church in a bustling suburb or a monastic house on the edge of a town. Julian would have shared with other anchoresses the paradoxical situation of having 'withdrawn' from the world only to find herself in a comparatively 'public' position, and at certain times of the day and season anyone could draw upon her time and energies to seek spiritual advice at her window. The potential psychological agonies of the anchoritic life were acknowledged by contemporary authors, and the dangers of falling into variants of *accidie* such as indolence, languor, apathy and despondency were cautioned against.[48] Some anchoress's cells were very small, most must have been rather dark, and their usual northerly outlook would have blighted them

---

[45] Ann K. Warren, *Anchorites and their Patrons in Medieval England* (Berkeley, 1985), pp. 1, 2. She provides a summary of the concepts of anchoritism and eremiticism in Christian history, pp. 7–14; also Rotha Mary Clay, *The Hermits and Anchorites of England* (London, 1914); E. A. Jones, 'Hermits and Anchorites in Historical Context', in *Approaching Medieval English Anchoritic and Mystical Texts*, ed. Dyas, Edden and Ellis, pp. 3–18; Christopher Cannon, 'Enclosure', in *The Cambridge Companion to Medieval Women's Writing*, ed. Carolyn Dinshaw and David Wallace (Cambridge, 2003), pp. 109–23; Liz Herbert McAvoy and Mari Hughes-Edwards (eds), *Anchorites, Wombs and Tombs: Intersections of Gender and Enclosure in the Middle Ages* (Cardiff, 2005), pp. 6–26; Liz Herbert McAvoy (ed.), 'Introduction: Place, Space and Body within Anchoritic Rhetoric', in *Rhetoric of the Anchorhold: Place, Space and Body within the Discourses of Enclosure* (Cardiff, 2008), pp. 111–26.
[46] A helpful annotated list is in Warren, *Anchorites and their Patrons*, Appendix 2, pp. 294–8.
[47] Clay, *Hermits and Anchorites*, pp. 146–55; Warren, *Anchorites and their Patrons*, pp. 110–13.
[48] Clay, *Hermits and Anchorites*, p. 124.

with a permanent chill. Recluses were not always as strictly enclosed as one might imagine – some kept gardens or gained permission to go on pilgrimage[49] – but as they were expected to live an enclosed life their spiritual reputation would have relied on them staying in the cell most of the time. The anchoress needed to 'learn to suffer, and to suffer well'. In so doing she sought spiritual reward, but stayed well within the parameters of socially sanctioned ways to lead a feminine life. In Chris Cannon's words, 'eagerness for self-torment is a very odd sort of empowerment and might be better described as a procedure for *furthering* social domination.'[50]

'Alternative femininity' is the least well-documented feminine way of being, and the most difficult to identify. Heretical women, of which there were significant numbers in East Anglia, were certainly transgressive in their choice of religious belief but it is more difficult to demonstrate that they were transgressive in their *femininity*, as many joined with their husbands and communities in adopting dissident spirituality.[51] Better candidates are the groups of 'sisters' who lived together in informal communities in Norwich and Ipswich and appear to have dedicated themselves to chastity, poverty or some kind of religious vow, although they were not formally recognised by the Church. Norman Tanner suggests that these informal clusters of spiritual sisters resemble Continental beguinages, but Gilchrist and Oliva feel the term 'beguine' may veil distinctive East Anglian forms of feminine piety.[52] Although some of these communities may have followed a rule which dictated their hours of rising and bedtime, their dietary practices, the wearing of hairshirts and the saying of constant prayers,[53] they stand outside of institutional structures and may have been self-governing. Such women had moved beyond conventional frameworks to adopt a more daring way of being a woman.

Julian stepped into a pre-determined non-marital role when she became a recluse. She needed the approval of her bishop, her church and her community and, even though she was probably not required to live by a rule in the way that nuns did, the norms and expectations surrounding the anchoritic life would have ensured that her conduct was regulated and observed by men in authority and more informally by her community. In these respects she chose a vocational framework for living. Yet Julian was not a standard English anchoress. If other recluses produced written work dealing with visionary experience then little or none has survived to the present.[54] If any other anchoresses of her time engaged

---

[49]  Warren, *Anchorites and their Patrons*, pp. 77–8.
[50]  Cannon, 'Enclosure', p. 117.
[51]  Shannon McSheffrey, *Gender and Heresy: Women and Men in Lollard Communities, 1414–1520* (Philadelphia, 1995); Norman P. Tanner (ed.), *Heresy Trials in the Diocese of Norwich, 1428–1431*, Camden Society 4th series 20 (London, 1977).
[52]  Tanner, *The Church in Late Medieval Norwich 1370–1532* (Toronto, 1984), pp. 64–6, 130–1; Gilchrist and Oliva, *Religious Women*, pp. 17, 71–4, 95–6.
[53]  B. Zimmerman, 'The White Friars at Ipswich', *Proceedings of the Suffolk Institute of Archaeology* 10 (1891–1900), pp. 196–20, at p. 198.
[54]  Although a recent article by Mary C. Erler makes out an excellent case for the late medieval visionary text, 'A Vision of Purgatory' as having been written by a Winchester anchoress. See Mary C. Erler, '"A Revelation of Purgatory" (1422); Reform and the Politics of Female Visions', *Viator* 38 (2007), pp. 321–47.

in high level and original theological thought then no trace remains of their ideas. To produce a substantial piece of writing of any sort, with or without the help of a secretary, was uncommon behaviour for women of Julian's day. Indeed, Julian is regarded as the 'earliest known woman writer of English'.[55] She may not have been well known for her written work during her own lifetime but the fact that she produced it is still remarkable. Like her contemporary Margery Kempe, in these respects her femininity was of the alternative sort although, unlike Margery, she combined her authorial bravery with an approved vocation, in this way softening the choices she made for herself as a woman of her time.

In answer to Barratt's call to reconstruct a social Julian, then, I have focused on considering the forms of femininities open to her, while trying to avoid excessive conjecture about her pre-reclusive life. Barratt is anxious that '[w]e do Julian a profound disservice if, with the laudable desire of making her accessible to our own time, we occlude the way in which she is firmly embedded in a specific historical era',[56] which is true in many ways, yet occlusion of biographical detail seems to have been just what Julian wanted. Julian's cell has long since crumbled away and the details of her life along with it. What we can say is that as a woman of her time she was at once conventional and extraordinary. Readings of Julian tend to be personal, and mine is no exception. I am content to let the pre-reclusive Julian go, to admire the choices she evidently made to become a anchoress, mystic, author and thinker, and ultimately to let the focus of scholarship rest on her work, not her life.

---

[55] *Writings*, ed. Watson and Jenkins, p. ix.
[56] Barratt, 'Lordship, Service and Worship', p. 177.

# 2

# 'A recluse atte Norwyche': Images of Medieval Norwich and Julian's Revelations

CATE GUNN

We know nothing conclusive about Julian's early life, but she indicates that she had been devout since her youth; if Julian's childhood and youth had been spent in Norwich, how would the experiences of her early life have fed her devotional life and possibly informed her visions? Among the evidence that Norman Tanner cites in support of his claim that Norwich may have been 'Europe's *most* religious city'[1] is the number of hermits and anchorites supported by the city in the high Middle Ages. Pre-eminent among these anchorites is Julian herself, the 'star attraction'[2] of the spiritual life of Norwich. But it is possible to look at the situation another way: while Julian may be proof of the religiosity of Norwich, could it be that the religious atmosphere, devotional practices and imagery of Norwich made Julian's spirituality possible and inspired her writing? The very buildings manifested both the economic importance and religious significance of the city: the magnificent Norman Cathedral challenged the dominance of the Castle; the splendid church of St Peter Mancroft overshadowed the marketplace. Every day in the city was punctuated by the ringing of bells of nearly sixty churches,[3] and the chanting and singing in religious houses provided a counterpoint to the noise and bustle of the marketplace. The impact of religion was auditory, olfactory and, above all, visual.

Every 'major European development in the practice of institutional religion' from the Benedictine monastic cathedral to the 'Great Hospital' of St Giles and the secular college of St Mary in the Fields was represented in Norwich;[4] the most important new movement in the high Middle Ages was that of the mendicant friars, all four major orders of which had houses in Norwich. Both Dominicans and Franciscans were dedicated to preaching to the people and used techniques such as colourful narrative stories or *exempla* to attract lay audiences; sermons were an important way of educating and inspiring people both religious and lay. One of the few pieces of information Julian gives about her early life is that she

---

[1]   Norman Tanner, 'Religious Practice', in *Medieval Norwich*, ed. Carole Rawcliffe and Richard Wilson (London, 2004), pp. 137–55 (137).
[2]   Ibid., p. 138.
[3]   Jonathan Finch, 'The Churches', in *Medieval Norwich*, ed. Rawcliffe and Wilson, pp. 49–72 (50 and 58).
[4]   Christopher Harper-Bill and Carole Rawcliffe, 'Religious Houses', in *Medieval Norwich*, pp. 73–119 (73–4).

heard 'a man telle of halye kyrke of the storye of Sainte Cecille' (*Vision*, 1.36),[5] presumably in a sermon. Julian may have been a nun at Carrow Priory, whose large church was used for preaching by resident and visiting clergy.[6] The story of Saint Cecilia recalled by Julian is contained in the famous *Legenda Aurea*, a collection of stories and *exempla* written by the Dominican Jacobus de Voragine. The Dominican church Julian may have known was destroyed by fire in 1413, but the large church built in the mid-fifteenth century is still standing, and the great size of its nave, as well as the preaching yard outside, are witnesses to the importance of the Dominicans' preaching mission in Norwich. The friars also provided intellectual stimulation; the Dominican friary ranked as a *studium* to which brethren were sent for further training from all parts of England. The Benedictine cathedral priory also had a reputation for learning, with one of the finest libraries in medieval England and a school for oblates, as well as having some responsibility for the grammar school.[7] Carrow Priory also had a library.[8]

The experience of religion in the fourteenth century, however, was much more than cerebral: Miri Rubin has described the intensely sensory nature of the Eucharist for lay people – incorporating sight, sound and smell,[9] while Eamon Duffy has written of the impact of images on the devotions and religious practices of late medieval England.[10] Michael Camille has suggested that images are 'taken for granted in our society' and that '[w]e probably see more of these in one day than a medieval person might see in a whole lifetime'.[11] But in one important area, the medieval person certainly encountered the colour and forms of images: where churches now present bare stone or whitewash, the medieval church was alive with murals and painted statues. Imagery was a part of everyday life – and the everyday world was incorporated into religious imagery. The Despencer retable, an altar piece made for Norwich Cathedral in the late fourteenth century, sets the Passion, Crucifixion and Resurrection among people – citizens of Norwich – clothed in late fourteenth-century dress. When Julian saw Christ dying on the cross and his flesh turning pale there was 'a dry, harre wind' blowing (*Revelation*, 16.10). Watson and Jenkins note that this is not a standard detail of Passion accounts but 'a cold east wind from the North Sea might have

5   All quotations will be taken from *The Writings of Julian of Norwich: A Vision Showed to a Devout Woman and A Revelation of Love*, ed. Nicholas Watson and Jacqueline Jenkins (Turnhout, 2006). References to both *A Vision* and *A Revelation* will be given in the text with section or chapter and line numbers.
6   Harper-Bill and Rawcliffe, 'Religious Houses', p. 98; Watson and Jenkins suggest 'there is a strong possibility she was a nun at the Benedictine convent at Carrow, a mile from the church of St Julian's, Conisford, in Norwich, where she was later enclosed as an anchoress', *Writings*, p. 4.
7   Norman Tanner, 'The Cathedral and the City', in *Norwich Cathedral: Church, City and Diocese 1096–1996*, ed. Ian Atherton *et al.* (London, 1996), pp. 255–80 (270–2).
8   Marilyn Oliva, *The Convent and the Community in Late Medieval England: Female Monasteries in the Diocese of Norwich, 1350–1540* (Woodbridge, 1998), p. 67.
9   Miri Rubin, *Corpus Christi: The Eucharist in Late Medieval Culture* (Cambridge, 1991), pp. 59–63.
10   Eamon Duffy, *The Stripping of the Altars: Traditional Religion in England c.1400–1580* (New Haven, 1992), pp. 155–63.
11   Michael Camille, 'The Language of Images in Medieval England, 1200–1400', in *Age of Chivalry: Art in Plantagenet England 1200–1400*, ed. Jonathan Alexander and Paul Binski (London, 1987), pp. 33–40 (33).

been a feature of many Good Fridays in fourteenth-century Norwich'.[12] Robert
Flood has also suggested that the 'sea grounde' with hills and dales, wrack and
gravel (*Revelation*, 10.16–17) is reminiscent of the Yare valley east of Norwich;[13]
whilst Flood tends to interpret Julian's visions in terms of her physical environment too literally, we should not ignore that environment. Like the painter of
the Despencer retable, Julian, in many ways, imagined the Crucifixion as taking
place in Norwich.

The Norwich in which Julian lived was full of the sights, sounds and smells
of religion, and these must have had an effect upon her spirituality; although
her writings convey a deep theological understanding and spiritual concern, the
visions she describes are intensely sensory. Towards the end of her vision, the
devil came to Julian, with his dreadful heat, stench and noise (*Vision*, 23.1–6).
Overall, however, the experience was primarily visual; like many Christian
mystics, Julian wrote of seeing God. Augustine wrote that 'sight is the principal sense by which knowledge is acquired';[14] perception was the paradigm
of knowledge, and metaphors of illumination and vision were used to express
intellectual and spiritual knowledge.[15]

Images played an important role in the regular devotional practices of
lay people also. The ubiquity of Gregory the Great's dictum that 'a picture is
displayed in churches on this account, in order that those who do not know
letters may at least read by seeing on the walls what they are unable to read
in books'[16] can be distracting – it prevents us from apprehending what the real
function of imagery in the churches of the Middle Ages was.[17] Lawrence Duggan
has argued persuasively that we must already know what pictures represent for
them to be meaningful, and suggests that pictures are read to deepen knowledge of what is already known and perhaps to gain new insight, rather than for
new information.[18] Richard Marks, in his exploration of the use and function of
imagery in parish churches in late-medieval England, suggests a move away
from a concern with the didactic purpose of images as 'pictorial "texts"' towards
a more affective function, stimulating personal piety.[19] In the early fifteenth-
century English dialogue *Dives and Pauper* it is argued that images are used
to recall the Passion of Christ and the saints, and to stir people to devotion as

[12] *Writings*, ed. Watson and Jenkins, p. 178.
[13] Robert H. Flood, *A Description of St Julian's Church, Norwich and an Account of Dame Julian's Connection with It* (Norwich, 1936), p. 36.
[14] 'Oculi autem sunt ad noscendum in sensibus principes', Augustine, *Confessions*, ed. James O'Donnell, 3 vols (Oxford, 1992), I, p. 140; *Confessions*, trans. R. S. Pine-Coffin (London, 1961), p. 241.
[15] Carolly Erickson, *The Medieval Vision: Essays in History and Perception* (New York, 1976), pp. 42–3.
[16] 'Idcirco enim pictura in ecclesiis adhibetur, ut hi qui litteras nesciunt saltem in parietibus uidendo legant, quae legere in codicis non ualent'. Trans. and quoted by Celia M. Chazelle, 'Pictures, Books and the Illiterate; Pope Gregory I's Letters to Serenus of Marseilles', *Word and Image* 6 (1990), pp. 138–53 (139).
[17] Camille suggests it is 'a commonplace in our perception of medieval art which requires some rethinking', in 'The Language of Images', p. 33.
[18] Lawrence G. Duggan, 'Was Art Really the "book of the illiterate"?', *Word and Image* 5 (1989), pp. 227–51 (243 and 47).
[19] Richard Marks, *Image and Devotion in Late Medieval England* (Stroud, 2004), p. 18.

well as to be a book for the unlearned.[20] Reginald Pecock, defending the use of images against the attacks of the Lollards, argued that one purpose of images was that they acted 'as rememoratijf signes of God and of hise benefetis, and of his holi lijf and passioun'.[21] I want to suggest that the images she was familiar with may have acted as rememorative signs for Julian.

Julian's younger contemporary, also from East Anglia, Margery Kempe, was certainly stirred to devotion by images. She was reminded of the passion of our Lord by a crucifix she saw in Leicester which 'was petowsly poyntyd & lamen-tabyl to be-heldyn'.[22] She was also moved by a pietà in Norwich at the sight of which she felt compelled to cry. She was gently rebuked by her companion who reminded her that Jesus had been long dead, to which Margery replied that 'hys deth is as fresch to me as he had deyd þis same day, & so me thynkyth it awt to be to ʒow & to alle Cristen pepil. We awt euyr to han mende of hys kendnes & euyr thynkyn of þe dolful deth þat he deyd for vs.'[23] This serves as a good explanation of the role of images of the Passion, such as crucifixes and pietàs, in the high Middle Ages: they served to remind the viewer that Jesus died for them, and that his death was a present necessity for their redemption. The iconography of the pietà – Mary with the dead Christ in her lap – developed in the fourteenth century and combined the representation of Mary as grieving mother with her 'role as *mediatrix* for mankind'.[24] It is not clear whether the church in which Margery saw the pietà was St Stephen's, which she had just left after a crying fit; there were pietàs in the churches of the Austin Friars and the Greyfriars which were the objects of devotion for people outside the mendicant communities,[25] and at the end of the fourteenth century an image of the pietà in Norwich Cathedral was attracting oblations.[26]

In her vision, Julian saw Mary 'gastelye in bodilye lyekenes' as 'a simpille maidene and a meeke, yonge of age' (*Vision*, 4.22); later she is shown Mary as she was as she conceived, in her sorrow under the cross and 'as sho is nowe, in likinge, wirshippe, and joye' (*Vision*, 13.21). Julian saw Mary in her eleventh revelation at the right side of Christ and the editors note that 'In late medieval painting and sculpture Mary is usually depicted on the right side of the cross, from Christ's perspective'.[27] However, what Christ shows to Julian is more than Mary at the Crucifixion: he shows his love for her, and it is through this love that he loves all humanity. Mary is not only the simple maiden, she is also seen in

20  *Dives and Pauper*, ed. P. H. Barnum, EETS o.s. 275 (London, 1976), vol. 1, pt. 1, p. 82.
21  Reginald Pecock, *The Repressor of Over Much Blaming of the Clergy*, ed. Churchill Babington, Chronicles and Memorials of Great Britain (Kraus reprint, 1966), p. 167; see also Marks, *Image and Devotion*, p. 16.
22  Margery Kempe, *The Book of Margery Kempe*, ed. Sanford Brown Meech and Hope Emily Allen (Oxford, 1997), ch. 46, p. 111.
23  Ibid., ch. 60, p. 148.
24  Marks, *Image and Devotion*, p. 123.
25  Harper-Bill and Rawcliffe, 'Religious Houses', p. 112.
26  Identified as 'sancta maria de compassione' in 1391: John R. Shinners, 'The Veneration of Saints at Norwich Cathedral in the Fourteenth Century', *Norwich Archaeology* 40 (1988), pp. 133–44 (138) .
27  *Writings*, ed. Watson and Jenkins, p. 202.

the manner of the Assumption and Coronation as the Queen of Heaven (*Revelation*, 25.33–4).

The visions Julian received were initiated by the crucifix held before her as she lay close to death. The church of St Edward and St Julian, to which Julian was attached as an anchorite, is recorded as having two 'portable' (*portatilis*) crosses in 1368.[28] Julian's 'parson' who attended her when she was believed to be dying brought such a cross, probably with a painted figure of Christ on it,[29] and set it before her, saying: 'Doughter, I have brought the the image of thy savioure. Loke thereupon, and comforthe the therewith in reverence of him that diede for the and me' (*Vision*, 2.22–4). The words he is recorded as saying in the later *Revelation* are slightly different (*Revelation*, 3.19–20), but both state that the image should be a comfort to the dying woman; it is a reminder that her saviour died for her redemption. Christopher Abbott points out that 'The church presents the crucifix to Julian precisely to activate and support her faith in Christ as saviour and redeemer.'[30] This scene is similar to that illustrated in the guides of a good death, *Artes moriendi*,[31] and recalls the grace Julian had desired in order that she may experience not only the pains but also the 'dredes and tempestes of feyndes' that would prepare her for when she was really dying (*Vision*, 1.27).

By the Middle Ages, the cross was the most important of Christian symbols. From the early tradition of presenting the cross as 'a statement of divine victory'[32] it had become a memorial of the Passion of the human Jesus, and in late-medieval piety in particular there was a desire to imaginatively participate in that Passion: through the cross, Christ became present to the devout viewer. For Julian the cross was at the heart of her spirituality; as an anchoress the crucifix would have been a constant presence in her cell, as it was for the sister of Aelred and the anchoresses for whom the thirteenth-century *Ancrene Wisse* was written (an English work Julian may have known). Aelred wrote in the *De Institutione Inclusorum*: 'On your altar let it be enough for you to have a representation of our Saviour hanging on the Cross; that will bring before your mind his passion for you to imitate'.[33]

The representation of the Crucifixion became increasingly affective during the high Middle Ages; a more dynamic representation of the suffering of Christ stressed his agony and intensified the emotional response of the viewer.[34] Denise

---

[28] *Inventory of Church Goods temp. Edward III* (Archdeaconry of Norwich), transcribed by Dom Aelred Watkin, 2 vols (Norfolk Record Society, 1947 and 1948), I, p. 24.

[29] See *Age of Chivalry*, ed. Alexander and Binski, Cat. no. 99, pp. 231–2 and Philip Lindley, *Image and Idol: Medieval Sculpture* (London, 2001), Cat. no. 19, pp. 38–9.

[30] Christopher Abbott, *Julian of Norwich: Autobiography and Theology* (Cambridge, 1999), p. 63.

[31] See Paul Binski, *Medieval Death: Ritual and Representation* (London, 1996; pb 2001), pp. 39–42.

[32] Colin Morris, *The Sepulchre of Christ and the Medieval West: From the Beginning to 1600* (Oxford, 2005), p. 132.

[33] 'Sufficiat tibi in altari tuo saluatoris in cruce pendentis imago, quae passionem suam tibi repraesentet quam imiteris': Aelred of Rievaulx, *De Institutione Inclusorum* in *Opera Omnia* 1, ed. A. Hoste and C. H. Talbot, CCCM, 1 (Brepols, 1971), §26; trans. as 'Rule of Life for a Recluse' in *Treatises, The Pastoral Prayer*, Cistercian Fathers Series 2 (Kalamazoo, MI, 1971), pp. 43–102 (73).

[34] Paul Binski, *Becket's Crown: Art and Imagination in Gothic England 1170–1300* (New Haven, 2004), p. 219.

Nowakowski Baker has suggested that 'undoubtedly Julian was familiar with the conventions of depicting the crucified Christ in affective spirituality',[35] and gives as an example a wall painting from St Faith's Priory in Horsham, near Norwich. Baker suggests that while the depictions of the Passion and Crucifixion 'shaped what Julian saw', it was the narrative provided by meditative exercises and the visualization induced by such meditation, rather than devotional art, that was the 'catalyst for her visions'.[36]

Julian's intellectual achievement is now recognized, as is the spirituality of her writing; but is it possible that the religious imagery she encountered could also have informed her spirituality? Paul Binski argues that depictions of the Crucifixion should not be seen as secondary to, or dependent on, changes in the discourse about the Passion; while 'certain aspects of crucifixion imagery had a distinct discursive basis'[37] the imagery itself could constitute a new understanding and signification, promoting and propelling the discourse. There may be a fear that, by discussing the affectivity of Julian's response and the emotionally charged visual content of her revelations, we may detract from her intellectual achievement and somehow be complicit in the dismissal of her as a weak and feeble woman, prey to visions and imaginings. Benedicta Ward insists that the *Revelations* are 'not … a description of the Crucified written to invoke pity and repentance; they are not in the tradition of the *Stabat Mater*, they are serious theology of the love that is God'.[38] I would question the implied absoluteness of the distinction between the affectivity of descriptions of the Crucifixion in the late medieval affective tradition, represented by the *Stabat Mater*, with its portrayal of the suffering of Mary witnessing the painful death of her son, and the 'serious theology' of Julian's *Revelations*. Pity and theology are not mutually exclusive. Images themselves can have intellectual content; in a recent paper, Bernard McGinn has questioned the inevitability of a tension between theology and iconography which has been posited by some art historians; by reference to Hildegard of Bingen, Joachim of Fiore and Henry Suso he argues for the importance of the illustrations they commissioned and directed within their theology. McGinn points out that Julian of Norwich 'did not feel compelled to illustrate, or to commission others to illustrate, the visions that God had given [her]',[39] but the visual importance of Julian's revelation and theology is indisputable; it is as though her whole being is rapt up in her gaze on the vision of God.

It is clear from Julian's description that the cross held before her had on it a figure of the dying Christ. It was the image of the dying Christ that inspired Julian's visions: she experienced a visceral understanding of his suffering. While her understanding of his redemptive sacrifice was spiritual and theological,

---

35 Denise Nowakowski Baker, *Julian of Norwich's* Showings: *From Vision to Book* (Princeton, 1994), p. 40.
36 Ibid., pp. 44 and 51; see also Anne Clark Bartlett, *Male Authors, Female Readers: Representation and Subjectivity in Middle English Devotional Literature* (Ithaca, 1995), p. 116.
37 Binski, *Becket's Crown*, p. 218.
38 Benedicta Ward, 'Julian the Solitary', in *Julian Reconsidered*, ed. Kenneth Leech and Benedicta Ward (Oxford, 1988), pp. 11–31 (29).
39 Bernard McGinn, 'Theologians as Trinitarian Iconographers', in *The Mind's Eye: Art and Theological Argument in the Middle Ages*, ed. Jeffrey F. Hamburger and Anne-Marie Bouché (Princeton, 2006), pp. 186–207 (187).

her quest for this understanding was provoked by the *affectus* of the image. In the Eighth Revelation, Julian wrote of three ways of 'beholding of his blessed passion' (*Revelation*, 21.1–2); *beholding* is more than seeing: it suggests observing and examining in order to come to an understanding, but the understanding is initiated in a visual apprehension. Julian saw the suffering of Jesus, and from that came to an understanding of his Passion and its meaning for 'us': that is, her fellow Christians (*Revelation*, 21.12–13). Through suffering with Christ, they will come to share his bliss in heaven. The other manners of 'beholding' are to do with 'the love that made him to suffer' (*Revelation*, 22.37–8), and 'the joy and the blisse that maketh him to like it' (*Revelation*, 23.6); Julian has moved beyond the observation of the Passion to an understanding of its purpose and teleology.

The triad of three beholdings is typical of much of Julian's writing: her understanding of theology is underpinned by an awareness of God as a trinity. As part of these three beholdings, she is shown three heavens; in the first heaven she 'saw in Crist that the father is' (*Revelation*, 22.11). This seems to recall a verse from St John's Gospel: 'Jesus saith … no man cometh unto the father, but by me' (John 14:6). In the First Revelation, Julian understood the Trinity in the suffering of Christ: 'For wher Jhesu appireth the blessede trinity is understand, as to my sight' (*Revelation*, 4.11–12).[40] Julian's theology was rooted in her incarnational spirituality, but over the years, as she contemplated her vision, she came to understand Jesus as embracing the Trinity.

The Trinity is an abstract concept and depicting it was theologically and technically difficult. Alexandra Barratt, who explores its iconography and the relevance of that imagery in the essay which follows this one, focuses primarily on manuscript illustrations but, as she points out, Norwich Cathedral was dedicated to the Holy Trinity. There would, therefore, have been a patronal image of the Trinity in the Cathedral, probably standing to the north of the High Altar,[41] that Julian may well have seen. Roberta Gilchrist refers to the High Altar as the 'location of the sacred' and although the laity were prohibited from the presbytery, the pilgrims' route through the ambulatory took them behind the altar, from where they could view relics.[42] Francis Blomefield suggests that the image was on the rood loft; he also describes the image as being of the 'Throne of Grace' type: 'the Almighty Father … being blasphemously represented by a weak old man; the Blessed Redeemer on the Cross, between his knees, and the Eternal Spirit, by a dove, on his breast'.[43] This form of the Trinity is found on the signet ring of William Alnwick as Bishop of Norwich in the fifteenth century.[44] What

---

[40] This passage – and others referring to the Trinity – are not included in the shorter and earlier *A Vision*; in her essay in this volume, ' "No Such Sitting": Julian Tropes the Trinity', Alexandra Barratt points out that *A Vision* makes only two references to the Trinity. See p. 42.

[41] William Page (ed.), *VCH Norfolk*, vol. 2 (1906; rep. for University of London Institute of Historical Research, Folkestone: Dawson, 1975), p. 321.

[42] Roberta Gilchrist, *Norwich Cathedral Close: The Evolution of the English Cathedral Landscape* (Woodbridge, 2005), pp. 244–6.

[43] It is not clear where Blomefield obtained his information, but clearly the very idea of an image of the Trinity could still give offence in the eighteenth century when Blomefield first wrote his account, *The History of the City and County of Norwich*, vol. 4 of *An Essay towards a Topographical History of the County of Norfolk* (London, 1806), pp. 29–30.

[44] My thanks to Rosemary Hayes for sending me a picture of this seal.

may be the earliest depiction of the Throne of Grace Trinity, possibly dating from the end of the eleventh century, has been recently uncovered in a painting above the chancel arch in St Mary's Church, Houghton, less than twenty-five miles west of Norwich.[45] In the church of Long Melford in Suffolk, dedicated to the Holy Trinity, the patronal image was housed in a 'goodly gilt tabernacle' to the north of the High Altar. It is described by the recusant churchwarden in his account of the church immediately before the Reformation as 'one fair large gilt image of the Holy Trinity',[46] which suggests a single image incorporating all three persons. Also in Long Melford church, there is still a medieval glass painting depicting the Trinity as three hares' heads, sharing three ears between them.

The image of the Holy Trinity in Norwich Cathedral was accorded due reverence in the fourteenth and fifteenth centuries: basins containing wax tapers burned continually before it.[47] The image was treated as a spectacle: in 1404 a jewel was bought for the body of Christ to be displayed at the feasts of the Holy Trinity and Corpus Christi, and in the sixteenth century gold shoes were made for the Trinity, and a tunic and crown were placed upon the second person of the Trinity 'at fit times'.[48] The elaborate costume of the second person – Christ – seems to be at odds with the usual portrayal of the Trinity as the 'Throne of Grace' where Christ is shown crucified and wearing only a loin-cloth. The image was at the High Altar, which received a steady income of donations, almost impervious to the fashions that came and went for other shrines in the cathedral. In the fourteenth century, these were the largest annual donations, amounting to over thirty pounds in 1386.[49] Offerings were boosted by papal indulgences,[50] and those living in the diocese were encouraged to visit the cathedral. Records of the heresy trials in Norwich show that Johannes Fynche was required to offer a wax candle weighing a pound to the image of the Holy Trinity in the cathedral in penance for the offence he had given to God and the Church.[51] Margery Kempe offered at the Trinity in Norwich as part of her preparations for pilgrimage to the Holy Land; she also offered 'in þe worshep of þe Trinite whan sche come to Norwych' on her return.[52] There is no suggestion that Margery thought the image of the Holy Trinity was thaumaturgic; rather, offering at it was one of a number of necessary tasks to be undertaken before embarking on a pilgrimage, and in thanksgiving on her return: it was part of her regular devotional life.

45  François Bœspflug, *La Trinité dans l'Art d'Occident (1400–1460): Sept Chefs-d'Œuvres de la Peinture* (Strasbourg, 2000), p. 25; see http://www.saintmaryschurch.org.uk/wallpaintings. htm and http://www.paintedchurch.org/hought.htm, both accessed 20 February 2008.
46  Roger Martin, 'The State of Melford Church and our Ladie's Chappel at the East End, as I did know it', in David Dymond and Clive Paine, *The Spoil of Melford Church: The Reformation in a Suffolk Parish* (Ipswich, 1992), p. 1.
47  William Page (ed.), *VCH Norfolk*, p. 322.
48  Ibid., p. 322.
49  Shinners, 'Veneration of Saints', p. 135.
50  There was a papal indulgence in 1400 for penitents visiting the three chief altars during the feast of the Holy Trinity: Page (ed.), *VCH Norfolk*, p. 322.
51  Norman P. Tanner (ed.), *Heresy Trials in the Diocese of Norwich, 1428–31*, Camden Society 4th series 20 (London, 1977), p. 188.
52  *Book of Margery Kempe*, ch. 26, p. 60 and ch. 43, p. 102.

As Barratt also points out in her own contribution, Julian eschews such pictorial explanations of the Trinity; it may, however, be worth asking whether a depiction of the Trinity – apparently static and hieratic – can in any way be linked to Julian's understanding of a dynamic Trinity relating with humanity. We should keep in mind Jeffrey Hamburger's claim that 'In the context of Christian doctrine, image and text were tied one to the other as Christ's visible humanity was indissolubly, if mysteriously, linked to his divinity as the Logos.'[53] Julian has an eschatological understanding of the Trinity: it will be fully revealed only at the end of time at the final judgement, when the power of the Trinity will make all things well; but in this life we come to an understanding of the Trinity through the incarnate Jesus, whose Crucifixion comprehends the Trinity.

The iconography of the Trinity is very varied; the Throne of Grace incorporates the Crucifixion but occasionally all three figures are represented anthropomorphically side by side.[54] In both these forms, God the Father is seated on a throne; Julian states that 'The sitting of the fader betokeneth the godhede' (*Revelation*, 15.232). In the parable of the Lord and Servant in Julian's Fourteenth Revelation, the lord is sitting in state when he sends the servant – who is both humanity and Christ – out to do his will (*Revelation*, 51.7–10). The servant falls and is raised again; in the Throne of Grace the figure of Christ is raised up on the cross and supported by God the Father. The relationship between father and son is dynamic rather than static, and Julian interprets it to understand the active engagement of the Trinity with the human soul. Her description of Christ the servant clothed and crowned and seated on a throne beside his father (*Revelation*, 51.273) does seem to be visually reminiscent of the crowning of the Trinity at the festival of the Holy Trinity, but Julian insists that that the son and father are not sitting 'as one man sitteth by another in this life – for ther is no such sitting, as to my sight, in the trinite' (*Revelation*, 51.275). Julian is rejecting too simplistic a visualisation of the relationship between father and son in heaven in favour of an allegorical understanding of the relationship of the persons of the Trinity.

In exploring the relationship between the Trinity and humanity, Julian frequently uses the term 'beclosed', which suggests the visual depiction of the Trinity as three figures enclosed in one image:

> We are beclosed in the fader, and we are beclosed in the son, and we are beclosed in the holy gost. And the fader is beclosed in us, the son is beclosed in us, and the holy gost is beclosed in us: all mighty, alle wisdom, and alle goodnesse; one God, one lorde. (*Revelation*, 54.18–21)

Christ unites divinity and humanity: 'And thus in Crist oure two kindes be oned. For the trinite is comprehended in Crist' (*Revelation*, 57.16–17); Julian

---

[53]  Jeffrey F. Hamburger, 'The Place of Theology in Medieval Art History: Problems, Positions, Possibilities', in *The Mind's Eye*, pp. 11–31 (24).
[54]  As Barratt points out in her contribution to this volume, this is 'extremely dubious from a theological viewpoint': p. 46.

emphasizes the co-inherence of the Trinity in Christ[55] while the image of the Throne of Grace presents the crucified Christ co-inhering within the Trinity. In painted versions of the Throne of Grace the figures are often enclosed within a mandorla, and three-dimensional images are also framed; a patronal image such as that at Long Melford would be enclosed within a tabernacle. The unity of the image presents a representation of the triune God: three in one. The representation of Christ's humanity in the Crucifixion and of his divinity 'sitting in rest in the godhed' (*Revelation*, 56.21) are central to Julian's theology; they are also contained in images of the Holy Trinity such as the one she may have seen in the cathedral in Norwich before her enclosure.

By placing the figure of the human, crucified Christ between the knees of God the Father on the throne of heaven, the Throne of Grace image represents both his humanity and his divinity. Such an image, which probably developed from a crucifixion showing the hand of God, 'gave prominence to God's acceptance of Christ's sacrifice. ... The emphasis of the message of the image was not at first on the Trinity but on the Father's sacrifice of his Son in an expiatory Death, a Death he offered to the world for its redemption'.[56] This understanding of the Trinity, with its emphasis on sacrifice and redemption, is in keeping with Julian's own trinitarian theology. It is, to use a phrase that Julian uses elsewhere in the *Revelation*, a 'marvelous medelur' (*Revelation*, 52.6–7) of triumph and suffering, which together expressed the paradox of redemption. Julian is struggling to express the ineffable in words, but the rich visual culture of the world she inhabited gave her access to a tradition of allegory which enabled her to transcend the limitations of language.

[55] J. P. H. Clark, 'Nature, Grace and the Trinity in Julian of Norwich', *Downside Review* 100 (1982), pp. 203–20 (206).
[56] Gertrud Schiller, *Iconography of Christian Art*, trans. Janet Seligman, 2 vols (London, 1972), 2, *The Passion of Jesus Christ*, p. 123.

# 3

## 'No such sitting': Julian Tropes the Trinity

### ALEXANDRA BARRATT

Devotion to the Trinity was growing in the fourteenth and fifteenth centuries: 'In 1334 Pope John XXII set aside the first Sunday after Pentecost as Trinity Sunday. Increasing devotion to the Trinity can also be seen in the many prayers addressed to the Trinity'.[1] Theology, however, did not necessarily keep pace. In his study of the doctrine of the Holy Trinity, Thomas Marsh has claimed: 'In spite of the formal, notional acknowledgement of the doctrine, a real understanding of God as Trinity practically disappeared from the Christian consciousness of the Middle Ages'.[2] This sweeping condemnation, however, ignores the notable contribution of Julian of Norwich, at the heart of whose *Revelation of Love* lies an attempt to come to terms with this central concept by radically reinventing it.

This preoccupation was not an overt part of her original reaction to her showings. As has been noted by others,[3] the Short Text, *A Vision Showed to a Devout Woman*, makes only two references to the Trinity. In Section 12, on the Three Heavens (kept and expanded in Chapters 22 and 23 of *A Revelation of Love*) Julian sets up a series of correspondences with the three Persons of the Trinity:

> For the firste heven, shewed Criste me his fadere, bot in na bodelye liknesse botte in his properte and in his wyrkinge [...] And in this thre wordes – 'It is a joye, a blisse, and ane endeles likinge to me' – ware shewed to me thre hevens as thus: for the joye, I understode the plesance of the fadere; for the blisse, the wirshippe of the sone; and for the endeles likinge, the haly gaste. The fadere is plesed, the sone is worshipped, the haly gaste lykes. Jhesu wille that we take heede to this blisse that is in the blissedfulle trinite of oure salvation. (*Vision*, 12.9–11; 31–6)[4]

And in Section 24, Julian alludes to the traditional Augustinian interpretation of the Trinity as might, wisdom and love, while stressing that the most immediate or accessible of these 'propertees', or attributes, is love, or the Holy Spirit:

---

[1]   Pamela Sheingorn, 'The Bosom of Abraham Trinity: A Late Medieval All Saints Image', in *England in the Fifteenth Century: Proceedings of the 1986 Halaxton Symposium*, ed. Daniel Williams (Woodbridge, 1987), pp. 273–95 (286).
[2]   Thomas Marsh, *The Triune God: A Biblical, Historical and Theological Study* (Dublin, 1994), p. 194.
[3]   For instance Grace Jantzen, *Julian of Norwich: Mystic and Theologian* (London, 1987), p. 108.
[4]   All quotations are taken from *The Writings of Julian of Norwich: A Vision Showed to a Devout Woman and A Revelation of Love*, ed. Nicholas Watson and Jacqueline Jenkins (Turnhout, 2006).

Though the persones in the blissede trinite be alle even in properte, luffe was moste shewed to me, that it is moste nere to us alle. And of this knawinge er we moste blynde. For many men and women leves that God is allemighty and may do alle, and that he is alle wisdome and can do alle. Botte that he is alle love and wille do alle, thar thay stinte [...] For of alle the propertees of the blissed trinite, it is Goddes wille that we hafe moste sekernesse in likinge and luffe. For luffe makes might and wisdome fulle meke to us. (*Vision*, 24.15–19; 27–9)

These brief references are the seeds from which grows her more developed trinitarian thought in *A Revelation of Love*. This much longer text was (probably) composed by Julian after many years spent in the anchorhold attached to the church of St Julian, which was (and is) only a short walk away from Norwich Cathedral. Like many a medieval institution, the cathedral priory was dedicated to the Holy and Undivided Trinity. Maybe this dedication served as a focus for Julian's meditations, especially if she followed the recommendations of at least one medieval text directed at anchoresses. The fifteenth-century *Myrour of Recluses* recommends meditation on the Trinity, specifically on its Augustinian properties of might, wisdom and goodness:

of þe myȝt of G[o]ddys mageste þat maade al the world of nauȝt for man; of the hy wysdom of sothfastnesse, whiche gouerneþ moost ordynatly his affect; and [of] þe greet mercy of his goodnesse, whiche delyuerede & bouȝte mankynde fro perpetuel deeþ; & of perfyt ryȝtwysnesse of equite, that schal fynaly rewarde or punsche euery good or wykkyd deede.[5]

The *Myrour* continues in terms that Julian would find unexceptionable, explaining how the human person is created in the trinitarian image:

God, by a special prerogatif [privilege] of love, maade man to þe ymage and lyknesse of hym-self [...] Wher-for, lykly yt was þat by þe conseyl of al þe Trinite [...] yt was seyd in þe bygynynge of þe world, "Make we man to þe ymage and oure liknesse" [...] as þouȝ he schold sey in this wyse, "Ryȝt as in the Godhede the Sone [is] of the Fadir, and the [Holy Goost is of the] Fader and of þe Sone togedire, ryȝt so in a maner yt is in a mannys soule" [...] Wherfore, a man may knowe, as þer ben þre myȝtes [faculties] and o substaunce in his soule, ryȝth so lyk in a manere þer bien three persones in the Godhede, and þo þre ben substancialy [in substance] on and þe same God.[6]

Whatever the reason, Julian has far more to say about the Trinity in *A Revelation of Love*. Indeed, the opening, which lists all the chapters to come (and which, of course, may not have been composed by Julian herself but by a later scribe), reads:

This is a revelation of love that Jhesu Christ, our endles blisse [glory], made in sixteen shewinges.

---

5 *Myrour of Recluses: A Middle English Translation of* Speculum Inclusorum, ed. Marta Powell Harley (Madison and London, 1995), p. 24. E. A. Jones considers the text of the Latin original in his essay also included in this volume.
6 *Myrour of Recluses*, p. 24.

Of which the first is of his precious crowning of thornes. And therin was comprehended [included] and specified the blessed trinity [...] in which all the shewinges that foloweth be groundide and oned. (*Revelation*, 1.1–7)

Essentially, this makes the Trinity the foundation of all the individual shewings.[7]
The list ends, too, with a reference to the Trinity, describing the Sixteenth and
final showing as 'that the blisseful trinity our maker, in Christ Jesu our saviour,
endlesly wonneth [dwells] in our soule' (*Revelation*, 1.47–8). This showing takes
place in Chapter 68, where Julian sees Jesus, 'highest bishoppe, solempnest
kinge, wurshipfullest lorde', sitting in the midst of her soul, and asserts that
'the blessed trinite enjoyeth without ende in the making of mannes soule' and
that 'if the blisseful trinite might have made mannes soule ony better, [...] he
shulde not have been full plesid with making of mannes soule' (*Revelation*, 68.
5–6; 17; 31–3).

The First Revelation, too, lives up to its description: when Julian sees Christ's
bleeding head in Chapter 4 she immediately comments:

in the same shewing, sodeinly the trinity fulfilled my hart most of joy. And so I
understode it shall be in heaven without end, to all that shall come ther. For the
trinity is God, God is the trinity. The trinity is our maker, the trinity is our keper,
the trinity is our everlasting lover, the trinity is our endlesse joy and oure blisse
[glory], by our lord Jesu Christ and in our lord Jesu Christ. And this was shewed
in the first sight [vision] and in all. For where Jhesu appireth [appears] the blessed
trinity is understand, as to my sight [in my opinion]. (*Revelation*, 4.6–12)

We can connect this with Julian's description in the Ninth Revelation, Chapter 22
(which develops a passage already present in *A Vision Showed to a Devout Woman*),
of Christ showing her the Father 'in no bodely liknesse [physical manifestation]
but in his properte [attributes] and in his wurking [function]: that is to sey, I saw
in Crist that the father is' (*Revelation*, 22.10–11). It also chimes with her remark
in Chapter 58 on our substance and our 'sensuality': our substance is in each of
the persons of the Trinity, but 'our sensualite is only in the seconde person, Crist
Jhesu, in whom is the fader and the holy gost' (*Revelation*, 58.53–4). We should
also bear in mind a biblical precedent, Saint Paul's words (2 Corinthians 5:19):
'God was in Christ, reconciling the world unto himself'.[8]

Julian describes the vision in Chapter 22 as a 'touch'. It is enigmatic but, if
nothing else, she is clearly dissociating herself here from any claim to represent the Trinity visually. Medieval art, however, was not so fastidious. One of
the commonest ways of representing the Trinity is the Throne-of-Grace Trinity
(also commented on by Gunn in the essay which precedes this one), which
does emphatically present the Father 'in bodily likeness'. Typically, it represents
God the Father as an old, bearded man, usually seated, displaying the Son in
the form of Christ Crucified. Sometimes the Holy Spirit, in the form of a dove,
hovers between the two figures. This iconographic type

---

7   The sentence is ambiguous: I take 'Trinite' as the primary referent of 'in which'.
8   See also Watson's and Jenkins's comments on this 'hermeneutic principle, that references to
Jesus also allude to the Trinity', *Writings*, ed. Watson and Jenkins, p. 134.

first appeared ... in the early twelfth century, and from the beginning had a very strong association with liturgical contexts ... It frequently illustrates the *Te igitur* of the canon of the Mass [and] flourished in the later Middle Ages to such an extent that Wolfgang Braunfels calls it *the* medieval form of the Trinity.[9]

Ironically, such representations, in which the figure of God the Father is usually much larger than, and almost envelops, that of the Son, could be seen as an exact reversal of Julian's perception that 'in Crist the father is': Christ seems enclosed, and certainly dominated, by God the Father. Instinctively or otherwise, Julian knew that this was highly problematic from a theological point of view, and she was not alone in this: as one art historian has commented, 'anthropomorphic representations of the Trinity, with their inevitable suggestion of tritheism, were constantly condemned by theologians'.[10] In Julian's own time, in late fourteenth-century England, the Lollards held strong views on this subject: 'Objects of especial antipathy were the anthropomorphic renderings of the Holy Trinity (on the grounds that God belonged to a different order of being from mortals and therefore was unrepresentable)', even though 'In respect of images of the Trinity the Lollards merely echoed the criticisms voiced by theologians from the middle of the thirteenth century'.[11]

Nonetheless, Julian is throughout her writings quite happy to use metaphorically words that refer literally to the faculty of sight, such as *saw, shewed, appereith, revelation* and *showing*. But in Chapter 51 of *A Revelation of Love* she expands her intuition that the Trinity cannot be represented visually in any satisfactory fashion. This chapter, of course, contains the 'wonderful example' of the Lord and the Servant and leads into Julian's most extended discourse on the Trinity. It culminates in the apotheosis of the servant, who is also Adam, as the Son or second person of the Trinity:

> Now stondeth not the sonne before the fader on the lefte side as a laborer, but he sittith on the faders right hand in endlesse rest and pees. (But it is not ment that the sonne sittith on the right hand beside [Sloane reads 'syde by syde] as one man sittith by another in this life – for ther is no such sitting, as to my sight, in the trinite. But he sittith on his faders right honde: that is to sey, right in the hyest nobilite of the faders joy.) (*Revelation*, 51.272–6)

This casual remark – the parentheses are of course contributed by the modern editors, but they are surely in the spirit of the text – opens up the possibility that, though much has been made of the influence of written texts on Julian, she was surely affected just as strongly by the visual culture of the time, as Gunn has already asserted. But what visual representations of the Trinity current in late fourteenth-century and early fifteenth-century England might Julian have seen which might have prompted this remark?

Art-historical agreement on the precise classification of the medieval iconography of the Trinity remains elusive. However, the Glossary in one recent refer-

---

9   Sheingorn, 'The Bosom of Abraham Trinity', p. 285, referring to *Die heilige Dreifaltigkeit* (Düsseldorf, 1954), p. xxxv.
10   G. McN. Rushforth, *Medieval Christian Imagery* (Oxford, 1936), p. 405.
11   Richard Marks, *Image and Devotion in Late Medieval England* (Stroud, 2004), p. 257.

ence work on images in medieval English manuscripts lists three standard ways of representing the Trinity in fifteenth-century English manuscripts, all of them anthropomorphic. The first, the 'Crucifix-Trinity as God the Father', shows him 'seated, supporting a Crucifix and sometimes blessing; usually with dove'. This iconographical type, which is sometimes called the Throne-of-Grace, Mercy Seat or *Gnadenstuhl* Trinity, has already been mentioned. The second represents 'Father and Son enthroned with dove, often with attributes of cross and orb'; common variations add 'clasping hands; trampling devil underfoot'. Thirdly there is 'Father, Son and Holy Ghost as three personified figures, with attributes, sometimes enclosed in one mantle'.[12]

Possibly Julian had in mind this third method of representing the Trinity, as three human male figures seated side by side.[13] This iconographic type was, of course, extremely dubious from a theological viewpoint (which did not prevent its appearance in, for instance, the Dutch Hours of Catherine of Cleves, c.1440).[14] It appears in several artistic media, and was particularly common in the fifteenth century. An historian of late-medieval English stained glass commented: 'The representation of the Trinity as three human beings was no innovation of the fifteenth century, though it is most frequent in that period', and proceeded to list several surviving English examples.[15] Sometimes this Three-Person Trinity is crowning the Virgin, in effect a representation of a four-fold Godhead: a stained-glass example, which can be quite precisely dated as 1470, survives in Holy Trinity Church, York. But Julian, by implication, refers to *two* men and two men *seated* ('as one man sittith by another'). She is, I believe, not merely rejecting anthropomorphic representations of the Trinity in general, but one iconographical tradition in particular: the so-called *Dixit Dominus* type.

The *Dixit Dominus* Trinity was firmly established from at least the thirteenth century.[16] It depicts two regal figures, usually with the Dove between them, sitting side by side, and takes its name from the first verse of Psalm 109, 'Dixit Dominus domino meo' ('The Lord said unto my lord'). In manuscripts it seems to occur more frequently than the Three-Person Trinity. Julian's comment, therefore, even if only made in passing to reject this iconographical type, suggests that she had some personal access not just to late-medieval visual culture in general, but specifically to illuminated psalters.

Most fourteenth-century English psalters divided the text of the psalms into ten sections, at the beginning of each of which stood an historiated initial: 'The initials fall at the beginning of the allotment of psalms for each day of the week (Psalms 1, 26, 38, 52, 68, 80, 97 and 109)'.[17] In the late thirteenth and early fourteenth centuries there was a standard repertory of subjects for each of these.

[12] *An Index of Images in English Manuscripts: From the Time of Chaucer to Henry VIII c.1380–c.1509*, ed. Kathleen Scott *et al.*, 3 vols (Turnhout, 2002), I, p. 105.
[13] This appears to be the view of Colledge and Walsh: see *A Book of Showings to the Anchoress Julian of Norwich*, ed. Edmund Colledge and James Walsh, 2 vols (Toronto, 1978), II, pp. 544–5.
[14] *The Hours of Catherine of Cleves*, introduction and commentaries by John Plummer (London, 1966), plates 32, 35, 36.
[15] Rushforth, *Medieval Christian Imagery*, p. 405.
[16] See also *An Index of Images in English Manuscripts*, I, 103 and II, 109.
[17] Lucy Freeman Sandler, *The Peterborough Psalter in Brussels and Other Fenland Manuscripts* (London, 1974), p. 95.

Psalm 109 had traditionally been interpreted as referring to the dual nature of Christ, or to the Father and the Son, so the opening of that psalm was often illustrated with a representation of the Trinity or of the Father and Son.

This exegetical tradition went right back to the New Testament, where extracts from Psalm 109 are quoted several times: Matthew 22:41–6, where Christ cross-questions the Pharisees and quotes the first verse; Acts 2:34–35, part of St Peter's speech at Pentecost, which cites the first two verses; and in the Epistle to the Hebrews, 1:13 and 10:13, where the anonymous author focuses on the second half of the first verse. Early psalm commentaries continued the tradition, notably Saint Augustine in his *Enarrationes in Psalmos* and the Greek Theodore of Mopsuestia (d. 428). Unorthodox though he was (he was condemned as a heretic and his works survive largely in fragments quoted by his opponents), Theodore's influence reached the West in an abbreviated and revised Latin version.[18]

Theodore promoted the Messianic interpretation of Psalm 109. He argued that in the Hebrew text of Psalm 109 the equivalents to 'Dominus domino' in the opening verse were both represented by the tetragrammaton, indicating divinity. From this it was clear that the psalmist is not speaking of a human being, 'sed de eo qui sit et Deus uerus et omnium Dominus, qui Christus est' (but of him who is both true God and Lord of all, who is Christ).[19] He therefore rejected the Jewish interpretation of the phrase 'domino meo' as meaning Abraham or David: rather, David is speaking to 'his lord', who he knows will be born of his seed. Theodore goes on to comment (cross-referring to Psalm 9:5) that this lord is said to 'sit' in order to symbolize his kingdom, rule and judgment. The Father is therefore sharing equality of honour with the Son and both sharing and handing over the power of judgment: the sharing of honour is indicated by the act of sitting at the right hand.[20]

This, then, was the theological basis for the *Dixit Dominus* image, of which there is a particularly splendid example at the opening of Psalm 109 in the Ormesby Psalter (Oxford Bodley MS Douce 366, fol. 147v – see Plate 1), executed in East Anglia in or around 1300.[21] The historiated initial *D* has been described as follows:

> Within the letter itself … sit God the Father and God the Son, in formal frontal positions, their hands raised in the ancient 'orans' position. They look straight ahead with solemn gaze. Almost identical ('for he who hath seen me hath seen the Father also'), they are dressed in long blue cloaks, tied with plain, knotted girdles, and long pink cloaks each fastened in the centre with a brooch of almond shape. Their long curly hair and neat beards are brown.[22]

---

18 Sandler, *The Peterborough Psalter*, pp. 137–8 n. 25.
19 *Theodori Mopsuesteni Expositionis in Psalmos*, ed. Lucas de Coninck, Corpus Christianorum Series Latina 88A (Turnholt, 1977), p. 351.
20 *Expositionis in Psalmos*, p. 352.
21 On the Ormesby Psalter, see Otto Pächt and J. J. G. Alexander, *Illuminated Manuscripts in the Bodleian Library, Oxford, Vol. 3: British, Irish and Icelandic Schools* (Oxford, 1973), Item 499 (fols 10–45, 58–69), late 13th–early 14th century; Item 536 (additions of historiated and other borders and initial), *c.*1310; Item 581 (fols 1–9, fols 46–57), *c.*1320–1330.
22 A. G. and Dr W. O. Hassall, *Treasures of the Bodleian Library* (London, 1976), p. 99.

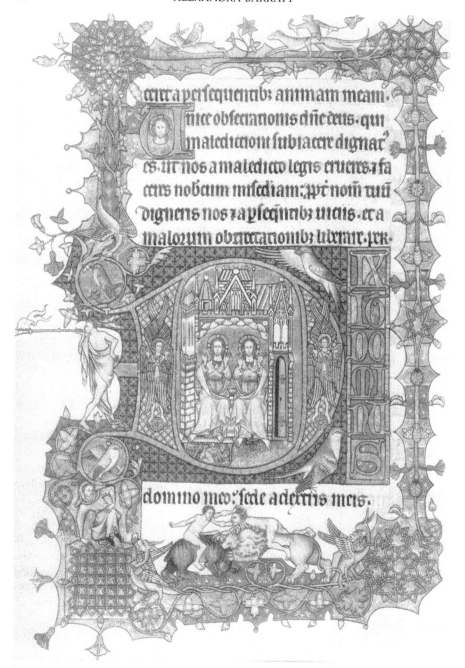

Plate 1. *Dixit Dominus* from the Ormesby Psalter, Bodleian Library, University of Oxford. MS Douce 366, fol. 147v.

Sir Sydney Cockerell, too, who was the first to describe the psalter in detail, stresses this aspect of the initial: 'The two first persons of the Trinity, identical in all respects, are seated side by side.'[23] Notably, there is no Dove, so this is strictly speaking a representation of God-the-Father and Son, rather than of the Trinity. In the twenty-four English psalters c.1300–1340 whose decorative schemes have been tabulated by Sandler, the Ormesby Psalter is one of only two to illustrate Psalm 109 in this way (the other is the Douai Psalter, Douai Bibl. Pub. MS 171).[24] In contrast, fifteen psalters represent the entire Trinity.

The psalter is so called after its donor, Robert Ormesby, who is represented on the *Beatus* page. There are painted 'the kneeling figures of a mitred ecclesiastic (no doubt the bishop of Norwich) and a Benedictine monk (Ormesby himself)'.[25] Joan Greatrex considers that the appearance of his name in a document dated 1336/7 'suggests that he may have been sub-prior' at Norwich.[26] William de Ormesby, who was rector of St Mary in the Marsh in the precincts of Norwich Cathedral, may have been Robert's brother:[27] he gave the priory a glossed bible, now Cambridge University Library MS Kk. 4. 3. The name 'Ormesby' appears at the end of a late thirteenth-century manuscript of Bartholomew Cotton's chronicle, which is still at Norwich Cathedral.[28]

Robert's donation was unusual. It was more lavish than the usual book donations made by monks, and it was to be placed in the choir, not in the library. 'Additions to the library', Joan Greatrex has pointed out, 'usually came through gifts, mainly from the monks themselves, who purchased books with their allowances, probably retained them for use, and eventually placed them in the library, as many of the inscriptions on the flyleaves explain.'[29] That Robert could afford such an expensive psalter suggests that he came from a wealthy family: 'such gifts may be held to imply some position in the world as well as access to a full purse', as Cockerell wryly remarks.[30] Possibly his was the family that held the lordship of Ormesby in Norfolk: in 1294 there is a record of a Sir William de Ormesby, his son John, and his son's sons Robert and William.[31]

The Ormesby Psalter had a complicated history, being decorated over three separate periods. Cockerell argued that 'it was written in Norfolk or Suffolk during the last years of the thirteenth century [and] it remained in quires for at least a quarter of a century, during which time the decoration proceeded intermittently'.[32] Heraldic evidence suggests that it was commissioned, as late

23 S. C. Cockerell and M. R. James, *Two East Anglian Psalters at the Bodleian Library* (Oxford, 1926), p. 20.
24 Sandler, *The Peterborough Psalter*, pp. 98–9.
25 Cockerell and James, *Two East Anglian Psalters*, p. 3.
26 Joan Greatrex, *Biographical Register of the English Cathedral Priories of the Province of Canterbury c.1066 to 1540* (Oxford, 1997), p. 546.
27 Greatrex, *Biographical Register*, p. 547.
28 N. R. Ker, 'Medieval Manuscripts from Norwich Cathedral Priory', *Transactions of the Cambridge Bibliographical Society* 1 (1949), pp. 1–28 (13).
29 Joan Greatrex, 'Monk Students from Norwich Cathedral Priory at Oxford and Cambridge, c.1300 to 1530', *English Historical Review* 106 (1991), pp. 555–83 (576).
30 Cockerell and James, *Two East Anglian Psalters*, p. 37.
31 Ibid., p. 36.
32 Ibid., p. 31.

as 1320, to mark a marriage between a Foliot and a Bardolf, which for some reason never took place.[33] Cockerell speculated: 'The book being again on the market and unfinished, Robert of Ormesby, then or soon afterwards a monk of Norwich, stepped in to acquire it. Under his direction it was brought to hasty completion.'[34] After its donation to Norwich Cathedral, it remained there for 200 years.

Robert of Ormesby gave the psalter to his priory with instructions that it was to lie in the choir before whomever happened to be sub-prior at the time: on fol. 1v is formally inscribed, in red, 'psalterium fratris Roberti de Ormesby monachi Norwyc' per eundem assignatum choro ecclesie sancte Trinitatis Norwici ad iacendum coram Suppriore qui pro tempore fuerit in perpetuum.'[35] As the priory church of the Holy Trinity was also the cathedral, it is entirely possible that Julian had seen this very manuscript lying open at this page in the choir – and never forgotten its 'pulsing vitality',[36] even if on reflection she came to problematize it.

If Julian had indeed seen this particular psalter – or any illuminated manuscript – she was in a privileged position. Alabasters and stained glass, for example, would be much more part of common visual experience than illuminated manuscripts, but they preferred to represent the Trinity differently. John A. Knowles has described the kinds of visual representations of the Trinity popular in later medieval English stained glass. The Throne-of-Grace Trinity, representing God the Father displaying Christ on the Cross, sometimes with the Dove hovering above Christ's head, was common, and survives into the incunable period in woodcuts. What Knowles calls the 'Corpus Christi subject' (by some others known as the Trinity Pietà), of 'God the Father supporting the dead Christ', is found in stained glass windows in York at Holy Trinity, St John's Mickelgate and at St Martin-le-Grand. This type is 'rare, but at the end of the fourteenth and beginning of the fifteenth centuries it seems to have enjoyed a considerable amount of popularity'.[37]

Carved alabaster panels were widespread in late-medieval England. Francis Cheetham, who has extensively investigated these English alabasters, has pointed out that the Trinity was a very popular subject and that more than eighty panels representing it survive, almost all variants on the Throne-of-Grace Trinity. First, there is the standard Throne-of-Grace Trinity, with a seated, old and bearded God the Father, with or without the Dove, inevitably a vulnerable addition in a carving:

[33] Ibid., p. 35.
[34] Ibid., p. 36.
[35] Ker, 'Medieval Manuscripts from Norwich Cathedral Priory', p. 12; and N. R. Ker, *Medieval Libraries of Great Britain: A List of Surviving Books*, 2nd edn (London, 1964), p. 285.
[36] Hassall and Hassall, *Treasures of the Bodleian Library*, p. 128.
[37] John A. Knowles, *Essays in the History of the York School of Glass-painting* (London and New York, 1936), pp. 171–2. This iconographic type, found on a number of Continental oil-on-wood panel paintings, survived well into the Counter-Reformation: there are, for instance, two well-known late sixteenth-century paintings using the same iconography by the Flemish painter Pieter Coecke van Aelst and by El Greco in the Prado, and an early sixteenth-century painting, 'The Trinity and Mystic Pietà', by Hans Baldung Grien (1484/5–1545) in the National Gallery, London.

Often all that remains is a dowel hole by which frequently the Dove was attached. In a number of examples, however, there is no sign of the Dove, in which case it was probably originally painted onto the alabaster, the paint being subsequent [sic] lost. But the possibility does arise that occasionally the Dove was not represented at all.[38]

The second type, known as the Bosom of Abraham Trinity, is similar, but the Father holds a napkin containing the souls of the saved: it 'contains the standard components of the Throne of Grace or Mercy Seat Trinity, that is, God the Father as an elderly, regal figure, God the Son as the crucified Christ supported symmetrically in front of God the Father, and God the Holy Spirit as a dove', but it is 'different from the Throne of Grace Trinities that are quite common in alabaster'.[39] In the third type, there are attendant angels but 'the symbol of the Holy Spirit is frequently absent'.[40] The fourth type, which is very uncommon, represents the Trinity 'as three separate individuals'.[41] The *Dixit Dominus* Trinity, with or without Dove, is not found in late medieval English alabasters.

Chapters 54 to 60 of *A Revelation of Love* are the heart of what Julian has to say on the Trinity. She develops a model – or perhaps one should say a model evolves – of the First and Second Persons as father and mother, but of the Holy Spirit as 'our good lord'. Just as the Holy Spirit is too often an afterthought in the iconography of the Trinity – many representations of the Trinity might as well be entitled 'Father and Son (and optional Dove)', as the Dove is often not prominent and sometimes is absent altogether – so he does not fit easily into the new paradigm. 'Father' and 'mother' are interdependent and mutually defining terms, but the phrase 'good lord' (the complexities of which I have discussed elsewhere) belongs to a quite different conceptual field, that of political rather than familial relationships.[42] Similarly, even allowing for the bizarre appearance to modern eyes of the anthropomorphic Trinities, the Holy Spirit as Dove seems visually out of place and can too easily be lost (literally, in the case of the alabasters).

Like the artist of the Ormesby Psalter, who omits him altogether, Julian has trouble fitting the Holy Spirit into her Trinitarian scheme. Or perhaps it is truer to say that she has trouble finding a metaphor for the Holy Spirit that can happily co-exist with her images of God our Father and our Mother. She has no problems with the functional aspects of the Spirit, who sits happily within the tradi-

---

38  Francis Cheetham, *English Medieval Alabasters* (Oxford, 1984), pp. 296–7.

39  Sheingorn, 'The Bosom of Abraham Trinity', pp. 274 and 275.

40  There is a small high-relief German alabaster, dated *c*.1430, by Hans Multscher (b. *c*.1400), now in the Liebighaus, Frankfurt, of a related type: an angel, not God the Father, supports the dead or dying Christ, God the Father stands by with his hand raised in blessing, and the Dove is represented between his head and that of Christ's.

41  'It is very uncommon in alabaster in the Trinities alone, but is to be found on a panel combining the Trinity with the Annunciation (Cat. 236). The only other recorded example in English alabaster is the Trinity in the Yorkshire Museum, York', Cheetham, *English Medieval Alabasters* (Oxford, 1984), p. 297 and plate 236, p. 310.

42  See my 'Julian of Norwich and the Holy Spirit, "Our Good Lord"', *Mystics Quarterly* 28 (2002), pp. 78–84, and 'Lordship, Service and Worship in Julian of Norwich', in *The Medieval Mystical Tradition in England: Exeter Symposium VII*, ed. E. A. Jones (Cambridge, 2004), pp. 177–88.

tional 'power-wisdom-love (or goodness)', or 'nature-mercy-grace' model (e.g. Chapters 56, 58, 59), in a formula like 'Oure fader willeth, oure mother werketh, oure good lorde the holy gost confirmeth' (*Revelation*, 59.24–5). And there is no doubt that she is convinced of the primacy of Love: 'For of alle the propertees of the blisseful trinite, it is Goddes will that we have most sekernesse and liking in love' (*Revelation*, 73.36–7); 'What, woldest thou wit thy lordes mening in this thing? Wit it wele, love was his mening' (*Revelation*, 86.13–14). It is the attempt to trope the Spirit that causes the problems.

Finally, it is interesting to reflect that the *Dixit Dominus* Trinity, even though firmly rejected by Julian at the rational level, might have subliminally suggested the basic Father-Mother model. For it presents two similar figures seated side by side, young rather than elderly, both with long hair and wearing fairly indeterminate clothing, so they look like two equal consorts.[43] For as Julian moves into her consideration in Chapters 59–63 of God's fatherhood and motherhood, the focus falls almost as much on a binary as on a Trinitarian godhead: 'As verely as God is oure fader, as verely is God oure moder' (*Revelation*, 59.10), he 'is very fader and very moder of kindes' (*Revelation*, 62.12). Sometimes she lays an almost exclusive emphasis on 'our swete, kynde, and ever lovyng Moder Iesus'.[44] In Chapter 68, though, balance is restored and Julian stresses that the whole Trinity, not just the Second Person, takes part in the creative act. Creation thus becomes much closer to the human experience of reproduction, in that it requires more than one participant.[45]

---

[43] Although the figures are bearded more often than not, in the Ormesby Psalter this is discreet.

[44] This phrase appears in the chapter heading to the Sloane manuscript version. See *A Revelation of Love*, ed. Marian Glasscoe (Exeter, 1976), p. 73.

[45] On this, see further Alexandra Barratt, '"In the Lowest Part of Our Need": Julian and Medieval Gynecological Writing', in *Julian of Norwich: A Book of Essays*, ed. Sandra J. McEntire (New York and London, 1998), pp. 239–56 (247).

# 4

# Julian of Norwich and the Varieties of Middle English Mystical Discourse

## DENISE N. BAKER

Writing near the end of the fourteenth century, the anonymous author of the *Cloud of Unknowing* warns his disciple that the language of spirituality is radically metaphoric:

> & þerfore beware þat þou conceyue not bodely þat þat is mente goostly, þof al it be spokyn in bodely wordes […] For þof al þat a þing be neuer so goostly in itself, neuerþeles ʒif ʒit it schal be spoken of, siþen it so is þat speche is a bodely werk wrouʒt wiþ þe tonge, þe whiche is an instrument of þe body, it behoueþ alweis be spoken in bodely wordes. Bot what þerof? Schal it þerfore be taken & conceyuid bodely? Nay, it bot goostly.[1]

The *Cloud* author's remark is usually regarded as a criticism of the sensational language of the first Middle English mystic, Richard Rolle (*c*.1300–49), and other literal-minded practitioners of contemplation. However, his words also provide a warning to those who study texts about mysticism: we must regard them as metaphoric discourse rather than as literal accounts of experience.

Over the last two decades, scholars have heeded the *Cloud* author's advice and focused greater attention on the language contemplative writers employ rather than any experience informing their texts. In his magisterial three-volume study, *The Presence of God*, for example, Bernard McGinn acknowledges that since readers can never have access to the mystic's consciousness, they can only explore the language he or she uses to describe it. Like the *Cloud* author, McGinn recognizes the metaphoric complexity of texts about mysticism and compares their deployment of language to poetry:[2]

> Mystical masterpieces … are often close to poetry in the ways in which they concentrate and alter language to achieve their ends … [and employ] verbal strategies in which language is used not so much informationally as transformationally, that is, not to convey a content but to assist the hearer or reader to hope for or to achieve the same consciousness.[3]

---

1 *The Cloud of Unknowing and Related Treatises on Contemplative Prayer*, ed. Phyllis Hodgson, *Analecta Cartusiana* 3 (Exeter, 1982), Chapter 61, p. 63.
2 For a discussion of Julian specifically as a poet, see Ena Jenkins' essay in this volume, pp. 181–91.
3 Bernard McGinn, *The Foundations of Mysticism*, vol. 1 of *The Presence of God: A History of Western Christian Mysticism* (New York, 1992), pp. xiv, xvii.

In his study of the apophatic tradition, *The Darkness of God*, Denys Turner also insists that one can only study the mystic's language. Despite the continuity of metaphors of interiority and ascent, of light and darkness, and of oneness with God in the Christian discourse of spirituality, he contends that the meaning of these metaphors is radically different for medieval and modern writers.[4] Thus, Turner argues, scholars must not only concentrate on the metaphoric language of a mystical text, but also articulate the different philosophical and theological principles informing it.

McGinn's and Turner's observations about the metaphoric language of mysticism provide a method for assessing Julian of Norwich's position in the Christian tradition of contemplation. Pertinent issues here are her familiarity with the tradition and which of her predecessors influenced her, especially during the twenty or more years during which she revised the Short Text into the Long. These issues are difficult to address not only because all medieval mystics share the common beliefs and vocabulary of Christianity, but also because the various strands of the contemplative tradition are so complex and interwoven. Julian of Norwich is usually identified as one of the group of five writers known as the Middle English mystics; this group also includes Richard Rolle, Walter Hilton, the anonymous author of the *Cloud of Unknowing* and Margery Kempe. Certainly, from the early 1320s, when Rolle left his father's home wearing his sister's tunics as a hermit's habit, to the death of Margery Kempe around 1440, the production and dissemination of texts about contemplation written in or translated into Middle English increased dramatically. These five writers participated in a 'flowering of mysticism' that began on the continent in the thirteenth century, but took root in England a century later.[5]

Recently, however, Nicholas Watson has questioned the critical practice of regarding the five Middle English mystics as a group.[6] This categorization, he argues, emphasizes their relationship to each other rather than their involvement in the broader context of the late medieval vernacular theology and culture. Such a grouping implies that the four authors who followed Rolle knew his works and each other's. In fact, this assumption holds true for three members of the group. The *Cloud* author, Hilton and Kempe were all familiar with Rolle; the two male authors knew each other's texts; and Kempe had heard of Hilton. Because the three male authors wrote works to guide religious or recluses in the practices of the contemplative life, it appears plausible that Julian of Norwich, who may well have been a Benedictine nun prior to 1373 and was certainly an anchorite at least by the early 1390s, might have been familiar with their writings. This assumption is bolstered by Julian's claim to be 'a simple creature unletterde' (*Revelation*, 2.1), which is usually interpreted to mean that she did

---

[4]  Denys Turner, *The Darkness of God: Negativity in Christian Mysticism* (Cambridge, 1995), pp. 1–8; for Turner's disagreement with McGinn's experiential definition of mysticism, see pp. 260–5. Wolfgang Riehle also studies the metaphoric language of mystical texts in *The Middle English Mystics*, trans. Bernard Standring (London, 1981).
[5]  The third volume in Bernard McGinn's *The Presence of God* is *The Flowering of Mysticism: Men and Women in the New Mysticism, 1200–1350* (New York, 1998).
[6]  Nicholas Watson, 'The Middle English Mystics', in *The Cambridge History of Medieval English Literature*, ed. David Wallace (Cambridge, 1999), pp. 539–65.

not know Latin rather than that she was illiterate. Thus, vernacular texts would seem to have been her primary source of spiritual guidance.

In this essay, however, I contend that Julian of Norwich is the odd person out in this group of Middle English mystics. Even though Margery Kempe visited Julian around 1413, she does not identify the anchorite as a writer; nor do either Hilton or the *Cloud* author ever mention her or allude to her texts. Furthermore, as I will show, both chronological and textual evidence make it very difficult to ascertain whether Julian of Norwich knew the works of her male counterparts.[7] Whatever resemblance the two versions of her text may have to those of the three male Middle English mystics may be due to their common participation in the rich discourse of the contemplative tradition rather than any direct influence. By examining the language these four authors employ to describe union, I will show that they make very different assumptions about the nature of God and of humankind's relationship to the divine.

The *terminus a quo* for the two versions of Julian's book, *A Vision Showed to a Devout Woman*, the Short Text, and *A Revelation of Love*, the Long Text, is the date of her visionary experience, May 1373. Although it is not clear how soon after this experience she composed the Short Text, Julian says that in 1388 and again in 1393 she achieved realizations that helped her to complete the Long Text. Watson speculates that *A Vision* may have been finished in the mid 1380s and *A Revelation* at any time between the mid 1390s and Julian's death after 1416.[8] Based solely on chronology, it is certainly possible that Julian might have known Rolle's English epistles, written in the last decade before his death in 1349, either before her visionary experience or while she composed one or other version of her book. However, she could not have read either book of Hilton's *Scale of Perfection* or the *Cloud of Unknowing* until after she completed her Short Text, even if it were finished as late as the mid 1380s, because these books were composed in the decade between 1386 and 1396. Hilton began the first book of the *Scale* sometime after he entered the Augustinian Canons in 1386. Clark argues that the *Cloud of Unknowing* refers to *Scale* I, placing it after 1386 but before Hilton's response to the *Cloud* in the second book of the *Scale*, which must have been finished by his death in 1396.[9] Thus, the possibility that Julian of Norwich could have known either book of the *Scale of Perfection* or the *Cloud of Unknowing* while she revised *A Vision* into *A Revelation of Love* depends on how soon she completed the Long Text after she achieved an understanding of the parable of the Lord and Servant in 1393. The closer to that date the revision

---

7    I do not discuss *The Book of Margery Kempe* since it was dictated several decades after Julian's death. For a thorough analysis of similarities and differences between these two women authors, see Liz Herbert McAvoy, *Authority and the Female Body in the Writings of Julian of Norwich and Margery Kempe* (Cambridge, 2004).

8    Nicholas Watson and Jacqueline Jenkins (eds), *The Writings of Julian of Norwich: A Vision Showed to a Devout Woman and A Revelation of Love* (Turnhout, 2006), p. 1 and p. 2. All references to Julian's writing will be from this edition, with section/chapter and line references appearing parenthetically in the main text.

9    John P. H. Clark, *The Cloud of Unknowing: An Introduction*, Analecta Cartusiana 119, 4 (Salzburg, 1995), I, pp. 86–92. In 'The Dating and Authorship of the *Cloud* Corpus: A Reassessment of the Evidence', *Medium Aevum* 71 (2002), pp. 81–100, Annie Sutherland argues that *The Cloud* was written in the late 1380s, rather than the early 1390s as Clark asserts.

was finished, the less likely it is that she would have had access to manuscript copies of Hilton's and the *Cloud* author's books.

While the chronological evidence about the plausibility of Julian's knowledge of her male counterparts' work is inconclusive, the textual evidence does not provide a stronger case because, despite their common indebtedness to the Christian contemplative tradition, each of these Middle English mystics represents one of many diverse strands of mystical discourse that had developed by the fourteenth century. Richard Rolle's language of union derives from the affective mysticism of the twelfth-century Cistercian Bernard of Clairvaux. The *Cloud* author writes in the tradition of the *via negativa*, the apophatic mysticism initiated by Pseudo-Dionysius in the fifth century, but as interpreted by Thomas Gallus 700 years later. Walter Hilton is most indebted to the introspective mysticism which developed from Augustine's *De Trinitate*. Although Julian of Norwich is also in the Augustinian tradition, her language of union differs significantly from Hilton's as well as from that of the two other male writers.[10] Thus, although it is possible that Julian knew works by her male counterparts, there is no decisive textual evidence that either version of her book was strongly influenced by any of them.

The earliest of the Middle English mystics, Richard Rolle, uses sensory imagery to describe the culmination of the third degree of love in contemplative union. In *Ego Dormio*, for example, he provides a detailed account of the experience:

> At þe begynnynge, when þou comest thereto, þi goostly egh is taken vp in to þe light of heuyn, and þare enlumyned in grace and kyndlet of þe fyre of Cristes loue, so þat þou shal feel verraily þe brennynge of loue in þi herte, euermore lyftynge þi thoght to God, and fillynge þe ful of ioy and swetnesse, so myche þat no s[eke]nesse ne shame ne anguys ne penaunce may gref þe, bot al þi lif shal turne into ioy. And þan for heynesse of þi hert, þi praiers turneth in to ioyful songe and þi þoghtes to melodi. Þan Jhesu is al þi desire, al þi delit, al þi ioy, al þi solace, al þi comfort, so þat on hym wil euer be þi songe, and [in] hym al þi rest. Þan may þou say 'I slepe and my hert waketh. Who shal to my leman say, for his loue me longeth ay?'[11]

For Rolle, the sensations of fire, sweetness and song are marks of contemplative union. While it is commonplace for mystics to use metaphors of sight involving light and darkness, Rolle emphasizes touch (fire), taste (sweetness) and hearing (song). These senses, especially touch and taste, are considered more corporeal and less intellectual than sight; therefore, they are often regarded as inappropriate for describing the spiritual. The *Cloud* author and Hilton, for example,

---

[10] For a more thorough discussion of these similarities and differences, see Denise N. Baker, 'The Image of God: Contrasting Configurations in Julian of Norwich's *Showings* and Walter Hilton's *Scale of Perfection*', in *Julian of Norwich: A Book of Essays*, ed. Sandra J. McEntire (New York, 1998), pp. 35–60. In a note to Chapter 32, ll. 33–38, of *A Revelation of Love* (p. 222), Watson and Jenkins point out that Julian's speculations about universal salvation contradict the conservative position stated by Hilton in *Scale II*, Chapter 3. Thus, although Julian may have known Hilton's second book, she was not in agreement with him on this issue.

[11] Richard Rolle, *Richard Rolle: Prose and Verse*, ed. S. J. Ogilvie-Thomson, EETS 293 (Oxford, 1988), pp. 31–2.

seem to criticize Rolle for the apparent literalism of the language he uses to describe spiritual union. However, Rolle is not as eccentric as their criticism implies, for he derives this emphasis on the physical effects of love from Bernard of Clairvaux.

From the time of Origen (c.185–252) Christian thinkers had grappled with the problem posed by the Bible's use of sensory language about God, particularly the physical and erotic language of the Song of Songs. Although Bernard does not employ the concept of the spiritual senses first proposed as a solution to this problem by Origen, he does not hesitate in his sermons on the Song to describe union with God in sensory terms. In fact, as Rudy demonstrates, 'Bernard inverts the traditional hierarchy: he places sight first and *lowest*, taste and touch last and *highest*. He seems to do so because references to these senses help him articulate the immediacy and mutuality of union with God.'[12] For Bernard of Clairvaux and those writing in his tradition of affective mysticism, sensory language is not at odds with the spiritual, for the body is an integral component of the human person.

Denis Renevey demonstrates how Rolle, though idiosyncratic, nonetheless follows such predecessors as Bernard of Clairvaux and William of Thierry in appropriating the language of the Song of Songs to express his own mystical experience.[13] As Annie Sutherland puts it, 'For Rolle, personal experience and biblical authority are diagnostically connected. In other words, rather than standing in a hierarchical relationship with each other, the two are mutually informing and validating'.[14] Rolle signals this debt with the Latin quotation of Song 5:2 that begins his English epistle: 'Ego dormio "et" cor meum vigilat'. He then refers to his source for the quotation as 'þe songe of loue'.[15]

Rolle's typical conjunction of sweetness and song may, in fact, derive from Bernard's commentary on the Song 1:2: 'Thy name is as oil poured out'. In sermon 19 he concords this verse with Psalm 33:9, 'Taste and see that the Lord is sweet', to characterize 'Thy name' as 'sweet'. Bernard further emphasizes the sweetness of God's name in sermon 15: 'Jesus is honey in the mouth, melody in the ear, a jubilee in the heart'.[16] Although these metaphors employ the physical sensations of taste and hearing, Bernard plays on the relationship between tasting and knowing implied in the Latin similarity between *sapio* (I know) and *sapere* (to taste). As Carruthers writes, 'even in these most ecstatic sermons of Bernard's human knowledge is created through natural psychological processes and sensory experiences, because tasting flavors is also a means of knowing, even knowing God'.[17] Since Rolle's strong devotion to the Holy Name is obvi-

---

12 Gordon Rudy, *Mystical Language of Sensation in the Later Middle Ages*, Studies in Medieval History and Culture (New York, 2002), p. 57.
13 Denis Renevey, *Language, Self and Love: Hermeneutics in the Writings of Richard Rolle and the Commentaries on the Song of Songs* (Cardiff, 2001). See also E. Ann Matter, *The Voice of My Beloved: The Song of Songs in Western Medieval Christianity*, Middle Ages Series (Philadelphia, 1990), pp. 183–5.
14 Annie Sutherland, 'Biblical Text and Spiritual Experience in the English Epistles of Richard Rolle', *Review of English Studies*, n.s. 56 (2005), pp. 697–711.
15 Rolle, *Richard Rolle*, p. 26.
16 Mary Carruthers, 'Sweetness', *Speculum* 81 (2006), pp. 999–1013 (1000).
17 Ibid., p. 1001.

ously indebted to Bernard, it is very likely that he was familiar with this conflation of sweetness and song. In the 'songe of loue,' the poem with which Rolle
ends *Ego Dormio*, he associates these terms with the name of Jesus:

> Ihesu, my dere and my drery, delites art þu to synge;
> Ihesu, my myrth, my melody, when wil þou cum, my kynge?
> Ihesu, my hele and my hony, my quert, my confortynge,
> Ihesu, I couait for to dey when hit is þe paynge.
> Langynge is in me lent, þat my loue hath me sent.
> Al wo fro me is went, sethen þat my hert is brent
> In Criste loue so swete …[18]

Rolle extols the sensations of song, sweetness and fire experienced in contemplative union because they increase the longing for the permanent vision of God
that will be possible only after death.

The metaphor of the fire of love is much more commonplace than
sweetness and song, Rolle may also have developed it from the Song of Songs 8:7:
'[Love's] flashes are flashes of fire, a most vehement flame. Many waters cannot
quench love, neither can floods drown it.'[19] The metaphor of fire is a multivalent
one, indicating both heat and light. In *Ego Dormio* he alludes to a purifying heat
when he claims 'þe fyre of loue hath brent away al þe roust of syn'.[20] Rolle also
uses fire to emphasize the intensity of love, either divine or human, as indicated
in the passage cited above about the third degree of love: 'þi goostly egh is
taken vp in to þe light of heuyn, and þare enlumyned in grace and kyndlet of
þe fyre of Cristes loue, so þat þou shal feel verraily þe brennynge of loue in þe
herte.'[21] Rolle uses the light produced by fire as a visual metaphor; since sight
was regarded as a more intellectual sense, light becomes a metaphor associated
with heaven and grace.

The *Cloud* author's directions to his disciple about the contemplative
method seem to be opposed to Rolle's somatic language. He contends that the
practitioner should situate himself between two clouds, of forgetting and of
unknowing. The cloud of forgetting is a metaphor for the apophatic or negative method of contemplation itself. In order to concentrate his attention on the
utterly unknown deity, the disciple must obliterate all thoughts from his mind
and 'put a cloude of forʒetyng bineþ þee, bitwix þee & alle þe creatures þat euer
ben maad'.[22] The second cloud is a metaphor for the absolute transcendence and
incomprehensibility of God:

---

[18] Rolle, *Richard Rolle*, p. 33.
[19] Sutherland provides this translation in 'Biblical Text and Spiritual Experience', p. 702.
Matter's translation of this verse is a more literal rendering of the Vulgate in *Voice of my
Beloved*, p. xxxiii: '[love's] lamps, lamps of fire / and of flames / many waters cannot extinguish
charity / nor rivers drown it'. John Alford asserts that Rolle always uses Songs 8:6–7 to describe
the highest state of love, in 'Biblical *Imitatio* in the Writings of Richard Rolle', *ELH* 40 (1973),
pp. 1–23 (22). Sutherland, however, contends that Rolle's biblical citations are not as schematic
as Alford claims: 'Biblical Text and Spiritual Experience', p. 707.
[20] Rolle, *Richard Rolle*, p. 32.
[21] Ibid., p. 31.
[22] *The Cloud of Unknowing*, Chapter 5, p. 13.

þis derknes & þis cloude is, howsoeuer þou dost, bitwix þee & þi God, & letteþ þee þat þou maist not see him cleerly by liȝt of vnderstonding in þi reson, ne fele him in swetnes of loue in þin affeccion. & þerfore schap þee to bide in þis derknes as longe as þou maist, euermore criing after him þat þou louest; for ȝif euer schalt þou fele him or see him, as it may be here, it behoueþ alweis be in þis cloude & in þis derknes.[23]

Interestingly, the *Cloud* author refers to the light of understanding and the sweetness of affection, invoking the senses of sight and taste as Rolle does, but perhaps making his metaphoric intent clearer by using phrases rather than the single words. Unlike Rolle, though, the *Cloud* author contends that neither understanding nor affection provides adequate access to the divine.

Despite his suspicion of the imagination and sensory language, the *Cloud* author again employs metaphors of sight and touch in describing the culmination of contemplative practice in the brief and sporadic penetration of the cloud of unknowing.[24] First of all, the apophatic exercise he teaches involves stirrings or impulses of affection that the contemplative is to direct continually towards God 'as sparcle fro þe cole' or 'as a scharp darte of longing loue'.[25] These metaphors emphasize the rapid succession of upward, piercing movements, sometimes expressed through the repetition of single words like *sin* or *love*, to indicate the pulsation of desire. The *Cloud* author recommends that his disciple repeat this effort until the transcendent deity beyond human conception responds:

Þan wil he sumtyme parauenture seend oute a beme of goostly liȝt, peersyng þis cloude of vnknowing þat is bitwix þee & hym, & schewe þee sum of his priuete, þe whiche man may not, ne kan not, speke. Þan schalt þou fele þine affeccion enflaumid wiþ þe fire of his loue, fer more þen I kan telle þee, or may, or wile, at þis tyme. For of þat werke þat falliþ to only God dar I not take apon me to speke wiþ my blabryng fleschely tonge; & schortly to say, alþof I durst, I wolde not.[26]

Like Rolle, the *Cloud* author uses both the light and the heat of fire as metaphors for illumination and love, but, alluding to Paul's words about his mystical experience in 2 Corinthians 12:4, he is reluctant to try to describe contemplative union in more detail. Thus, despite the *Cloud* author's realization of the limitation of language to discuss spiritual experience, he employs the same words as Rolle does in describing the culminating experience of contemplation, although he acknowledges more explicitly the figurative nature of this language.

The spiritual programme of the two books of Hilton's *Scale of Perfection* is closer to Rolle's than the *Cloud* author's. Like Rolle, Hilton is instructing an anchorite on the traditional stages of contemplative progress, rather than the more advanced apophatic method of the *Cloud* author. In contrast to Rolle,

---

23  Ibid., Chapter 3, p. 9.
24  Two excellent discussions of the *Cloud* author's use of figurative language are Alastair Minnis, 'Affection and Imagination in "The Cloud of Unknowing" and Hilton's "Scale of Perfection"', *Traditio* 39 (1983), pp. 323–66; and J. A. Burrow, 'Fantasy and Language in *The Cloud of Unknowing*', in *Essays on Medieval Literature* (Oxford, 1984), pp. 132–47.
25  *The Cloud of Unknowing*, Chapter 4, p. 12; Chapter 6, p. 14; Chapter 12, p. 21.
26  Ibid., Chapter 26, p. 34.

however, Hilton more fully articulates the principles informing contemplative practice and places himself in the tradition of introspective mysticism derived from Augustine's interpretation of the soul as the image of God and the conception of contemplative ascent as a journey into the self and upward toward God.[27] In *Scale* I Hilton advises the anchorite that she should engage in introspection, 'that is for to entre into thyn owen soule bi meditacion, for to knowe what it is, and bi the knowynge therof for to come to the goostli knowynge of God. For as Seynt Austyn seith: "Bi the knowynge of mysilf, I schalle gete the knowing of God".'[28] When the contemplative looks within, however, she finds that the image of God has been disfigured by sin. This recognition of the foul image of sin compels the contemplative to begin the process of destroying the ground of sin upon which it rests. The subsequent chapters of Book I therefore instruct the anchorite on how she can eradicate sin and restore the image of God to her soul. For Hilton, then, introspection begins a process of reform. The *Cloud* author, in contrast, discourages introspection because it reveals the 'foule stynkyng lumpe' of the sinful soul that must be put under the cloud of forgetting.[29]

Hilton begins Book II of the *Scale of Perfection* by reiterating the definition of the soul as an image of God and recounting the disfiguration of that image through original sin. In this book he divides reform into two types: the reform in faith necessary for salvation and the reform in feeling that is achieved through the contemplative process and culminates in union with God. Although Hilton speaks of contemplative ascent as a movement inward and upward, he agrees with the *Cloud* author that the soul must recognize that it is incorporeal and that God is incomprehensible. Using the metaphor of sight, as do his two predecessors, Hilton describes the apex of the contemplation as illumination:

> [Jesus] openeth the innere iye of the soule whanne He lightneth the reson thorugh touchynge and schynynge of His blyssid light, for to seen Hym and knowe Him; not al fulli at oones, but litil and litil bi dyverse tymes, as the soule mai suffre Hym. He seeth Hym not what He is, for that mai no creature doon in hevene ne in erthe; ne he seth Him not as He is, for that sight is oonli in the blisse of hevene. But he seth Him that He is: an unchaungeable beynge, a sovereyn might, sovereyn soothfastnesse, and sovereyne goodnesse, a blissid lyf, and an eendelees blisse. This seeth the soule [...] with a wondirful reverence and a privei brennande love, with goostli savour and heveneli delite, more cleerli and more fulli than mai be written or seid.[30]

Contemplation, for Hilton, is like the act of staring at the desired object from a distance without hope of achieving complete comprehension in this life. The sight of the deity only reveals humankind's insignificance because, compared to God, 'mankynde is as nought'.[31] Though the means for achieving contemplative

---

[27] See Turner, *Darkness of God*, Chapters 3 and 4, pp. 50–101, for an excellent discussion of Augustine's introspective mysticism.

[28] Walter Hilton, *The Scale of Perfection*, ed. Thomas H. Bestul, TEAMS (Kalamazoo, MI, 2000), Book I, Chapter 40, p. 74.

[29] See *The Cloud of Unknowing*, Chapter 43, p. 45.

[30] Hilton, *Scale*, Book II, Chapter 32, p. 212.

[31] Ibid., Book II, Chapter 37, p. 227.

union is different, Hilton agrees with both Rolle and the *Cloud* author in using light and fire as metaphors to signify this moment of illumination. In the next chapter, though, Hilton consciously explains the meaning of these metaphors of ascent and interiority, light and fire; as do his predecessors, he associates light with truth and reason and fire with love and affection. Hilton's discussion is similar to the *Cloud* author's analysis of the figurative nature of the language in Chapters 45 to 62 and reveals the influence of *Cloud* on *Scale* II.

Although they subscribe to different theories of contemplation, the three male Middle English mystics are similar in several respects. All wrote guidebooks addressed to recluses to instruct them about the stages in a spiritual progression that culminates in an experience of contemplative union. All three agreed that this experience is one reserved for the spiritual elite, those in contemplative life, rather than all Christians. All three described the apex of this process using metaphors of bright light and burning fire that appeal to the senses of sight and touch. If we now finally turn to Julian of Norwich's *Revelation of Love* we will see how different her conception of union is from that of her male colleagues.

Julian of Norwich addresses her *Revelation of Love* not to an audience of contemplatives but rather to her 'evencristen', her fellow Christians. She recounts and interprets the visionary experience she had in May 1373 so 'that they might alle see and know the same that I sawe, for I wolde that it were comfort to them' (*Revelation*, 8.23–4). In the Fourteenth Revelation she discusses union with God in paradoxical language: 'Hyely owe we to enjoye that God wonneth in oure soule, and mekille hyly we owe to enjoye that oure soule wonneth in God. Our soule is made to be Goddes wonning; and the wonning of oure soule is God, which is unmade' (*Revelation*, 54.7–9). Rather than using the metaphors of bright light and burning fire, as her three male counterparts do, Julian intensifies the intimacy between the soul and God with her metaphors of mutual enclosure. However, her statement seems to be a contradiction: how can the soul be situated in God and God situated in the soul simultaneously? As unusual as her wording sounds, Julian's conception of mutual enclosure is influenced by Augustine's introspective mysticism. As Turner puts it, 'the truth Augustine discovered was that to discover his own inwardness was the same thing as to discover God and that to discover God was to discover his own inwardness – either discovery was the discovery of his true selfhood'.[32] Although Julian, like Hilton, subscribes to the Augustinian model, she does not emphasize the disfiguration of the image of God by sin nor the distance between humankind and the deity as he does.

Furthermore, while all three of the male mystics regard the union with God as the culmination of an arduous spiritual progress reserved for a few elites, Julian instead presents the double conjunction of the soul within God and God within the soul as common to all who will be saved. Julian uses the terms *substance* and *sensuality* to refer to the two parts of the soul corresponding to Augustine's higher and lower reason.[33] She situates the substance, or higher part of the soul,

---

[32] Turner, *Darkness of God*, p. 70.
[33] The *Cloud* author and Hilton also use *sensuality*, but the word has a much more negative resonance for them. See *The Cloud of Unknowing*, Chapter 66, p. 66, and Hilton, *Scale*, Book II, Chapter 13, p. 159.

in God and the image of God in the sensuality, or lower part of the soul: 'For I saw full sekerly that oure substance is in God. And also I saw that in oure sensualite God is' (*Revelation*, 55.19–20). Julian explains creation as a process occurring in two stages. The substance of the soul is first created as a substance in God: 'And I sawe no difference between God and oure substance, but as it were all God. And yet my understanding toke that oure substance is in God; that is to sey, that God is God and oure substance is a creature in God' (*Revelation*, 54.13–15). Thus God is the 'grounde in whome oure soule standeth'. In a second stage of creation, the substance of the soul is joined to the sensuality when it is embodied; at that point the image of God unites the two parts of the soul and becomes the 'mene that kepeth the substance and the sensualite togeder, so that it shall never departe' (*Revelation*, 56.10–11). Thus, paradoxically, the soul is both enclosed by and enclosing God. Not only does the substance of the soul rest within God as the ground of its being, but the image of God resides within the soul from the moment of its embodiment with the sensuality.

The concept of God's immanence as the image within the soul is, of course, the basis for the Augustinian tradition and the enabling premise of Hilton's introspective mysticism. However, the notion of the substance of the soul grounded in God, although implicit in Augustine, becomes most pronounced in the mystical writings of the late Middle Ages. Julian's references to the ground of the soul reveal the same concern with 'the exemplary or virtual preexistence of the soul in God' that McGinn identifies as 'an important theme of the new mysticism of the thirteenth century … a notion that served as at least part of the foundation for new modes of conceiving *unio mystica*.'[34] Julian refers to this exemplary pre-existence of the soul in the second person of the Trinity as she explains the 'godly wille' of those who shall be saved: 'For that ech kinde that heven shall be fulfilled with behoveth nedes of Goddes rightfulhede so to be knit and oned in him, that therein were kepte a substance which might never nor shulde be parted from him, and that thorow his awne good will in his endlesse forseeing purpose' (*Revelation*, 53.14–17). As illluminated by Jenkins later in this volume, Julian uses metaphors of knitting and a knot to describe the entanglement of substance that this union entails:

> [T]his deerwurthy soule was preciously knit to [Crist's soul] in the making. Which knot is so suttel and so mighty that it is oned into God, in which oning it is made endlessly holy […] all the soules that shalle be saved in heven without ende be knit in this knot, and oned in this oning, and made holy in this holyhede'.
>
> (*Revelation*, 53.50–4)

For Julian, then, the pre-existence of the soul's substance in the Logos, the second person of the Trinity, is an ontological rather than a mystical union. It is an eternal and essential conjunction rather than a temporary one.

Julian's conception of union and the language she uses to discuss it are very different from that of the three male Middle English mystics. Although there is no evidence that Julian knew the works of the continental mystics like Hadewijch

---

[34] McGinn, *Flowering of Mysticism*, p. 214.

of Antwerp, Mechthild of Magdeburg, Marguerite of Porète or Meister Eckhart, to whom McGinn attributes this emphasis on the pre-existence of the soul in God, further investigation of the similarities and differences between her ideas about God as the ground of being and those of her continental predecessors are warranted.[35]

---

[35] Bernard McGinn, 'Love, Knowledge and Unio Mystica in the Western Christian Tradition', in *Mystical Union and Monotheistic Faith: An Ecumenical Dialogue*, ed. Moshe Idel and Bernard McGinn (New York, 1989) p. 75; Turner, *Darkness of God*, p. 162.

# 5

## Saint Julian of the Apocalypse

DIANE WATT

### The Solitary in her Community

In both the earlier *A Vision Showed to a Devout Woman* and the longer *A Revelation of Love*,[1] Julian of Norwich relates that she was denied a specific revelation concerning the spiritual destiny of a close friend or relative:

> And when God allemightye hadde shewed me plentyouslye and fully of his goodnesse, I desired of a certaine person that I loved howe it shulde be with hire. And in this desire I letted myselfe, for I was noght taught in this time. And than was I answerde in my reson, als it ware be a frendfulle meen: 'Take it generally, and behalde the curtaysy of thy lorde God as he shewes it to the. For it is mare worshippe to God to behalde him in alle than in any specialle thinge.' I assented, and therwith I lered that it is mare wyrshippe to God to knawe alle thinge in generalle than to like in anythinge in specialle. And if I shulde do wisely efter this techinge, I shulde nought be glad for nathinge in specialle, na desesed for na manere of thinge, for alle shalle be wele. (*Vision*, 16.12–21)

From the passage in *A Vision* alone, it might be inferred that Julian is seeking information about whether or not this woman will go to heaven. In *A Revelation*, this passage is subtly reworded so that we no longer know that the person is female: 'I desired to wit of a serteyn creature that I loved if it shulde continue in good leving, which I hoped by the grace of God was begonne' (*Revelation*, 35.2–3). At the same time, however, we are given additional information about her: evidently, like Julian, she has committed her life to divine service in some way. And the nature of Julian's request is also specified, since it is now clear that she is enquiring about her friend's state of grace in her lifetime, rather than after her death. Both versions agree, however, that Julian was denied this knowledge on the grounds that it was a 'specialle thinge' (*Vision*, 16.17; *Revelation*, 35.7), or as *A Revelation* puts it, a 'singular desyer' (*Revelation*, 35.4), a desire to know about an individual rather than a general truth. In *A Vision*, this moment of comprehension is immediately followed by a revelation that Julian herself

---

[1]   All in-text references to the Short Text and Long Text (hereafter cited as either *A Vision* or *A Revelation*) are by section or chapter and line to *The Writings of Julian of Norwich:* A Vision Showed to a Devout Woman *and* A Revelation of Love, ed. Nicholas Watson and Jacqueline Jenkins (Turnhout, 2006).

'shulde sinne' (*Vision*, 16.22), one that she is not yet ready to comprehend, but which emphasizes her relationship with her fellow believers and humankind in general. The context in *A Revelation* changes, but in referring to the woman as a 'creature' (*Revelation*, 35.2), a term unmarked by gender which Julian increasingly uses to refer to herself, she stresses the similarities between their experiences. She thus underlines her message that the fate of one Christian is in a sense the fate of all.

This relatively minor episode has received little critical attention hitherto, but it raises a number of questions about Julian's vocation, her status within her own community at the time of her showings and her relationship to other women visionaries in the English medieval tradition.[2] There is an influential strand of scholarship that argues that Julian of Norwich should not be located within a specifically feminine mystical and prophetic tradition. According to this viewpoint, despite her identification with the Virgin Mary in both versions of her work, and her extended discussion in *A Revelation of Love* of Christ as mother, Julian's theology and writing transcends her sex.[3] This argument, in fact, has a solid foundation: in Julian's own works. In transforming *A Vision* into *A Revelation*, Julian herself stresses the universality of her message, and represents herself not as 'a woman, lewed, febille, and freylle' (*Vision*, 6.36–37), but as a Christian sinner, a creature, an every*man*. In this essay, however, I consider what happens if we ignore Julian's redirection in *A Revelation* and explore her relationship to other women prophets in England in the later Middle Ages, focusing particularly on both the recluse, then nun and, later, prioress, Christina of Markyate (*c*.1096–after 1155), and Julian's younger East Anglian lay contemporary, Margery Kempe (*c*.1373–after 1439).

Critics are still undecided about whether Julian was a nun or a laywoman at the time of her showings in 1373. What does seem probable is that she was not yet an anchoress. From her description in *A Vision*, her sickbed (where she was tended by her mother and other companions, and to which was summoned her priest to attend her death, and who came accompanied by a boy) could be in a room in either a convent or a domestic home. Nicholas Watson and Jacqueline Jenkins are of the view that Julian of Norwich was a nun from the Benedictine convent of Carrow in Norwich, where she would have been consecrated as a young girl.[4] One piece of evidence that they cite in support of their argument is a reference in the showings to Christ thanking Julian for her 'service' in her youth (*Vision*, 8.53; cf. *Revelation*, 14.1). Benedicta Ward, on the other hand, sees Julian as a laywoman at the time of her visions, and suggests that she was a widow and had had children.[5] I have argued elsewhere for another possibility: that Julian,

---

2   In this article I revisit, develop and revise my brief discussion of Julian of Norwich in the context of Margery Kempe and other medieval women prophets in *Secretaries of God: Women Prophets in Late Medieval and Early Modern England* (Cambridge, 1997), pp. 28–33. Some paragraphs and sentences have been borrowed and adapted from that analysis. I am grateful to Boydell and Brewer for permission to reuse this material.
3   See, for example, the claim that 'the references to mothering and pregnancy in *A Revelation* are theological, not autobiographical', in *Writings*, ed. Watson and Jenkins, p. 4.
4   *Writings*, ed. Watson and Jenkins, p. 4.
5   Benedicta Ward, 'Julian the Solitary', in *Julian Reconsidered*, ed. Kenneth Leech and Benedicta Ward (Oxford, 1988), pp. 11–35.

aged thirty at the time of her visions, was single and childless, either living in
her parents' home or in service with another family.[6] The obvious comparison to
draw here is with Elisabeth Paston (1429–1488), daughter of Agnes and William
Paston I, who did not marry until she was almost thirty.[7]

The fact that Julian chooses to tell us so little about herself, her background,
her life experiences and her relationships with others means that what she does
say takes on enormous significance. Julian only mentions a handful of people
in her writings: the priest who comes to her sickbed, the boy at his side, a
man of religion to whom she first mentions her visions, her mother, and the
woman about whose fate she seeks assurances from God. Who was this devout
woman who, like Julian, devoted herself to divine service? Was she a nun (a
sister in Julian's own convent perhaps), an anchoress, or a vowess or other pious
laywoman? Was she a relative (an aunt, sister, cousin, even Julian's own mother
or, just conceivably, her child)? Could she even have been Julian's companion or
servant (we know from the evidence of later wills that Julian had female servants after she entered the anchorhold)?[8] And what does Julian's intercession on
her friend's behalf reveal about Julian's status in her own community, whether
religious or lay? Was Julian, at the time of the visions in 1373, already regarded
as a holy woman, approached by others with prayers and petitions and for spiritual reassurance because her reputation was established and well known? In
other words, did she ask God about this woman's spiritual state because she had
in turn been asked to do so by the woman herself? Or had Julian in her former
service to God simply shared her devotions, rituals and prayers with another
like-minded woman, so that when she received her showings she remembered
this woman, and for her own peace of mind petitioned God on her behalf?

Felicity Riddy has argued that 'to see Julian as a solitary is to ignore a central
feature of her self-representation, which is relational'.[9] In this essay I want to
take Riddy's view further, and suggest that, whatever the reality of Julian's life
before (and indeed after) her showings, she was never isolated, but – in her role
as holy woman and intercessory – always part of a larger spiritual community
and tradition. To understand this role, then, we have to look at other examples of
late medieval English visionaries. One interesting comparison is with Christina
of Markyate. Christina not only received revelations from God concerning her
own spiritual state, but also, crucially, was blessed with a gift of prophecy, which
enabled her to give guidance to those around her. She was able, for example,
to predict whether or not the sick would recover from their illnesses (*Life of
Christina of Markyate*, pp. 140–3 and 146–9).[10] She also warned people about their
wrongdoings and had insight into the sins that they kept hidden in their hearts

[6]    Diane Watt, *Medieval Women's Writing: Works By and For Women in England, 1100–1500*
(Cambridge, 2007), ch. 4.
[7]    See my discussion of this in *The Paston Women: Selected Letters*, ed. Diane Watt (Cambridge,
2004), pp. 4–5.
[8]    See *Writings*, ed. Watson and Jenkins, Appendix B, pp. 431–5.
[9]    Felicity Riddy, '"Women Talking About The Things of God": A Late Medieval Sub-Culture',
in *Women and Literature in Britain, 1150–1500*, ed. Carol M. Meale (Cambridge, 1993), pp. 104–27
(115).
[10]   All in-text references (hereafter *Life*) are to *The Life of Christina of Markyate: A Twelfth Century
Recluse*, ed. and trans. C. H. Talbot (Oxford, 1959; repr. Toronto, 1998).

(*Life*, pp. 134–5, 140–1 and 190–1). Much closer to Julian is, of course, Margery Kempe. Margery Kempe shared with Christina of Markyate an ability to fore-tell future events, and she was also able to reveal whether the sick would be healed or if their illnesses would prove fatal (*The Book of Margery Kempe*, ch. 23, pp. 53–4).[11] She too could see the secrets of people's hearts, discern true piety from hypocrisy, and suggest how sinners might reform their lives (e.g. *Book*, ch. 24, pp. 55–8). Her gift of prophecy gained her many followers and the dying called for her to be with them in their final hours to help them prepare for judgement (*Book*, ch. 72, pp. 172–3). It is exactly this sort of tradition – a tradition not exclusively female, but often associated with women – into which Julian's request concerning her companion falls. Even before her 1373 illness and show-ings, it would appear that Julian saw her own long-established service to God as encompassing a prophetic and intercessory role.

### Hidden Secrets: Apocalyptic Visions, the Last Things and Julian's Thirteenth Revelation

In the thirty-third chapter of *A Revelation of Love*, part of her Thirteenth Revela-tion, Julian recalls another, related, showing that she was, at first, denied – in this case a general rather than a specific revelation, concerning the fate of sinners after their deaths:

> And yit in this I desyered as I durste that I might have had full sight of hel and of purgatory. But it was not my mening to take prefe of onything that longeth to oure faith. For I beloved sothfastly that hel and purgatory is for the same ende that holy church techeth for. But my mening was that I might have seen for lerning in alle thing that longeth to my faith, wherby I might live the more to Goddes wurshippe and to my profite. And for ought that I culde desyer, I ne culde se of this right nought. (*Revelation*, 33.1–7)

Julian is here careful to emphasis the orthodoxy of enquiries (she does not intend them as a test) and of her showings – absence thereof – and their implications. She goes on to remind the reader that she knows that 'the deville is reproved of God and endlessly dampned' (*Revelation*, 33.7–8), as are those 'that be of the devilles condition in this life' (*Revelation*, 33.9) and the Jews who put Christ to death and were not converted (*Revelation*, 33.17–19). At the same time, however, she does not specify any who are damned eternally apart from the devil himself, keeping alive the possibility that before the final judgement salvation remains open to all. This implication makes her assertion 'But I saw not sinne' near the beginning of the Thirteenth Revelation seem all the more bold (*Revelation*, 27.22).

A significant strand of medieval prophecy is the vision of the otherworld or revelation of the last things: heaven, hell and purgatory. These visions draw on the imagery of Scripture and, in particular, the Book of Revelation. Apoca-

---

11  All in-text references (hereafter *Book*) are to *The Book of Margery Kempe*, ed. Sanford Brown Meech and Hope Emily Allen, EETS o.s. 212 (Oxford, 1940; repr. 1997).

lyptic descriptions of the sufferings of intransigent bishops and kings are found, for example, in the revelations of Hildegard of Bingen (1098–1179), Bridget of Sweden (1303–1373) and Catherine of Siena (1347–1380). Moreover, the relevance of such visions to nuns, for whom saying prayers for the dead was an important duty, is manifest. In England in the twelfth century, Aelred of Rievaulx reported that the sisters of Watton in Yorkshire were 'often taken in ineffable raptures' and would offer prayers for their dead sisters until they were granted a vision to assure them of their salvation.[12] However, laywomen might also experience similar revelations concerning whether the living would go to heaven, hell or purgatory and have visions of the otherworld and the fate of the dead. Even while she was still living in her parents' house, Christina of Markyate received assurances not only of her own salvation, but also of those close to her (*Life*, pp. 78–9). These continued, of course, when she became a recluse and once she had taken her vows (e.g. *Life*, pp. 158–9 and 178–83).

In direct contrast to Julian of Norwich, Margery Kempe received revelations concerning the fate of the dead and was able to advise friends and relatives of the deceased on how the sufferings of those in purgatory could be reduced by pious acts, such as almsgiving (*Book*, ch. 19, pp. 46–7 and ch. 23, pp. 53–4). Yet, while she rejoiced in knowing who would be saved, her revelations concerning the damned caused her such distress and despair that, despite the Lord's warnings, she convinced herself that she was experiencing diabolic delusions:

> Sche wolde not heryn it ne beleuyn þat it was God þat schewyd hir swech thyngys & put it owt of hir mende as mech as sche myth. Owr Lord blamyd hir þer-for & badde hir beleuyn þat it was hys hy mercy & hys goodnesse to schewyn hir hys preuy cownselys, seying to hir mende, 'Dowtyr, þu must as wel heryn of þe dampnyd as of þe sauyed.' Sche wolde ȝeuyn no credens to þe cownsel of God but raþar leuyd it was euvyl spiryt for to deceyuyn hir.
>
> (*Book*, ch. 59, p. 144; cf. ch. 23, pp. 54–5)

As a result, God punished her for her lack of faith. Elsewhere, Christ acknowledges Margery Kempe's prayers for the salvation of:

> alle laȝerys, & [...] alle presonerys [...] alle lecherows men & women [...] alle Iewys & Saraȝenys & alle hethyn pepil [...] alle þe pepil þat is now in þis worlde leuyng & [...] alle þo þat arn for to come in-to þis worldys ende.
>
> (*Book*, ch. 84, p. 204)

Also quite distinct from Julian of Norwich's showings is *A Revelation of Purgatory*, written in the first half of the fifteenth century by a visionary of Winchester, in all probability a lay anchoress, as Mary C. Erler has recently argued; this gives a graphic account of the pains endured by the dreamer's friend, a sister of Nunnaminster called Margaret:[13]

---

[12]  Giles Constable, 'Ælred of Rievaulx and the Nun of Watton: An Episode in the Early History of the Gilbertine Order', in *Medieval Women*, ed. Derek Baker (Oxford, 1978), pp. 205–26 (206); see also Sharon Elkins, *Holy Women of Twelfth Century England* (Chapel Hill, NC, 1988), pp. 106–11.

[13]  Mary C. Erler, '"A Revelation of Purgatory" (1422): Reform and the Politics of Female

And þan me þoʒt þer came out oþer two deuelles, of þe which one hadde sharp rasours, and he ferd as he wold al to-kyt hyr fleishe, and so he didde to my syght. And me þoʒt he pared away al hyr lyppis, and he toke a grete hoke of iren and smote þroʒ-out hyr hert, and þat oþer devill melted lede and brymstone and al maner stynkynge venym that man myʒt thynk.[14]

It also provides detailed instructions about what prayers, pilgrimages and masses will speed her into heaven.

Julian of Norwich's showings are clearly related to but distinct from these visions of the otherworld. Like Margery Kempe, she is pained by the knowledge of damnation. In her Thirteenth Revelation in Section Fourteen of *A Vision*, she wonders about the damage brought about by sin: '"A, goode lorde, howe might alle be wele for the grete harme that is comon by sinne to thy creatures?"' (*Vision*, 14.2–3). As part of the answer (which endorses the notion of the *felix culpa* or fortunate fall), Julian is granted understanding that there are two types ['parties'] of truth:

> The ta party is oure saviour and oure salvation. This blissed party is open and clere and faire and light and plentious. For alle mankinde that is of goode wille or that shalle be es comprehended in this partye. Hereto ere we bidden of God and drawen and consayled and lered inwardlye be the haly gaste and outwarde by haly kyrke by the same grace [...] The tother parte is spared fra us and hidde: that is to saye, alle that is beside oure salvation. For this is oure lordes prive consayles, and it langes to the ryalle lordeship of God for to have his prive consayles in pees, and it langes to his servantes for obedience and reverence nought to wille witte his councelle. Oure lorde has pite and compassion of us, for that sum creatures makes tham so besy therin. And I am seker if we wiste howe mekille we shulde plese him and ese oureselfe for to lefe it, we walde.
>
> (*Vision*, 14.15–30; cf. *Revelation*, 30.1–15)

Margery Kempe, who is described in her *Book* as one of 'owyr Lordys owyn secretarijs whech he hath indued wyth lofe' (*Book*, ch. 28, p. 71), clearly envisages herself as a divine councillor, who, as we have seen, has access to his 'preuy cownselys'. Julian of Norwich draws on similar imagery of contemporary secular kingship.[15] But, in contrast to Margery Kempe, she contends that God's servants, Christians such as herself, should not seek access to his confidences, and that attempts to do so are ill-advised, inappropriate and displeasing to God. Knowledge pertaining to salvation is available to all Christians, including Julian; that which is not is locked away. It is, then, a crucial aspect of Julian's self-

Visions,' *Viator* 38 (2007), pp. 321–45 (324–5). Erler offers an important re-evaluation of the text, which stresses that its attacks on ecclesiastical corruption operate within an orthodox framework. Erler also stresses the importance of women's friendship and female intercession.

14  *A Revelation of Purgatory by an Unknown Fifteenth-Century Woman Visionary: Introduction, Critical Text and Translation*, ed. Marta Powell Harley, Studies in Women and Religion 18 (Lewiston, NY, 1985), p. 67.

15  See *Writings*, ed. Watson and Jenkins, p. 94, l. 25n, where the editors observe that 'the expected word here would be [not "prive" but] "privetes", which often means "heavenly secrets"'. As we will see, 'privetes' is used by Julian elsewhere.

identification as mystic and visionary that her knowledge of divine things is partial and restricted.

In the longer version of the Thirteenth Revelation, the concern with divine secrets and what can and cannot be known by those living remains a central focus. In Chapter 27 of *A Revelation of Love*, Julian, returning to the question of why God allows sin, refers to 'an high, mervelous previte hid in God, which privite he shalle openly make knowen to us in heven' (*Revelation*, 27.33–34). This leads, in Chapter 32, to a startling apocalyptic prophecy:

> There is a deed the which the blissful trinite shalle do in the last day, as to my sight. And what the deed shall be and how it shall be done, it is unknowen of alle creatures which are beneth Crist, and shall be tille whan it shalle be done. The goodnesse and the love of our lorde God wille that we witte that it shall be. And the might and the wisdom of him, by the same love, wille heyle it and hide it fro us, what it shalle be and how it shalle be done [...] This is the gret deed ordained of oure lorde God fro without beginning, tresured and hid in his blessed brest, only knowen to himselfe, by which deed he shalle make all thing wele. For right as the blessed trinite made alle thing of nought, right so the same blessed trinite shalle make wele alle that is not welle. (*Revelation*, 32.19–30)

Because the specific nature of this deed remains unknown to Julian, she continues to struggle with the Christian doctrine 'that many creatures shall be dampned' (*Revelation*, 32.33–4), namely the fallen angels, heathens and Christians who die outside the state of charity (*Revelation*, 32.34–7). Despite her repeated insistence that she believes as Holy Church teaches, she nevertheless intimates that universal salvation may yet become a reality.[16] Alluding to Luke 18.26–7 ('And they that heard it said, who then can be saved ...'), Julian is reassured by the Lord, '"That that is unpossible to the is not unpossible to me"' (*Revelation*, 32.41–2). The absence of a showing of a general hell seems implicitly to admit the theologically radical – and heterodox – possibility that, in Julian's understanding, hell does not exist.

At the end of *A Revelation* Julian talks about how, on the Day of Judgement, for all who are saved, pain and sorrow will pass away: 'And not only we shalle receive the same blisse that soules afore have had in heven, but also we shall receive a new, which plentuously shalle beflowe oute of God into us and fulfille us' (*Revelation*, 75.15–17). Again the language is apocalyptic, echoing the Book of Revelation 21.1, 'And I saw a new heaven and a new earth ...'. This bliss appears to be associated with the fulfilment of Julian's prophecy in Chapter 32 concerning the 'gret deed' (*Revelation*, 32.27).[17] Julian goes on to describe the dread that will accompany this bliss, so that 'the pillours of heven shulle tremelle and quake' and ultimately 'alle heven, alle erth, shall tremelle and quake whan the pillers shall tremelle and quake' (*Revelation*, 75.24–5 and 38–9).

[16] Nicholas Watson, 'Visions of Inclusion: Universal Salvation and Vernacular Theology in Pre-Reformation England', *Journal of Medieval and Early Modern Studies* 27 (1997), pp. 145–87; pp. 160–6.
[17] *Writings*, ed. Watson and Jenkins, p. 360, ll. 15–17n.

Julian's apocalyptic visions are, then, concerned with salvation rather than with damnation. But Julian's showings are also concealings. What God does not reveal to Julian is, she implies, even more important than what he does. Whereas the visions and revelations of Christina of Markyate, Margery Kempe and the anonymous visionary of *The Revelation of Purgatory* affirm traditional salvation theology, Julian's showings challenge it. Her repeated references to the teaching of Holy Church, her repeated insistences that she is only talking about those who will be saved, are carefully and crucially included to protect her from accusations of heresy.

## Communities of Believers and Readers

Neither Christina of Markyate nor Margery Kempe were isolated seers; rather, both were members of communities of ecstatics within (and to some extent outside of) the societies in which they moved; and in the case of Margery Kempe, this community included Julian of Norwich herself. Christina of Markyate was one to whom others came for advice and spiritual help in times of need, but others around her shared her gift of prophecy, including Roger the hermit, with whom she lived for some years, and Sueno, canon of Huntingdon (*Life*, pp. 82–3, 96–7, 100–1 and 106–9). Some members of her circle were granted visions, such as her closest associate for many years, Geoffrey, abbot of St Albans (*Life*, pp. 152–5). Similar observations can be made about Margery Kempe, three centuries later. During her lifetime, Norwich was a centre of religious enthusiasm, orthodox as well as heretical, and Margery Kempe was not on her own. In her *Book*, Margery Kempe describes her introduction to Richard Caister, vicar of St Stephen's Church in Norwich, to whom were ascribed miracles and great works in his lifetime and who after his death in 1420 was revered as a popular saint (*Book*, pp. 38–40, 147, and 320 n. 142/29–31). Margery confided in him at length about her revelations, even prophesying his death (*Book*, pp. 39–40), and he, in turn, supported her against her enemies. She also consulted William Southfield, a Norwich Carmelite, whom she describes as 'a good man and an holy leuar,' and of whom it is recorded elsewhere that he received divine visitations (*Book*, ch. 18, p. 41 and p. 278 n. 41/2sq). The anchorite of the Friar Preachers in Lynn, who acted as one of her principal confessors, is reported to have encouraged her in her pilgrimage to Jerusalem. He foresaw, in considerably accurate detail, 'be þe spiryt of prophecye,' some of the tribulations and blessings she would experience (*Book*, ch. 18, pp. 44; ch. 21, p. 60 and ch. 30, pp. 76–7). He is also represented by Margery Kempe as skilled in the discernment of spirits; she confided her revelations to him when she dared do so to no other 'for he cowde most skyl in swech thyngys'(*Book*, ch. 21, p. 50; cf. ch. 18. pp. 44–5).

Margery Kempe's account of her meeting with Julian, by now, of course, an anchoress, is justifiably well known. According to this account, Margery Kempe approached 'Dame Ielyan' on the instructions of the Lord (*Book*, ch. 18. p. 42). The meeting took place in around 1413, when Julian would have been seventy and Margery Kempe forty. Margery Kempe makes no mention of Julian's visionary writings, which has led critics to speculate about whether she had read or even knew of them.[18] Instead she describes how she confided to Julian her spiritual feelings, meditations, conversations with the Lord and revelations 'to wetyn yf þer wer any deceyte in hem, for þe ankres was expert in swech thyngys & good cownsel cowd ʒeuyn' (*Book*, ch. 18, p. 42). Julian is represented not as a mystic or visionary, but as one knowledgeable about the discernment of spirits. Kempe relates Julian's circumspect but encouraging words, which include the assurance that 'þe sowle of a rytful man is þe sete of God, & so I trust, syster, þat ʒe ben,' and a prayer that she may be granted perseverance and patience in the face of hostility (*Book*, ch. 18, p. 43). Kempe records that she and Julian conversed about God for the 'many days þat þei were to-gedyr' (*Book*, ch. 18, p. 43). Nevertheless, in recounting this episode she concentrates on Julian's side of the exchange. This is in line with what she reveals of her encounter with William Southfield, whom she also consults to find out if 'sche wer dysceyued be any illusyons or not' (*Book*, ch. 18, p. 41); here, too, her own words are not recorded in detail. However, it contrasts with what we are told of the revelations concerning the Virgin Mary that she confides to her anchorite confessor in Chapter 21 (*Book*, ch. 21, p. 50).[19] Even more strikingly, it contrasts with the extended account of her visions that she confesses to Richard Caister, including those 'boþen of qwyk & of ded & of hys own self' (*Book*, ch. 17, p. 39).

It is possible that here *The Book* simply avoids duplication, and that the reader is meant to assume that Margery Kempe revealed similar things to Julian of Norwich and William Southfield as to her confessor and Richard Caister. But had Margery Kempe consulted Julian of Norwich about her revelations concerning the fate of the living and the dead, as she did Richard Caister, Julian would surely have advised her to dismiss them. Because, in Chapter 36 of *A Revelation*, Julian of Norwich reveals that when 'we by oure foly turne us to the beholding of the reproved' (*Revelation* 36.37–8), Christ redirects his children to contemplate him. It is not unfeasible, then, that Margery Kempe would have been circumspect in what she confided to Julian; in other words, that she was, if only at times, careful to avoid conflict or debate with those within her community whose support she sought.

Margery Kempe's account of her meeting with Julian of Norwich is revealing about the spiritual community of which both women were part, a spiritual community for which prophetic knowledge of judgement and salvation had considerable urgency. It also tells us something about the status of Julian in her local community of Norwich in her own lifetime, and specifically in the decades after she first received her showings. Here we see a Julian who is respected by her peers, and particularly by another visionary who perhaps wants to present herself as Julian's heir, but certainly wants to seek her authorization. Margery Kempe, for one, sees herself as part of the same social and pious community as Julian – a community centred on the city of Norwich and its spiritual networks

---

[18]  But see the discussions in Watt, *Medieval Women's Writing*, ch. 4; and *Writings*, ed. Watson and Jenkins, pp. 12–13.
[19]  According to a scribal note, Chapter 22 is misplaced and should be read before Chapter 17, in other words, in the context of Kempe's accounts of her consultations with Caister, Southfield and Julian: *Book*, ch. 16, p. 38.

and vibrant religious culture – and as part of the same visionary tradition. But Margery Kempe also appears to be sensitive to the differences between herself and Julian. She seems to be aware that, while both emerge from a prophetic tradition that is concerned with the last things, the doctrine of damnation and the fate of the souls of the dead, their showings and beliefs diverge in important respects.

If we turn to thinking about the reception of Julian of Norwich's showings, it is interesting to consider whether those who read Julian's *A Vision*, and in particular *A Revelation*, placed much emphasis on her universalist apocalypticism, or whether they, like Margery Kempe, chose to ignore it. The evidence of the reception of Julian's work is patchy, and it is analyzed more fully elsewhere in this volume, so here I focus on two seventeenth-century fragments produced by recusant nuns on the continent.[20] Both of these fragments refer to the prophetic Thirteenth Revelation of the longer text of Julian's work. In the first, written by Margaret Gascoigne, a nun of Cambrai in the 1630s, the sentence '"Lette me alone, my deare worthy childe, intende (or attende) to me, I am inough to thee; rejoice in thy Saviour and Salvation"' (the lines come from *Revelation*, 36.39–40) becomes, alongside '"thou my God art inough to me"' (*Revelation*, 5.31–32), the basis for a meditation on personal salvation.[21] Gascoigne acknowledges her debt to the book of revelations of 'Julian the Ankress of Norwich', but her own concern is not the possibility of universal salvation or a questioning of why sin is allowed to exist, so much as a fear of her own sinfulness and its consequences. As she puts it, 'it seemeth to my naturall judgement that my case is almost damnable'.[22] In contrast, in the second fragment, which appears in the Upholland Manuscript, and was written by an anonymous nun of Cambrai, more of Julian's text is preserved, including warnings against 'seeking and desiring to know and understand the secrets of allmighty god'.[23] This text, headed 'SAINT JULIAN',[24] extracts and paraphrases the Thirteenth Revelation of Julian's longer version, and gains particular prophetic power in a context of Catholic persecution: 'Holy Church shall be shaked in sorrow and anguish, and tribulation in this world, as a man shaketh a cloath in the wind'.[25] Yet even here, the text is edited and reworked to remove the strongest assertions of universalist apocalypticism. There is no reference to Julian not seeing sin, no great deed to be done on the last day, and no struggle to understand damnation.[26]

---

20  Both are also considered briefly by Elisabeth Dutton in her essay later in this volume.
21  *Writings*, ed. Watson and Jenkins, Appendix D.1, pp. 443–4 and 441 and *passim*.
22  Ibid., Appendix D.1, pp. 440–1.
23  Ibid., Appendix D.2, p. 447; this phrase is an addition to *Revelation* 30.
24  Ibid., Appendix D.2, p. 446.
25  Ibid., Appendix D.2, p. 446 (cf. *Revelation* 28.4–6).
26  Ibid., Appendix D.2, pp. 446–8, and note especially the cuts to *Revelation* 27 and 32.

## *Conclusion*

Julian of Norwich's *A Vision* and *A Revelation* are both indebted to a tradition of medieval prophecy that encompasses apocalyptic revelation and visions of heaven, hell and purgatory. Julian acknowledges her own assumption that, like women visionaries such as Christina of Markyate or Margery Kempe, she will receive such showings, and she will be able to determine the fate of the living and the dead. But she also distances herself from such traditions and expectations when she asserts that she is denied specific knowledge concerning her friend, and that she sees neither sin nor hell. Instead she develops her own far more theologically daring universalist apocalypticism. Indeed, it might be argued that Julian's universalist beliefs evolve from her early anxieties about the fate of her friend. Margery Kempe's account of her meeting with Julian of Norwich may reveal in its omissions and silences her awareness of the chasm between their respective beliefs and practices and, unusually, her unwillingness to confront this. Later recusant nuns also struggled to reconcile the implications of Julian's showings, and especially of her Thirteenth Revelation as it appears in the longer text, with their own faith and experience. When Julian, at the end of *A Revelation*, announces 'This boke is begonne by Goddes gifte and his grace, but it is not yet performed, as to my sight' (*Revelation*, 86.1–2), she suggests that it is neither completed nor perfected. Thus, she entrusts it to her readers to 'perform', whom she invites to pray with her 'for charite' (*Revelation*, 86.2). In so doing, she rhetorically places the book into the hands of her spiritual community, now and in the future. Yet, at the same time, she relocates it within the medieval prophetic tradition. For these lines also convey the idea that the book will only be completed and perfected with the fulfilment of its predictions on the Day of Judgment. Ultimately, 'Saint' Julian's prophecies concerning the great deed and other secrets cannot be fully 'performed' until the Apocalypse itself.

# 6

## Anchoritic Aspects of Julian of Norwich[1]

### E. A. JONES

That we know next to nothing about our author has long been a truism of Julian studies. Serenus Cressy tells us that, for all his searching, he 'could not discover any thing touching her, more than what she occasionally sprinkles in the Book it self'.[2] For Colledge and Walsh she is 'an enigmatic figure'; for Grace Jantzen she is likewise 'an enigma'; for Christopher Abbott she has 'a certain "disappeared" quality', and in their recent edition Watson and Jenkins are able to offer only 'a fragmentary biography'.[3] The fragments for such a biography are admittedly few, as McAvoy also points out in her introduction to this volume: four wills (which, since the disastrous Norwich Central Library fire of 1994, have effectively become three), the account, in her *Book*, of Margery Kempe's visit to consult 'Dame Ielyan' about her 'wondirful reuelacyons' in 1413, and of course the testimony of Julian's book(s) themselves.[4] All but the last identify Julian as an anchorite, as do the rubricators of the Amherst and Paris manuscripts of her *Vision* and *Revelation*.

What, though, does this mean? At one level, the response to this question ought to be, as Langland's Ymaginitif might have put it: there are books enough to tell men what anchoritism is. There are indeed now a number of good general introductions to the anchoritic vocation in the Middle Ages.[5] But studies of

1   Thanks to the Bodleian Library Oxford and Eve McClure at the Norfolk Heritage Centre for the supply of photographic material; Kate Harris at Longleat House and Roberta Gilchrist for answers to my queries; Ralph Hanna for a copy of his Dygon essay, and Fr John-Julian OJN and Cate Gunn for sharing unpublished material with me. My title is a 'steal' from Alexandra Barratt, whose 'Anchoritic aspects of *Ancrene Wisse*', *Medium Aevum* 49 (1980), pp. 32–56, similarly seeks to interrogate some of what 'goes without saying' in a canonical anchoritic text.
2   Quoted in *The Writings of Julian of Norwich*: A Vision Showed to a Devout Woman *and* A Revelation of Love, ed. Nicholas Watson and Jacqueline Jenkins (Turnhout, 2006), p. 450. References to Julian's texts themselves will be to *A Vision* and *A Revelation* respectively and section/ chapter and line numbers will appear parenthetically in the main text.
3   *A Book of Showings to the Anchoress Julian of Norwich*, ed. Edmund Colledge and James Walsh (Toronto, 1978), p. 41; Grace Jantzen, *Julian of Norwich: Mystic and Theologian* (London, 2000), p. 3; Christopher Abbott, *Julian of Norwich: Autobiography and Theology* (Cambridge, 1999), p. 2; *Writings*, ed. Watson and Jenkins, p. 4.
4   The wills and Kempe's visit are discussed below. For the quotations from the latter here, see *The Book of Margery Kempe*, ed. Sanford Brown Meech and Hope Emily Allen, EETS o.s. 212 (Oxford, 1948; repr. 1997), ch. 18, p. 42.
5   Rotha Mary Clay, *The Hermits and Anchorites of England* (London, 1914); Ann K. Warren, *Anchorites and their Patrons in Medieval England* (Berkeley, 1985); Roberta Gilchrist, *Contemplation and Action: The Other Monasticism*, The Archaeology of Medieval Britain (London, 1995), ch. 5; and my own 'Hermits and Anchorites in Historical Context', in *Approaching Medieval English*

Julian seem not to have made much use of them – perhaps another instance of the tendency Nicholas Watson has discerned for critics too easily to think of Julian as just 'a voice without a context'.[6] For historicization, most writers turn instead to another literary text, whose relevance as 'context' ought to require more examination than it is sometimes given. At least since 1905, when Dean William Inge introduced both works to a wider public in one of his Westminster lectures on mysticism, Julian has been discussed alongside *Ancrene Wisse*.[7] In some respects this is not unreasonable: though a product of the early thirteenth century, the *Wisse* was certainly still being read in the fifteenth (albeit most of the readers we know about were not in fact anchorites). That other early classic of anchoritic guidance, Aelred's *De Institutione Inclusarum*, was likewise newly translated into English in the late fourteenth and again in the mid fifteenth century. No doubt these works had much to offer, *mutatis mutandis*, to the late-medieval anchorite. But it is precisely the *mutanda* – the subtle modulations required when reading the text in the new circumstances of a different period – that we need to know more about if the comparison is not to contribute to a flattening out of the texture of Julian's anchoritic context.

In this chapter, accordingly, I am going to turn for illustration to the lived experience of other female anchorites of the late fourteenth and fifteenth centuries. For those aspects of the anchoritic life less accessible through the documentary record – what might be termed the anchoritic mentality – I will use a guidance text less well-known than Aelred and *Ancrene Wisse*, but more closely contemporary with Julian. The *Speculum Inclusorum* probably dates from the second decade of the fifteenth century, towards the end of Julian's life and writing career. It was written in Latin for an audience primarily of male anchorites, but translated into English in mid-century for a new audience 'naamly' of 'anchoresses'.[8]

Although I am going to argue that we have more context than is often acknowledged for Julian's experiences as an anchorite, I want to preface this essay with some words of caution about three 'facts' that seem to me to be too often accepted and repeated uncritically. All three may be verified by further research, but further research there needs to be.

*Julian's cell.* No visitor to the cell at the church of St Julian in Conisford can fail to be impressed by the materiality of this fact about Julian's existence. It is worth recalling, however, that this is a reconstruction whose form is conjectural (stone

---

*Anchoritic and Mystical Texts*, ed. Dee Dyas, Valerie Edden and Roger Ellis (Cambridge, 2005), pp. 3–18. See also Liz Herbert McAvoy and Mari Hughes-Edwards (eds), *Anchorites, Wombs and Tombs: Intersections of Gender and Enclosure in the Middle Ages* (Cardiff, 2005) and Liz Herbert McAvoy (ed.), *Rhetoric of the Anchorhold: Space, Place and Body within the Discourses of Enclosure* (Cardiff, 2008).

6   'Julian of Norwich', in *The Cambridge Companion to Medieval Women's Writing*, ed. Carolyn Dinshaw and David Wallace (Cambridge, 2003), pp. 210–21 (211).

7   William Ralph Inge, *Studies of English Mystics: St Margaret's Lectures 1905* (London, 1906), Lecture II. *Ancrene Wisse* is also used for illustration in the introduction to *Revelations of Divine Love Recorded by Julian of Norwich*, ed. Grace Warrack (London, 1901).

8   *Speculum Inclusorum auctore anonymo anglico saeculi xiv*, ed. Livarius Oliger, Lateranum n.s. 4/1 (Rome, 1938); *Myrour of Recluses*, ed. Marta Powell Harley (Madison, 1995). For the audience of the latter, see l. 395. I am working on a new, parallel-text edition.

does not appear to have been common, for example), and whose site is not accepted by all.[9]

*The Carrow connection.* Although the old view that, before becoming an anchorite, Julian must have been a nun at the Benedictine nunnery of Carrow (which was less than a mile from her cell) has lost ground, belief in a link persists. The commonly held view is put most baldly by Watson and Jenkins: 'Julian's cell was in the gift of the Carrow nuns'.[10] This is a lot more than the evidence allows us to say. We know that the advowson of St Julian's belonged to Carrow. That is, the Priory held the right of presenting their candidate to the bishop for appointment as rector whenever a vacancy should occur. Whether the nuns had any say in the process that led to Julian's enclosure there is mere speculation.

*Julian's name.* It seems to be universally assumed that Julian was not our author's given name. It is stated that she would have taken a new name when she became an anchorite, choosing 'Julian' on account of the dedication of the church where she was to spend the rest of her life. The oddity of a woman's choice of a male saint's name is sometimes noted. There is not space here to examine the evidence for and against the practice, but my impression is that it was not normal but exceptional for an anchorite to take a new name on profession.[11] The odd 'choice' of name becomes less odd when one recalls that 'Julian' was simply the equivalent of modern 'Gillian', and as such a common enough woman's name in the Middle Ages.[12]

Rather than dwelling on what we do not know, however, I shall spend the rest of this essay reviewing those aspects of Julian's anchoritic experience that we do know something about, and which may illuminate, and be illuminated by, contemporary anchoritic practice.

## The legatee

There are three wills that certainly contain bequests to Julian: in 1404 Thomas Emund, a Norfolk chantry priest with connections in Norwich, left 12d to Julian, anchorite at the church of St Julian, and 8d to Sarah who lives with her; in 1415 John Plumpton, citizen of Norwich, left 40d to the (unnamed) anchorite at St Julian's, 12d to her maidservant (*ancille sue*), and 12d to her former maid, Alice; and in 1416 Isabel Ufford, widow of the Earl of Suffolk, left 20s to Julian, recluse at Norwich.[13] In addition, the bequest of the rector of St Michael's Coslany in Norwich of 2s to 'Julian anakorite' in 1394 almost certainly also refers to our Julian. A chantry priest, a merchant, an aristocrat and a career cleric: the range

---

9   Georgia Ronan Crampton, *The Shewings of Julian of Norwich* (Kalamazoo, 1994), p. 9; Roberta Gilchrist and Marilyn Oliva, *Religious Women in Medieval East Anglia*, Studies in East Anglian History 1 (Norwich, 1993), p. 76.
10   *Writings*, ed. Watson and Jenkins, p. 4.
11   I investigate this subject more fully in E.A. Jones, 'A Mystic by Any Other Name: Julian(?) of Norwich', *Mystics Quarterly* 33, 3–4 (2007), pp. 1–17.
12   Elizabeth Gidley Withycombe (ed.), *Oxford Dictionary of English Christian Names*, 2nd edn (London, 1950).
13   The wills are translated in *Writings*, ed. Watson and Jenkins, pp. 431–5, where references to the original texts will also be found.

of testators who remembered Julian is a perfect illustration of Ann Warren's contention that material support for the anchoritic vocation was present 'at every point in the medieval social system'.[14]

## The householder

The bequests are particularly valuable for their reminder that the anchoritic life could not be lived in splendid isolation. The prescriptive texts give considerable attention to this aspect of the anchoritic experience: we recall Aelred's advice as to the choice of servants (one young and strong, one old and sensible), and the provisions in Part 8 of Ancrene Wisse for their instruction and discipline. But records of anchorites' servants are few and far between. In 1415 Henry Lord Scrope made a bequest to Elizabeth, formerly the servant of the anchorite of Hampole.[15] Around 1300, the female anchorite of St Chad's in Chester was represented in a lawsuit by her maid, Cecil.[16] A bequest in 1496 of 12d to the 'ancras' of Faversham, included also 4d to 'the ancaras' women', while in 1505 a bequest to the anchoress of 6s 8d was accompanied by 3s 4d to 'her woman' and 20d to her servant.[17]

The inclusion – and naming – of Julian's maids in two of the four bequests to her is therefore unusual, and may imply that they enjoyed a degree of status by their association with her. They also allow us more of a glimpse than we usually get into the intimate world of the reclusory. No other source makes us ask just what might have been involved when an anchoress came to appointing a new maidservant. Above all, they remind us that the anchorite, in addition to her roles as spiritual athlete and intercessor for the world, was also the head of a small household. Julian's whole theodicy, of course, turns on her rhetorically persuasive yet theologically daring 'example' of a servant whose eagerness to fulfil his master's desire is simultaneously his undoing and the making of him. Ideas of lordship and service in Julian have been explored revealingly by Alexandra Barratt.[18] Alongside the Lord and Servant exemplum, she draws attention to the Short Text's early showing of Mary as 'a simpille maidene and a meeke, yonge of age, in the stature that sho was when sho conceivede' (Vision, 4.22–3), who says meekly, 'Lo me here, Goddes handemaidene' (4.29–30) (where 'handemaidene' translates the Vulgate ancilla) – and whose meekness exalts her above 'alle that God made' (Vision, 4.31). Service is not demeaning, but part of a 'nexus of obligation, honour, service, love and reward'[19] that Barratt situates specifically in the 'Bastard feudalism' of late-medieval social relations. She goes on to

---

14  Warren, Anchorites and their Patrons, p. 279.
15  Foedera, Conventiones, Literae, et Cujuscunque Generis Acta Publica etc., ed. Thomas Rymer, 20 vols (London, 1704–32), vol. IX, p. 275.
16  British Library, MS Harley 2162, fol. 61v.
17  Leland L. Duncan (ed.), Testamenta Cantiana, Archaeologia Cantiana (London, 1906), p. 128.
18  Alexandra Barratt, 'Lordship, Service and Worship in Julian of Norwich', in The Medieval Mystical Tradition in England: Exeter Symposium VII, ed. E. A. Jones (Cambridge, 2004), pp. 177–88.
19  Ibid., p. 184.

suggest that Julian herself must very likely have come from the aristocratic or gentry background in which such language would be natural. This is not in itself improbable, but for a material basis for some complex reflections on service and dependence, with a special focus on the relationship between superior and *ancilla*, Julian need have looked no further than her own anchoritic ménage.

The nature of the relationships within this household community is lost to us, though speculation in this area is tempting. Several authors have wanted to identify the 'certaine person that I loved' (*Vision*, 16.1), about whose welfare Julian tells us she was concerned, with her maid Alice. Felicity Riddy goes on to suggest that she – as likely as the male confessor who is usually assumed – could have been the amanuensis who helped Julian write her book.[20] Alice, rather than Sara, tends to be the subject of such conjectures because of the appearance in a late fourteenth-century Norwich document of an Alice Hermyte.[21] This is the only known reference to a woman hermit in medieval English sources. That the designation might be used for the sub-anchoritic status of one of Julian's servants with spiritual ambitions is an interesting and not impossible suggestion, as again McAvoy points out in her introduction.[22]

For further insights into the anchoritic household (including its spiritual dimension) we must look to another example. Katherine Ditton was anchorite at St Michael's church, St Albans, by 1421, when she was received into the fraternity of the Abbey there. She was the recipient of frequent bequests from local people over the next decade, most often to her alone, but in 1426 to her and her companions (*consodalibus*); in a will of 1424 her companions are named as Joan Gerard and Agnes Vertesaws, and in 1433 Thomas Lundon left money to her and Philip Gerarde her servant.[23] On 11 June 1437 Ditton made her own will, leaving small bequests to the high altar, priest, lights and fabric of St Michael's. The residue of her goods she left to her executors who were, besides a nephew named John, her servants and companions Joan Gerard and Agnes Verdesaus.[24]

## The dynast

This is not the last we hear of one of these women. In 1452, Dame Agnes, anchorite of St Michael's, received a legacy of a load of logs, provided she paid for their carriage; and in his will of 1472 a London lawyer, John Wardale, made several bequests to anchorites, including 6s to Agnes Vertesawce, anchoress of St

---

[20] Felicity Riddy, 'Julian of Norwich and Self-Textualization', in *Editing Women*, ed. Ann M. Hutchison (Cardiff, 1998), pp. 101–24 (108–9).

[21] Norman P. Tanner, *The Church in Late Medieval Norwich 1370–1532* (Toronto, 1984), p. 202.

[22] It is made (*inter alia*) by Watson and Jenkins in *Writings*, p. 5; Tanner, *The Church in Late Medieval Norwich*, p. 202 n. 55; Colledge and Walsh call it 'a friendly nickname' (p. 34). The name Alice was, of course, exceptionally common.

[23] W. Brigg (ed.), *The Herts Genealogist and Antiquary* (Harpenden, 1895–99), i.106, i.67, ii.91. See also my 'Christina of Markyate and the *Hermits and Anchorites of England*', in *Christina of Markyate: A Twelfth-Century Holy Woman*, ed. Samuel Fanous and Henrietta Leyser (London, 2004), pp. 229–53 (233 and 245–6).

[24] Hertford, Hertfordshire Archives and Local Studies, 1AR, fol. 31v.

Michael's.[25] Some fifty years after she had first appeared in Ditton's household, Agnes had evidently succeeded her mistress as principal occupant of the cell. She died in 1478, but there continued to be anchorites at St Michael's into the sixteenth century, our last reference being dated 1531.[26]

Such long sequences are unusual in the anchoritic record: most cells seem to have been occupied for the lifetime of a single occupant only. Another exception is Julian's cell at Conisford.[27] There are bequests to a female recluse at St Julian's throughout the 1420s: these are probably not to Julian but to a successor. She is unnamed, as is the recipient of bequests (perhaps the same woman, perhaps her successor) in the 1440s. More details emerge in 1444, when Thomas Wetherby of Carrow left 10s to the anchorite of St Julian's, and further sums to her two servants: 6s 8d to Agnes (presumably the senior) and 40d to Margaret.[28] In 1449, however, Agnes the anchorite at Conisford and her servants were the recipients of bequests from John Chese.[29] She is recorded there until 1475. This Agnes, like her Hertfordshire namesake, may have followed her mistress into reclusion.

## The counsellor

Margery Kempe visited Norwich in 1413, anxious 'to wetyn yf sche wer dysceyued be any illusyons or not' (*Book*, ch. 18, p. 41). She came primarily to consult Richard Caister, who subsequently became her champion, and the Carmelite William Southfield, a noted visionary, whose words of reassurance left her 'mech comfortyd boþe in body and in sowle [...] and gretly strengthyd in hir feyth' (*Book*, ch. 18, p. 42). The divine instruction to visit Julian came only subsequently (did one of the men refer her on?), but to her Margery seems to have poured out her heart, showing her

> þe grace þat God put in hir sowle of compunccyon, contricyon, swetnesse & devocyon, compassyon wyth holy meditacyon & hy contemplacyon, & ful many holy spechys & dalyawns þat owyr Lord spak to hir sowle, and many wondirful revelacyons whech sche schewyd to þe ankres to wetyn yf þer wer any deceyte in hem, for þe ankres was expert in swech thyngys & good cownsel cowd ȝevyn.
>
> (*Book*, ch. 18, p. 42)

The measured wisdom of the advice that Julian gives Margery in answer over the 'many days that þei were to-gedyr' (*Book*, ch. 18, p. 43) has drawn universal praise.

---

[25] The first of these bequests was communicated to Rotha Clay by William Page for inclusion in the second edition of her *Hermits and Anchorites*. Although the details given here are preserved in her notes, the reference has disappeared. For Wardale, see The National Archives: Public Record Office, PROB 11/6, fols 41r–v.

[26] For Agnes's obit, see London, British Library MS Cotton Nero D 7, fol. 137r. For St Michael's generally, see Jones, 'Christina of Markyate', as before.

[27] See the lists in Tanner, *The Church in Late Medieval Norwich*, pp. 200–1. There were anchorites at St Julian's into the 1520s.

[28] Norwich, Norfolk Record Office, NCC Wylbey, fol. 31r.

[29] NCC Aleyn, fol. 24v.

Margery's most faithful supporter, though, was her confessor, who was an anchorite at the Dominicans in Lynn. Male anchorites may have played this essential role of spiritual direction and counsel more frequently than on the few occasions which have left a trace in the record. Margery's consultation with Julian, however, provides a rare example of a female anchorite occupying a position of spiritual authority. But it is not unique. For another instance we can turn to one of the most illustrious personages of early fifteenth-century chivalry: Richard Beauchamp, earl of Warwick. His first wife, Elizabeth Berkeley, died in her mid-thirties in 1422, having given him only three daughters. He remarried in 1423, and at the same time refounded the chantry at Guy's Cliff (near Warwick) in the hope 'that God wold send hym Eyre male'.[30] The 'Rous Roll', which records the story, explains further:

He did hyt by the styrryng of a holy anchoras namyd dam Em Rawghtone dwellyng at all halows in the northestrete of york and for hyt to her apperyd our lady vii tymes in on yer and seyd that in tyme to cum hyt shuld be a regal collage of the Trinyte of a kynges fundacone.[31]

Emma Raughton is recorded as anchoress of All Saints North Street through the 1430s.[32] Beauchamp did not only consult her on domestic/dynastic matters. The 'Beauchamp Pageant' repeats the Guy's Cliff story as part of the text accompanying its illustration of the French coronation of Henry VI:

Of the which coronacion in Fraunce and also the said erle to have the rule of his noble persone unto he were of the age of xvj yeres, it was the will and ordenaunce of Almyghty God, as our Blessed Lady shewed by revelacion unto Dam Emme Rawhton, recluse at All Halowes in Northgate Strete of York.[33]

Nor was Raughton the only anchoress whose advice Beauchamp sought. In early 1421, he had sent one of his chaplains to speak with an anchoress at Winchester. We do not know the subject of the consultation, but Beauchamp was evidently impressed by what he heard, since in May of the same year, while he was in London attending the parliament, he sent for her and (extraordinarily) she came, he laying out £2 6s 8d for her travel and accommodation expenses and 'in providing her with a suitable reward'.[34]

---

[30] *The Beauchamp Pageant*, ed. Alexandra Sinclair (Donington, 2003), p. 39. Henry Beauchamp was born in 1425. Beauchamp's dealings with anchorites are also discussed by Warren, *Anchorites and their Patrons*, pp. 203–6.
[31] *The Rous Roll: with an historical introduction on John Rous and the Warwick Roll*, ed. Charles Ross (repr., Gloucester, 1980), no. 50.
[32] Two squints in the west end of the south aisle of the church have been interpreted as having a connection with Raughton, and a reconstruction of her cell has been erected on the site.
[33] *The Beauchamp Pageant*, ed. Sinclair, p. 144. Discussed in Nancy Bradley Warren, *Spiritual Economies: Female Monasticism in Later Medieval England* (Philadelphia, 2001), pp. 111–12.
[34] Charles Ross, *The Estates and Finances of Richard Beauchamp Earl of Warwick*, Dugdale Society Occasional Papers 12 (1956), p. 15. For the Winchester anchoress see now Mary C. Erler, '"A Revelation of Purgatory" (1422): Reform and the Politics of Female Visions', *Viator* 31 (2007), pp. 321–45. In addition to detailing the milieu and social and spiritual networks in which the anchoress participated, Erler argues that she was probably the author of the earlier fifteenth-century *A Revelation of Purgatory*. My thanks to Professor Erler for a copy of her essay.

As important as the similarities between these cases, however, are the differences. Beauchamp goes to his anchoresses for guidance *from God*: Raughton's communications sit squarely in the 'feminine' genre of visionary prophecy discussed by Diane Watt in the previous essay. Such deference to female visionaries carries some irony in a man who played a prominent role in the trial and condemnation of Joan of Arc.[35] Kempe, by contrast, is interested in what *Julian* has to say. Playing Alphonse of Pecha to Margery's St Bridget, Julian here takes on the clerical roles of spiritual direction and the discerning of spirits.

## *The visionary*

The 'Life' of John of Bridlington (d. 1379) includes a well-known encounter between the saint and a visionary anchoress. Obliged to travel into Richmondshire on monastery business, John makes a diversion to visit a recluse there. On his arrival, she excitedly tells him about the vision she has had the previous night: an eagle of wondrous beauty had circled her dwelling, holding in its beak a document bearing the legend *Ihesus est amor meus* (Jesus is my love). She interprets her vision as presaging John's visit: he is the eagle, who has transferred his affections from the things of this world to the love of God. The saint, exasperated at these 'inane words', leaves at once.[36]

That English sources are rather nervous of visions, especially when they are had by women visionaries, is well established.[37] Although there are signs of a softening in clerical attitudes from the late fourteenth century (following the canonisation of Bridget), such nervousness is still in evidence in the early fifteenth-century *Speculum Inclusorum*. The author acknowledges that anchorites' meditations might lead them to 'have some foretaste of the sweetness of future bliss in enjoyment of God's goodness and his exceptional beauty, in the revelation of things to come, in conversation with angels, and in some kind of vision of the Almighty himself and his ineffable consolation'.[38] (We have already seen that Emma Raughton was sought out for her revelations 'of things to come'.) But the anchorite so blessed should beware Satan transfigured into an angel of light, to 'sotylly deceyve & leede folk into errour', and should also take care 'lest þe gretnesse of reuelacion or sum oþir gracious ȝefte or schewynge of God swelle or bolne so greetly in a man þat he sette ovir-mochil by hymself'.[39] The remedies are (to the second) humility of heart and (to the first) a careful attention to the articles of the Creed, which should be understood and believed implicitly, so that 'nothing þat longiþ to þe feyth be disputyd ne be othir-wise beleeuyd

---

[35]  As noted by Warren, *Spiritual Economies*, pp. 163–4.
[36]  *Nova Legenda Anglie*, ed. Carl Horstman, 2 vols (Oxford, 1901), vol. II, pp. 71–2.
[37]  See, for example, Watson, 'Julian of Norwich', in *The Cambridge Companion to Medieval Women's Writing*, Dinshaw and Wallace (eds), pp. 210–21 (218–19).
[38]  *Speculum Inclusorum*, ed. Oliger, p. 113; my translation (the Middle English text is defective at this point).
[39]  *Myrour of Recluses*, ed. Harley, ll. 1155–6 and 1168–70. Subsequent line references are to this edition.

þan was byforn [...] but euery man knytte hym stedefastly & myȝtyly, wiþ-
oute hesitacion or doute, to þe byleve of oure modyr Holy Cherche' (*Myrour*,
ll. 1210–14). One is reminded of Julian's famous apologia-cum-modesty topos-
cum-protestation in *A Vision*, Section 6. The most suitable (and by implication
the safest) subjects for meditation are:

> þe werkes of Crist for mannes profyt, fro þe firste salutacion of þe angel to þe
> Blessyd Virgine vn-to þe sendynge doun of the Holy Goost. But among alle oþer
> þinges, ofte to remembre hertly on þe glorious passion of Oure Lord Ihesu moost
> prikkeþ and sterith synful man to compunccion of herte. (*Myrour*, ll. 830–6)

This is the world of affective Passion meditation that Julian's revelations sound
as if they are going to inhabit before Jesus (and they) change their *chere*. A reader
who had persevered with Julian's book no further than this might easily have
written a description of one variety of mystical experience that occurs later in
the *Speculum*:

> Some in devout prayers before a crucifix or in meditation on his glorious passion
> have had their heart so filled with sweetness, and become so drunk with the
> delight of divine love, that for all the pleasures of the world they would not
> forego that spiritual joy.[40]

## The reader

The question of Julian's 'intellectual formation' has always been a vexed one:
estimations of the degree of her participation in the literate culture of the late
Middle Ages have ranged between the two poles marked out by her own description of herself as 'a simple creature unletterde' (*Revelation*, 2.1) and Colledge and
Walsh's woman of formidable biblical, theological and rhetorical learning.[41] On
the assumption that Julian received at least some of her intellectual formation
within the anchorhold,[42] how might it have taken place?

The author of the *Speculum Inclusorum* tells his audience of male anchorites
that they are called to practise the contemplative life, which consists in three
things: fervent prayer, devout meditation and edificatory reading (*edificatoria
leccione*).[43] When the text was translated for a female audience, these exercises
were tellingly redefined as consisting in 'feruent preiere, in deuout meditacion,
and in *edificatyf spekynge* (þat is to sey, in speche strecchinge vn-to vertu)'.[44]
But evidence for book ownership by late-medieval anchoresses is not entirely

---

40 *Speculum Inclusorum*, ed. Oliger, p. 128 (not in Middle English text). One of the author's
other examples is a thinly veiled allusion to Rolle.
41 The phrase 'intellectual formation' is borrowed from Colledge and Walsh's discussion in
*Book of Showings*, pp. 43–59.
42 This is now more or less universally accepted. For Colledge and Walsh's discomfort on this
point, see Riddy, 'Julian of Norwich and Self-textualization', pp. 106–7.
43 *Speculum Inclusorum*, ed. Oliger, p. 85.
44 *Myrour of Recluses*, ed. Harley, ll. 564–6; my italics. In the single manuscript in which the text
survives, the two chapters of the Latin original which discuss anchoritic reading are absent.
This seems, however, to be the result of damage to the manuscript.

wanting. In 1451, Thomas Cumberworth, a former sheriff of Lincolnshire, left to the recluse at Greestone Steps Lincoln, besides six yards of blanket, six yards of linen and thrice the alms that a prioress might expect, 'my roll of prayers'.[45] In 1425, Alice the anchorite by St Leonard's Exeter was left a book of Sunday sermons written in English.[46]

In 1417 the London vowess Margery de Nerford left the anchoress outside Bishopsgate her choice from the books that she had not bequeathed elsewhere.[47] Nerford was of Norfolk gentry origins and sole heir of property in Norfolk and Suffolk. She vowed chastity in 1383 at the age of twenty-five, and took up residence in a tenement in Threadneedle Street. She would have passed through Bishopsgate every time she left London to visit the country house she kept in Hackney. The anchorite to whom she made her bequest was almost certainly Margery Pensax. She had been enclosed at Hawton in Nottinghamshire, but in 1399 was given permission to relocate to another cell in a place of her choosing. She was enclosed at Bishopsgate within the year, and was still there in 1414, and probably for several years after. At her death she bequeathed one of the extant copies of the *Scale of Perfection* to Syon Abbey. The copy of the *Scale* may not have come from Nerford's collection; indeed, Ralph Hanna has suggested that Pensax might even have been the woman recluse for whom Hilton wrote it (Hawton is only 10 km from Thurgarton).[48]

A generation later, the Bishopsgate reclusory was occupied by another book-owner and donor with connections south of the river. Joan the anchorite's name appears in five books now in Oxford libraries, where she is identified as joint donor with John Dygon, who became the fifth incumbent of the reclusory attached to Sheen Charterhouse in the mid 1430s, and who wrote the donation notices.[49] They gave a volume of miscellaneous excerpts from theological authors for the use of 'those students ... wishing to preach the word of God' at Exeter College; three other books containing biblical commentary and preaching materials were given to Joan's son Thomas Grenewode for life, and then to Magdalen College; and an incomplete copy of Bridget's *Revelations* was destined for the next recluse of Sheen, with reversion to Magdalen. What the relationship was between the two anchorites, and what relation Joan had to the books distributed, is not known. The books that include her name represent only a portion of the nineteen that are known to have been Dygon's. These others are similarly dominated by preaching material and general theology, of a sort one might expect to find in the private collection of an Oxford graduate, diocesan administrator and dedicated parish priest like Dygon. But a small subset matches the contem-

[45] Andrew Clark (ed.), *Lincoln Diocese Documents, 1450–1544*, EETS o.s. 149 (1914), p. 50. The recluse was a woman named Matilda. See Warren, *Anchorites and their Patrons*, p. 221 and n. 80.

[46] G. R. Dunstan (ed.), *The Register of Edmund Lacy, Bishop of Exeter, 1420–1455: Registrum Commune*, vol. 4, Devon and Cornwall Record Society n.s. 16 (1971), p. 4.

[47] Mary C. Erler, *Women, Reading and Piety in Late Medieval England* (Cambridge, 2002), pp. 48–67, on which the whole of this paragraph is based.

[48] Erler, *Women, Reading and Piety*, p. 170 n. 52. Ralph Hanna, 'John Dygon, Fifth Recluse of Sheen: His Career, Books and Acquaintance', in *Imagining the Book*, ed. Stephen Kelly and John J. Thompson (Turnhout, 2006), pp. 127–41 (136).

[49] The whole of this paragraph is based on Hanna's important recent survey.

plative, and specifically solitary, interests represented in the joint bequests by Bridget's *Revelations*, the Latin *Ancrene Wisse* and the later anchoritic guidance text ascribed to 'Walter the Recluse', Fishlake's Latin *Scale*, Petrarch on the solitary life, and the earliest-known English translation of Thomas à Kempis. Hanna suggests with probability that this 'apparent discovery and transmission of a sophisticated literature of the contemplative life' should be attributed to the 'intellectual deepening' of Dygon's retirement to the reclusory. That this intellectual deepening was shared with his fellow anchorite is a tempting thought, but if Dygon and Joan maintained a book-mediated relationship to parallel the Grenehalgh/Sewell liaison of a half-century later, they were (for us, sadly) more codicologically discreet about it.[50]

Whatever else he may have become, the Carthusian James Grenehalgh was Joanna Sewell's spiritual director before she entered Syon. Arrangements for the spiritual direction of anchorites are generally obscure; we would certainly like to know more about this aspect of Julian's anchoritic experience. A generation later, though, elaborate and careful provision was made for another Norwich anchoress. When Emma Stapleton was enclosed at the house of the Carmelites in 1421, the provincial of the order appointed a team of five friars – including a noted Oxford theologian – as overseers of her spiritual development.[51]

## *The author*

Ashmole MS 59 in the Bodleian Library Oxford may (with due deference to Julian's rival claim) contain the earliest-known piece of writing by an English anchoress. The volume is a miscellany of pieces in prose and verse, written throughout in the hand of the well-known scribe and pioneer of the London book trade, John Shirley. He gives the poem in question the title 'A devoute and holy salutacion of oure ladye made by an holy Ankaresse of Mannsffeld'. The woman meant may well be the anchoress of Mansfield Woodhouse (Notts.) who was the recipient of bequests in 1403 and 1411.[52] The five-stanza poem on the Joys of Mary is found in two other manuscripts, and in one of them appears to be ascribed to Lydgate.[53] The copy in Ashmole 59 has no particular claim to textual authority, and indeed in a couple of places is almost certainly corrupt. Nevertheless, while it would be overstating the case to say that the authorship of the anchoress of Mansfield has the ring of truth about it, it does not seem to be the kind of attribution that would be made lightly – certainly not as casually, and as frequently, as are attributions to Lydgate. The poem begins thus:[54]

50   For the now notorious Grenehalgh and Sewell, see Hanna, 'John Dygon', p. 135. The classic account is Michael G. Sargent, *James Grenehalgh as Textual Critic*, Analecta Cartusiana 85, 2 vols (Salzburg, 1984).
51   Clay, *Hermits and Anchorites*, p. 137; Warren, *Anchorites and their Patrons*, pp. 213–14.
52   A. Gibbons, *Early Lincoln Wills*, Lincoln Record Society 1 (Lincoln, 1888), pp. 103, 118.
53   Carleton Brown and Rossell Hope Robbins (eds), *Index of Middle English Verse* (New York, 1943), no. 1046. See Alexandra Barratt (ed.), *Women's Writing in Middle English* (London, 1992), pp. 277–9.
54   Barratt, *Women's Writing*, p. 277. She replaces thorns with 'th'. 'See' (l. 4) is an emendation of MS 'place'.

Heille, glorious Virgyne, grounde of al oure grace.
Heyle, mayde and moder in virgynitee.
Heyle, whame the Sone of God cheesse for his place,
Sent frome above þane frome the Faders see.
Heyle, with thyne ere conceyvinge, sente to thee
By Gabriell, he thus to thee seyinge:
'Heyle, ful of grace, Marye, God is with thee.'
Heyle, with thine humble herte ther obeyinge.

Four further stanzas treat the remaining Joys (Nativity, Resurrection, Ascension and Assumption). The verse is as accomplished as Julian's prose, but it is not exceptional.

Although the anchoress of Mansfield cannot compete with Julian on any terms except perhaps date, some familiar questions pose themselves. Her poem runs through the commonplaces of Marian iconography: where did she learn them, how and from whom? She displays full command of versification and enough rhetorical figures to satisfy even Colledge and Walsh: what was the 'intellectual formation' that made such techniques available to her and how did it take place? And how did her poem find its way to a wider audience?

### Connections and conclusions

John Shirley, who recorded the work of the anchoress of Mansfield (or attributed the poem to her), was a member of the household of Richard Beauchamp, and served as his secretary at least from 1420, the year before Beauchamp consulted the Winchester anchoress. Isabel Ufford, who made a generous bequest to Julian, was Beauchamp's sister. One of her executors was Sir Miles Stapleton, whose daughter Emma was enclosed, with careful arrangements for her supervision, at the Carmelites in Norwich in 1421. John Chese, who left money in his will to Julian's successor Agnes, also remembered two other anchorites – one of them Joan Grenewode, the anchoress of Bishopsgate. The co-owner of Joan's books, John Dygon, occupied the Sheen reclusory, with which the *Speculum Inclusorum* is probably associated. And there are a few hints that the author of the *Speculum* may have read or heard of Julian.

I am aware that the belief that everything is connected is a sign of delusion, and do not intend to develop these observations into a sustained argument. Nevertheless, the degrees of separation among many of the key figures in this essay are strikingly few. Whether these examples might offer support to Watson and Jenkins's intriguing hypothesis of an 'irregular community' of 'lovers of God'[55] – from whose ranks, they suggest, Julian's early readers and dissemi-nators may have come – is something for further investigation. The evidence presented in this essay does, however, seem to me to demonstrate that Felicity

---

[55] *Writings*, ed. Watson and Jenkins, p. 12.

Riddy's comment, 'To see Julian as a solitary is to ignore a central feature of her self-representation, which is relational', is based on a false antithesis.[56] But there is much still to be done before we reach a full understanding of the networks that helped to create and sustain Julian's anchoritic identity.

---

[56] '"Women Talking about the Things of God": A Late Medieval Sub-Culture', in *Women and Literature in Britain, 1150–1500*, ed. Carol M. Meale (Cambridge, 1993), pp. 104–27 (115). In fairness, Riddy has done some of the work of righting this herself: see her 'Self-textualization', as before.

# 7

## Julian of Norwich and the Liturgy

ANNIE SUTHERLAND

At the very outset of the Short Text of her Revelations,[1] Julian of Norwich tells us:

> I desirede thre graces be the gifte of God. The first was to have minde of Cristes passion. The seconde was bodelye syekenes. And the thrid was to have of Goddes gifte thre woundes. (*Vision*, 1.1–3)

Within the context of late medieval affective spirituality, the first of these requests seems entirely conventional, yet Julian positions it explicitly outside the devotional framework of the Church:

> Notwithstandinge that I leeved sadlye alle the peynes of Criste as halye kyrke shewes and teches […] noughtwithstondinge alle this trewe beleve, I desirede a bodilye sight, wharein I might have more knawinge of bodelye paines of oure lorde oure savioure. (*Vision*, 1.9–14)[2]

Although the second request is expressed in extreme terms ('I wolde that this bodilye syekenes might have beene so harde as to the dede': *Vision*, 1.21–2) and is without exact contemporary parallel, in its emphasis on physical mortification it does not sound entirely out of keeping with the trends of contemporary spirituality.[3] Julian, however, is quick to tell us that:

> This two desires of the passion and of the seekenes, I desirede thame with a condition. For methought that it passede the comene course of prayers.
> (*Vision*, 1.30–1)[4]

---

[1]  All references to the Short Text (*A Vision Showed to a Devout Woman*) and to the Long Text (*A Revelation of Love*) will be taken from *The Writings of Julian of Norwich:* A Vision Showed to a Devout Woman *and* A Revelation of Love, ed. Nicholas Watson and Jacqueline Jenkins (Turnhout, 2006).

[2]  Julian deletes this comparison between her visionary desire and the teaching of the Church from the corresponding chapter of the *Revelation of Love* (2.5–16).

[3]  It should be noted that such emphasis on physical mortification is not entirely characteristic of Julian's writings. See, for example, *Revelation*, 6.33–7.

[4]  This is expressed more carefully in *A Revelation*, which deletes any suggestion that Julian's prayers go beyond or surpass conventional practice ('For methought this was not the commune use of prayer'; *Revelation*, 2.29).

She does not apply this 'condition' to her third request (for the wounds of 'contrition', 'compassion' and 'wilfulle langinge to God': *Vision*, 1.40–1) and that she does not claim her desire for this third grace 'passede the comene course of prayers' is perhaps because the states of contrition, compassion and the longing for God are such staples of the late medieval devotional life.[5]

According to Julian, however, a visionary experience of the Passion beyond the 'techinge of haly kyrke' and a physical illness 'so harde as to the dede' cannot be defined by the terminology of contemporary devotion. Nor, she infers, can her desire for these graces be judged to fall within the boundaries of 'comene' intercessory practice. It is precisely this relationship between Julian's visionary experience and the patterns of contemporary prayer (specifically liturgical and quasi-liturgical) which I explore in this essay, suggesting that, while wider intercessory and meditative practices can shed some light on Julian's literary and liturgical affinities, there are inevitably aspects of her devotional life and language which remain idiosyncratic and enigmatic.[6]

Throughout *A Vision* and *A Revelation*, we find sustained emphasis on the importance and efficacy of prayer. In *A Vision* we are told that 'it is Goddis wille that we pray' and that prayer 'anes the saule to God' (*Vision*, 19.30–4). And in *A Revelation* Christ tells Julian that all 'living prayer' is pleasing to him; we should, he says, 'pray interly' and 'continually' (*Revelation*, 41.33–40) in order to reach that state of unity which is 'the fruit and the ende of oure prayer' (*Revelation*, 42.7). However, it is only in *A Vision* that these reflections on prayer are tied to any specific liturgical practice and, even then, this is achieved by reference to only the most generic of intercessory models:

> For in this oure lorde lered me [...] to hafe of Goddes gifte faith, hope, and charite, and kepe us therein to oure lives ende. And in this we say Pater noster, Ave, and Crede with devotion, as God wille giffe it. (*Vision*, 19.6–8)[7]

Indeed, while recognition of the value of continual prayer is central to Julian's mystical enterprise, any sustained description of the precise form which that prayer might take is less important.[8] In fact, one is often left with the impression

---

5  These three wounds remain exempt from any condition in *A Revelation*: see 2.36–7. Denise Nowakowski Baker makes a similar point regarding the conventionality of Julian's third request. See Denise Nowakowski Baker, *Julian of Norwich's* Showings: *From Vision to Book* (Princeton, 1994), pp. 21–2.

6  By 'quasi-liturgical' I mean those texts which draw on the sequences of the liturgy in encouraging private and personal devotional experience.

7  Edmund Colledge and James Walsh suggest in their edition of Julian's texts that Julian is 'probably alluding to the people's devotions during Mass: 'In the *Lay Folk's Mass Book* they are directed to recite the Our Father, Hail Mary and Creed at the beginning of Mass ... during the offertory ... at the elevation ... and at the end of Mass': *A Book of Showings to the Anchoress Julian of Norwich*, ed. Edmund College and James Walsh, 2 vols (Toronto, 1978), p. 258. This is possible, but as Watson and Jenkins point out more straightforwardly, these are simply 'the three prayers all Christians were supposed to know': *Writings*, ed. Watson and Jenkins, p. 102.

8  It may be that, in her apparent lack of attention to the precise form that prayer should take, Julian is reacting against the literary extravagance of some medieval intercessory practice. See, for example, the comments in Edmund of Abingdon's *The Mirror of Holy Church*, where the *Pater Noster* is lauded as surpassing other, more extravagant prayers; 'And þare-fore a hundrethe thousande er dyssayuede with multyplicacione of wordes and of Orysouns; ffor when þay wene þat þay hafe grete deuocyone, þane hafe þai a fulle fleschely lykynge, ffor-thy þat ilk a

that the most meaningful prayer is that of silent, unscripted contemplation, 'an high, unperceivable prayer' (*Revelation*, 43.18).[9]

Yet we do know that the physical ritual of spoken prayer was significant to Julian. When, in Section 23 of her *Vision*, she is visited by the 'fende' 'with his heete and with his stinke', she comforts herself by setting her eyes on the cross and tells us that '*my tunge* I occupied with speche of Cristes passion and rehersinge of the faith of haly kyrke' (*Vision*, 23.12–13; italics mine), by which, perhaps, we are to understand that she recited such prayers as the aforementioned 'Pater noster, Ave, and Crede'.[10] Narrating the same occurrence in the longer *Revelation*, Julian again emphasizes the reassuringly physical nature of spoken prayer:

> And oure good lorde God gave me grace mightily to trust in him, and to comfort my soule with *bodely spech*, as I shulde have done to another person that had been traveyled. (*Revelation*, 69. 8–10; italics mine)[11]

However, given Julian's silence as to what exactly her 'bodely' prayer entails, it is left to us to speculate on what form her intercessions might have taken and on the liturgical (and quasi-liturgical) background that might inform her writings.

As *Ancrene Wisse* informs us, the life of the anchoress was dominated by prayerful interaction with God. Not only would the anchoress have followed a pattern of private devotions (a point to which this chapter will return), but it is also very probable that she would have been closely familiar with the ecclesiastical liturgy celebrated on a daily basis in the church adjoining her cell. Indeed, echoes of liturgical language and syntax can be heard throughout both of Julian's texts.[12] Most obviously, Julian's prose recalls the phrasing of the *Pater Noster* with which she would have been familiar by means of private devotion and public liturgy.[13] But given the centrality, in Julian's experience, of the Passion of the incarnate Christ, it is not surprising that many of her liturgical echoes can

---

fleschely lykynge delytes þame kyndely in swylke turnede langage. and þare-fore I walde þat þou war warre, ffor I say þe sykerly þat it es a foule lychery for to delyte þe in rymes and slyke gulyardy.' See C. Horstmann (ed.), *Yorkshire Writers – Richard Rolle of Hampole and His Followers*, new edition with preface by A. C. Bartlett (Cambridge, 1999), vol. I, p. 232. All references will be to this revised edition.

[9]   It is possible that in the lack of detail as to *how* exactly she prayed, Julian is protecting herself against accusations of pride. Bear in mind, for example, the comments found in the anonymous late-medieval devotional compilation *þe Holy Boke Gratia Dei*: 'þas deuocions þat þou has thorugh grace sterand be noght knowyn of oþer, hide þaim in þat þou mai with will & dede for drede of vany-glorie'. See *þe Holy Boke Gratia Dei*, in *Richard Rolle and þe holy Boke Gratia Dei*, ed. Sister Mary Luke Arntz (Salzburg, 1981), p. 109, ll. 25–7.

[10]  In both *A Vision* and *A Revelation*, the fiend is presented as 'jangeling' as though he were two men: 'And alle was softe mutteringe, and I understode nought whate thay saide'; *Vision*, 23.5–6; cp. *Revelation*, 69.341–5. One might interpret the fiend's incomprehensible noise as a parody of the ordered and devout 'rehersinge' of liturgical prayer. Watson and Jenkins make a similar point in *Writings*, p. 340.

[11]  In this narration in *A Revelation*, it is noteworthy that the 'feende' scorns 'bidding of bedes which are saide boistosly with mouth, failing devout intending and wise diligence, the which we owe to God in oure prayer' (*Revelation*, 69.7–8). Presumably, Julian's 'bodely spech' is accompanied by appropriately 'devout intending'.

[12]  I am assuming that Julian had lived as an anchoress for several years prior to her composition of *A Revelation*. The situation vis à vis *A Vision* is more ambiguous, but I speculate that it was written at around the time of enclosure.

[13]  For examples, see *A Vision*, 15.32–3; and *A Revelation*, 33.26–7, 43.3, etc.

be traced back to the Canon and Order of the Mass and to the liturgy of Holy Week.[14] To take just one example, we might note that on more than one occasion in *A Revelation* we find the syntactical structure 'by ... in' and 'in ... by' used in articulating our relationship with Christ. So, in Chapter 4 we read:

> The trinity is our maker, the trinity is our keper, the trinity is our everlasting lover, the trinity is our endlesse joy and our blisse, *by our lord Jesu Christ* and *in our lord Jesu Christ*. (*Revelation*, 4.8–10; italics mine)

And in Chapter 55, Julian tells us that she:

> saw that Crist, *us alle having in him that shall be saved by him*, wurshipfully presenteth his fader in heven with us. (*Revelation*, 55.2–3; italics mine)

Although such a prepositional articulation of our relationship with Christ recalls partially the tripartite division found in Romans 11:36 ('For of him, and by him, and in him are all things'), it may well be that Julian has in mind the wording of the Canon of the Mass, recorded thus in the Sarum Missal:

> Per ipsum. Et cum ipso. Et in ipso. Est tibi deo patri omnipotenti. in unitate spiritus sancti omnis honor et gloria.[15]

It is, however, typical of Julian that she does not reproduce exactly the tripartite liturgical formula, but replaces it with a bipartite structure, echoing contextual material allusively rather than duplicating it straightforwardly.

Of course, the location of such liturgical echoes presupposes that Julian possessed a degree of Latinity, and I do not think that this presupposition is necessarily problematic. For although we need not (and probably should not) imagine a fluently Latinate Julian, it seems highly unlikely that an anchoress fed on a daily basis with the traditions of the liturgy would not have ingested something of its language. Further, it may well have been that at some point Julian benefited from clerical or monastic help in 'decoding' the liturgy, and that this assistance proved of continual support in her development of liturgical understanding.[16]

---

14  Of course, the Passion had been long regarded as providing the anchoress with appropriate meditative material. See, for example, Goscelin of St Bertin's late eleventh-century *Liber Confortatorius* in *Goscelin of St. Bertin: The Book of Encouragement and Consolation [Liber Confortatorius] – The Letter of Goscelin to the Recluse Eva*, ed. Monika Otter (Cambridge, 2004), Book III, p. 99). See also Aelred of Rievaulx's *De Institutione Inclusarum*, ed. John Ayto and Alexandra Barratt, EETS o.s. 287 (Oxford, 1984), ch. 17, pp. 47–51 (The Vernon Manuscript), ch. 14, pp. 21–2 (MS Bodley 423).

15  'Through whom, and with whom, and in whom, in the unity of the Holy Spirit, all honour and glory be to you God, Father Almighty', in *The Sarum Missal edited from Three Early Manuscripts*, ed. J. Wickham Legg (Oxford, 1916), p. 224. Unless otherwise specified, all translations from Latin are my own. Since the Sarum Rite was the most widely used liturgy in medieval England, it is this that I have chosen for the purpose of exploring liturgical traces in Julian's writings.

16  For further exploration of the relationship between Norwich-based recluses and the clergy and religious orders, see Norman Tanner, *The Church in Late Medieval Norwich 1370–1532* (Toronto, 1984), esp. pp. 62–64. See also p. 33 for brief reference to a kind of 'personal supervision' given by one priest to another. It is tempting to speculate that similar 'supervision' might have played some part in Julian's life.

For Julian's writings do not simply echo liturgical language and syntax; they could also be argued to demonstrate a grasp of doctrinal issues highlighted through biblical readings used in the liturgical calendar. Far from insignificant in this context is Julian's recognition of the importance of the fact that Christ died only once. Foregrounded in the New Testament Epistle to the Hebrews ('Neither by the blood of goats, or of calves, but by his own blood, [he] entered *once* into the holies, having obtained eternal redemption ... we are sanctified by the oblation of the body of Jesus Christ *once*'; Hebrews 9:12 and 10:10), Julian echoes such thought in both *A Vision* ('For I wate wel that he suffrede nought botte anes': *Vision*, 10.24–5) and *A Revelation* ('... the swete manhode of Crist might suffer but onse': *Revelation*, 22.28).

The Sarum Missal records that Hebrews 9:11–15 was one of the Passion Sunday readings and it is perfectly possible that Julian's familiarity with its theological resonances was prompted by its liturgical positioning immediately prior to Holy Week.[17] In both *A Vision* and *A Revelation*, however, Julian seems to wrestle with the singularity of the Passion; recognizing that Christ's one sacrifice is sufficient, she also suggests that in his infinite love Christ would willingly have suffered (and indeed, died) more than once:

> And in these wordes – 'If I might suffer more, I wolde suffer more' – I saw sothly that as often as he might die, as often he wolde, and love shulde never let him have rest tille he had done it. (*Revelation*, 22.21–3; cf. *Vision*, 12.19–22)[18]

In wrestling thus with Christ's willingness to suffer more than the necessary once, it may be that Julian is influenced by the dual linear and circular impetus of the liturgy. Taking us from Advent to the end of the Trinity sequence by means of a progressing calendar, the liturgy emphasizes a divinity whose actions can be located in linear, historical time. And this is a linearity of which Julian reveals herself to be aware:

> All that he hath done for us, and doeth, and ever shalle, was never cost ne charge to him ne might be, but only that he did in oure manhede, beginning at the swete incarnation, and lasting to the blessed uprising on Ester morow.
>
> (*Revelation*, 23.15–17)

But in providing us with a repeated pattern of meditative celebration and lament, the liturgy reminds us of a God who, in his perpetual activity, lies beyond the conventions of linear time. Indeed, this is a dual impetus which is particularly apparent in the context of the Passion. For while Julian would have encountered the full liturgy of Holy Week only once a year, she would have heard

---

[17]  *Sarum Missal*, ed. Wickham Legg, p. 86.
[18]  In reference to Christ's words, Watson and Jenkins point out that the liturgy for Good Friday contains the words 'What more should I do for you and have not done?' *Writings*, ed. Watson and Jenkins, p. 194, note on ll. 4–5. See *Sarum Missal*, ed. Wickham Legg, p. 113. Julian's Christ seems to offer a theoretical answer this question with 'If I might suffer more, I wolde suffer more'.

and watched the vivid Eucharistic enactment of Christ's death on a much more regular basis.

Of further significance in the context of Julian's familiarity with the liturgy of Holy Week is *A Vision*'s allusion to the words of St Paul in Philippians 2:5 ('For let this mind be in you, which was also in Christ Jesus'). Claiming that the 'shewinge of Criste paines filled me fulle of paines', Julian states, 'Botte ilke saule, aftere the sayinge of Sainte Paule, shulde "feele in him that in Criste Jhesu"' (*Vision*, 10.22–3).

In suggesting that an appropriate response to Christ's Passion involves such Pauline empathy, she echoes Palm Sunday's vivid processional recollection of the entry into Jerusalem, one of the culminating points of which was (and is) a reading from Philippians 2:5–11, followed by St Matthew's account of the Passion. Indeed, this Philippians passage also informs *A Revelation*'s example of the lord and servant, wherein we learn that the humble servant, whom the lord loves greatly, is to be 'hyely and blissefully rewarded without end, above that he shulde have be if he had not fallen' (*Revelation*, 51.48–9).[19] Further, a servant whose fall is preceded by his sudden 'stert[ing] and runn[ing] in gret hast for love to do his lordes wille' might be understood to recall Christ in his humble yet dramatic entry into Jerusalem prior to his crucifixion (*Revelation*, 51.1–12).

From the entry of Christ into Jerusalem (celebrated on Palm Sunday) to the death of Christ on the cross (mourned on Good Friday), the liturgy of Holy Week gives us a vivid sense of the chronology of the Passion.[20] This is a chronology which would also have been impressed upon Julian if, as is surely likely, she had followed her own pattern of private liturgical devotion in addition to following the public liturgy of the Church. For late-medieval Primers, apparently intended for personal use, not only built their devotions around the conventional seven daily offices, but were also frequently accompanied by the Hours of the Cross, encouraging very specific and directed meditation on the narrative sequence of Christ's Passion.[21]

Indeed, a chronological awareness of this narrative seems to lie at the heart of much Middle English writing on the Passion. Turning our attention away from the formal sequences of the ecclesiastical liturgy and towards the devotions outlined in those quasi-liturgical texts which proliferated in the later Middle Ages, again we find ourselves asked repeatedly to consider the unfolding

---

19  For further liturgical background to the Lord and Servant, one might explore Advent's recollection of Isaiah 42:1–9 ('Behold my servant, whom I uphold, my servant, in whom my spirit delights …') and Epiphany's recollection of Isaiah 52:13 ('Behold, my servant shall prosper, he shall be exalted and lifted up, and shall be very high'). See *Sarum Missal*, ed. Wickham Legg, p. 16 and p. 39.

20  It is worth noting that Matthew 21:1–9 (the entry of Christ into Jerusalem) is also read on the first Sunday of Advent. Such repetition of biblical narrative highlights the liturgy's celebration of a God who acts both within and without the linear sequentiality of time.

21  For exploration of the role of such devotions in anchoritic life, see Bella Millett, '*Ancrene Wisse* and the Book of Hours', in *Writing Religious Women: Female Spiritual and Textual Practices in Late Medieval England*, ed. Denis Renevey and Christiania Whitehead (Cardiff, 2000), pp. 21–40. If Julian did follow such Primer-based devotions, we cannot be sure that they would have been in English, since vernacular Primers do not seem to have been common much before the fifteenth century. For exploration and exemplification of the Primer see *The Prymer or Lay-Folks Prayer Book*, ed. H. Littlehales, EETS o.s. 105 and 109 (London, 1895–7).

drama of Christ's sacrifice. Take, for example, *The Privity of the Passion* (the northern English abbreviated version of Johannes de Caulibus' *Meditationes Vitae Christi*) which instructs its audience, 'Begynne nowe thy meditacyone at the begynnynge of Cristes passyone and pursue it feruently to þe laste Ende',[22] and which, drawing on the tradition of the Hours of the Cross, facilitates such meditation by dividing the events of the Passion according to the liturgical hours.[23] In fact, so thoroughgoing is *The Privity*'s assimilation of the crucifixion narrative to liturgical time that it reverses the hierarchy between biblically recorded event and liturgically ordered recollection of that event. Rather than simply offering us the seven hours as a meditatively convenient means of recalling and ordering the events of the passion, it presents Christ's Passion as having been suffered within liturgical time:

> Thow haste now herde me reherse here þe manere of his crucyfyenge, his passione and his bitternes, and his rewefull dede, *the wilke he sufferde in þe houre of vndrone and of none* [...] And nowe I will reherse the schortely whate be-fell *aftyr þat he was dede at þe houre of none* &c. (Italics mine)[24]

Without claiming that Julian was necessarily familiar with this particular text, it is nevertheless abundantly clear that she lived and prayed in a devotional environment which encouraged a vivid awareness of the chronology of the Passion.

That Julian was alert to schematic trends in meditation is suggested by her retrospective division of her Passion-based revelations into five categories:

> For oure curteyse lorde shewed his passion to me in five manneres: of which the furst is the bleding of the hede, the seconde is discolouring of his blessed face, the thirde is the plentous bleding of the body in seming of scorging, the fourth is the depe drying – theyse four as it is before saide for the paines of the passion – and the fifte is this that was shewed for the joy and the blisse of the passion.
>
> (*Revelation*, 23.6–11)

While the basis of this division is not solely chronological (seeming rather to reflect a shifting and kaleidoscopic perspective on the body of Christ), it does

---

[22] *Yorkshire Writers*, ed. Horstmann, vol. I, p. 198. See also the edition and translation of *The Privity of the Passion*, in *Cultures of Piety: Medieval Devotional Literature in Translation*, ed. A. C. Bartlett and T. H. Bestul (New York, 1999), translation (pp. 85–106) and Middle English (pp. 194–211).

[23] For this division according to liturgical hours, see *Yorkshire Writers*, ed. Horstmann, vol. I, pp. 198–218. Such division of the events of the Passion according to the liturgical hours is, of course, commonplace. See, for example, Goscelin of St Bertin's *Liber Confortatorius*, ed. Monika Otter, Book III, p. 99. See also the Meditations on the Passion attributed to Richard Rolle, in *Richard Rolle: Prose and Verse*, ed. S. Ogilvie-Thomson, EETS 293 (Oxford, 1988), p. 75, ll. 242–5 (Meditation B).

[24] *Yorkshire Writers*, ed. Horstmann, vol. I, p. 207. *The Mirror of St Edmund* also orders private devotions according to the liturgical hours. Although not as detailed as the *Privity* in its devotional recommendations, the *Mirror* does recommend meditation on the Passion at every hour. So, before 'matyns', one should think of the birth of Christ and 'sythyne eftyrwarde of his passione'; before 'pryme', one should think of 'þe passione of Ihesu and of his Ioyfull ryssynge'; before 'vndrone', one should think of 'þe passione and of þe witsondaye', etc. (*Yorkshire Writers*, ed. Horstmann, vol. I, p. 235).

recall the sequential emphasis of contemporary devotion. And this sequential emphasis is recalled elsewhere in both *A Vision* and *A Revelation*, in which Julian's showings focus first on the bleeding, crowned head of Christ, and second on 'a parte of his passion: dispite, spitting, solewing, and buffeting, and many languring paines' (*Revelation*, 10.2–3; cf. *Vision*, 8.2–3). They turn then to a consideration of Christ's 'scorging [...] with sharpe smitinges all about the sweete body' (*Revelation*, 12.2–3; cf. *Vision*, 8.21–2), before exploring 'a parte of his passion nere his dying' (*Revelation*, 16.1; cf. *Vision*, 10.1). This exploration is followed by Christ leading 'forth the understanding of his creature by the [...] wound into his sid' (*Revelation*, 24.2–3) and then, by his looking 'downe on the right side' and bringing to Julian's mind 'where our lady stode in the time of his passion' (*Revelation*, 25.1–3).[25]

Such divisions recall the devotional categories of texts such as the 'Meditations on the Passion', ascribed to Richard Rolle, and *The Privity of the Passion*. In the former, for example, the speaker thanks Christ for 'al þat shame and anguyshe þat þou suffred when þay spitten in to þy face', for 'þat shame and shendshipe þat þou suffreddeste in þy buffetynge', for his scourging 'ful stronge and smert' and for 'al þat blode þat þou so plenteuously bled in þy coronynge'.[26] And in the latter, we are asked to meditate at Prime on Christ's beating 'withe scharpe knotty schourges' and on how 'his heued was thurghe-prikkede with scha[r]pe thornes thurghe his blesside brayne [...] and beholde his blyssede face all rynnande with rede blode'. At Midday, we are asked to consider the sorrow of his mother, and at None 'þe howre of his ded'.[27]

Yet, given this devotional and liturgical context, what is remarkable about Julian's writings is the manner in which they resist, even subvert, a straightforwardly chronological reading of Christ's death. Perhaps most notably, Julian does not provide us (and neither is she herself provided) with any introduction to the suffering body of Christ; making no mention of the Last Supper, the betrayal, the questioning or the bearing of the cross, she tells us simply that during her first revelation she was 'sodeynlye' confronted with Christ's bleeding head:

> And in this, sodenly I saw the red bloud trekile downe from under the garlande, hote and freshely, plentuously and lively, right as it was in the time that the garland of thornes was pressed on his blessed head.
>
> (*Revelation*, 4.1–3; *Vision*, 3.10–12)

Such a sudden and sharply focused 'close up' on the suffering Christ is set in stark relief by the wealth of preparatory meditation recommended in contemporary quasi-liturgical material and foregrounded explicitly in the liturgy itself, and serves to emphasize Julian's very particular position in late-medieval devo-

---

[25] In *A Revelation*, the crowned head introduces the first revelation, the 'dispite, spitting, solewing, and buffeting' the second. The fourth explores the 'scorging' and the eighth considers 'a parte of his passion nere his dying'. In the tenth, Julian considers the wound in Christ's side and in the eleventh, Christ points us towards Mary at the foot of the cross.

[26] *Richard Rolle: Prose and Verse*, ed. Ogilvie-Thomson, pp. 69–83 (Meditation B), esp. 72.138–9; 73.177–8; 73.191–2; 75.266–7.

[27] *Yorkshire Writers*, ed. Horstmann, vol. I, pp. 198–218, esp. pp. 203, 204, 206.

tion. It is particularly noteworthy that at no point does she see, envisage or narrate the act of crucifixion. Indeed, she moves from a consideration of Christ's 'scorging' (*Revelation*, 12.2–3; *Vision*, 8.21–2), endured prior to his crucifixion, to the showing of 'a parte of his passion nere his dying' and a reference to his position on the 'rode' (*Revelation*, 16.1–10) without any allusion to the Crucifixion itself.[28] That she should make no mention of this event is all the more striking when one considers the prominence granted it in contemporary devotional material such as *The Privity*: '... as wode mene they threwe hym wyde opyne one þe crosse, and strenede oute his armes with gret violence on euery side'.[29]

Even more remarkable is the fact that, although Julian makes reference to Christ having died ('For that same time that oure blessed saviour died upon the rode, it was a dry, harre wind, wonder colde as to my sight' (*Revelation*, 16.9–11),[30] she states unequivocally that she did not witness this death:

> And I loked after the departing with alle my mightes and wende to have seen the body all dead. But I saw him not so. And right in the same time that methought by seming that the life might no lenger last, and the shewing of the ende behoved nedes to be nye – sodenly, I beholding in the same crosse, he changed in blisseful chere. (*Revelation*, 21.5–9)

The bold idiosyncrasy of this claim is all the more dramatic when viewed in the light of the liturgy of the Mass and of Holy Week, and when situated beside devotional traditions enshrined in such late medieval treatises as *A Talking of the Love of God*: 'A: swete Ihesu deore lemmon. Nou þou diȝest for me hongynge on Rode tre. & letest þin hed falle doun. þat del hit is to se'.[31]

Indeed, Julian's writings are characterized by the manner in which they allow Christ's Passion to fade in and out of narrative focus.[32] For example, startled by the first revelation's dramatic visualization of Christ's bleeding head, Julian tells us that she was equally 'sodeinly' (*Revelation*, 4.6) drawn into a consideration of the nature of the Trinity, which led to a vision of the young Virgin Mary 'ghostly in bodily likenes' (*Revelation*, 4.25).[33] At the beginning of Chapter 5, she refers back briefly to 'this sight of the head bleeding' as providing a context for her 'ghostly sight of [Christ's] homely loving' (*Revelation*, 5.1–2), but it is not until

---

[28] *A Vision* does not refer to Christ on the 'rode' but does refer to the 'wringinge of the nailes' (10.18).
[29] *Yorkshire Writers*, ed. Horstmann, vol. I, p. 205.
[30] For the stretching of Christ on the cross, see also the *York Play of the Crucifixion* in *The York Plays*, ed. R. Beadle, York Medieval Texts, Second Series (London, 1982). For devotional analogues to this 'wonder colde' weather, see, for example, *A Talking of the Love of God*: 'þer þow hongedest reuþly. so cold and so blodi, ...' in *A Talkyng of þe Loue of God*, ed. Sr. Dr. D. W Westra (The Hague, 1950), p. 52, ll. 10–11; and *The Privity*: 'Be-holde hym here besyly thus betyne & all tremlynge for colde: for, as þe gospell sais, þe wedire was colde' in *Yorkshire Writers*, ed. Horstmann, vol. I, p. 203. For devotional analogues to the wind, see, for example, the *Meditations on the Passion* found in Cambridge University Library, MS. Cambr. Ll I. 8: 'þi heere meuyth with þe wynde clemyd with þe blood', in *Yorkshire Writers*, ed. Horstmann, vol. I, p. 85. For further reference to the wind and cold in Julian, see *A Revelation*, 17.37–9.
[31] *A Talkyng of þe Loue of God*, ed. Westra, p. 52, ll. 12–14.
[32] Baker makes similar observations regarding Julian's episodic and intermittent narration of the Passion. See *Julian of Norwich's Showings*, pp. 48–51.
[33] These Trinitarian and Marian ruminations are not found in the corresponding Section 3 of *A Vision*.

Chapter 7 that we are presented once more with a vividly focused image of the suffering Christ: 'The gret droppes of blode felle downe fro under the garlonde like pelottes, seming as it had comen oute of the veines' (*Revelation*, 7.10–12).[34] Such fading in and out of focus contributes to our sense of the Passion in both texts as surprisingly decontextualized. Not only does Julian resist presenting us with a consistently observed narrative, but she does not allow us much sense of Christ's suffering as having been endured in a particular place, at the hands of particular people. In her relative silence as to the environment of the Passion (the most that she tells us is that it was cold and wet), Julian does not recall the biblically inspired awareness of location exhibited in the liturgy of Holy Week, and evades the precision of contemporary devotional references to, for example, 'the mount of Caluarie'.[35] Further, in speaking of the pain inflicted on Christ ('dispite, spitting, solewing, and buffeting'; *Revelation*, 10.2–3) without mentioning those who inflicted it, the *Revelations* distinguish themselves from the contemporary trend of naming and demonizing the Jews.[36] And that this is an unconventional omission of which Julian is aware is suggested in Chapter 33 of *A Revelation*, when she tells us:

> For I had sight of the passion of Crist in diverse shewing: in the furst, in the secunde, in the fourth, and in the eighth, as it is before saide, wherin I had in part feling of the sorow of oure lady and of his tru frendes that saw his paines. But I saw not so properly specified the Jewes that did him to deth.
>
> (*Revelation*, 33.14–18)[37]

In thus implicitly acknowledging – while withstanding – the trends of contemporary devotion, Julian allows her visions to focus on the suffering Christ (albeit 'swemly, and darkely': *Revelation*, 10.8) to the exclusion of all distractions. In so doing, she emphasizes to us the arguably quite deliberate idiosyncrasy of her visionary experience.

It is in Chapter 6 of *A Revelation* that we might be said to reach the heart of Julian's devotional and intercessory theory and practice. Having recounted her first revelation, inspired by Christ's coronation with a 'garland of thornes' (*Revelation*, 4.3), Julian is led to reflect on 'the custome of our prayer' and tells us that she sees 'how that we use, for unknowing of love, to make many meanes' (*Revelation*, 6.2–4). In other words, she suggests that we are distracted in our intercessions by unnecessary attention to the mediating devices by which we might worship God. She elaborates thus on these 'meanes':

---

[34] Like *A Revelation*, *A Vision* also speaks of a 'gastelye sight of [Christ's] hamly lovinge' (4.2) and takes its time in returning to 'the face of the crucifxe that hange before me' (8.1–2).

[35] *Richard Rolle: Prose and Verse*, ed. Ogilvie-Thomson, p. 66, l. 103 (Meditation A). As well as alluding to the weather, Julian also refers to 'where our lady stode in the time of his passion', but she does not expand descriptively on this (*Revelation*, 25.2–3).

[36] For the naming of the Jews in contemporary devotions, see, for example, *Richard Rolle: Prose and Verse*, ed. Ogilvie-Thomson, p. 65, l. 60 (Meditation A).

[37] In addition to the Jews, Pilate also seems to have been a stock character in late-medieval Passion meditation. He is mentioned in *A Revelation* but it is not within the context of his condemning Christ to death, nor, indeed, within the specific context of the crucifixion. Rather, Pilate is one of two whom Julian mentions as not knowing Christ, the other being 'Saint Dionisy of France, which was that time a paynim' (18.21–2).

We pray to God for his holy flesh and for his precious bloud, his holy passion, his dereworthy death and worshipful woundes: and all the blessed kindnes and the endlesse life that we have of all this, *it is of his goodnes*. And we pray him for his sweete mothers love that him bare: and all the helpe that we have of her, *it is of his goodnes*. And we pray for his holy crosse that he died on: and all the helpe and all the vertu that we have of that crosse, *it is of his goodnes*. And on the same wise, all the helpe that we have of special saintes, and of all the blessed company of heaven, the dereworthy love and the holy endles frenshipe that we have of them, *it is of his goodnes*. (*Revelation*, 6.9–18; italics mine)

In elaborating thus, only to emphasize repeatedly the simplicity of God's good-ness which lies at the true centre of prayerful living, Julian seems to suggest that the Passion-based, Marian and hagiographic emphases of contemporary devo-tion are complicating distractions.[38] However, having established and affirmed the divine 'goodnes' which is the goal of all intercessory practice, Julian expresses herself content that we should use the 'meanes' which 'God of his goodnes hath ordained', [o]f which the chiefe and principal meane is the blessed kinde that he toke of the maiden' (*Revelation*, 6.19–21). She concludes: 'Wherfor it pleseth him that we seke him and worshippe him by meanes, understanding and knowing that he is the goodnes of all' (*Revelation*, 6.22–4). In a characteristically careful manoeuvre, Julian has at once distanced herself from the intercessory conven-tions of affective devotion while at the same time registering the appropriate-ness of meditative devices ('meanes') when deployed within an overarching awareness of the fundamental 'goodnes' of God. And it is this dual awareness of the mystical life as surpassing the 'comene course of prayers' while remaining appropriately modulated by its conventions that renders Julian's voice so litur-gically and devotionally allusive, yet at the same time so uniquely distinctive.

---

[38] For God as the source of all goodness, see the *Order of the Mass*: 'Deus pater fons et origo tocius bonitatis ...' in *Sarum Missal*, ed. Wickham Legg , p. 226. In drawing attention to the potential distraction of mediating devices in prayer, Julian has something in common with the *Cloud* author who emphasizes that the meditations of those 'þat contynuely worchen in þe werk of þis book' are 'as þei were sodein conseites & blynde felynges of þeire owne wrechidnes, or of þe goodness of God, wiþoutyn any menes of redyng or heryng comyng before, & wiþoutyn any specyal beholdyng of any þing vnder God'. *The Cloud of Unknowing and Related Treatises*, ed. P. Hodgson (Exeter, 1982), ch. 36, 40/15–19.

# PART II
# MANUSCRIPT TRADITION
# AND INTERPRETATION

# 8

## Julian's Second Thoughts: The Long Text Tradition

### BARRY WINDEATT

> This boke is begonne by Goddes gifte and his grace, but it is not yet performed, as to my sight. (*Revelation*, 86.1–2)[1]

The survival of two versions of the text of Julian of Norwich – both judged authentic by modern scholarship – provides an opportunity to chart the development of a mystic mind and a contemplative writer in their recording of how Julian responds to the challenge of interpreting her original revelatory experience.[2] Only one mid fifteenth-century manuscript – London, British Library MS Additional 37790 – preserves the shorter form, in a compendium of contemplative reading (outlined by Marleen Cré at the start of her essay), while the fuller version, some six times longer, survives complete in three post-Reformation manuscripts.[3] Development in form and content between these two extant versions of Julian's text is so extensive that there may well have been intervening versions that do not survive. Some personal and circumstantial details about the showings as an event are included in the shorter version (*A Vision Showed to a Devout Woman*) but go unrecorded in the longer text (*A Revelation of Love*), arguably because the former is nearer in composition to the experience.[4] Such internal evidence points to the *Vision* being an authorial recension of Julian's work, and one that precedes the longer version (*A Revelation of Love*) rather than

---

1   All references to Julian's texts will be taken from *The Writings of Julian of Norwich: A Vision Showed to a Devout Woman and A Revelation of Love*, ed. Nicholas Watson and Jacqueline Jenkins (Turnhout, 2006) and will be cited by section or chapter and line.
2   On the two versions, see: Denise Nowakowski Baker, *Julian of Norwich's Showings: From Vision to Book* (Princeton, NJ, 1994); Marion Glasscoe, 'Visions and Revisions: A Further Look at the Manuscripts of Julian of Norwich', *Studies in Bibliography* 42 (1989), pp. 103–20; Barry Windeatt, 'Julian of Norwich and Her Audience', *Review of English Studies*, n.s. 28 (1977), pp. 1–17; '"Pryvytes to us": Knowing and re-vision in Julian of Norwich', in *Chaucer to Shakespeare: Essays in Honour of S. Ando*, ed. Toshiyuki Takamiya and Richard Beadle (Cambridge, 1992), pp. 87–98; 'Julian of Norwich', in *A Companion to Middle English Prose*, ed. A. S. G. Edwards (Cambridge, 2004), pp. 67–81.
3   On the manuscripts, see: *Julian of Norwich's Revelations of Divine Love: The Shorter Version from B.L. Add. MS 37990*, ed. Frances Beer (Heidelberg, 1978); *A Book of Showings to the Anchoress Julian of Norwich*, ed. Edmund Colledge and James Walsh, 2 vols (Toronto, 1978); *Julian of Norwich: Showing of Love: Extant Texts and Translation*, ed. Sr Anna Maria Reynolds and Julia Bolton Holloway (Florence, 2001). These manuscripts are also discussed by Elisabeth Dutton in this present volume.
4   The priest who brings a crucifix is accompanied by a child and addresses Julian as 'daughter' (*Vision*, 2.20–2); the posture of Julian's head and hands on her sickbed are described (*Vision*, 2.33–5); and Julian's mother is at her bedside (*Vision*, 10.26–8).

being abridged from it (even though *A Vision* is preserved in an anthology that includes abridgements of other contemplative works).

The showings, which start when a dying Julian sees the blood on a painted crucifix begin to trickle and spread, prompt her to a lifetime of subsequent meditation, of which *A Revelation* is the outcome. Julian's visions focus on uniquely detailed insights – as in her First Revelation of the blood on Christ's forehead – but in *A Revelation* this visuality is also enhanced by distinctively dynamic perceptions (Christ's blood spreads like herring scales, for example, and it streams down like rain pouring over eaves: *Revelation*, 7.17–20). In her Second Revelation in the Short Text Julian records seeing 'alle his blissede face a time closede in dry blode' (*Vision*, 8.4–5), but in *A Revelation* this has become:

> And one time I saw how halfe the face, beginning at the ere, overyede with drye bloud till it beclosed into the mid face. And after that the other halfe beclosed on the same wise, and therewhiles it vanished in this party, even as it cam.
>
> (*Revelation*, 10.4–7)

What is first recorded as the face unchangingly covered in blood comes to be remembered through precisely detailed observation of how the two sides of Christ's face discolour alternatingly. The fuller version rewrites a conventional devotional image – a static account of Christ's bloodied face – into the uniquely dynamic experience of an arrestingly strange vision which focuses on the changing coloration of Christ's suffering face. Whether or not the vision of the alternatingly blood-stained halves of Christ's face formed part of Julian's visions in the first instance which have simply been passed over in her less descriptive shorter text, the more detailed account develops in conjunction with Julian's 'feer whether it was a shewing or none' (*Revelation*, 10.27) and her prolonged uncertainty in understanding it which, however, she candidly allows to remain part of her record of how she comes to interpret her revelation. As more is understood more is visualized and, overall, *A Revelation* presents images caught with a photographic precision by a painterly eye, along with the outcome of meditation on the fuller visual details that it records. Julian knows very well that she is not seeing the Passion ('For I wiste welle he sufferede but onys, but as he wolde shewe it me and fille me with minde': *Revelation*, 17.41–2), but is receiving instead a visionary insight – as in her Fourth Revelation – into the Passion's implications: 'the bleding continued a while till it might be seen with avisement' (*Revelation*, 12.6). It is the pursuit of such implications through contemplative understanding that *A Revelation* represents in its content, style and form.

What had started in *A Vision* as the story of Julian's visions becomes in *A Revelation* the history of how she comes to understand them. As an authorial re-edition of the earlier text – and something of a journal recording intervening meditation – *A Revelation* now includes within itself so much extended commentary analyzing the earlier narrative of Julian's revelatory experience as to shift the balance and revise the focus of the earlier account and refashion its genre. In essence *A Vision* had presented a narrative self-account of an experience. In *A Revelation*, however, the unity of a narrative line gives way to the more exploratory continuum of a meditative commentary that foregrounds all the analytical subtleties of a contemplative and theologically informed mind that discerns patterns, categorizes and sub-divides. Indeed, it is commentary that comes to constitute the continuity of the text in *A Revelation*. Both the Thirteenth and Fourteenth Revelations prompt Julian to such an extended excursus of commentary that a narrative history of the fifteen revelations received on the first day can barely re-establish itself before commentary on the completed revelations as a whole takes over until the text's conclusion. With understanding come careful attempted categorizations of the different roles of bodily sight, spiritual sight and 'worde formede in my understanding' (*Revelation*, 9.24–5), distinctions already present in a *Vision* but much refined in *A Revelation*. Julian's perplexing but key revelation of the lord and servant is presented inseparably from the anxious process of how she learns to interpret it and then applies the interpretation, but this is only the most prominent instance of a process that characterizes Julian's text throughout and in which three levels are distinguished. First comes 'the beginning of teching that I understode therin in the same time' as the revelation (*Revelation*, 51.64). Crucially follows 'the inwarde lerning that I have understonde therein sithen', combined with an overview of the whole revelation which is brought 'oftimes frely to the sight of my understonding' (*Revelation*, 51.64–7), although Julian records difficulty in separating these phases of insight.

Although Julian dates her subsequent breakthroughs in interpreting that 'love was his mening' to 'fifteen yere after and mor' (*Revelation*, 86.12) and her decoding of the lord and servant example to 'twenty yere after the time of the shewing, save thre monthes' (*Revelation*, 51.73), she implies many other illuminations subsequent to the original revelatory experience. Of her first showing Julian records that 'the bodely sight stinted, and the gostely sight dwelled in my understonding' (*Revelation*, 8.19–20), and this is more largely true of how she stores and interprets her recollections. In retrospect, and before describing the Sixteenth Revelation, Julian declares only in the Long Text:

> Now have I tolde you of fifteen shewinges, as God whitsafe to minister them to my minde, renewde by lighteninges and touchinges, I hope of the same spirite that shewed them alle. (*Revelation*, 65.29–31)

These 'lighteninges and touchinges' are alluded to in various contexts and fashions. In Julian's extensive added meditation on her First Revelation, for example, she introduces a new subject with 'And to the understonding of this, he shewde this open example' (*Revelation*, 7.27), which is the honour a great lord does a poor servant by being 'homely' with him. 'This bodely exsample' (*Revelation*, 7.33–4), as Julian terms it, has apparently been 'shewed' subsequent to the original revelations. Her being 'lerned in the gostely shewing of our lord God that he meneth so' (*Revelation*, 8.32) also implies subsequent insights. Recording her anxiety over the Second Revelation, Julian remarks, 'And then diverse times our lord gave me more sight, wherby that I understode truly that it was a shewing' (*Revelation*, 10.27–9), and this hint of subsequent 'lighteninges and touchinges' is the context for her interpretation ('It was a figur and a liknes …': *Revelation*, 10.27–9). Towards the end of the Eleventh Revelation a sentence present in the Long Text but not in the Short is introduced with the words, 'And to mor understanding, he shewed this exsample' (*Revelation*, 25.26), which apparently refers to illumination received subsequent to the original revelations. During her extended meditative commentary on the Thirteenth Revelation Julian declares 'And farthermore he gave special understanding and teching of working and shewing of miracles, as thus ...' (*Revelation*, 36.49–50) and reports Christ's direct speech, which is not part of her shorter report in *A Vision*. In other places any subsequent 'lighteninges and touchinges' are seemingly withheld ('And as to this, I had no other answere in shewing of oure lorde but this': *Vision*, 32.41), although more divine speech is reported. In such references Julian acknowledges the culminative nature of the process of meditation implicit in her text, to be taken alongside her record of understandings insisted upon as concurrent with the original experience of revelation ('For thus as I shall say cam to my mind in the same time': *Revelation*, 6.9; 'And in alle that time that he shewd this that I have now saide in gostely sight, I saw the bodely sight lasting': *Revelation*, 7.9–10).

In *A Revelation* the modern reader gains access to a work that – for all its formal textualization and its alertness to Julian's fellow Christians – retains something of the layered, interleaved structure of a private working draft, perhaps never widely circulated. It has not been restructured into a logical linearity for the benefit of readers who have not shared its author's experience and is criss-crossed with references to revelations not yet narrated (as when the meditation on the Second Revelation refers forward to the Eighth in 10.52–3). This sense of a commentary in progress is inseparable from the challenge to interpretation reflected in the accumulating content and impetus of Julian's revelations as she revises them between the Short and the Long texts. In most of the revelations there are absent from *A Vision* but present in *A Revelation* (and presumably added as the outcome of intervening meditation) passages reflecting some transformative shift in understanding of the original revelation which is conveyed in changes of plane and in intensification of awareness as to how imagery may express this. Each revelation where this occurs is distinct in method and effect – although there is some reiterated symbolism of blood and lordship – but the impetus in revelation after revelation establishes a pattern characteristic of the stage of Julian's text which *A Revelation* represents.

In the First Revelation the supplemented visual intensity of seeing the blood spreading out over Christ's forehead ('quick and lively, and hidous and dredfulle, and swete and lovely': *Revelation*, 7.23–4), far from being vivid and gruesome for its own sake, comes to be understood as an 'open example' of divine favour:

> It is the most wurship that a solempne king or a gret lorde may do to a pore servante if he wille be homely with him, and namely if he shew it himselfe [...] both in previte and openly. (*Revelation*, 7.27–30)

In addition, this perception of privilege in intimate access prompts a rapturous transport of self-forgetfulness: 'This bodely exsample was shewde so high that this mannes hart might be ravished and almost forget himselfe for joy of this grete homelyhede' (*Revelation*, 7.33–5).

In the Second Revelation Julian's realization – only recorded in the Long Text – of the seeing and seeking, both having and wanting God in this life, moves into her striking vision of what it is like on the floor of the sea ('hilles and dales grene [...] with wrake and gravel'; *Revelation*, 10.17–18), which she understands to signify that if we truly grasped God's continual presence with us we should be safe, whether beneath the waves or in whatever element. Julian's vivid and imaginative exploration into a different plane is a means of conveying a necessary transformation of spiritual awareness, just as her expansion in *A Revelation* of the Third Revelation ('I saw God in a pointe': *Revelation*, 11.1) strives to expand her readers' alertness to the gap between divine and human perspectives ('by our blindhede and our unforsighte, we say these thinges be by happes and aventure [...] in the sight of our lord God is no happe ne aventure': *Revelation*, 11.10–13).

In its prototype in *A Vision* Julian's Fourth Revelation focuses on Christ's profusely bleeding body, as at the Flagellation, with the follow-up thought that, just as God has made abundance of waters on earth, so we are to apply his plenteous blood to wash us of sin. In *A Revelation* this is transformed by a surreal visionary understanding of the potent blood streaming through hell, earth and heaven with a dynamic purposiveness: bursting the bonds of hell and delivering the saved; overflowing the earth and purifying sin; ascending into heaven 'bleding, preying for us to the father' (*Revelation*, 12.23). In comparable vein in her Sixth Revelation ('our lorde saide: "I thanke thee of thy servys [ ...] and namely of thy youth"': *Revelation*, 14.1–2), Julian has added, after meditation, a passage recording a visionary transformation of insight into the original showing:

> my understonding was lifted uppe into heven, wher I saw our lorde God as a lorde in his owne house, which lorde hath called alle his derewurthy frendes to a solempne fest. (*Revelation*, 14.2–4)

Here, Julian's imagery of lord and servant works doubly, conveying not only the privilege in God's favour but also the implicit worth honoured in the human soul by the same token. Always careful to offset any anthropomorphic visualizing of her revelations ('I saw the lorde taking no place in his awne house, but I saw him ryally reigne in his house': *Revelation*, 14.4–5), Julian's understanding is of no material feast but of the solace of drawing near 'with mervelous melody of endelesse love' to the face of God, 'which glorious chere of the godhede fulfilleth alle heven of joy and blisse' (*Revelation*, 14.7–9). And it is to the divine countenance that Julian returns in an added passage that represents her meditative conclusion to her richly expanded and interpolated Eighth Revelation of the gruesome agonies of Christ's dying and drying body. In *A Vision* Julian had simply recorded a change in Christ's countenance and that 'the chaunginge of his chere changed mine [...] And I was fulle merye' (*Vision*, 11.18–20). But, in the expanded version, this change of facial expression has been developed to reflect a transformation from this world to the next:

> we, wilfully abiding in the same crosse [...] sodeynly he shalle change his chere to us, and we shal be with him in heven. Betwene that one and that other shalle alle be one time, and than shall alle be brought into joy. (*Revelation*, 21.13–16)

If Christ were to show us now the divine countenance no pain could aggrieve us, and hence 'for this litille paine that we suffer heer, we shalle have an high, endlesse knowing in God, which we might never have without that' (*Revelation*, 21.23–4).

The meditative insights into some succeeding revelations recorded only in *A Revelation* present Julian's comparably transformative realizations of the implications for spiritual understanding of the original showings. To her Ninth Revelation (where Christ declares, amongst other things, 'If I might suffer more, I wolde suffer more': *Revelation*, 22.21) Julian's intervening meditations record how she wanted to learn 'how often he wolde die if he might. And sothly the nomber passed my understanding and my wittes' (*Revelation*, 22.24–5). With contemplation Julian comes to see that for Christ, who might effortlessly perform any marvel ('if he saide he wolde for my love make new hevens and new erthes, it ware but litille in regarde': *Revelation*, 22.30–1) this divine offer to die so repeatedly beyond our comprehension 'is the highest profer that oure lorde God might make to mannes soule, as to my sight' (*Revelation*, 22.30–4). Or, again, in the differences between the Short and Long Text versions of the Tenth Revelation are revealed some of the contemplative transformation in understanding that Julian has accomplished during the stages represented by the two texts. The core idea of this revelation in both texts is that 'our goode lorde loked into his side and behelde' while saying 'Lo, how I loved the!' (*Revelation*, 24.1, 11). For Julian in *A Vision* this is as if he had said 'My childe, if thow kan nought loke in my godhede, see here howe I lette open my side' (*Vision*, 13.2–3). Yet by *A Revelation* Julian's contemplation records something altogether different in implication. First, Christ's own gazing at his side guides Julian towards a perception that opens out into a mysterious transformation of spiritual dimension and miraculous space: 'And ther he shewed a fair, delectable place, and large inow for alle mankinde that shalle be saved to rest in pees and in love' (*Revelation*, 24.3–4). Even more remarkably, where *A Vision* offered solace ('if thow kan nought loke in my godhede'), *A Revelation* records instead at the equivalent point: 'And with this swete enjoyeing he shewed to my understanding, in part, the blessed godhede, as farforth as he wolde that time' (*Revelation*, 24.7–8), before expanding *A Vision*'s brief locution into a rapturous prose poem in which Christ hymns his love for the human soul ('as if he had saide: 'Behold and see that I loved thee so much': *Revelation*, 24.16).

Just as this Tenth Revelation goes back to, yet transcends, devotion to Christ's wounded side among his five wounds, so the Eleventh Revelation 'brought to my minde where our lady stode in the time of his passion' (*Revelation*, 25.2–3), although, with intervening meditation, Julian adds in *A Revelation* a more spiritual understanding ('But hereof am I not lerned to long to see her bodely presens while I am here, but the virtuse of her blissed soule': *Revelation*, 25.15–16). Yet, after years of meditative reflection, the record in *A Revelation* of contemplative attainment is inseparable from an added sense of uncompleted process and inexpressibility. In the Twelfth Revelation 'our lorde shewed him more glorified as to my sight than I saw him before' (*Revelation*, 26.1–2) and, as Ena Jenkins also identifies in her essay later in this volume, voices a prose poem that defines himself in relation to the soul ('I it am that thou servest! I it am that thou longest

...!'). But, whereas the response to this revelation in the earlier text is to record confidence in what contemplation can attain ('And in this was I lerede that ilke saule contemplatife to whilke es giffen to luke and seke God shalle se hire [i.e. Mary] and passe unto God by contemplation') (*Vision*, 13.23–24), in *A Revelation* this has been revised into 'Wherin I was lerned that oure soule shalle never have reste tille it come into him' (*Revelation*, 26.2–3) and, after the divine locution, *A Revelation* has added a passage acknowledging its inexpressibility and wonder:

> The nomber of the words passeth my wittes and my understanding [...] For therin is comprehended I can not telle what! But the joy that I saw [...] passeth alle that hart can think or soule may desire. (*Revelation*, 26.8–11)

Equally transformative is Julian's rewriting of her final revelations in the sequence, changes that both draw upon, yet transcend, conventional devotional imagery and Julian's own recurrent symbolism. In the record of her Fifteenth Revelation ('Sodeynly thou shalte be taken ... ') it is only in *A Revelation* that Julian includes both her vision of the soul leaving a decomposing body and her subsequent meditations:

> And sodeynly oute of this body sprong a fulle fair creature, a litille child, full shapen and formed, swift and lifly and whiter then the lilye, which sharpely glided uppe into heven. (*Revelation*, 64.25–8)

However, Julian's careful temporal introduction of this passage implies the concurrence of this later-recorded vision with the original showing ('And in this time I sawe a body lyeng on the erth': *Revelation*, 64.24). Just as the image of the soul as a child quitting the corpse derives from traditional iconography, so in her concluding Sixteenth Revelation (of Christ sitting enthroned in the city of our soul) Julian builds on her pervasive symbolism of divine lordship. In a meditation present only in *A Revelation* but recording insights ostensibly dated to the original revelatory experience, 'understanding was geven in the same time by example of a creature' (*Revelation*, 68.19–20) who is prompted by seeing the panoply of treasures and realms possessed by a lord to seek out that lord's dwelling and presence:

> And thus I understonde sothly that oure soule may never have rest in thing that is beneth itselfe [...] yet may it not abide in the beholding of itselfe, but alle the beholding is blissefully set in God, that is the maker, wonning therin.
>
> (*Revelation*, 68.23–7)

Despite all such signs of scrupulous revision between *A Vision* and *A Revelation*, Julian confronted problems in both form and content when moving from seeing into writing. These problems are compounded when accumulated insights from subsequent reflection become incorporated into her text, and still challenge us today when reading it. By comparison with the Long Text, the revelations in the Short Text are quite sparely recounted; they open with less by way of introduction or context and are unlocated in time. Julian's account of the revelations in the earlier text does not present a connected thematic sequence. There, the showings may appear fragmentary and even disjointed: a succession of

segments, without much foreground, background or overall perspective, and in
no apparent order. Absence of sub-division in *A Vision*'s text may retain Julian's
earlier sense of her experience as a stream of revelatory consciousness within
which boundaries between revelations are still merging and emerging to her
perception, and with such boundaries an understanding of relative priority and
significance that eventually enables the demarcation and numbering of revelations. As visions, Julian's showings are strikingly dissimilar in length, type and
content. Not all focus on the Passion, and in the Long Text Julian later categorizes these as a sub-group ('For I had sight of the passion of Crist in diverse
shewing: in the furst, in the secunde, in the fourth, and in the eighth': *Revelation*,
33.14–15). Not all revelations are primarily visual, and much of *A Revelation*'s
commentary is distinctively auditory, recording Julian's understanding of what
is attributed to divine direct speech not recorded in *A Vision*. Julian's revelations
prompt distinct kinds of contemplative revision and reflection, for part of the
character of *A Revelation* may be understood as a pondered commentary upon,
and exegesis of, the record of a vision in the Short Text that *A Revelation* has
edited.

The words in *A Vision* document the core testimony of Julian's revelations.
These remain at the heart of *A Revelation*, but around the text of *A Vision* the
later text frames the apparatus of an edition of the original version, an apparatus
created both through formal textualization and through numerous interpolations of extended meditative commentary on the showings' content ('And in
this swete word, as if he had said ...': *Revelation*, 25.3–4). In *A Revelation* (but not
in *A Vision*) are the division into numbered chapters and the numbering of the
revelations. Absent from *A Vision* too is the opening chapter setting out a table of
contents (although this may well derive from scribal editing, as may the chapter
summaries in MS Sloane 2499).[5] Together with such articulation of divisions
comes more sense in *A Revelation* of a chronological continuum, smoothing over
some of the transitions in the earlier account. Also in *A Revelation* a timetable
of the two days' showings is added in retrospect ('the furst beganne erly in the
morninge [...] the goode lorde shewde the sixteenth revelation on the night
folowing': *Revelation*, 65.31; 66.1–2), which is significant in introducing an authorial overview, absent before, of how her experience shaped and paced itself to
a climax ('it lasted – shewing by processe, fulle fair and soberly, eche folowing
other': *Revelation*, 65.32–3). Interconnections between revelations are already
being noted in *A Vision* but, by the phase of development represented in *A
Revelation*, Julian's meditations are interlinked by precise cross-references facili-
tated by numbering of the revelations: 'And the ground of this was shewed in
the furst, and more openly in the thirde, wher it seyth ... ' (*Revelation*, 35.15–16,
analyzing the Thirteenth Revelation). More largely, *A Revelation*'s text is shaped
by an added sense of perspective and overview. The special significance of the
First Revelation in itself and in relation to the whole sequence of subsequent

---

[5]   The summaries preceding chapters in the Sloane MS (but absent from the Paris MS) occasionally refer to the author in the third person: 'Of the mekenes of this woman ...' (ch. 9); 'This
blissid woman saw God ...' (ch. 81; cf. also chs 51, 66, 69), although this may indicate only that
summaries deriving from Julian have been edited, rather than wholly invented.

showings is brought out explicitly ('this was shewed in the first sight and in all': *Revelation*, 4.10–11; 'For the strength and the grounde of alle was shewed in the furst sight': *Revelation*, 6.55). When Julian writes of her First Revelation, 'and herefore was this lesson of love shewed, with alle that foloweth, as ye shall see' (*Revelation*, 6.54–5), she seems to write in knowledge of her late understanding: 'Thus was I lerned that love is oure lordes mening' (*Revelation*, 86.16–17). In a passage not in *A Vision*, meditating on the Ninth Revelation, Julian perceives that 'oure curteyse lorde shewed his passion to me in five manneres' and recalls these as the First, Second, Fourth and Eighth Revelations, with the Ninth as the fifth manner (*Revelation*, 23.6–11). After an overview of the first day of fifteen showings Julian comments in the Long Text about her final revelation before she has narrated it, 'which sixteenth was conclusion and confirmation to all the fifteen' (*Revelation*, 66.2–3), and so lends shape and structure to her visionary sequence in this version.

The whole project of revising the shorter text into the altogether more analytical and patterned prose of *A Revelation* embodies in itself a kind of re-edition. The major part of *A Vision*'s shorter text is absorbed into the longer version: some passages undergo re-expression but much phrasing remains relatively unchanged and little material is positively discarded. Sounding closer to speech and possibly to dictation than *A Revelation*'s patterned periods, the often terse statements of Julian's shorter version survive into the fuller text, although in revision Julian has surrounded these sentences with formulations of the understanding of those initial statements that she has come with contemplation to perceive. The terseness of *A Vision* is carried forward into new contextualizations, where it is framed by distinctions and qualifications. In moving towards *A Revelation* it is as if Julian works on and from a copy of *A Vision* in front of her (or an amanuensis might have done so, if Julian were dictating). Thus, the text of *A Revelation* may be imagined to have evolved through intensive accumulation onto a version of *A Vision* of interlineated expansions and interleaved commentary in the form of interpolation of new passages, of new sentences into existing passages, and of new clauses into sentences surviving from *A Vision*. Commenting on the Fourth Revelation, that we should wash ourselves in Christ's blood, Julian amplifies:

> For it is most plentuous *as it is most precious and that by the vertu of the blessed godhead*. And it is our owne kinde *and all blissefully overfloweth us by the vertu of his precious love*. (*Revelation*, 12.12–15, my emphasis)

The italicised words – present only in the later text – have set the brief, original statement in a more spiritual dimension, matched stylistically through more developed syntactical patterns. Julian's expansion of her initial comments on Mary's sorrows at the Passion similarly sets *A Vision*'s original observation within a more developed spiritual awareness and corresponding syntax in *A Revelation*:

> For Crist and she was so oned in love that the gretnes of her love was cause of the mekillehede of her paine. *For in this I saw a substance of kinde love, continued by grace, that his creatures have to him, which kinde love was most fulsomly shewde in his*

*swete mother, and overpassing.* For so mekille as she loved him more then alle other, her paine passed alle other. *For ever the higher, the mightier, the swetter that the love is, the more sorow it is to the lover to se that body in paine that he loved.*

(*Revelation*, 18.1–7, my emphasis)

Exploring and deepening her original visions' analysis of love as of sin, such revisions between the texts point to ways of working that probably character-ized intervening stages of Julian's text between *A Vision* and *A Revelation* that happen not to survive, for the style created by Julian's contemplative revisions pervades her work:

*And for the tender love that oure good lorde hath* to alle that shalle be saved, he comforteth redely and swetly, mening thus: '*It is soth that sinne is cause of alle this paine*, but alle shalle be wele, [Sloane adds 'and alle shall be well'] and alle maner of thing shalle be wele.' (*Revelation*, 27.26–9)

Such a technique of interpolating and commenting allows for noticeable qualification and realignment of problematic passages. This development in understanding by adaptive expansion in the later text can be seen in the Fifth Revelation, which shows how the passion vanquishes the malice of the devil. Julian tells how 'I saw oure lorde scorne his malis and nought his unmight' (*Revelation*, 13.19), but with meditation she evidently feels the need to correct potential misunderstandings of her vision of God's scorning the fiend's malice. Her original revelation of that scorning remains in her text, but Julian prefaces it in *A Revelation* with careful scruple ('But in God may be no wrath, as to my sight': *Revelation*, 13.14–15), and a little later in the chapter Julian again inter-venes in the fuller text to clarify:

And ther I sawe him scorne his malis, it was be leding of my understanding into oure lorde: that is to say, an inwarde shewing of sothfastnesse, without changyng of chere. (*Revelation*, 13.25–7)

With subsequent meditation, the original showing's visualization of God's scorn has come to trouble Julian with its potential to mislead. Her resolution, however, is to retain the vividly visual core of her initial perception alongside the subse-quent contemplative commentary that offsets it, and to round off her Fifth Reve-lation with a concluding section only present in the longer text. The original report in *A Vision* is presented as if narrating a particular historic moment ('I saw our Lord'), but by interpolating a final section of contemplative commentary Julian builds in a transformative shift in dimension that recurrently character-izes the Long Text: her realization of the continuing and the endless which is in God that we can only endeavour to perceive within our time-bound context. This is the passage that begins 'And ther I saide "he is scorned", I ment that God scorneth him: that is to sey, for he seeth him now as he shall do withoute ende' (*Revelation*, 13.34–5).

Many key differences that distinguish the Long Text from the Short are the outcome of moves to edit Julian's visions for a readership wider than the audience implied in *A Vision*. Indication in *A Vision* that the text is directed at contemplatives (see, for example, *Vision*, 4.37–8) does not survive into *A Revela-*

*tion*; throughout, references in the earlier text to 'he' or 'thou' have been trans-posed into the first-person plural in *A Revelation*. In presenting its record of the revelations, the later text moves beyond contexts where *A Vision* aligns itself defensively with orthodox church teaching and authority. Alertness to a sense of sin and to the devil are never far away in *A Vision*, along with some fear of the deceptiveness of visions. Just before Jesus declares that 'Sinne is behovely' in the Thirteenth Revelation, *A Revelation* records that Jesus 'in this vision enformed me of alle that me neded' (*Revelation*, 27.8–9) but omits a passage here in *A Vision* which declares more defensively: 'I saye nought that me nedes na mare techinge. For oure lorde, with the shewinge of this, hase lefte me to haly kyrke [...] I [...] wilfully submittes me to the techinge of haly kyrke' (*Vision*, 13.40–3). Comparably, near the beginning of the Fourteenth Revelation concerning prayer *A Revelation* drops a section in *A Vision* including 'And that es as I hafe under-standide be the techinge of haly kyrke [...] And in this we say Pater noster, Ave, and Crede' (*Vision*, 19.5–8). By the stage of *A Revelation*, Julian no longer feels the need to express such conventional orthodoxies.

Julian's alertness to sin's perils is seen throughout her text's development, but her statements about sin in the Short Text tend to be more strident and disorganized than they become in *A Revelation*. With intervening contemplation Julian evidently gains control of what had previously seemed uncontrollably problematic, and this is reflected stylistically. In analyzing sin near the close of the Thirteenth Revelation *A Vision* gives the impression of a series of observa-tions noted hurriedly, and driven by Julian's urgent preoccupation with sin as danger:

> For alle thinge is goode botte sinne, and nathinge is wikked botte sinne. Sinne es nowthere deed no liking. Botte when a saule cheses wilfully sinne – that is, paine – as fore his God, atte the ende he hase right nought. That paine thinke me the herdeste helle, for he hase nought his God: in alle paines a saule may hafe God botte in sinne. (*Vision*, 18.7–11)

In *A Revelation* these jottings have been refashioned into:

> And to me was shewed none harder helle than sinne. For a kind soule hateth no helle but sinne [...] And whan we geve oure intent to love and meknesse by the werking of mercy and grace, we be made alle fair and clene.
>
> (*Revelation*, 40.33–6)

Here, Julian's achievement of her mature view on sin is reflected in syntax that first puts into a nutshell the content of the earlier text and then expands on that teaching – expansive too in style and spirit – on the role of love and grace. Overall, *A Revelation* reflects how Julian comes to see that the very ignoring of sin by her revelations is a token of its utter insubstantiality, and hence she omits from the revised text her lengthiest explicit discussion of sin in *A Vision*, an outburst in which she apostrophizes sin indignantly ('A, wriched sinne! Whate ert thowe? Thowe er nought. For I sawe that God is alle thinge: I sawe nought the': *Vision*, 23.23–4). This can be dropped from *A Revelation* because Julian's understanding of sin becomes implicit in a more assured analysis of the spiritual progress of humanity in her fuller text.

With comparable assurance Julian revises her discussion after the Sixteenth Revelation of the proper balance between love and dread of God, developing a confidence based on a refined understanding of the experience of love and grace. Of the various types of dread described in *A Vision*, the third is doubtful dread:

> For though it be litille in the selfe, and it ware knawen it is a spice of dispaire. For I am seker that alle doutefulle dredes God hates, and he wille that we hafe tham departed fro us with trewe knawinge of luffe. (*Vision*, 25.11–13)

But in *A Revelation* this is revised into:

> Doubtfulle drede, inasmoch as it draweth to dispair, God wille have it turned in us into love by tru knowing of love; that is to sey, that the bitternesse of doubt be turned into swetnes of kinde love by grace. (*Revelation*, 74. 11–13)

The fuller understanding explored in *A Revelation* characteristically turns upon a transformation accomplished by means of love, and through a realization that the two responses which seem at variance with each other are in truth interrelated within us ('Love and drede are bredren, and they are roted in us by the goodnesse of oure maker': *Revelation*, 74.17–18).

Near the heart of Julian's reinterpretation of her showings into *A Revelation* lie her contemplative revisions of what, on the evidence of the rewriting they prompt, were her most problematic Thirteenth and Fourteenth Revelations ('And in theyse same wordes, I saw an high, mervelous previte hid in God': *Revelation*, 27.33). Here are found expansions of what may seem jotted outlines of thinking in *A Vision*. Meditating on the spiritual thirst of Christ, Julian simply records in the earlier text that this is 'the falinge of his blisse, that he has us nought in him als haelye as he shalle thane haffe' (*Vision*, 15.15–16). However, by the time *A Revelation* is written, the thirst as failing of bliss has been rewritten through intervening meditation into Christ's 'love-longing to have us all togeder, hole in him to his endlesse blisse, as to my sight' (*Revelation*, 31.15–16). This, in turn, has prompted interpolation of a meditative sequence which, after cross-reference to previous showings ('namely in the twelfth [...] And that shewde he in the ninth': *Revelation*, 31.21–5), concludes: 'For as verely as ther is a properte in God of ruth and pite, as verely ther is a properte in God of thurst and longing' (*Revelation*, 31.34–5) before rejoining the original argument retained from *A Vision* ('And alle this was seen in shewing of compassion': *Revelation*, 31.42). Over succeeding pages, single sentences from *A Vision* provide cues for contemplations now recorded through interpolated sections exploring the understandings Julian has attained on the interface between orthodoxy and the universalist optimism of her revelations. In a passage from *A Vision* which is replaced in *A Revelation*, Julian has already accepted what she cannot know now:

> I am well payed that I wate it noght [...] It is Goddes wille that we witte that alle shalle be wele in generalle. Botte it is nought Goddes wille that we shulde witte it nowe, botte as it langes to us for the time. And that is the techinge of haly kyrke. (*Vision*, 15.27–31)

In *A Revelation* the corresponding sections reflect a far-reaching rethinking of this state of unknowing, with an added section opening mysteriously: 'There is a deed the which the blissful trinite shalle do in the last day ...', and closing: 'This is the gret deed [...] tresured and hid in his blessed brest, only knowen to himselfe, by which deed he shalle make all thing wele' (*Revelation*, 32.19, 26–9). Enlarging with contemplation on an assurance from *A Vision* that 'the same blissed trinite shalle make wele alle that es nought wele' (*Vision*, 15.22–3), *A Revelation* develops a section recalling church teaching on condemnation of heathens and others to hell, and worrying that therefore 'methought it was unpossible that alle maner of thing shuld be wele, as oure lorde shewde' (*Revelation*, 32.39–40). Yet here Julian also meditates her way to recognition that what seems impossible to us is not impossible for God's great deed, 'in which dede he shalle save his worde in alle thing and he shalle make wele all that is not welle' (*Revelation*, 32.47–8). Recurring to her earlier text for a sentence ('It is Goddes wille that we hafe grete rewarde to alle the dedes that he has done': *Vision*, 15.23–4), Julian develops from it with the outcome of intervening meditation, adding a further section on acceptance of what we cannot yet know and understand: 'But evermore us nedeth leve the beholding what the dede shalle be [...] Than shalle we only enjoye in God and be welle apaide both with hiding and shewing' (*Revelation*, 33.24–8).

'Both with hiding and shewing' in its intensely inward focus as a personal testimony in first-person narrative, the text of *A Revelation* cannot but have an intrinsically autobiographical quality, while striving to transcend individuality and present itself as the progress of a soul. Julian's studied anonymity and self-effacement give her text a distinctive voice, at once individual yet universal. Any context in place, circumstance or social status had already been occluded from *A Vision*, so it is ironic that with a few added words the scribal colophon to *A Vision* which names Julian 'that is recluse atte Norwiche' has undone all her self-abnegation and enabled her identification. All reference in this text to the author's being a woman disappears from *A Revelation*, which retains Julian's self-denigrations as a simple creature 'unlettered' or 'that coude no letter'. Although these features may reflect contemporary anxieties about women's authorship, they also form part of a larger trend between *A Vision* and *A Revelation* to dwell less on the author than the message, and to universalize that message. Nonetheless, the actuality of Julian's exact age of thirty-and-a-half years at the time of the showings is retained in *A Revelation* from *A Vision*, while the precise dating of the revelations to a day in May 1373 – and later to the hours ('aboute the oure of four [...] tille it was none of the day or paste': *Revelation*, 65.32–3) – lends the historicity of a documentary deposition to an account of what transcends time and defies description. Any overt or overarching metaphors of spiritual progress as a journey or ascent are eschewed, and Julian does not analyze advancement for herself or her readers through progressive stages of contemplation. Her text is not structured by teaching any meditative programme for Julian's readers to follow and apply for themselves. It is as an uncompleted project shared with the reader that *A Revelation* subsumes any more direct claim to didactic intent in *A Vision*, instead providing the record of a contemplative movement towards greater understanding. In essence, Julian offers her own experience as a witness, and her only claim on her reader lies in her conviction that her testimony's value lies not in any endorsement of herself but in its import for all.

Today, when most readers of the Long Text will be 'tho that be hethen – and also man that hath received cristondom and liveth uncristen life' (*Revelation*, 32.36–7), to chart the movement between *A Vision* and *A Revelation* enables us to explore the record of a painful *inward* pilgrimage, which accommodates without compromise a self-authenticating personal vision that seemingly conflicts with authority and convention. Inseparable from Julian's visionary insights into the courteous homeliness towards humanity that God showed in taking on human flesh is her revelatory understanding – worked through between *A Vision* and *A Revelation* – that the Incarnation carries ennobling implications for humankind. It is only in the later text that Julian adds the transformative example in John of Beverley of a saint who, despite a youthful fall, is rewarded 'overpassing that he shuld have had if he had not sinned or fallen' (*Revelation*, 38.27–8). It is also in *A Revelation* that Julian records her insight into her Sixteenth Revelation's implication concerning divine satisfaction at the making of man's soul:

> For I saw in the same shewing that if the blisseful trinite might have made mannes soule ony better, ony fairer, ony nobeler than it was made, he shulde not have been full plesed with making of mannes soule (*Revelation*, 68.30–3).

It is in *A Revelation* that Julian's lord and servant example draws these themes into triumphant synthesis, serenely occluding a whole tradition of human self-blame and guilt for the Fall. It is also in *A Revelation* that an undeveloped draft in *A Vision* about how all creation is desolated at the hour of the Crucifixion ('thay that luffed him nought sufferde paine for failinge of comforthe of alle creatures': *Vision*, 10.48–9) is transformed into a numinous account of devotional process. A pagan observer of this desolated creation (and one who will become a saint) – convinced that a suffering universe witnesses to its self-sacrificingly suffering creator – takes a first step in devotion and 'did write on an awter: "This is an awter of the unknowen God"' (*Revelation*, 18.25).

Just such a spiritually transformative awareness is conveyed in the Second Revelation by Julian's vision (absent from her shorter text) of being led down to the bottom of the sea and there understanding that, if only we had a sense of God's constantly being with us, it would be like inhabiting a different plane or element ('if a man or woman were there, under the brode water, and he might have sight of God – so as God is with a man continually – he shoulde be safe in soule and body': *Revelation*, 10.18–20). To this an anecdote in Gervase of Tilbury's *Otia Imperialia* offers some parallel, in recalling the widespread folk belief that our sky forms the surface of the sea in another world overhead, from which the inhabitants occasionally swim down. As Gervase relates, one day a congregation 'straggling out of their parish church after high mass' are dumbfounded to see a ship's anchor caught fast on a tombstone in the churchyard, 'with its rope stretching up and hanging in the air'.[6] In some versions of the legend a sailor

---

[6]   Gervase of Tilbury, *Otia Imperialia*, ed. and trans. S. E. Banks and J. W. Binns (Oxford, 2002), p. 81.

swims down to free the anchor, but cannot survive in our element and drowns. Yet in another tradition, developed in a poem by Seamus Heaney, the sailor is enabled to ascend again, having experienced – like Julian of Norwich, and hence her readers – a visionary change of plane from a foray into another world:

> A crewman shinned and grappled down the rope
> And struggled to release it. But in vain.
> 'This man can't bear our life here and will drown,'
>
> The abbot said, 'unless we help him.' So
> They did, the freed ship sailed, and the man climbed back
> Out of the marvellous as he had known it.
>
> 'Lightenings', viii (*Seeing Things*, 1991)[7]

---

7   Seamus Heaney, *Open Ground: Poems 1966–96* (London, 1998), p. 364.

# 9

## 'This blessed beholdyng':
## Reading the Fragments from Julian of Norwich's
## A Revelation of Love in London,
## Westminster Cathedral Treasury, MS 4

MARLEEN CRÉ

Julian of Norwich's writings have come down to us in a limited number of manuscripts, only two of which are medieval. London, British Library MS Additional 37790 (Amherst) was written around 1450, most likely in an English charterhouse. It is an anthology of five complete authorial texts in Middle English interspersed with shorter extracts and compilations.[1] In this manuscript Julian's Short Text, *A Vision Showed to a Devout Woman*, follows Richard Misyn's Middle English translations of Richard Rolle's *Emendatio vitae* and *Incendium amoris* and is itself followed by the Middle English translation of Ruusbroec's *Vanden blinkenden steen* and M. N.'s Middle English translation of Marguerite Porète's *Mirouer des Simples Âmes*, all of which describe and provide instruction regarding the contemplative life. The second medieval manuscript that preserves some of Julian's writing is London, Westminster Cathedral Treasury MS 4 (W), a manuscript of unknown provenance datable to around 1500.[2] The single text contained in this manuscript is a compilation which is entirely made up of fragments from existing texts: commentaries on Psalms 90 (*Qui habitat*) and 91 (*Bonum est*), probably by Walter Hilton,[3] Books I and II of Hilton's *Scale of Perfection* and *A Revelation of Love*, the long version of Julian's text.

What both manuscripts have in common is that they place *A Vision Showed to a Devout Woman* (in full) as well as *A Revelation of Love* (in fragments) in context, aligning or juxtaposing the texts with other texts written by mainly contemporary contemplative authors. As neither the Amherst anthologist nor the compiler of the Westminster compilation account for their decisions in a prologue in

---

[1]  See M. Cré, *Vernacular Mysticism in the Charterhouse: A Study of London, British Library, MS Additional 37790*, The Medieval Translator 9 (Turnhout, 2006).
[2]  Though the manuscript is owned by Westminster Cathedral, it is on temporary deposit in Westminster Abbey Library. For a description of the manuscript see H. Kempster, 'The Westminster Text of *A Revelation of Love*', *Mystics Quarterly* 23 (1997), pp. 178–9.
[3]  See *An Exposition of Qui habitat and Bonum est in English*, ed. Björn Wallner, Lund Studies in English XXIII (Lund, 1954), pp. xxxix–xliv. References to *Qui habitat* (*QH*) and *Bonum est* (*BE*) are by page and line numbers and will appear parenthetically in the main text.

which the intended readers are addressed,[4] any information about their intentions needs to be gleaned from the texts themselves, and from the contents and placement of the adjacent texts.[5] The *Revelation* fragments in Westminster have so far largely been treated in isolation.[6] In this essay, therefore, I would like to reassess the compiler's selections from *A Revelation* in the context of the compilation as a whole, following onto and interacting with the selections from the *Qui habitat* and *Bonum est* expositions and from the *Scale of Perfection*. This means seeing the compilation in positive terms, as a text with a clear focus on one particular theme – contemplation – written using fragments of existing texts chosen in the service of this theme,[7] rather than in the negative terms of loss and simplification of the source texts, and repression of some of their material.[8] In preferring 'choice' over 'repression' as an approach to the compilation, we come to focus on the compiler's editorial activity in a different way, not defining his omissions as censorship of his sources, but his selections as appreciation of what the source texts have to say on the topics of his interest.[9]

The text-internal evidence of the Westminster compilation warrants treatment of it as one coherent text rather than as a haphazard collection of purple passages. With themes, motifs and metaphors recurring in the selections from

---

4    This suggests that, like Amherst, the compilation was intended to be used in the same circle in which it originated. That none of the fragments in W are attributed to their authors may seem like an indication of the same, yet Hilton's works are unattributed in most manuscripts, as is Julian's Long Text.
5    For the place of *A Vision* in the Amherst anthology see Cré, *Vernacular Mysticism*, pp. 99–122.
6    See Kempster, 'The Westminster Text', and 'A Question of Audience: The Westminster Text and Fifteenth-Century Reception of Julian of Norwich', in *Julian of Norwich: A Book of Essays*, ed. Sandra J. McEntire (New York and London, 1998), pp. 257–89, which only contain minor references to the Hilton texts making up the larger part of the compilation. In Watson and Jenkins' new edition of Julian of Norwich's writings, the introduction describes the *Revelation* fragments as integral to the compilation, but the edition included in Appendix A remains –understandably but regrettably – decontextualized. See *The Writings of Julian of Norwich: A Vision Showed to a Devout Woman and* A Revelation of Love, ed. Nicholas Watson and Jacqueline Jenkins (Turnhout, 2006), pp. 13–14 and pp. 417–31. References to this edition of the 'Westminster Revelation' (*WR*) are by page number. In the quotations from W, I reproduce the manuscript's spelling. The compilation as a whole is transcribed and discussed in M. Cré, 'Westminster Cathedral Treasury MS 4: A Fifteenth-Century Spiritual Compilation' (unpublished MPhil diss., University of Glasgow, 1997) and 'Authority and the Compiler in Westminster Cathedral Treasury MS 4: Writing a Text in Someone Else's Words', in *Authority and Community in the Middle Ages*, ed. Donald Mowbray, Rhiannon Purdie and Ian P. Wei (Stroud, 1999), pp. 153–76.
7    This is exactly the activity ascribed to the *compilator* ( as opposed to the *scriptor*, *commentator* and *auctor*) in Bonaventure's *Prologue* to his *Sentences* commentary. The *compilator* adds together, or arranges the statements of other men, adding no opinion of his own (*addendo, sed non de suo*). See A. J. Minnis, *Medieval Theory of Authorship: Scholastic Literary Attitudes in the Later Middle Ages* (London, 1984), p. 94.
8    In focusing on the compiler's omissions, Kempster inevitably defines the Westminster fragments in terms of loss. Kempster's comment that 'it is significant that neither of the two earliest extant copies of [Julian's] work reproduce [the Long Text's] unusual integration of mystical prose genres' also, in fact, disregards the existence of the Long Text copy that the Westminster compiler worked from, which was apparently not the same as the ones that in the sixteenth and seventeenth centuries ended up among Catholic exiles on the Continent. Kempster, 'A Question of Audience', p. 270 and 'The Westminster Text', p. 185.
9    I view with some caution Kempster's interpretation of the *Revelation* passages as having been edited to be made easily digestible by lay readers committed to the mixed life. 'A Question of Audience', *passim*.

all source texts, the compilation weaves a richly coloured and patterned textual tapestry. The formal characteristics of the manuscript corroborate the text-internal findings. The manuscript is written in one hand, and, as the *Revelation* fragments start on the verso side of folio 72, they were intended to form an integral part of the compilation, and were not coincidentally bound together with the Hilton material. In addition, marginal annotations occur throughout the manuscript, which means that its late seventeenth- to early eighteenth-century readers considered the compilation as one text. On the basis of the script, W is dated to around 1500. The dialect of the text suggests that the extant copy was made of an earlier original (the compiler's autograph?) written around 1450 in south-east England, adjacent to London.[10] The provenance of the manuscript is unknown, as are both its intended and actual readership. Thus the text itself will be the starting point of an analysis that attempts to recover the compiler's editorial strategies.[11]

The *Qui habitat* exposition is, perhaps not coincidentally, the only text of which the larger part has been selected. Its relative weight on the compilation as a whole, therefore, is considerable. It is striking that the *Qui habitat* passages the compiler has left out are all on sin and temptation. He does not select verse or exposition (apart from the occasional relic passage) of 90:6 ('ffro þe Arewe fleoinge in þe day, fro þe neodes goinge in þesternes: fro in-renninge, and fro þe mydday fend': *QH*, 17.2–4), nor of 90:7 ('A þousand schal fallen fro þi syde, and ten þousend from þi riht hand: soþliche, to þe þei schul not neihȝen': *QH*, 23.14–16), and the second half of 90:10 ('þe scourge schal not neiȝen in þi tabernacle': *QH*, 32.9–10), and of 90:12 ('leest happilich þou hurte þi fote at a ston': *QH*, 38.5–6).

In some cases he selects the exposition, but not the verse itself, such as 90:3 ('Ffor-whi he haþ delyuered me from þe snare of hunters: & from a scharp word': *QH*, 7. 8–9, exposition on ff. 4v–6v). He includes the exposition of the first half of 90:5 ('His soþfastnes schal vnbigo þe with a scheld': *QH*, 13.14, exposition on ff. 9r–v), 90:8 ('Soþliche with þin eȝen þou schal beholden: & þe ȝeldyng of synnes þou schalt sen': *QH*, 25/13–14, exposition on ff. 10r–12v), and 90:16 ('in lengþe of dayes i schal fulfille him: & I schal schewen to him myn hele': *QH*, 48.15–16, exposition on ff. 24r–25r).

The compilation's themes are triggered by the psalm verses and their expositions which the compiler does select. He borrows *Qui habitat*'s discussion of contemplation from the exposition of Psalms 90:1 ('He that wonyth in þe helpe of the hyeste: in helyng of god of heuen he shall dwel': f. 1r; cf. *QH*, 2.2–3), 90:2 ('he shall sey to our lord: my vptakar art thou, my refute, my god, I shall hope in hym': ff. 1v–2r; cf. *QH*, 3.8–9), 90:4 ('Our lorde god shall with hys shulders vmbeshadowe the and vnder his feders þou shalt hope': f. 6v; cf. *QH*, 10.8–9), 90:9 ('Lord thou arte my hope, and þou haste sett me in my refute moste hyeste':

---

[10] See *Of the Knowledge of Ourselves and of God: A Fifteenth-Century Spiritual Florilegium*, ed. James Walsh and Eric Colledge (London, 1961), p. vii.

[11] Textual analysis of the Hilton passages suggests that W may have originated within (the sphere of influence of) Syon Abbey, and thus that it was not necessarily written for or used by a lay audience. From this analysis it could also be concluded that the decisions discussed as editorial strategies are indeed the compiler's own.

f. 12v; cf. *QH*, 29.7–8), the first half of 90:10 ('Iuell shall not comm to þe': f. 15r; cf. *QH*, 32.9), 90:11 ('he hath sent his angels for to kepe the in all thy weyes': f. 16r; cf. *QH*, 36.7–8), the first half of 90:12 ('in their handis they bere þe vp': f. 17r; cf. *QH*, 38.5), part of 90:14 ('Sothly for he hopyth in me. Therfor I shall delyuer hym for he knoweth my name': f. 18v; cf. *QH*, 43.8–9) and 90:15 ('for he cryed to me, I shall here him. I am with hym in tribulacion. I shall delyuer hym, and I shal gloryfie hym': f. 21r; cf. *QH*, 45.20–46.2).

The compiler, then, is concerned first and foremost with contemplation, defined in terms of enclosure and ascent, played out in the metaphors of Psalms 90:2, 90:3 and 90:9, as well as in sensory terms (seeing, being shown, feeling).[12] In leaving out those expositions describing sins and temptations, he writes a text that is spiritually optimistic at heart, stressing the favourable workings of God's grace and the possibility of union with God, the positive outcome of conversion and the contemplative's humility and loving desire:

> And þou art my god. I wyll haue noo god but only þee þat haste so moche done for me. For though I may not see þee as þou art, ne feele þee as þou art in thi blessed kynde, neuerþelesse, by the effecte of þi graciouse workyng in me þat þou hast doo so myche for me, I see þe and feele þee as I se þe sonne and fele þe hete of it by shynynge of þe beames. Ryght so I do se þee and feele þee by thi yeftis of grace, for sothely þat thyng þat toke me vp fro þe fylth of synne and hath strengthed me thorough swetnes of deuocion for to loue hym, that thynge is my god, what þat it be. (ff. 3v–4r; cf. *QH*, 5.3–6.1)

In the description of contemplation as the knowledge and (later) the receiving of God's name, the *Qui habitat* fragments introduce the themes of the intricate relationship between knowledge and love of God and God's gift of himself – here in this passage referred to as 'the yeftis of the holy gooste' – a God who is trinitarian, Father (might–memory), Son (wisdom–wit) and Holy Ghost (goodness–love):

> I shall departe with hym the yeftis of the holy gooste, and I shall make hym free and wyllynge for to loue. And for he knowethe my name I shall defende hym [...] He þat knowyth my full name, þat I am ihesu god, he knowyth me and he louyth me, for my name is both god and man. He knowyth my name through the lyght of grace yeuen vnto hym as souereyne goodnes, souereyne wysedom, souereyne might, endelesse beynge, and blessed life and ioy vnspekable. He knowith my name, for I am all this. I do all thyng þat I do wysely and godly, and ryghtfully.
> (ff. 18v–19v; cf. *QH*, 43.13–16 and 44.6–13)

The scope of the compilation, largely defined in the *Qui habitat* fragments, is completed in the *Bonum est* fragments. The compiler has selected from the

---

12 The understanding of knowledge of God as 'sight' of him is deeply embedded in religious and mystical writing in general. See Santha Bhattacharji, 'Medieval Contemplation and Mystical Experience', in *Approaching Medieval English Anchoritic and Mystical Texts*, ed. Dee Dyas, Valerie Edden and Roger Ellis, Christianity and Culture: Issues in Teaching and Research 2 (Cambridge, 2005), pp. 51–2. Therefore the use of metaphors of sight cannot just be traced back to 91:16 'I schal schewen to him myn hele', only the exposition of which has been selected. See ff. 24r–25r; cf. *QH*, 49.3–50.4.

exposition of Psalms 91:1 ('It is good to shryue to our lord god and synge to his name': f. 25r; cf. *BE*, 51.2–3), 91:2 ('for to shewe thy mercy at morowe and þi soþfastnesse by nyght': f. 26r; cf. *BE*, 54.6–7), 91:3 ('In a ten-stringed sautri: with song in þe harpe': f. 29r; cf. *BE*, 57.11–12), 91:4 ('ffor why, lord god, þou haste delyted me in thy makyng, and in the werkes of thy handys I shall ioye': f. 31r; cf. *BE*, 60.11–12) and 91:5 ('Lorde God hou wonder grete ben thi werkys and full depe ar thy thoughtis made': f. 32v; cf. *BE*, 62.8–9). That the compiler selects only the exposition of these spiritually affirmative passages is in keeping with the optimism of the *Qui habitat* selections. The *Bonum est* fragments round off the compilation's treatment of contemplation with their discussion of the apparent withdrawal of grace, and the necessity to accept it as one of God's gifts:

> He is not angri with god, demyng in hym hardnesse, ne he dispeyryth not in hym selfe for drede of his wyckednesse, for it is all for yevyn. But he a bydith in this derke nyght, and shewyth to our lord full trustily his sothfastnes. And he thynkith þat thus shulde it be here in this lyfe, ffor this is sothfastnes. He knowyth well þat grace is withdrawen for hym in on maner, but it is yeuen to hym on an oþer maner as god wyll, not so swetely nor so felably as it was, but more preuyly, more myghtyly and more godly. (ff. 28r–v; cf. *BE*, 56.9–57.5)

Thus, the compilation's themes are set in these linear borrowings from the *Qui habitat* and *Bonum est* expositions, in which the compiler has gone through the text from beginning to end, copied the spiritually affirmative passages and left out the ones on sin, temptation and the lover of the world's attitudes.

The compiler's editorial choices in the *Scale* fragments show him working with his source text in a different way to ensure thematic continuity with the psalm exposition selections. He handpicks passages from Book I, Chapters 40 to 43, 68 and 70 and Book II, Chapters 27, 28, 30, 32 to 39, and 41 to 46, yet instead of presenting them in the order in which they occur in the full text, he jumps to and fro between books and shuffles passages between chapters.[13] It is clear that the compiler knew Hilton's *Scale* well (his effortless movement between Books I and II illustrates which passages he associated with one another), and it is significant that he chose passages from the text's 'more mystical' chapters, which describe the soul's 'reformation in feeling' (f. 56v; cf. *Scale* II, 3022). More than in the *Qui habitat* and *Bonum est* fragments, he made changes to the text to adapt it to his needs.[14]

The picture emerging from the compiler's selections and omissions of sentences within those selections is not unambiguous. In some instances it would seem that he is indeed, as Kempster argues, adapting the passages for a lay audience. In Book I, Chapter 41, Hilton includes a sequence of four quota-

---

[13] See table 3 in the Appendix to Cré, 'Authority and the Compiler', pp. 166–9.
[14] Interestingly, W is one of three manuscripts Hussey could not assign to any group in his assessment of Book II manuscripts of the *Scale*. See S. S. Hussey, 'The Text of *The Scale of Perfection*: Book II', *Neuphilologische Mitteilungen* 65 (1964), pp. 75–92 (87). In what follows, the readings found in W will be compared those found in *Walter Hilton: The Scale of Perfection*, ed. T. H. Bestul, TEAMS (Kalamazoo, 2000), based on London Lambeth Palace, MS 472 (L). Reference to the *Scale* are by book and line numbers. There is evidence to suggest that the Hilton texts in W might derive from a manuscript copy antecedent to L.

tions from St Paul, which he translates and expounds to illustrate that contemplatives have to work with the gifts they have been given by God in order to be 'safe': that is, to ensure that they come to the bliss of heaven. The compiler does not select the Latin scriptural quotations here, but he does select the exposition, in which this passage gives examples of the kinds of spiritual work contemplatives might do:

> As som by dedis and werkes of mercy, somm by grete penaunce, and som by dyuerse gracis and yeftes of deuocion shalbe saufe and com to þe blysse of heuyn. (f. 37v; cf. *Scale* I, 1101–3)

Lambeth Palace, MS 472 (L) has the following phrase after 'penaunce': 'summe by sorwes and wepynges for here synnes al here lyiftyme, sum by prechynge and techynge' (I, 1101–2). The reference to abundant sorrow and weeping for one's sins may have been left out because of the perceived excess in such behaviour; the reference to preaching and teaching may have been cut because these are activities not usually performed by laypeople. W's 'Þe moste speciall prayer þat þe soule vsyth and hath moste conforte in is þe pater noster, and psalmes and ympnes and oþer seruice of holy churche' (ff. 54v–55r) is a condensed version of a longer passage, which in L reads:

> The moste special praiere that the soule useth and hath most confort in, I hope, is the Pater Noster, *or elles psalmes of the sautier; the Pater Noster for lewid men*, and psalmes and ympnes and othere servyce of Holi Chirche *for lettred men*.
> (II, 3167–9 my emphasis signalling the phrases absent in W)

One might wonder, too, whether the omission of the distinction between prayers for the lettered and the unlettered in W is the result of a levelling of the field and the making available of devotional and contemplative material (including this compilation) to laypeople. Yet there are other editorial choices that seem to contradict this reading – choices indicative of a specialised audience. There is one passage that, taken in isolation and without previous contemplative knowledge and practice, might well confuse unprepared lay readers:

> A Soule þat hath goostly syght of god, it takyth no grete hede of stryvyng for vertues. He is not besy aboute them specially, but he settyth al his besynes for to kepe þat syght and beholdyng of god that he hath, for to kepe his mynde stable þerto, and bynde his loue only to it þat it fall nat therfro, and forgett all oþer thyngis as meche as it may. And when it doth this, than god is maister in þe soule. (f. 50r; cf. *Scale* II, 2554–8)

The 'forgetting' of the virtues is not a condition of contemplation. It is the result of the soul's spiritual progress, which makes it experience practising the virtues differently. As the full text of the *Scale* puts it:

> Thanne bringeth love into the soule the fulheed of vertues, and turneth hem alle into likynge and softenesse as it were withoute wirkynge of the soule; for the soule striveth not mykil for the getynge of hem as it dide bifore, but it hath hem esili and felith hem restfulli, oonli thorugh the gifte of love that is the Holi Goste.
> (*Scale* II, 2535–39)

Instead of simplifying their source text, decontextualized passages like these complicate the reading of the compilation. It is improbable that this is how a compiler working on a text for lay readers would serve his audience. An audience of readers committed to the contemplative life and with previous knowledge of it seems more plausible here. Indeed, for an audience of enclosed nuns (Bridgettines) or monks (Carthusians) – not unlikely, given W's textual associations – the omissions of references to continual weeping, teaching and preaching, and to the difference between prayers for the lettered and the unlettered would make sense as well.

Overall, the *Scale* selections are thematically continuous with the preceding passages. Like the psalm commentary fragments, they describe and discuss knowledge of the soul and of God in visual as well as trinitarian terms and using the metaphor of God's gift of himself (God being both the gift and the giver: see f. 44v; cf. *Scale* II, 2336–7). They also focus on the apparent withdrawal of God's grace (ff. 57r–58v; cf. *Scale* II, 3025–41 and II, 1815–24), on charity as one of God's gifts (ff. 59r–60v; cf. *Scale* I, 1923–31 and I, 1982–96, with omissions), on the soul's following of Christ (ff. 60v–63v; cf. *Scale* I, 1997–2008 and II, 3240–67), and end with a description of the spiritual realities that can be seen when the eye of the soul is opened (ff. 66r–72r; cf. *Scale* II, 3452–9, 3463–98, 3500–9 and 3511–55, with omissions). They do differ from the preceding passages in tone, however. The *Scale* passages could be called the compilation's most treatise-like part, speaking 'of the knowledge of ourselves and of God',[15] the soul's loss of the image of the Trinity through sin, its reformation-in-feeling through God's grace leading to the recovery of the image in contemplation, all in dry and clear prose which is appealing in its analytical soundness as it allows the reader to see the underlying structure of contemplation in its constitutive elements and defining mechanics. Indeed, the function of the *Scale* fragments in the compilation seems to be the careful analysis of the spiritual phenomenon that the psalm commentary fragments suggest and announce and the *Revelation* fragments illustrate and make tangible. It is not coincidental that, whereas the Latin verses of *Qui habitat* and *Bonum est* are carefully excised in the psalm commentary fragments, Latin scriptural quotations followed by the translation into Middle English have been left in here. Thus, the doctrine of the *Scale* fragments is authorized by the 'holy fadirs' (f. 36v; cf. *Scale* I, 1077) and Saynt Paule (f. 37v; cf. *Scale* I, 1097) and not by the experiential feel of the psalmist's poetry or by the underlying visionary experience in the fragments from *A Revelation*.

When read in the context of the *Qui habitat*, *Bonum est* and *Scale* fragments that precede them, the fragments from *A Revelation* cannot be described as a simplification of the full text. Of course, as so much of the text has not been selected, they do not convey a message as carefully nuanced and complete as Julian's original, but even so, the internal logic of the compiler's selections[16]

---

[15] This is a title written in the top margin of f. 35v, where the *Scale* selections start, in a late seventeenth- or early eighteenth-century hand, adopted as the title of the compilation as a whole in Walsh and Colledge's 1961 translation.

[16] Apart from his shuffling of passages borrowed from Revelation 1, the compiler returns to linear selection from the full text. See Kempster, 'A Question of Audience', pp. 273–82 and 'The Westminster Text', pp. 186–95.

as well as their (most probably intended) effect as the culmination of the text, makes them much more than 'a purely didactic text [constructed] from the full Long Text, which then nestles unobtrusively at the end of a collection of extracts traditionally ascribed to Walter Hilton'.[17]

Thematically, indeed, the *Revelation* fragments can be argued to follow seamlessly on from the *Scale* fragments, which, as has been pointed out above, end with an enumeration of spiritual realities the contemplative beholds when the eye of the soul is opened, starting with 'the kynde of all resonable soulis' (f. 66v; cf. *Scale* II, 3464) and ending with 'a lytil of þe preuytees of þe blessed trynyte' (f. 71v; cf. *Scale* II, 3550). The opening scenes of the *Revelation* fragments, of the first-person narrator being shown 'þe wisdom and the trewthe of oure blessed lady saynt mary' (f. 72v; *WR*, p. 418) and later 'a lytil thyng þe quantite of a hasyl nott' (f. 74v; *WR*, p. 419) also have trinitarian undertones in their echoes of Father (memory–might), Son (reason–wit) and Holy Ghost (love–goodness–will). Mary saw 'her god so gret, so hygh, so myghty and so good' (f. 73r; *WR*, p. 419); the showing of the hazelnut makes Julian see that God is 'Sothly the maker, þe keper and þe louer' (f. 74v; *WR*, p. 419). The selections return to the theme of the soul's knowledge of God, who 'wyll be knowen' (f. 75r; *WR*, p. 419), and who gives himself to us in his goodness 'that commyth downe to vs, to þe loweste party of our nede' (f. 78r; *WR*, p. 420).[18] They also address the soul's feeling of spiritual barenness in 'þe tyme þat he wyll suffer þe soule to be in traueyle' (f. 81r; *WR*, p. 421). Yet they add more to the compilation than the thematic completion and elaboration of themes addressed before.

The compiler's selections from *A Revelation* start with an interesting double *mise en abîme*.[19] The first-person narrator describes how God showed her the wisdom and the truth of the Virgin Mary's soul, which the narrator understands as Mary's beholding of God at the Annunciation, marvelling that the Creator wanted to be born of a simple creature that he himself created. Mary the beholder is beheld by the visionary; the divine Father created Mary, who will give birth to the divine Son. This scene, powerful in its simplicity, plunges the readers into *A Revelation* on folio 72v, after a pause of half a blank page of vellum on folio 72r. The empty space signals that the showing, and the *Revelation* fragment group as a whole, in some way stands apart from the preceding text. The narrator's 'I' reads differently from the same pronoun on the preceding pages as the didactic and meditative mode has been replaced by the language of first-hand experience.[20] The vocabulary of seeing has taken on a startling

17  Kempster, 'A Question of Audience', p. 187.
18  The *Revelation* fragments play with the theme of the gift in a theologically subtle way: the redeemed soul is offered to the Father by the Son, yet is at the same time given by the Father to the Son in reward for his suffering. See f. 85r; *WR*, p. 422 and f. 100r; *WR*, p. 427.
19  The term originally derives from heraldry, and was used to describe the placement at the centre of an escutcheon of a smaller copy of the same escutcheon, at the center of which there could be another still smaller copy of the escutcheon, etc. Here the term is used more generally to mean the containment of a situation within another identical situation.
20  Though it is true that the word 'vision' does not occur in the *Revelation* extracts, the words 'beholdynge', 'see', 'syght', 'shewyng' retain a strong visionary undertone. That these words are indeed referring to the narrator's visionary experience is made explicit in the phrase introducing the borrowings from *A Revelation* 9: 'Also in the nyneth shewyng our lord god seyd

directness that contrasts with the use of conventional visual metaphors in the earlier descriptions of contemplation.[21] Stumbling over the threshold of half an empty piece of vellum, the readers happen upon a scene that cannot but catch their attention and make them aware that here they witness the experience of someone whose 'goostely eye' was 'opened in beholdynge' (f. 15v; cf. *QH*, 34.2). Thus, the readers behold the beholder behold Mary beholding her God that is her creator, who wanted to be born of her that was created: the *mise en abîme* is extended to include them.[22]

This meditative inclusion of readers into the text is replicated at the very end of the *Revelation* fragments, and of the compilation as a whole, in a sentence that explicitly invites them to meditate on 'this blessed beholdyng': 'It is godis wyll that we sett the poynt of our þought in this blessed beholdyng as often as we may and as long' (f. 112v; *WR*, p. 431).[23] Strictly speaking, the 'blessed behol-dyng' might only refer to the preceding locution from Revelation 15, but it can also be read to refer to all of the Julian fragments as well as to the text as a whole. The locution itself, too, takes the readers back to *Qui habitat*'s invocations of God – 'my vptakar art thou, my refute' (f. 2r; cf. *QH*, 3.8–9) – that conceptualize God as a high place in which they can be enclosed and be safe from all discomfort, whether occasioned by sin or temptation. Thus the text itself, in its thematic and verbal associations, supports its own call for meditative reading of it:

> Sodeynly þou shalt be taken fro all þi peyne and fro all thy seykenesse, fro all þi disese and fro all þi woo. And *þou shalt cum vp a boue*, and þou shalt haue me to þi mede and rewarde, and *þou shalt be fulfilled of ioye and of blysse. And þou shalt neuer more haue no maner of peyne, neþer no maner of seykenesse, no maner of myslykyng, ne no wantyng of wyll*, but euer in ioye and blysse withouten ende. What shulde it þan greue the to suffer a whyle, sithen it is my wyll and my wurship.
>
> (f. 112r–v; *WR*, p. 431; my emphasis)

The *Revelation* fragments, in addition to taking the text to its experiential conclu-sion, fold it back to its beginning, inviting the readers to read it again, to concen-trate on its teachings, but also to draw its teachings together by 'making them their own' in the internalizing process that is meditative reading.[24]

The *Revelation* fragments hark back to the *Qui habitat* and *Bonum est* frag-ments in more ways than one, and it seems fair to say that the compiler's choice of passages from *A Revelation* was determined by the themes and modes of

---

to her thus' (f. 83v; *WR*, p. 422), perhaps the compiler's instruction to the scribe inadvertently copied, yet more likely a reminder of the source text for the compilation's original audience.

[21]  See, for instance, two passages quoted earlier: ff. 3v–4r (cf. *QH*, 5.3–6.1), quoted on p. 119, and f. 50r (cf. *Scale* II, 2554–8), quoted on p. 121.

[22]  The creation–creature–birth *mise en abîme* may also be extended in the metaphor of contem-plation as the birth of Jesus in the soul, implied in the theme of the pure soul being given the name of Jesus on f. 19v.

[23]  Kempster's interpretation of this passage as 'as often and as long as is possible in the hustle and bustle of an active life' ('The Westminster Text', p. 202) can also be paraphrased as 'as often and as long as is possible amid the duties of a monastic or anchoritic life', in which personal devotions would also need to find a place beside manual work, the liturgy of the hours, meals and sleep.

[24]  See Mary Carruthers, *The Book of Memory: A Study of Memory in Medieval Culture*, Cambridge Studies in Medieval Literature 10 (Cambridge, 1990), pp. 168–9.

the psalm commentary selections. Both include performative and locutionary passages absent from the *Scale*: first-person prayers that can be adopted by the readers as their own and passages representing the words of God, either quoted directly or represented 'as if' spoken by him (expository locutions).[25] Triggered by the voices speaking in the psalms, and part of the showings given to the first-person narrator in *A Revelation*, these passages make both the contemplative and God present as active players in the spiritual relationship and, in the words of the *Scale*, 'are nought else but swete letters sendyng made betwene a louyng soule and god' (f. 66r; cf. *Scale* II, 3383–4). Indeed, whether intentionally or not, instead of being defined by the visions of the suffering Christ, the *Revelation* fragments in W are characterized by the less spectacular visions of Mary's soul, the hazelnut and God in a point, but also, and perhaps to greater effect, by God's locutions and Julian's reaction to them.[26]

Another theme not found in the *Scale* passages, though dominant in the selections from *Qui habitat*, is enclosure:

> The shuldres of oure lorde ben his mercy and sothefastenes, vndir the whyche he shall vmbeshadowe þee. And that is þe mercyfull foryeuynge of thi synnes, and sothfastly yeuynge the grace of vertuouse kepyng the safly fro þine enemyes as the henne kepyth her byrdis vnder þe shadowe of her wyngis.
>
> (f. 6v–7r; cf. *QH*, 10.10–14)

In the *Revelation* fragments, too, the body of Christ is described as a safe enclosure in which contemplatives can rest:

> Also with glad chere our lord loked into his syde and behelde, enioyenge. And with his swete lokynge he ledde furthe þe vnderstondyng of his creaturys by þe same wounde in to his syde, withyn. And þere he shewed a feyre, delectable place, and large I now for all man kynde þat shall be sauf to reste in pees and loue. (ff. 86v–87r; *WR*, p. 423)

Related to enclosure is the theme of the Motherhood of God, announced in the *Qui habitat* passage in the reference to the hen that keeps her chicks under its wings, and fully elaborated in the compiler's selections from Chapters 59 to 64 of Julian's Long Text on folios 103v to 111v (*WR*, pp. 428–31).[27]

As it opens and closes with fragments from texts that share an affective, effusive tone and address themes that are not dealt with in the *Scale* passages,

---

[25] The *Qui habitat* fragments close with a long expository locution stretching from f. 18v to f. 25r; cf. *QH*, 43.8–50.4 (with omissions).

[26] The (expository) locutions in the *Revelation* passages are found on f. 74v; *WR*, p. 419 ('It lastyth ... of god'), f. 83r; *WR*, p. 422 ('Se I am ... amys'), f. 83v; *WR*, p. 422 ('Art þou ... more', repeated in part on ff. 86r–v; *WR*, p. 423 and on f. 105r; *WR*, p. 429), ff. 87v–88r; *WR*, p. 422 ('loo how I louyd thee ... loue thee', partly repeated on f. 106r, *WR*, p. 429), f. 89v; *WR*, p. 424 ('I am grounde besekist it', partly repeated on ff. 90v, 92r–v; *WR*, pp. 424–5), f. 94r; *WR*, p. 425 ('beholde and se ... prayeste me'), ff. 102v–103r; *WR*, p. 428 ('I it am ... trew desyres', partly repeated on ff. 105v–106r; *WR*, p. 429 and on f. 107v; *WR*, p. 430), ff. 111r–v; *WR*, p. 431 ('I kepe þee full surely') and ff. 112r–v; *WR*, p. 431 ('sodeynly þou shalt ... my wurship').

[27] The incorporation of this theologically subtle discussion is another argument against the judgment of the compiler's activity as simplifying Julian's message.

the compilation could be said to be enclosed by the *Qui habitat* and *Revelation* passages and could itself be interpreted as its readers' verbal enclosure. Through reading it and meditating on it, and by living its precepts in their everyday lives, they can place themselves in God's protection. In the *Qui Habitat* fragments, the words of Scripture are described as providing protection, hence enclosure:

> vnder his fedirs shalte þou hope. Þe fedirs of our lorde ar wordis of holy wryte endited by þe holy gost in conforte of chosen soules trauelyng in derkenes of þis lyf, the whiche wordes yf they be truely fastened in a meke soule, then they bere vp þe soule in to þe eyre. With thees wordis shalt þou defende thy selfe ayenst all sharpe wordes of euyll men, and ayenste all false wordes of þe fende.
>
> (ff. 8r–v; cf. *QH*, 12.4–9 and 10–12)

The words of the compilation, too, could have been felt by its readers as a form of enclosure, reinforcing their material enclosure within convent, monastery or anchorhold walls, or substituting for it for lay readers, and could have 'all wounden and lapped'(f. 27r; cf. *BE*, 55.6) them, bringing them closer to God, who 'for loue wrappith vs and wyndith vs helpith vs and ablyth vs and hangith aboute vs for tender love' (f. 73v; *WR*, p. 419).

The compilation in Westminster Cathedral Treasury MS 4 is a dense and rich text, as it draws its metaphors and discussions, its voices and locutions, from four source texts. The *Revelation* fragments make an important contribution to this richness as the experiential account that completes the compilation and at the same time tells its readers how to approach the compilation by directing them to the text again and inviting them to meditate on it. As an integral part of the text, the *Revelation* fragments can only be fully assessed when read in the context of the selections from the *Qui habitat* and *Bonum est* expositions and the *Scale*. Philologically interesting though an isolated analysis of the *Revelation* fragments may be, a contextual reading of them proves more revealing of their links with and echoes of themes in the other texts. It may also be more rewarding not only because it is how the readers of W would have read them but also because it gives present-day readers of Julian an idea of the spiritual and contemplative background, knowledge and interests from which her medieval readers approached her texts and appreciated what she had to say to them.

# 10

## The Seventeenth-Century Manuscript Tradition and the Influence of Augustine Baker

### ELISABETH DUTTON

Although she wrote from the isolation of an anchoritic cell, Julian aimed at some form of publication, where '"publication" is short for public conversation.'[1] In her *Revelation*[2] she insists on an audience: the visions are for the good of all her fellow Christians.[3] But evidence about the circulation and readership of Julian's text in the first two centuries of its life is extremely limited and ambiguous.[4] And the Long Text presents particular difficulties:[5] although the Short Text is preserved entire in the medieval 'Amherst' manuscript, London, British Library, MS Additional 37790, the only manuscript witness to the Long Text which might be considered medieval – Westminster Cathedral Treasury MS 4 – contains only a limited number of short extracts, in an order different from that in which they appear in the Long Text and, in the estimation of Edmund Colledge and James Walsh, written in 'colourless' English.[6] It is not clear how easily medieval or Renaissance readers could have had access to the full Long Text, nor how closely any circulating text would have resembled what the medieval anchoress wrote.

The earliest manuscripts in which the Long Text survives in its entirety belong to the seventeenth century: at some frustratingly undeterminable point

---

1 Felicity Riddy, '"Publication" before Print: The Case of Julian of Norwich', in *The Uses of Script and Print, 1300–1700*, ed. Julia Crick and Alexandra Walsham (Cambridge, 2004), pp. 29–49 (43).
2 All references to Julian's writing, unless otherwise stated, will be taken from *The Writings of Julian of Norwich: A Vision Showed to a Devout Woman and A Revelation of Love*, ed. Nicholas Watson and Jacqueline Jenkins (Turnhout, 2006) and will be cited by section or chapter and line.
3 Of the *Revelation* she writes: 'I was lerned to take it to alle min evencristen, alle in generalle and nothing in specialle' (*Revelation*, 37.5–7).
4 Riddy suggests that Julian's book may follow a model of publication which mixes the 'sea of talk' with words on the page: 'Julian spoke about love at the window of her cell ... and someone asked for a copy of the book. Its author's emphatic wish that "it schulde be to euery ilke manne the same profytte that I desired to my selfe" must also have been a licence to pass it on.' She suggests that there may have been numerous copies of *A Revelation* which have not survived: 'the domestic copies ... were eventually discarded by uninterested heirs, or used to light the fire, or perhaps even read to bits': '"Publication" before Print', p. 49.
5 On the relationship between the Short Text and the Long Text, see Windeatt's essay in this volume. This present essay will deal almost exclusively with the Long Text.
6 *A Book of Showings to the Anchoress Julian of Norwich*, ed. Edmund Colledge and James Walsh, 2 vols (Toronto, 1978), p. 27. On the Westminster and Amherst manuscripts, see Marleen Cré's essay which precedes this one.

before this a copy, or copies, passed into the hands of Benedictine nuns. It is possible that *A Revelation* went into exile with religious communities during the Reformation, since the extant Long Text manuscripts were owned by and probably copied in English Benedictine houses in France. Paris, Bibliothèque Nationale Fonds Anglais MS 40, is early seventeenth-century: it was preserved and possibly produced by the nuns of Our Lady of Consolation in Cambrai. British Library Sloane MS 2499 (Sloane 1) is also early seventeenth-century and is a much plainer manuscript, possibly in the hand of Clementina Carey who founded Cambrai's daughter house in Paris, Our Lady of Good Hope. British Library Sloane MS 3705 (Sloane 2) is later seventeenth-century. These three manuscripts each contain the full Long Text of *A Revelation*, and that alone: together with a printed version published in 1670 by Serenus Cressy, based on the Paris manuscript, they are the earliest surviving versions of the full Long Text. The Long Text as it now survives is therefore a seventeenth-century text – or rather, texts, since the Paris manuscript preserves a markedly different version of *A Revelation* from that found in the Sloane manuscripts. Divergences between the Paris and Sloane textual traditions may perhaps be taken to indicate the considerable effect of scribes, compilers, glossators and readers in the years between the composition of *A Revelation* and its reappearance in France. It is also possible that some of the divergences are the result of authorial reworking of the Long Text.

Differences between Paris and Sloane are to do with both language and content. Linguistically, there are lexical differences which may be modernizations: Glasscoe has argued that Paris frequently modernizes readings in Sloane 1, citing: *dwelleth* for *wonyth*, *verely* for *sekirly*, *great* for *mekil*, *drede* for *vggyng*, *undertake* for *underfongyn*.[7] Sloane 1 sometimes modernizes, sometimes preserves archaic forms: it is an 'eclectic mixture' but most of its modernizations are 'well-informed and perceptive'.[8] Sloane 2 also frequently modernizes readings in Sloane 1 – for example *fellow christians* for *evyn christen*, *certain* for *sekir*, *here was I taught* for *here was I lernyd*. Sloane 2 is otherwise identical to Sloane 1 and probably copied from it. Paris, however, differs from Sloane much more radically. Linguistic differences may also be the result of dialectal variation. Hoyt S. Greeson has argued that Sloane 1 was copied in Norfolk, in the vicinity of Norwich.[9] Felicity Riddy notes 'sporadic northern vowels and words' in the Paris manuscript and 'unmistakable northern features' in the language of Sloane.[10]

Colledge and Walsh have drawn attention to the presence of Scottish and Northumbrian women among the Cambrai nuns who copied Sloane, and have

7   *Julian of Norwich: A Revelation of Love*, ed. Marion Glasscoe (Exeter, 1976; various repr.), p. ix. All references to this edition will appear parenthetically in the main text.
8   *Showings*, ed. Colledge and Walsh, p. 26.
9   Hoyt S. Greeson, 'Glossary to the British Library Sloane 2499 Manuscript', in *Julian of Norwich, Showing of Love: Extant Texts and Translation*, ed. Sr Anna Maria Reynolds and Julia Bolton Holloway (Florence, 2001), pp. 627–82.
10  Felicity Riddy, 'Julian of Norwich and Self-Textualization', in *Editing Women*, ed. Ann M. Hutchison (Toronto, 1998), pp. 101–24 (111). For details of the northern features of the manuscripts, see *Showings*, ed. Colledge and Walsh, pp. 28–33.

suggested that the northern forms were introduced by the Sloane scribes.[11] But it is more probable that Sloane's northern features may also be taken with its preservation of older linguistic forms to support a different hypothesis: Sloane closely imitates a very early exemplar in a northern dialect, and either Julian or a possible amanuensis were from the north of England.[12] Northern forms may then have survived in *A Revelation* until it was affected by a vital development in the history of the English language – the establishment of a more southerly form as the written standard. Watson and Jenkins argue that Paris presents *A Revelation* 'not in its original local dialect, but in a version of the East Midlands dialect that by 1420 was becoming standard for the copying of works intended for wider circulation'.[13] Processes of standardization may offer an alternative to modernization in accounting for some Paris readings. The shift towards standardization of written English in the first half of the fifteenth century may also account for the lack of northern forms in Westminster. Although it is the earliest extant witness to the Long Text, it was copied around 1500, after the establishment of a written standard, so its lack of support for the language of Sloane need not undermine the likelihood that Sloane's northernisms may be Julian's northernisms preserved. This likelihood may be strengthened by the consideration that Amherst, the earliest manuscript of all, though preserving the Short Text only, does preserve it with numerous northern forms.[14] It can be argued, therefore, that Julian, a northerner who moved into Norwich, or possibly her northern amanuensis, wrote both Long and Short texts in northern dialect: Amherst and Sloane have preserved some of these, but the scribes of Westminster and Paris, or the exemplars from which they copied, have in most but not all cases standardized Julian's dialect.[15]

Sloane may, perhaps, claim to be more authentically 'Julian' linguistically, and 'many dialectal or untranslated forms seem important to the thought of *A Revelation*'.[16] But Paris may have other claims to authority. Paris contains phrases and sometimes whole passages which do not occur in either Sloane manuscript. Sometimes these are phrases which seek to clarify ideas, rather than simply gloss individual words. Are these omissions from Sloane, or interpolations into Paris? On these questions rests the weight of the debate as to whether the Sloane

11 *Showings*, ed. Colledge and Walsh, p. 28.
12 Whereas Margery Kempe repeatedly draws attention, in her *Book*, to her use of an amanuensis to overcome the problem of her illiteracy, *A Revelation* makes no mention of an amanuensis. However, amanuenses were employed not just by the illiterate but also by the upper classes: an amanuensis 'separates reading and composition from the manual labour of writing and frees up time for prayer, study and meditation' (Riddy, 'Self-Textualization', p. 109).
13 *Writings*, ed. Watson and Jenkins, p. 11.
14 *Julian of Norwich's Revelations of Divine Love: The Shorter Version ed. from BL Add. MS 37790*, ed. Frances Beer (Heidelberg, 1978), pp. 19–20.
15 On northern forms in Paris see Riddy, 'Self-Textualization', p. 123 n. 37.
16 *Writings*, ed. Watson and Jenkins, p. 40: they note the superiority of Sloane's 'oning' over Paris's more abstract 'union', which loses the numerical connection with 'noughting', another important Julian term; also Sloane's 'wonninge' (being at home) as subtly different from Paris's 'dwelling' (staying somewhere). For a fuller discussion of Julian's theologizing diction, see the introduction to *Julian of Norwich: A Revelation of Love*, introduced, edited and modernized by Elisabeth Dutton (Plymouth, 2008).

or the Paris tradition should be viewed as closer to that elusive holy grail, the author's original.

Watson and Jenkins make a compelling case, using supporting evidence from Amherst, for Paris's preservation of authorial phrases and passages which Sloane has omitted: they argue of Sloane that 'somewhere in the history of its text are scribes who (in the early chapters) abbreviated material deliberately, sometimes left material out accidentally, and had to reconstruct readings whose sense had been lost'.[17] They cite several examples of Sloane's apparently wilful abbreviations, alterations and omissions, including Sloane's reshaping of Chapter 2, in which Paris's brief phrase 'The second was bodilie sicknes', supported by Amherst, is expanded by Sloane to 'The second was bodily sekenesse in youth at thirty yeeres of age': Sloane then omits, at the end of the chapter, Paris's phrase, also supported by Amherst: 'This sicknes I desyred in my jowth, that I might have it whan I ware xxxth yeare olde'. This certainly looks like wilful scribal alteration, 'as if a scribe had found the deliberate structure of Julian's exposition irritating.'[18] The 'deliberate structure' which Watson and Jenkins find in Julian is an aspect of their portrayal of her as a highly formal prose writer whose sentences display rhetorical and logical balance and whose exposition proceeds by carefully progressing points: in this portrayal they follow Colledge and Walsh and, like Colledge and Walsh, they draw their evidence from Paris.

Glasscoe, however, interprets Paris's fuller sentences differently, arguing that many of them must be read as interpolations, additions which are often made at the expense of a prose rhythm 'more felicitous' in Sloane 1. She cites from the seventh chapter in Sloane:

> our lord God shewed our lady Saint Mary in the same tyme; that is to mene the hey wisedom and trewth she had in beholding of hir maker [Paris adds: This wisdom and truth made her to behold her God] so grete, so hey, so mightie and so gode. This gretenes and this noblyth of the beholding of God fulfilled her of reverent drede. (Sloane, ed. Glasscoe, p. 8)[19]

The repetitious syntax of Paris – *this wisdom ... made, this gretenes ... fulfilled* – obstructs the flow of meaning even as it presumably seeks to clarify it: the 'explanatory insistence' of Paris 'impedes the cadence' of Sloane 1's reading, in which the reader can 'move easily from the statement of what was seen to its inward effect'.[20] The suggestion may be that in such cases what Sloane 1 represents is closer to the Julian original    more difficult at a literal level, perhaps, but also more elegant – and Paris represents some form of interpreted version, with interpolated explanatory phrases. These interpolations would be unlikely to be the work of the Paris scribe: their language is medieval, and the Paris scribe was 'a not very intelligent copyist, anxious to transcribe faithfully';[21] they would therefore have accrued to Julian's text at earlier stages in its transmission.

---

17  *Writings*, ed. Watson and Jenkins, p. 40.
18  Ibid., p. 38.
19  Cited by Glasscoe in Sloane, ed. Glasscoe, p. ix.
20  Ibid., p. x.
21  *Showings*, ed. Colledge and Walsh, p. 26.

But if Paris is the work of a plodding copyist carefully preserving what is before her, whether authorial or not, there can be no doubt that Sloane 1, or an exemplar at some earlier stage in its transmission, has been copied somewhat carelessly. There are many phrases and passages absent from Sloane 1 but present in Paris which may be accounted for by scribal carelessness, according to principles of homoeoteleuton, or 'eyeskip'. The careless scribe who, at some point in Sloane's transmission, lost thirty lines of Julian's text because of eyeskip, is a highly probable figure, though not even the appearance of homoeoteleuton is entirely uncontroversial where the resultant reading still makes sense. Glasscoe quotes as an example of eyeskip from Sloane's forty-sixth chapter:

> But our passand lif that we have here in our sensualite knowith not what ourself is; [Paris adds: but in our faith. And whan we know and see, verely and clerely, what ourselfe is] than shal we verily and clerly sen and knowen our lord God in fulhede of ioy. (Sloane, ed. Glasscoe, p. 48)[22]

The passage omitted ends with the same words – 'what ourself is' – as those after which it started, so it is easy to see how a transcriber might have accidentally left them out, the eye skipping from one phrase to the other in the exemplar. The fuller text of Paris clarifies one aspect of A Revelation's meaning here. It indicates that in this physical life we cannot know ourselves fully, and it explicitly connects our capacity to know ourselves with our capacity to know God. It does not, however, clarify what might appear to be the bigger question here, namely where and when we shall achieve such knowledge if not in this life. Implicitly, it seems we must assume that this knowledge is to come in some way after death or possibly at the end of time: both Sloane and Paris go on to indicate that we shall know ourselves fully only at 'the last point, in which pointe this passing life and alle manner of wo and paine shall have ane ende' (Revelation, 46.8–9; cp. Sloane, ed. Glasscoe, p. 48). But the context of this passage does not invite a reflection on knowing ourselves so that we can know God, nor does it emphasise a learning process by which, when we have mastered one lesson (ourselves) then we can master another (God), although the syntax of Paris – 'And whan … than …' might suggest this. The context indicates clearly that Julian's concern at this point is not with temporal development but with the shifting perspective between the mortal and the divine. Julian's meditation here springs out of her interrogation of the 'two judgements', one of God and one of Holy Church, by which we are judged: the two, though different, co-exist – although we live now on earth 'oure kindely substance is now blisseful in God, and hath bene sithen it was made' (Revelation, 45.34–5). What is important at 'the last point' is not that we learn something, or even that anything changes, for all that woe and pain cease: what is important is that in a moment ('than'), we shall be able to see things through God's eyes.

Sloane's briefer, simpler syntax emphasizes this through its juxtaposition of 'here' and 'than', and has strong Pauline echoes: 'For now we see through a glass, darkly, but then face to face' (1 Corinthians 13:12). These echoes are prob-

---

[22]   Cited by Glasscoe in Sloane, ed. Glasscoe, p. x.

ably not accidental, since Paul, like Julian, is contrasting earthly knowledge with the divine, and since the Pauline passage has been more directly quoted not much earlier, in Chapter 43: 'And than shal we sen God face to face' (Sloane, ed. Glasscoe, p. 46). Paul goes on to connect knowledge of God and knowledge of oneself, though in a rather different way from Paris – 'but then shall I know even as I am known' – and Paris's additional phrases have obscured the syntactical echoes of Corinthians which help to interpret the *Revelation*'s meaning at this point. A few lines later, Paris again displays its interpretive drive to make knowledge of God follow knowledge of self:

> And therfore it longeth properly to us, both be kinde and by grace, to long and desyer with alle oure mightes to know oureselfe [Paris adds: in which full knowing we shall verely and clerely know oure God] in fulhede of endlesse joy.
>
> (*Revelation*, 46.10–12; cp. Sloane, ed. Glasscoe, pp. 48–9)

Since the simpler Sloane reading is an unlikely example of eyeskip, it seems that the differences between Paris and Sloane here are deliberate and interpretive – and it is by no means clear that Paris is superior.

The following passage may perhaps have been omitted from Sloane by a scribe who understood the meaning of 'soule' to be, as was common in Middle English, 'food' or 'meal', and the 'purse' as therefore an image of the bowels:

> A man goeth upperight, and the soule of his body is sparede as a purse fulle fair. And whan it is time of his nescessery, it is openede and sparede ayen fulle honestly. And that it is he that doeth this, it is shewed ther wher he seith: 'He cometh downe to us, to the lowest parte of oure nede'. (*Revelation*, 6.29–33)

This striking passage, which in Paris is contextually congruent and which resonates with Julian's later comments on God's goodness as evident in his intimate duties as mother in Chapters 55–62, may perhaps be authorial but omitted from Sloane by a censoring scribe in a milieu troubled by the association of excretion with the divine.[23]

There are also a very few passages present in Sloane 1 but not in Paris, and of them Glasscoe asserts that a very high proportion may also be explained by homoeotoleuton on the part of the Paris scribe or an earlier Paris exemplar.[24] But, as Glasscoe also points out, there are some substantial differences which cannot be accounted for in this way,[25] of which perhaps the most immediately obvious is Sloane's more developed reading apparatus. While the first chapter in both Paris and Sloane is an annotated table of contents outlining the sixteen revelations, and both manuscript traditions divide the text further into eighty-six chapters, only Sloane provides expanded headings at the beginning of each chapter explaining that chapter's contents. While both the table of contents and

[23] For a full examination of this passage, see Liz Herbert McAvoy, ' "… a purse fulle feyer": Feminising the Body in Julian of Norwich's *A Revelation of Love*', *Reading Medieval Studies* 34 (2004), pp. 99–113.
[24] Sloane, ed. Glasscoe, p. x.
[25] Ibid., p. x.

the division of the text into eighty-six chapters appear to be authorial,[26] Sloane's expanded chapter headings are unlikely to be Julian's own. It is instructive to compare the heading to Chapter 4 – the beginning of the First Revelation – and the description of the First Revelation in the table of contents. First, the table of contents:

> Of which the first is of his precious crowning of thornes. And therin was compre-
> hended and specified the blessed trinity, with the incarnation and the oning
> betweene God and mans soule, with many fair shewynges and techinges of
> endlesse wisdom and love, in which all the shewinges that foloweth be groundide
> and oned. (*Revelation*, 1.3–7)

The Sloane heading to Chapter 4, which ostensibly introduces the First Revelation, reads:

> *Here begynnith the first revelation of the pretious crownyng of Criste etc. in the first*
> *chapter; and how god fulfilleth the herrte with most ioy, and of his greate meekenesse,*
> *and how the syght of the passion of Criste is sufficient strength ageyn all temptations of*
> *the fends, and of the gret excellency and mekenesse of the blissid virgin Mary – the iiii*
> *chapter.* (Sloane, ed. Glasscoe, p. 4)

Naturally this details the contents only of Chapter 4, while the summary of the First Revelation in the table of contents, although fairly general in expression, clearly alludes to material from the whole revelation. But the Sloane heading is also very different in character from the account of the First Revelation, although the 'precious crownyng of thornes' is the starting point for both. Whereas the table of contents offers a complex theological understanding of the First Revelation, with allusion to the Trinity, the unity of the souls of God and man, and the all-encompassing nature of these two concepts, the chapter heading offers a devotional interpretation of the fourth chapter, highlighting Christ's Passion as strength, and Mary's virtue as example for the believer.

Each chapter heading remarks devotional aspects of the text it precedes, and where the chapter begins a new revelation this devotional interpretation may be compared with the more theological, ordering nature of the table of content's description of the revelation. The chapter headings might well have been prepared for a female religious community of the kind which may have produced the Sloane manuscripts,[27] although it would have been an earlier community: the evidence of language and of textual variants in the headings of Sloane 1 and Sloane 2 indicates that they were extant long before these manuscripts were copied. The chapter headings were probably not, however, prepared by Julian as *A Revelation*'s author, and they may guide the reader in ways which were not those intended by Julian herself – that is to say more devotionally than theologi-

---

[26] Riddy, 'Self-Textualization', pp. 114–16.
[27] See also the Sloane heading to Chapter 66, which may be compared with the summary of the Sixteenth Revelation in the table of contents: the chapter heading has the tone of someone entrusted with the *cura animarum*, and Riddy discerns a clerical voice, 'Self-Textualization', p. 118.

cally, perhaps.[28] That each individual chapter is given a separate heading in the
Sloane manuscripts places greater emphasis on chapter divisions throughout the
Sloane text than on the more structurally fundamental division of Julian's religious experience into sixteen showings. The chapters provide smaller gobbets
for the reader, but if the chapter headings in Sloane are encouraging selective
reading, they do so against Sloane's own explicit warning:

> And beware thou take not on thing after thy affection and liking and leve another,
> for that is the condition of an heretique. But take every thing with other [...]
> And thou, to whome this booke shall come, thanke heyley and hartily our savior
> Crist Ihesu that he made these shewings and revelations for the, and to the, of
> his endles love, mercy and goodnes, for thine and our save guide and conduct to
> everlestyng bliss; the which Ihesus mot grant us. Amen. [Sloane 2 adds: Here end
> the sublime [...] revelations [...] vouchsafed to a dear lover of his and in her to
> all his dear friends and lovers whose hearts like hers do flame in þe loue of our
> dearest Jesu]. (Sloane, ed. Glasscoe, pp. 135–6)[29]

The passage explicitly seeks to limit *A Revelation*'s readership to those who are
in a position to read and understand the complete text. Passages are not to
be selected for meditative reading independent of their context. Textually, the
passage's 'I' need not be Julian: the showings are said to have been made 'to the',
not 'to me', and certainly the Sloane 2 addition seems interpolated: even given
that mystical writers such as Margery Kempe do speak of themselves in the third
person, it seems unlikely Julian would explicitly establish herself as a model of
flaming love for God. That this passage appears only in the Sloane manuscripts
also suggests that it is not authorial, but indicates something about the way in
which a scribe early in the transmission of Sloane intended *A Revelation* to be
read: that it is a reading model which seems to work against the textual apparatus unique to Sloane – namely the chapter summaries which might facilitate
selective, devotional reading – may suggest that from very early in its history *A
Revelation* was being edited and adapted for reading in many different ways.

   The readers of whom the modern Julian scholar must be most aware are the
seventeenth-century nuns who copied the extant manuscripts, for they are the
readers who are identifiable and whose influence on the text is certain, though
its character must be carefully traced. The evidence of MS St Joseph's College,
Upholland, is important here. The Upholland manuscript contains short extracts
from the *Revelation*, copied by the Cambrai nuns between 1670 and 1684,[30] alongside extracts from medieval and post-Reformation spiritual classics translated
by Father Augustine Baker, OSB, spiritual guide to the Cambrai nuns. The *Revelation* extracts, being in English, are of course not translated but are modernized and adapted in various ways, possibly by Baker: since Baker died in 1641

---

[28] This is discussed further in Elisabeth Dutton, *Julian of Norwich: The Influence of Late-Medieval
Devotional Compilations* (Cambridge, forthcoming 2008).
[29] See *Showings*, ed. Colledge and Walsh, p. 734 n. 29 for textual variants.
[30] For this dating see Elisabeth Dutton, 'Augustine Baker and Two Manuscripts of Julian of
Norwich's *Revelation of Love*', *Notes and Queries* 250, 3 (2005), pp. 329–37 (331). This article also
argues for Upholland's derivation from a Paris-style exemplar (332).

he cannot have been directly responsible for the anthology in its present form, but it is possible either that he selected the *Revelation* extracts and modernized them, or that he modernized more of *A Revelation* and a later compiler selected the extracts represented. Whatever the precise degree of Baker's involvement in the creation of Upholland – and it is likely that it was large – he was certainly a vital influence in the spiritual formation of those who read *A Revelation* and transmitted it to us: the selection of material in Upholland, and the nature of its adaptation, yield evidence as to how *A Revelation* was read by the exiled Benedictine nuns who preserved it.

Upholland constitutes four extracts from the Twelfth Revelation (Christ glorified, by which Julian is taught the joy which the soul shall have in God) and the Thirteenth Revelation (a consideration of how Julian is hindered by sin).[31] Upholland includes Christ's surprising statement that 'Synne is behouely', but Julian's theological discussion of sin as having no substance is omitted. Upholland's editor is uninterested in a philosophical characterizing of sin, except insofar as it is a cause of Christ's compassion on us: the focus is on God's 'prive conncelle' and human dependence on divine revelation. Upholland's text is concerned with knowing – what can and cannot be known, and God's will to reveal Himself to us; its appreciation of knowing, however, is focused on the human viewpoint, rather than the divine, Julian's discussion of which it omits.

Baker's numerous writings reveal an interest not in academic knowledge but in mystical 'knowing', a knowing which comes not from books but from the direct experience of God:

> No man is able by profoundnesse of his Learning, by yᵉ Subtilty or acutenesse of his Understanding, not by any meer Human industries, Perfectly to Comprehend or Understand; but it is only Learned & understood by experience by him, to whom yᵉ Divine Goodnesse & liberality shall please to impart yᵉ same experience & knowledg.[32]

To Baker, the image of divine privity is potent, although his focus on human knowledge ensures that his discussion of God's secrets, which we may imagine might have drawn him to the passages of *A Revelation* in Upholland, would surely twist *A Revelation*'s image. At the beginning of his exposition of *The Cloud of Unknowing*, Baker explains the reason that he has called his commentary *Secretum Sive Mysticum*:

> both because it Containeth Mystick matters (& *Mysticum* and *Secretum* are both of one Sence and Meaning), and such as S. Denis ... forbiddeth to be Communicated to such as do more use their externall Senses then internall & Spirituall exercises; as also because it Conteineth / Certain Particular Passages wᶜʰ the Author hereof doth not think fit to be made known to All.[33]

In Baker's hands, then, the divine secrets are the preserve not uniquely of God

31  The Upholland extracts are edited in *Writings*, ed. Watson and Jenkins, pp. 446–8.
32  Augustine Baker, *Secretum*, ed. John Clark (Salzburg, 1997), p. 1.
33  Ibid., p. 2.

but rather of a contemplative oligarchy. The 'secret' in which he is interested is not the mysterious thought of God's mind by which all shall, in the end, be made well; it is the secret of the mystic's knowing of God. For this reason, Baker might have commented upon *A Revelation* here in the way that we find in Upholland. The 'I it am' locutions are selected, but the penultimate locution – 'I it am that holy church precheth the and techeth thee' (*Revelation*, 26.7) – is removed: if *A Revelation* is to be presented as the articulation of a *mysticum*, then it is better to leave out anything which asserts that the knowledge it offers might be accessible to all through the teaching of the church. What follows in *A Revelation* would be much more in accord with Baker's concern with mystical experience, and it is edited in Upholland to lend emphasis to this interest:

> The nomber of the words passeth my wittes and my understanding and alle my mightes, for they were in thee highest, as to my sight. For therin is comprehended I can not telle what [Upholland adds: so that it cannot be expressed]. But the joy that I saw in the shewing of them passeth [Upholland: exceedingly surpasseth] alle that hart can think or soule may desire. And therfore these wordes [Upholland adds: (the meaning of them)] be not declared here. But every man, after [Upholland: one, according to] the grace that God geveth [Upholland: hath giuen] him in understandyng and loving, receive [Upholland: let them receaue] them in our lordes mening. (*Revelation*, 26.8–13)

The substitution of *one* for *man* is an innocent alteration such as might be made for the benefit of a female audience of Cambrai nuns; the expansion of *passeth* to *exceedingly surpasseth* modernizes but also emphasizes the loftiness of the vision-ary's ecstasy as she receives her showings. The addition of the phrase 'so that it cannot be expressed' is unnecessary, but shows the editor's particular interest in this point; the glossing of *these words* as *the meaning of them* is a clarifying gloss on the apparent paradox that words which have just been recorded are then said not to be *declared*; again, it shows an interest in this passage as a witness to the problems of recording mystical experience in words. The alteration of *the grace that God geveth* to a past tense, and of *receive* to *let them receaue*, functions less than innocently to reduce the optimistic inclusivity of all other *Revelation* witnesses at this point. Upholland's readers, in order to understand the divine mystery of Christ's locutions here recorded, must draw on the stock of grace in understanding and loving which God has granted them before they come to this text. The contemplative who has progressed enough in her way of life may be able to grasp the meaning when she begins to read revelations, but she who has not will not. This is in contrast to the present tense reading, which suggests that God will give grace for understanding as the reader reads – previous spir-itual grooming is not required, and this is implied also in the immediacy of the imperative *receive* these words, as contrasted with Upholland's distant jussive *let them receive*.

There may be a stronger reason than lack of interest for Upholland's omission of much of Julian's discussion of sin. Baker discusses sin as a pastoral rather than theological issue, insisting that the contemplative not allow the mind to become weighed down in a consideration of sin, because during ... the time th$^t$ y$^e$ Soul is in such Case about sins & in worthy remorse for them, She is not So apt for y$^e$ work of Immediate Love or Resignation towards God.[34]

Baker downplays discussion of sin in his spiritual counsel. Richard Lawes notes Baker's advice, 'extremely unusual in the Catholic Church of his period', that only those who have committed mortal sin should confess more than monthly: weekly confession was the norm for seventeenth-century nuns. Baker's counsel against frequent scrupulous examinations of conscience is based on a conviction that the cycles of anxiety-generation and reassurance-seeking in confession may prove 'compulsive and unhelpful'.[35]

Upholland includes a passage from *A Revelation* in which Julian's curiosity about sin is portrayed as unhelpful, if not dangerous. Upholland's reworkings clarify some obscure Middle English syntax while interpolations emphasize the dangers of curiosity about sin:

> And thus in my foly before this time, often I wondred why, by the grete forseeing wisdom of God, the beginning of sinne was not letted [Upholland: hindred or preuented]. For then thought me that alle shulde have be wele.
>
> This stering was mekille to be forsaken [Upholland: Thys steryng thought in my mind I should haue forsaken, and not haue yealded vnto it ], and [Upholland: yet] nevertheless morning and sorow I made therfore withoute reson and discretion [Upholland: nevyrthelesse it caused me to mourne and sorrow withou3te dyscrecion] (*Revelation*, 27.4–8)

Baker was concerned that meditation upon sin 'hath in it images about Creatures', and for this reason must be eschewed by the contemplative seeking the image-less cloud of unknowing; Julian realises, however, that sin of itself has no substance, and she notes that in all her visions she does not see sin (*Revelation*, 11.18). Julian's statement that sin may be known by 'the gret harme that is come by sinne to thy creatures'(*Revelation*, 29.3) seems to confirm Baker's opinion about the imaging of sin, but since Julian has a rather different view of images from either Baker or the *Cloud*, for her this is not the reason why questions should not be asked about sin. For Julian, it is simply the case that her visions 'enformed me of alle that me neded' (*Revelation*, 27.9) and that, while it is therefore right to examine and interrogate closely those visions, to enquire beyond their scope is to trespass on the divine privity. Upholland edits out the discussion of sin which ensues: it presents as a prohibition of enquiry into sin what was written as a prohibition of overmuch enquiry into the thoughts of God.

A compiler may wield considerable influence on the reading of a text by the selection and arrangement of material, as Cré effectively demonstrates in her discussion of the Westminster compilation in the essay which precedes this one. The reader of Upholland is influenced also by interpolations, annotations and modernizations not entirely different in kind from those already observable in

---

34  Ibid., p. 139.
35  Richard Lawes, 'Can Modern Psychology Help us Understand Baker's *Secretum Sive Mysticum*?', in *That Mysterious Man: Essays on Augustine Baker OSB 1575–1641*, ed. Michael Woodward (Abergavenny, 2001), pp. 245–59 (226).

the Paris and Sloane manuscripts, though perhaps more marked: comparison of Upholland with Paris facilitates a more certain identification of particular phrases as later, non-authorial interpolations than is possible with the full Long Text manuscripts. In Upholland we may observe clearly processes of omission and interpolation by which Julian's text is being edited to shape its reading by seventeenth-century nuns: the differences between Paris and Sloane make it clear that these processes were underway long before Upholland was prepared for the Cambrai community, but the extant evidence will not, alas, allow the reconstruction of an authorial original by the reversal of these processes. However, Julian insisted that her visions were for all, and even acknowledged that they might have more meaning for her readers than for herself.[36] Divergences in the manuscript traditions of the *Revelation*, therefore, give valuable clues as to the ways the text has been read and interpreted since its 'publication' and so, perhaps, with the manuscripts as with individual readings we do well ourselves not to 'take on thing and leve another'.

---

[36] '[I]n as much as ye love God the better, it is more to you than to me' (*Revelation*, 9.1–2).

# 11

## Julian of Norwich's 'Modernist Style' and the Creation of Audience

### ELIZABETH ROBERTSON

Given the prominence of Julian of Norwich's writing in the canon of English literature, it is surprising how little we know about her audience in general. Neither historical nor manuscript evidence reveals much about her contemporary audience. To determine who read or heard her work, either as a written or oral composition, we need to consider such questions as who Julian was, who wrote down her story in its short form and then in its longer and more considered version, for whom she intended these versions, and who actually received them. Despite the fact that these questions yield only fragmentary and ambiguous answers, we can still learn about Julian's audience by looking carefully at the accounts themselves. Not only does Julian tell us to whom she addresses her work – to her 'evencristen' (although who these might be is itself not as clear as it might seem) – but also the *idea* of an audience is very much part of Julian's formulation of her account of her visions. She describes an audience that is both general and universal rather than particular and individual and that imagined audience, everywhere inscribed in her accounts, is fundamental to the text's meaning. Julian's goal, especially in her Short Text (also in a somewhat different way in the Long Text), is to recount a series of visions she had of Christ in such a way that we, the audience, experience those visions just as she did – and she invents a variety of stylistic strategies to achieve this goal.[1] These stylistic techniques, as I shall argue, have much in common with 'modernist' style as defined by Eric Auerbach, and have the effect of dissolving the distance between both Julian and her vision and Julian and her audience. It is apt to call Julian's work a 'Showing,' the word she so often uses in her text, since Julian's modernist style, one shaped by her understanding of what it means to see, is committed above all to showing rather than telling her audience what she has seen.

---

1   All references to Julian's texts, *A Vision Showed to a Devout Woman* (Short Text) and *A Revelation of Love* (Long Text), will be to *The Writings of Julian of Norwich:* A Vision Showed to a Devout Woman *and* A Revelation of Love, ed. Nicholas Watson and Jacqueline Jenkins (Turnhout, 2006), unless otherwise stated.

## Julian's Actual Audience

Historical and manuscript evidence tell us so little about who Julian was and about her intended audience that we can only finally make conjectures about the actual audience of the accounts of her visions.[2] If we knew whether or not she entered her anchorhold from the secular life or from a convent we might be able to narrow her primary audience down to enclosed religious or, more specifically, to enclosed nuns.[3] Since it was nuns who preserved her accounts even through the vicissitudes of the Reformation, the manuscripts that remain (none of them Julian's original) suggest that her primary and most enduring reading audience consisted of *nuns*.[4] However, although her extant manuscripts are associated with enclosed religious and even though she at times directs her thoughts specifically to those who are 'contemplative' we still do not know that nuns were her *only* audience.[5] Indeed, her repeated address to her 'evencristen' suggests she intended both of her accounts to be available to everyone and anyone.

Most significant to an understanding of Julian's audience is the fact that she was an anchoress.[6] Margery Kempe's is the only name we have of an actual contemporary audience member: her visit to Julian in her anchorhold tells us that Julian was known as a visionary beyond her local community.[7] However, whether or not Margery and her advisors knew her *written* accounts is unknown. The visit also tells us that one of Julian's fundamental activities was advising lay spiritual audiences. An anchoress is always on the border between two communities, as signalled by her two windows, one looking into the Church and one looking out to the community. Julian may well have been beloved by both the enclosed spiritual community to which her anchorhold was attached

[2]   For a brief discussion of the manuscripts, see McAvoy's introduction to this volume and the essays by Cré and Dutton, in particular. For a fuller treatment see Barry Windeatt, 'Julian of Norwich', in *A Companion to Middle English Prose*, ed. A. S. G. Edwards (Cambridge, 2004), pp. 67–81.
[3]   Both Benedicta Ward and Felicity Riddy have considered it possible that Julian was a layperson before she entered the anchorhold. See Benedicta Ward, 'Julian the Solitary', in Kenneth Leech and Benedicta Ward, *Julian Reconsidered* (Oxford, 1988), pp. 11–35; and Felicity Riddy, '"Women Talking about the Things of God": A Late Medieval Sub-Culture', in *Women and Literature in Britain: 1150–1500*, ed. Carol M. Meale (Cambridge, 1993), pp. 104–27, especially p. 111. Watson and Jenkins disagree, as do Edmund Colledge and James Walsh in the introduction to their edition, *A Book of Showings to the Anchoress Julian of Norwich* (Toronto, 1978). Like other contributors to this present volume, although the evidence is inconclusive, I am inclined to agree with Ward and Riddy.
[4]   For a discussion of the association of Julian's manuscripts with nuns, see *Writings*, ed. Watson and Jenkins, Introduction, pp. 10–17; and Windeatt in 'Julian of Norwich', p. 69. See again Dutton's essay.
[5]   Julian addresses contemplatives in *Vision*, 4.38–40, and 13.23–4. Lynn Staley views the Short Text as addressed to female contemplatives. See her 'Julian of Norwich and the Crisis of Authority', in David Aers and Lynn Staley, *The Powers of the Holy: Religion, Politics and Gender in Late Medieval English Culture* (Pennsylvania, 1996), pp. 107–78, especially pp. 107–32. Felicity Riddy, on the other hand, argues the text is addressed to a broader audience: '"Publicaiton", before Print: The Case of Julian of Norwich', in *The Uses of Script and Print: 1300 –1700*, ed. Julia Crick and Alexander Walsham (Cambridge, 2004), pp. 29–49, esp. p. 44.
[6]   On Julian as an anchoress, see the essay by E. A. Jones in this present volume.
[7]   Margery Kempe, *The Book of Margery Kempe*, ed. Sanford Brown Meech and Hope Emily Allen, EETS o.s. 212 (Oxford, 1948; repr. 1997), ch. 18, pp. 42–3.

(the advowson of St Julian's at Conisford belonged to the Benedictine convent at Carrow, and perhaps these nuns were among her first audience) and the variety of laypeople, from the spiritually committed to the idly curious, who visited her. She probably intended her visions to be shared by both those communities.

Julian's status as an anchoress also points us to a different context for assessing her literacy, for her primary engagement with the world might have been as much through oral communication as through the written text.[8] Julian's extensive intellectual range, from her deep knowledge of Augustine to her acquaintance with philosophical debate (perhaps even that of Duns Scotus), suggests that she read widely.[9] However, the fact that her writings are remarkably devoid of direct reference (as Vincent Gillespie demonstrates later in this volume), might suggest a secondary knowledge of her sources gained not through reading written works, but rather through listening to speakers and advisors reading texts to her and/or discussing them with her. That she describes herself as 'a woman, lewed, febille and freylle (*Vision*, 6.36) and as 'a simple creature unletterde' (*Revelation*, 2.1), may simply mean that she does not know how to read Latin, or that she may be downplaying her more extensive knowledge either out of humility or in order to avoid being accused of being a Lollard woman preacher. She may, however, merely be telling us that she was indeed unlettered – that is, unacquainted with the written text. Her ruminating meditations on simple biblical phrases might suggest a nun's experience with *lectio divina*, but a spiritual advisor may also have taught her the habit of rumination. Even if Julian could not read or write, she could have received a superb education aurally by listening avidly to her spiritual advisor and to the visiting theologians and preachers who poured through the unusually sophisticated religious community of Norwich.[10]

It is also possible that she learned to read and write only after she entered the anchorhold; her comparison in the later text of pondering the image of the lord and servant to learning the ABC suggests that the process of learning to read was in the forefront of her mind even when that version was composed.[11] Most critics also agree that her writing shows no signs of the presence of an amanuensis. The Short Text, however, seems rhetorically closer to speech than the Long Text, and much of its simplicity in comparison to the Long Text implies that it could easily be Julian's own work. Nonetheless, as Barry Windeatt has suggested, the text may not have been written down by Julian, but rather dictated to a scribe; he and Felicity Riddy also raise the possibility that a male spiritual advisor may have collaborated with her to produce the more theologically complex and

8   For a discussion of the importance of Julian's placement within an oral community, again see Riddy, '"Women Talking about the Things of God"', pp. 104–27.
9   J. P. H. Clark discusses Julian's acquaintance with a number of philosophical issues in a series of essays: 'Fiducia in Julian of Norwich', *Downside Review* 100 (1982a), pp. 79–91; 'Predestination in Christ according to Julian of Norwich', *Downside Review* 100 (1982b), pp. 203–20 and 'Time and Eternity in Julian of Norwich', *Downside Review* 109 (1991), pp. 259–76.
10   For a discussion of the vibrancy of Norwich as an intellectual religious community, see Norman P. Tanner, *The Church in Late Medieval Norwich 1370–1532* (Toronto, 1984), especially pp. 18–57.
11   See *Revelation*, 51.228–31.

rhetorically smooth longer version of her showing.[12] Given the closeness of most anchoresses to their spiritual advisors, it is entirely possible that Julian's written texts may have been collaborative productions produced primarily through oral communication. Julian does not directly mention the name of an advisor but does refer once to a 'religiouse person' who, after initial skepticism, came to believe in her revelation (*Vision*, 21.6). Given Julian's probable experience of oral intellectual communication, she may have had both a listening and a reading audience in mind. Indeed, the written accounts may well have been secondary to her oral performance of their content through the window of her anchorhold. Moreover, the dearth of extant medieval manuscripts could suggest that Julian was not especially interested in producing a written account and that her oral interactions, such as the exchange she had with Margery Kempe, were of equal importance to her.

The Sloane manuscript includes an endnote that may suggest that Julian's audience eventually became limited because of the radical theology it contained. The note says:

> I pray almyty God that this booke com not but to the hands of them that will be his faithfull lovers, and to those that will submitt them to the feith of holy church, and obey the holsom vnderstondyng and teching of the men that be of vertuous life, sadde age and profound lernyng; for this revelation is hey divinitye and hey wisdam, wherfore it may not dwelle with him that is thrall to synne and to the devill. And beware thou take not on thing after thy affection and liking and leve another, for that is the condition of an heretique. But take everything with other. And trewly vnderstonden all is according to holy scripture and growndid in the same, and that Ihesus, our very love, light, and truth shall shew to all clen soules that with mekenes aske perseverantly this wisdom of hym.[13]

This rubric implies that Julian's work could lead to heresy if read partially or without intellectual rigor. Such a rubric seems particularly apt to the climate of fear of vernacular theology produced by Arundel's constitutions of 1409, and it is tempting to think that Julian's work failed to reach the broad audience she intended specifically because of a radical potential that may have prevented her manuscripts from being circulated in her lifetime. After the Reformation, dissemination of the written text would be further compromised by the Protestant desire to repress Catholic works, especially those that celebrated the Marian or the miraculous and mystical.

While it may be that Julian's primary, early, actual audiences were aural ones, a treatise written in the 1630s by Margaret Gascoigne, a nun at Cambrai (and already discussed by Watt) tells us how one early *reader* of her text understood Julian. According to Watson, Margaret takes sentences from the Long Text as springboards for her own meditation.[14] In addition, on her own deathbed, she

---

[12]  Windeatt, 'Julian of Norwich', pp. 78–9; and Felicity Riddy, 'Julian of Norwich and Self-Textualization', in *Editing Women*, ed. Ann Hutchinson (Toronto, 1998), pp. 101–24.

[13]  The Sloane manuscripts have been edited by Marion Glasscoe in *Julian of Norwich: A Revelation of Love* (Exeter, 1970; various repr.). This quotation is on p. 103. It is also cited in *Writings*, ed. Watson and Jenkins, p. 11 and in the textual notes, p. 415.

[14]  See *Writings*, ed. Watson and Jenkins, p. 15.

imitates Julian's near-death experience and asks that a crucifix be brought before her with Christ's promise to Julian written underneath. Margaret ruminates on Julian's sentences as if they were passages from the Bible. More particularly, however, her reading practice suggests that Margaret identifies so strongly with Julian that there is little difference between herself and the author. Christ's words are spoken as much to her as to Julian. Although her training as a nun would encourage such rumination of a text, what is striking about Margaret's meditation is that she feels at ease in entering Julian's narrative as if it were her own. I argue that such a response emerges less from her training in monastic rumination than from the fact that Julian's style, to which I now turn, encourages just such an interaction with her work.

## Julian's 'Modernist' Style

Although the avowed audience of Julian's writing is made up of her 'evencristen', the meaning of this term remains uncertain. By 'even', does she mean those, like her, who are devoted to a rigorous form of the contemplative life, or does she intend 'even' to mean 'equal', in the sense of sharing with her the status of being human? While her specific addresses in the Short Text to those interested in contemplation suggest that Julian may have had a narrow audience in mind when she embarked upon her writing, her text – certainly as it develops – ultimately concerns a much broader one. That wider audience is as much inside the text as outside it, however, since Julian's stylistic strategies pull readers into her work as her 'evencristen'. Julian positions herself in relationship to her audience as one who does not claim authority over the materials she wishes us to experience, but rather one whose compositional style allows us to become co-participants with her in that experience. I will briefly touch upon a variety of stylistic elements that contribute to Julian's dissolution of her own authority and her ability to empower her readers and listeners to join with her as witnesses of her showing. First, she presents her visions from multiple perspectives in a way that induces the reader to join in the production of one or more meanings of the experiences described. Second, she disrupts temporal linearity in order to create an immanence of meaning available to all. Third, she creates a narrative voice both assured and reassuring while at the same time claiming no authority over her readers or listeners or her vision itself. Fourth, she obscures the relationship between exterior events and inner meditation so that the inner world and the outer world merge, thus reinforcing her attempts to create an all-inclusive vision without boundaries. Fifth, she uses inclusive diction and quotidian imagery that create a sense of a community of which she is a part and an account of her vision that is accessible to everyone in that community. Finally, and perhaps most importantly, she uses visual techniques through which she invites the reader to witness with her 'moving images'.[15] These stylistic elements, I suggest, shatter the distance between Julian as writer

---

15  I adopt the term James Simpson uses in his discussion of late medieval saints' lives in his book, *The Oxford English Literary History Volume 2: 1350–1547: Reform and Cultural Revolution*

and her audience whether that audience is a listener or a reader, of the past or of the present.

Erich Auerbach's characterization of modernist literary style, through an analysis of Virginia Woolf's *To The Lighthouse*, helps bring into focus those elements of Julian's style that concern audience. These stylistic features include what Auerbach calls a 'multipersonal representation of consciousness', the disintegration of the continuity of exterior events, and the use of layered time strata.[16] Unlike in stream-of-consciousness narrative, however, the narrator of a multipersonal representation of consciousness does not claim authority over her subject matter:

> [T]he writer as narrator of objective facts has almost completely vanished ... the author at times achieves the intended effect by representing herself to be someone who doubts, wonders, hesitates, as though the truth about her characters (or subject) were not better known to her than it is to them or to the reader.[17]

Auerbach distinguishes Woolf from other modernists such as Flaubert, who 'with his knowledge of an objective truth never abdicated his position as the final and governing authority'.[18] Auerbach's modernist writer further abandons a sense of teleology, preferring to

> render the continuous rumination of consciousness in its natural and purposeless freedom ... he submits much more than was done in earlier realistic works to the random contingency of real phenomena; and even though he winnows and stylizes the material of the real world ... , he does not proceed rationalistically, nor with a view of bringing a continuity of exterior events to a planned conclusion.[19]

Auerbach demonstrates how Woolf, while telling a narrative in one time, interweaves three excurses from different times and places. Finally, he describes how the relationship between inner and outer is obscure in Woolf, where 'the exterior events have actually lost their hegemony' and, instead, 'serve to release and interpret inner events'; this is in contrast to writers of an earlier period for whom, in his view, 'inner movements preponderantly function to prepare and motivate significant exterior happenings'.[20] In Woolf, 'The stress is placed entirely on what the occasion releases, things which are not seen directly but by reflection'; the reader is immersed in a 'layered structure of a consciousness engaged in recollection'.[21]

Whilst Auerbach notes that many male writers differ from Woolf, in that they

---

(Oxford, 2002), pp. 383–457. I shall focus more specifically on the cinematic animation and movement of Julian's images.

[16] Eric Auerbach, 'The Brown Stocking', in *Mimesis: The Representation of Reality in Western Literature* (Princeton, 1953), pp. 536 and 545.

[17] Ibid., pp. 534–5.

[18] Ibid., pp. 535–6.

[19] Ibid., p. 538.

[20] Ibid., p. 538.

[21] Ibid., pp. 541 and 542. Auerbach uses this phrase to describe Proust, but it seems especially applicable to Julian.

tend to display 'unipersonal subjectivism' and almost always control their narrative, bringing it to a clearly sighted end,[22] what he fails to recognize is that the doubtful, wondering, non-teleological, non-hegemonic style he describes is not particularly the province of male writers; nor is it exclusively modern, but rather one that occurs in numerous women writers – and even long before Woolf's time, in the writing of Julian of Norwich. Auerbach also fails to discuss how such a style is intimately connected to a radical understanding of audience.

While there are, of course, significant differences between Woolf and Julian, not least the fact that Woolf wrote novels and Julian an autobiographical account of a mystical encounter, the two authors have in common a number of stylistic attributes that have particular implications for an understanding of the author's relationship to her audience. In both cases, the author grants the reader as much agency, control or understanding as she herself has, while at the same time sharing with us the depth and intricacy of her own thought. Using Auerbach's discussion as a guide, I shall briefly delineate further specific aspects of Julian's style that have particular implications for her shaping of her audience.

Firstly, Julian, like Woolf, manipulates time in such a way that she focuses upon what Auerbach calls the 'symbolic omnitemporality of an event fixed in a remembering consciousness'.[23] Where Woolf creates a multipersonal consciousness through the presentation of characters whose mental worlds merge with one another, Julian does so by offering us multiple viewpoints on her vision. Julian's work is usually understood as progressing over time from a short, naïve account of a vision that was written down fairly close to the events to a long, measured, more theologically complex 'revelation' formulated and written down after long years of meditation, study and reflection. The later version should not, however, be considered a replacement of the earlier version; rather it is an amplification of it, as Barry Windeatt demonstrates clearly in his essay included here. The two accounts together produce multiple perspectives that ultimately dislodge the authority of the narrating 'I', transferring the task of producing the meaning of the events into the hands of the audience.

Julian's style in both versions, when the two are considered both as a whole and individually, is fundamentally dilatory – a stylistic attribute often associated specifically with the feminine.[24] When Julian returns to an aspect of her vision in the long version, she does so only to dilate it, that is, to add additional perspectives to it, or more precisely, to broaden the vision of it so as to be more inclusive. Neither account takes primacy over the other; rather the Long Text simply fills out one moment of consciousness. For example, in the Short Text she describes how 'I sawe the rede blode trekille downe fro under the garlande alle hate, freshlye, plentefully, and livelye, and methought that it was in that time that the garlonde of thornes was thyrstede in his blessede hede' (*Vision*, 3.10–12). It is not until the seventh chapter of the long version that she expands upon the bleeding:

---

22  Ibid., p. 536.
23  Ibid., p. 544.
24  See, for example, Patricia Parker's paradigmatic discussion of this attribute in her *Literary Fat Ladies: Rhetoric, Gender, Property* (London and New York, 1987), especially pp. 8–36.

> And in alle that time that he shewd this that I have now saide in gostely sight,
> I saw the bodely sight lasting of the plentuous bleding of the hede. The gret
> droppes of blode felle downe fro under the garlonde like pelottes [...] The plentu-
> oushede is like to the droppes of water that falle of the evesing of an house after a
> grete shower of raine, that falle so thicke that no man may number them with no
> bodely wit. And for the roundhede, they were like to the scale of hering.
>
> (*Revelation*, 7. 9–17)

The vision itself has not changed; she has simply attempted to capture again its
intensity by amplifying her rhetorical range. Even within the Long Text alone,
her methods are dilatory. Her meditation in Chapter 51 on the lord/servant
image returns to the image again and again to look at it from different angles,
considering placement of the figures, then the colours, then the clothing. Dilation creates the sense that Julian's visions can never fully be recounted. Her style
enacts the openness she wishes to create as she invites the audience to join with
her in deepening meditations on the multiple possible interpretations generated
by the vision before us. Indeed, all the aspects of Julian's style I wish to discuss
here might be gathered under the general term of dilation, for Julian's fundamental impulse is to open her visions wide.

The seemingly repetitious spiral-like structure of Julian's argument furthers
her desire to dilate her account so that the audience is drawn into her visions
as if they were happening before them. Windeatt describes the frustrations of
seeking a clear narrative structure in her work:

> The text apparently maintains a relatively straightforward narrative for roughly
> its first half, although already in the thirteenth showing, Julian is moving into
> digressive reflection and losing the thread of her narrative of a single experi-
> ence ... Julian's insertion of this later reflective vision within the continuum of
> her original account represents ... an exploration of problems as they suggest
> themselves regardless of self-conscious artistic constraints of form, symmetry and
> narrative continuity ... A sense of its own narrative continuity no longer controls
> the book, the first text has been turned inside out by those pressures ... Instead,
> the narrative of the original one day's visionary experience is held in fractured
> form within what is now the real continuum of the meditations on the visions.
> This continuum is itself unconnected with specific time or space since is it the
> product of Julian's whole intervening period of contemplation.[25]

Julian seems simply to be losing the thread and lapsing into repetition.[26] But
repetition is not accidental to her style; rather repetition enhances the immanence of Christ's meaning that she strives to recreate for her audience.

Julian not only violates temporal order, but also linear order. She often tells
us, for example, that there are six things, or three parts, or five aspects, but
she rarely completes the enumeration and the lists merge, blend and replicate
themselves with subtle alterations. Julian's shattering of linear logic reinforces

---

[25] Barry Windeatt, 'The Art of Mystical Loving: Julian of Norwich', in *The Medieval Mystical
Tradition in England: Exeter Symposium I*, ed. Marion Glasscoe (Exeter, 1980), pp. 55–71 (58–60).
My interest in Julian's style was inspired long ago by this wonderfully perceptive early essay
by Windeatt.

[26] Windeatt discusses Julian's repetitiousness: ibid., p. 62.

her refusal to claim authority over her readers and further reflects her assumption that understanding is reached by a continual process of analysis of each moment that will always be in flux. Julian furthermore does not exhibit a clear sense of boundary between herself and her readers.[27] Indeed, it is Julian's aim to dissolve boundaries altogether to create a community which, although made up of discrete individuals, is a unified whole.

By maintaining multiple chronological perspectives at once, Julian aims to integrate the past, present and future into a single immanent moment ever-present before her and her audience. As Windeatt writes, 'The showings are recorded in the past tense, but the meditations are expressed in a present tense that is timeless and that opens out into infinity to reflect in syntactical patterns the purposes of God'.[28] Teaching, understanding and revelation also occur simultaneously; as she writes of her contemplation of the Lord/Servant parable: 'The furst is the beginning of teching that I understode therin in the same time. The secunde is the inwarde lerning that I have understonde therein sithen. The third is alle the hole revelation, fro the beginning to the ende [...] And theyse thre be so oned, as to my understanding, that I can not nor may deperte them' (Revelation, 51.64–68). Watson aptly calls this technique her 'trinitarian hermeneutic',[29] and what this stylistic technique does for the audience is to place it with Julian at the centre of the immanence she wishes to recreate. She famously ends her work by proclaiming that her work 'is begonne by Goddes gift and his grace, but it is not yet performed' (Revelation, 86.1–2), and surely it is to be performed not just by Julian, but also continually by her audience.

Just as Woolf inhabits a narrative voice that doubts and wonders, Julian's narrative voice both wonders and hesitates to claim final or complete knowledge of the events she presents. For example, after her discussion of the Lord/Servant parable, Julian stresses the partial nature of her understanding of her vision: 'In this that I have now saide was my desyer in perty answered, and my grete fere somdele esed' (Revelation, 53.7–8).[30] Her understanding is limited and her quest for understanding never-ending. Despite her optimistic assurance of a community where she, her audience and Christ are all one, her knowledge is only partial, as she indicates in her repeated use of the word 'pertye'. Like Woolf, Julian provides partial glimpses of the truth – never the whole, never the definitive. Her stress on the incompleteness of her vision reveals her humility at the same time that it indicates her belief that truth is found only from the perspective of the collective. In her claim that 'alle shalle be wele, and alle maner of thinge shalle be wele' (Vision, 13.61), Julian reiterates the importance of creating a whole, both by acknowledging the variety of the particular (all manner of things) and by embracing it in an inclusive whole (all).

Most importantly, she repeatedly subordinates her judgment of the revelations to that of the reader while at the same time granting final interpretive authority

27  Windeatt discusses Julian's relationship to her readers: ibid., p. 65.
28  Ibid., p. 68.
29  Nicholas Watson, 'The Trinitarian Hermeneutic in Julian of Norwich's Revelations of Love', in Julian of Norwich: A Book of Essays, ed. Sandra McEntire (New York, 1998), pp. 61–90.
30  Windeatt points to this passage as a sign of Julian's lack of confidence and uncertainty in 'Art of Mystical Loving', p. 63.

to God: 'But I trust in our Lord God almighty that he shall, of his goodnes and for your love, make you to take it more ghostely and more sweetly than I can or may tell it' (*Revelation*, 9.26–8). In contrast, in keeping with Auerbach's description of a male author in control of his narrative who is ever-present as a guiding teleological force, the author of *The Cloud of Unknowing* sprinkles his narrative with hortatory commands and inserts his own authoritative voice in phrases such as 'I think I know that', 'I deem it better that you think'.[31] In a privileged relationship to his subject matter, he has more knowledge than his readers despite the fact that he acknowledges the incompleteness of his knowledge in the face of God. Julian, however, deliberately subordinates herself to her readers:

> Alle that I saye of myselfe, I meene in the persone of alle mine evencristene [...] And therefore I preye yow alle [...] that ye leve the behaldinge of the wrechid sinfulle creature that it was shewed unto, and that ye mightelye, wiselye, lovandlye, and mekelye behalde God, that of his curtays love and of his endles goodnes walde shew generalye this vision in comforthe of us alle'. (*Vision*, 6.1–7)

Julian is present only as one who facilitates, but does not mediate, a direct connection between the reader and her subject matter, God. She herself dissolves in the face of what she presents.

Julian's recurrent diction referring to human unity serves her desire to dissolve the boundary between herself and her readers in the creation of a universal 'we'. The most frequently used words are 'all', 'love', 'oneing', 'general' and 'common', implying that Julian's work is not for any one individual, but for everyone, for the general, and her concept of the general is of a community joined by love, a community 'oned'. In a discussion of the 'publication' of Julian's work, Riddy argues in this context: 'This private-public divide – special versus general, singular versus common – is not spatial: it does not have to do with accessibility versus inaccessibility, or with hidden versus disclosed; it has to do with "what is individual or pertains only to an individual, versus what is collective."'[32] Julian stresses her intention to recount her visions for the profit of the general of which she is a part: 'And so is my desire that it shulde be to everilke manne the same profitte that I desirede to myselfe, and therto was stirred of God in the firste time whan I saw itte, for it is common and generale, as we are all ane. And I am sekere I sawe it for the profitte of many oder' (*Vision*, 6.13–16).

Julian's repetitive use of the self-negating term 'nought' might suggest her desire to enter into an apophatic form of mystical union with Christ, as Vincent Gillespie and Maggie Ross have argued.[33] But if we look closely at her particular use of this word, she seems to wish to emphasize her desire for the dissolution of

---

[31] See *The Cloud of Unknowing and Related Treatises on Contemplative Prayer*, ed. Phyllis Hodgson, *Analecta Cartusiana* 3 (Exeter, 1982).

[32] Riddy, ' "Publication" before Print', pp. 44–5.

[33] Vincent Gillespie and Maggie Ross, 'The Apophatic Image: The Poetics of Self-Effacement in Julian of Norwich', in *The Medieval Mystical Tradition in England: Exeter Symposium V*, ed. Marion Glasscoe (Cambridge, 1992), pp. 53–77.

mediation between herself, her audience and God rather than desire for dissolution of herself alone. As she says:

> I say not this to them that be wise, for they wit it wele. But I sey it to you that be simple, for ease and comfort; for we be alle one in love [...] For if I looke singulery to myselfe I am right nought; but in general I am, I hope, in onehede of cherite wth alle my evencristen. (*Revelation*, 9.2–8)

'Noughting' herself leads her to merge not just with God, but also with everyone who together make up God. Furthermore, that dissolution of self takes place not by denying the world but by embracing it. Julian's meditations are thus quite different from the negative theology advocated in *The Cloud of Unknowing*, in which all earthly things are to be forgotten in the quest for union with God, for, in her vision, things of the earth are always before her. As Gillespie and Ross point out: 'Julian here emphasizes once again that the way (but not the means) to apophatic union is through our bodies and created things, not by rejecting or destroying them.'[34] She does not leave this world behind but rather seeks to show how the world is always already infused with God's meaning. Her noughting, therefore, is paradoxical for she wishes first to dissolve the distance between herself and her audience and then the distance between that larger whole and God. Ultimately her dissolution of her singularity into the general is what allows her to join with Christ.

The familiarity, simplicity and accessibility of Julian's quotidian imagery further attempts to bring her audience closer to her visions. She compares Christ's blood to the scales of a herring and the flowing of the blood to plenteous rain from the eaves. As other contributors also pointed out, the hazelnut is her most famous image:

> And in this, he shewed me a litille thinge the quantite of a haselle nutte, lygande in the palme of my hande, and to my understandinge, that it was as rounde as any balle. I lokede theropon, and thought: 'What maye this be?' And I was answerde generaly thus: 'It is alle that is made.' I merveylede howe that it might laste, for methought it might falle sodaynlye to nought for litille. And I was answerde in mine understandinge: 'It lastes and ever shalle, for God loves it. And so hath alle thinge the beinge thorowe the love of God'. (*Vision*, 4.7–13)

Julian develops this image by comparing the hazelnut to the Virgin Mary who, despite her 'created littleness', was chosen as God's handmaiden. Through this comparison, Julian invites anyone, even those who consider themselves too humble or too sinful to participate in God's love. She particularly grants the woman writer and the woman reader legitimacy by showing how even those considered little and inferior, like Mary, might be especially chosen by God. At the same time, by casting herself as ceaselessly restless in her desire for God, she acknowledges those who have not yet found grace and stresses that everyone must actively strive to participate in God's love.

In the development of this image, as so often throughout her work, Julian

---

[34]  Ibid., p. 75 n. 49.

blurs the distinction between outer and inner events. She begins by contemplating an external object and then moves inward into her spirit. She asks a question 'in her mind', but we do not know whether she receives an answer externally or internally. She then tells us her next question is answered in her understanding. This movement from the external to an inner space of the soul, from a bodily sight to a 'gastely' reinforces her dissolution of boundaries in her creation of a whole infused with God; God is always already inside and outside and both within and without her and us.

It is not only the content of Julian's images that is significant for defining her relationship to her audience, but it is also the very notion of the image itself, for to Julian, imagery takes precedence over analysis or interpretation in what Roland Maissoneuve calls her 'symbolic vision'.[35] Although critics have observed that the use of concrete, sensual imagery is common in the work of late medieval mystics such as Richard Rolle, and especially in that of female mystics, Julian's interest in the image is distinctive in that it is predominantly visual, and more precisely cinematic.[36] Discussing the difficulties Julian faced in 'turning shewing into writing', Windeatt concludes that her 'cinematically vivid, montage-like series of images and impressions, sensations and heard words, is so singular and deconstructive of traditional expectation as to pose real challenges to interpretation.'[37] Julian wishes us to observe and experience with her exactly what she observes without mediation.

Julian's account of her experiences begins with the contemplation of an image, the cross, and what emerges from that sight is her 'showings', events that have both physical and spiritual meaning, but which are repeatedly based on visual perception. Julian asks for only one showing, a 'bodilye sight, wherein I might have more knawinge of bodelye paines of oure lorde oure savioure, and of the compassion of oure ladye, and of alle his trewe loverse that were belevande his paines' (*Vision*, 1.13–15). Julian wishes to be present at Christ's Passion. Such a desire is in keeping with literature written for female contemplatives, such as *Ancrene Wisse* or Aelred of Rievaulx's 'Letter to his sister on the Reclusive Life', which urge the female contemplative to place herself within the Passion, to observe Christ's suffering first-hand with Mary. Whether we name her work 'showings', 'visions' or 'revelations', the importance of the word Julian uses repeatedly herself, 'showing', should not be underestimated. It is not until the Long Text that we learn that she had sixteen showings specifically; in the earlier text one showing blurs into another and the divisions between them are unclear, a confusion which contributes to her habit of dilation for, in the end, it is a single but all-inclusive vision that matters, one that embraces potentially infinite numbers of particular visions.

[35] Roland Maissoneuve, 'The Visionary Universe of Julian of Norwich: Problems and Methods', in *The Medieval Mystical Tradition in England: Exeter Symposium I*, ed. Marion Glasscoe (Exeter, 1980), pp. 86–98 (87).
[36] See Wolfgang Riehle's discussion of these features in his *The Middle English Mystics* (London, 1981).
[37] Windeatt, 'Julian of Norwich', p. 73.

Julian's visual imagination begins with a description of a static image in what Windeatt calls 'quasi-photographic detail', and then the image moves:[38]

> The persone sette the crosse before my face, and saide [… ], 'Loke thereupon, and comforthe the therewith in reverence of him that diede for the and me.' [...] I assended to sette mine eyen in the face of the crucifixe [...] After this my sight begane to faile, and it was alle dyrke aboute me in the chaumber, and mirke as it hadde ben night, save in the image of the crosse that helde a comon light, and I wiste nevere howe [...] But in this I desirede never ne bodely sight ne no manere shewinge of God, botte compassion [...] With him I desirede to suffere [...] And in this, sodaynlye I sawe the rede blode trekille downe fro under the garlande alle hate. (*Vision*, 2.22–31; 3.6–10)

Julian's vision's close focus on the cross is so intense that it instigates an all-inclusive dilation of the eye such that the object itself becomes infused with light and all around it goes black. The object then takes on life and movement as it bleeds. It becomes a 'moving' image as Christ bleeds, dries out and becomes discoloured. Julian then shifts from 'bodily sight' to 'gastelye sight' through which she understands God's love.

While Julian's meditations lead her to engage with a living Christ, they begin by her consideration of images common and available to any Christian: Christ on a simple wooden crucifix, Christ discoloured, Christ bleeding, Mary mourning Christ, a lord and a servant. This differs from the visions of other female mystics where Christ appears from nowhere, engages in conversation, offers gifts (such as the ring of his foreskin), and appears in different ages and forms. Her initial vision is not paranormal. That the cross becomes infused with light and the space around it becomes completely dark might be attributed to a physiological visual disturbance. The movement of her images might themselves be slowed down into single frozen frames of familiar images of Christ in different stages of his Passion. Julian's visions are grounded in an initial observation of something in this world and emerge from her contemplation of familiar devotional objects that become defamiliarized only when they move.

Julian asserts her belief in the spiritual efficacy of devotional objects such as the cross when she states:

> Methought I wolde have bene that time with Mary Maudeleyne and with othere that were Cristes loverse, that I might have sene bodilye the passion of our lorde that he sufferede for me, that I might have sufferede with him as othere did that loved him. Notwithstandinge that I leeved sadlye alle the peynes of Criste as halye kyrke shewes and teches, and also the paintings of crucifexes that er made be the grace of God aftere the teching of haly kryke to the liknes of Cristes passion [...] noughtwihstondinge alle this trewe beleve, I desirede a bodilye sight.
>
> (*Vision*, 1.6–13)

As Watson has suggested, in this passage Julian may well be engaging with contemporary discussion about the role of images in orthodoxy, perhaps to defend herself against those who might associate her with those Lollards who

38 Ibid., p. 73.

both valorize women as preachers and deplore the veneration of images.[39] By placing the cross at the centre of her meditations, Julian joins with others in the 1380s who celebrate the veneration of devotional objects, especially the cross.[40] In addition, the passage also suggests that devotional images were an important part of Julian's experience. As well as the simple cross she makes use of other images too, a number of which bear resemblance to paintings, as Barratt and Gunn persuasively argue in their own contributions to this present volume. Sarah Stanbury, too, reminds us of the ubiquity of devotional images in this period: 'the parishes and cathedrals of Chaucer's world (late fourteenth-century England) were saturated with images, their walls painted with life-sized sequences from the lives of the saints, choir screens and pulpits decorated with images of saints and apostles, and windows glazed with scenes from both Old and New Testaments.'[41] While Stanbury here describes Chaucer's London, given Norwich's reputation in this period as an especially religiously active town, Julian's life whether in or outside the convent would have included the sight of many images. Indeed, whilst Barratt links Julian's vision of the Lord and Servant, to the *Dominus Dixit* image found in the Ormesby Psalter, I suggest that it could just as easily have emerged from her observation of a wall painting:

> I sawe two persons in bodely likenesse, that is to say, a lorde and a servant [...]
> The lord sitteth solempnely in rest and in pees. The servant stondeth before his lorde reverently, redy to do his lordes wille. The lorde loketh upon his servant full lovely and sweetly, and meekly he sendeth him into a certaine place to do his will. The sevant not onely he goeth, but sodenly he sterteth and runneth in gret hast for love to his lordes wille. (*Revelation*, 51.6–9)

After describing the position of two figures in a static tableau, Julian finds they begin to move – as if an actual pictorial image imprinted in her mind then began to take on a life of its own. Later, Julian fills out the painting by describing the landscape the two inhabit, the clothing of both and the colour – the lord's a wide blue cape, the servant's a 'whit kirtel, singel, olde, and alle defauted' (*Revelation*, 51.142). Although, as Lynn Staley has shown, this parable draws on Julian's absorption of a host of scriptural references, almost all the details of the lord/servant parable in Julian's rendering of it are visual and could have been taken from a painting.[42] Indeed, the ante-reliquary chapel of Norwich Cathedral has a fourteenth-century wall painting with a figure of Christ in a blue mantle.[43]

Throughout her account, Julian repeatedly asserts that, as with her desire to reduce the distance between herself and her audience, she wishes to be with

---

[39] Watson argues that Julian's defence of her orthodox views of imagery implies that Julian must have written that passage during a time of intense attacks on the Lollards and therefore quite later than her initial vision of 1373. See Nicholas Watson, 'The Composition of Julian of Norwich's *Revelations of Love*', *Speculum* 68 (1993), pp. 637–83.

[40] Sarah Stanbury summarizes the debate in 'Visualizing', in *A Companion to Chaucer*, ed. Peter Brown, (Malden, 2000), pp. 459–79 and refers to Tomas Brinton and Walter Hilton in this context on p. 463.

[41] Stanbury, 'Visualizing', p. 465.

[42] See Staley, 'Crisis of Authority', p. 164.

[43] See *The Shewings of Julian of Norwich*, ed. Georgia Ronan Crampton (Kalamazoo, 1994), footnote to l. 1896. I am grateful to C. David Benson for alerting me to this wall painting.

Christ without anything between herself and the object of her sight: 'For to I am substantiallye aned to him I may nevere have full reste ne varray blisse: that is to say, I be so festenede to him that thare be right nought that is made betwyxe my God and me' (*Vision*, 4.16–19). Just as she wishes to diminish her own mediatory role between herself and her audience, she emphasizes that her vision was directly from God without mediation: 'it was himselfe that shewed it me, withouten any meen' (*Vision*, 3.14). This desire is in keeping with her comment about devotional objects – it is not that she wishes to do away with images, but rather that she wishes to go *through* the image to the thing itself – Christ – without the mediation of an object or a painting, without even the mediation of the eye.[44]

Of the many features of Julian's style that shape her relationship to her audience, it is finally her visual imagination that most significantly determines the kind of audience she engages. Reinforced by her repetitive use of the words 'shew' and 'behold', Julian asks the reader to join her as a witness of an event – to be shown something rather than to be told about it; and her 'modernist' stylistic strategies, including her self-effacement, her presentation of herself as doubting, hesitating or wondering, her violation of linear teleology, her layering of time strata, are all designed to produce that witnessing. On the one hand, she acts like a film director, deliberately 'splicing, pacing, shaping what has been seen, and creating continuity in her edited later version'.[45] On the other hand, in her commitment to the apophatic, to 'noughting', Julian works to dissolve her directorial role and the distance it implies between self and other. Julian, finally, is not just modernist in her style but post-modern in her cinematic imagination, an imagination that both creates and embraces an audience which is one and the same with herself.[46] In this regard, she makes a strenuous spiritual demand upon her audience – to respond, interpret and act directly and without assistance, upon the vivid showings before them.

---

44  Here, consciously or otherwise, Julian appears to engage with late medieval discussions regarding vision, which argued that objects themselves emitted rays ('species') which interacted with rays emitted from the eye (extramission and intramission). Ockham, however, rejected the doctrine of the multiplication of 'species', because 'for him the species in the medium would constitute an obstacle to vision of the object from which the species radiated'. See Alexander Broadie's review of Katherine H. Tachau's *Vision and Certitude in the Age of Ockham: Optics, Epistemology and the Foundations of Semantics, 1250–1345* in *Speculum* 65, 4 (1990), pp. 1061–3 (1062). For a superb discussion of the debates about nature of optics in the period see Suzannah Biernoff, *Sight and Embodiment in the Middle Ages* (New York, 2002). Whether or not she knew of these optical theories, Julian nonetheless rhetorically strives to recreate such directness of vision.

45  Windeatt, 'Julian of Norwich', p. 73.

46  I would like to thank Nicholas Watson for answering questions about Julian I had at the beginning of this project, Alexander Stewart for discerning comments about the manuscript contexts, Karen Jacobs and Stephen Shepherd for stimulating discussions about contemporary visual theory, Sarah Stanbury and Holly Crocker for helpful advice about medieval vision theory and Jennifer Jahner, Karen Jacobs, Gerda Norvig, Karen Robertson and Jeffrey Robinson for discussions about the essay as a whole.

# 12

## Space and Enclosure in Julian of Norwich's
## A Revelation Of Love

### LAURA SAETVEIT MILES

> A writer's domestic interior opens a window onto both author and text, reminding us that what we may at first perceive to be the timeless and universal truth of writing cannot be so neatly extricated from the complex particularities of its spatial and material origins.[1]

As much as a person is the product of her surroundings, her interiors and her movements, so a text is shaped by the space in which it was composed. We know, because she tells us, that Julian experienced her visions in May 1373 while resting in a sickbed. We do not know where she wrote her first account of those visions, the Short Text of *A Vision Showed to a Devout Woman*, finished in the 1380s, perhaps later. By the time she was fifty she was enclosed in an anchorhold, and this is where we know she composed the Long Text, *A Revelation of Love*.[2] In the case of this second, longer text, the link between 'inner mind and inner dwelling'[3] is unavoidable: *A Revelation of Love* cannot be extricated from the space of the anchorhold in which it was written any more than Julian could have been once she was ritually enclosed in the 'domestic interior' of her cell. Yet for Julian the relationship between text and the 'theater of composition'[4] is complicated by the presence of another interior beyond inner mind and inner dwelling. Her divine visions, beginning with the core experience of May 1373, became their own experiential world which could be returned to in her mind and by means of her written accounts over the next forty-odd years, and they likewise contained within themselves distinct structures of interiority. The domestic interior of the anchorhold is thus joined by visionary space as a valuable pair of windows onto an author about whom we know so little.

Other essays in this Companion focus on the historical and social implications of Julian's enclosure in the anchorhold or on the meaning of the images

---

[1] Diana Fuss, *The Sense of an Interior: Four Writers and the Rooms that Shaped Them* (London, 2004), p. 2.

[2] The time-line of Julian's visions and writings is explained in *The Writings of Julian of Norwich: A Vision Showed to a Devout Woman and A Revelation of Love*, ed. Nicholas Watson and Jacqueline Jenkins (Turnhout, 2006), pp. 1–4. All references to *A Vision* and *A Revelation* will be taken from this edition and will be cited by section/chapter and line number.

[3] Fuss, *Sense of an Interior*, p. 1.

[4] Ibid., p. 1.

in the Long Text, which was composed within that setting; my own purpose, however, is to concentrate on the intersection of the two. This essay, therefore, will consider the Long Text as a product of the anchorhold and examine how it negotiates a tripartite system of enclosures: the physical space of the anchorhold, the visionary space of the revelation and the authorial space of the text. How do these three spaces create or influence each other? How can we better understand Julian's physical enclosure as an anchoress by means of the visions' enclosing images, and better understand the visions' enclosing images by means of her physical enclosure? In exploring these questions, this essay will evaluate Julian's physical relationship to her community as an anchoress, her theological relationship with God and mankind as expressed in the spatial images of her visions, the extent to which the effects of anchoritic enclosure are exhibited in the Long Text and, lastly, Julian's unique use of visionary space when compared to texts written by other medieval visionary women.[5] As I will demonstrate, an understanding of *A Revelation of Love* as a product of the anchorhold is crucial to a nuanced interpretation of the spatial imagery in Julian's visions, and the key to comprehending how she is able to include so warmly her fellow Christians – her 'evencristen', as she refers to them, those saved souls of humanity – within her theology.

When the anchoress was enclosed in her cell with the binding power of her vow and the words of the funeral rite, she entered a space not of this world.[6] Her new room was a transitional space between earth and heaven, between church and community, a private fortress which she could not leave, nor could anyone enter – except God. The anchoress replaced any former worldly duties such as child-bearing and house-keeping with an ascetic life of prayer and penance under the keen eye of Christ. Yet, though she was dead to the world, her cell's physical attachment to the main parish church meant that she was also paradoxically trapped at the bustling centre of the very world she had rejected. Unlike the nun who tended to seclude herself in a rural convent, the late-medieval anchoress was a true 'urban recluse'. As one Latin dictionary defines it, *reclusio qua quis ad vacandum Deo in cella se includit* ([reclusion is] the seclusion whereby someone encloses himself or herself in a cell in order to be free for God).[7] This freedom for God was a privilege which connected the anchoress even more intimately with her parishioners, as she was expected to use that divine access to bring a new sense of holiness to the heart of the community. She accepted the spiritual responsibilities of praying for their souls, providing counsel and serving as a model of extreme sanctity; in return, the community often supported her with bequests and gifts. Thus the anchorhold could have provided for the medieval

---

5   I explore several of these angles in 'Julian of Norwich and St Bridget of Sweden: Creating Intimate Space with God', in *The Rhetoric of the Anchorhold: Place, Space and Body within the Discourses of Enclosure*, ed. Liz Herbert McAvoy (Cardiff, 2008), pp. 128–40. Some sentences have been adapted from that analysis, and I would like to thank University of Wales Press for permission to reuse this material.

6   For detailed analysis beyond this brief overview, see Grace M. Jantzen, *Julian of Norwich: Mystic and Theologian* (New York, 1987) and Anneke B. Mulder-Bakker, *Lives of the Anchoresses: The Rise of the Recluse in Medieval Europe* (Philadelphia, 2005).

7   Charles Ducange, *Glossarium Mediae et Infimae Latinitatis* (Paris, 1842), vol. 5, p. 620; cited and translated by Mulder-Bakker, *Lives of the Anchoresses*, p. 6.

holy woman a potentially liberating option of living symbiotically instead of antagonistically within society, of escaping from but not shirking humanity, and of enjoying the Church's sanction to follow Christ without fear.[8]

A helpful way of thinking about the complexities of the anchorhold space is to think of it as a paradigmatic example of Michel Foucault's 'heterotopia', an 'effectively enacted utopia' which adheres to five principles, of which the last three are particularly significant.[9] The first of these three principles, which states that 'the heterotopia is capable of juxtaposing in a single real place several spaces, several sites that are in themselves incompatible',[10] helps to explain how, within Julian's anchorhold in particular, there existed simultaneously a site for heaven on earth as well as a site of visionary (re-)experience that achieved an intimacy with God otherwise unreachable in this world. While, according to the next principle, a 'heterotopia begins to operate at full capacity when men arrive at a sort of absolute break with their traditional time',[11] the anchorhold similarly brings the anchoress out of marketplace time into her own 'hetero-chrony' of God-time: a mélange of liturgical schedule, personal time of life and death, and universal eschatological time. For Julian, we can also add to these the time of her vision and the time of writing.[12] And, according to Foucault's final principle, 'heterotopias always presuppose a system of opening and closing that both isolates them and makes them penetrable,' but usually 'the heterotopic site is not freely accessible like a public place'. Moreover (and, perhaps, most pertinently here), often 'the individual has to submit to rites and purifications'.[13] This 'system of opening and closing' highlights the anchorhold's unique contradiction of isolated yet centralized physical space coexisting with penetrable spiritual space, a contradiction brilliantly reconciled by a text which speaks with a truly heterotopic voice from within the anchorhold itself.

How Julian felt about this seeming paradox of physical isolation at the centre of society can be better understood when it is paralleled with another range of spatial paradoxes contained in her visions. Many of the most powerful images Julian presents in her texts invoke complex constructions of space as a theological medium for representing the relationship between the individual soul and the divine, between all of humanity and the divine, and between the individual soul and humanity. Far from simply static enclosures, however, these spatial images demonstrate the simultaneity of God's unknowable infinitude with the very measurable scale of human reality and the concrete world. The first such

[8]  See Liz Herbert McAvoy, *Authority and the Female Body in the Writings of Julian of Norwich and Margery Kempe* (Cambridge, 2004), pp. 70–1.
[9]  Michel Foucault, 'Of Other Spaces', trans. Jay Miskowiec, *Diacritics* 16, 1 (1986), pp. 22–7; p. 24.
[10]  Ibid., p. 25.
[11]  Ibid., p. 26. For a discussion of Julian's use of the adverb *sodenly* and the conflated timescale of her visions, see Vincent Gillespie and Maggie Ross, 'The Apophatic Image: The Poetics of Effacement in Julian of Norwich', in *The Medieval Mystical Tradition in England: Exeter Symposium V*, ed. Marion Glasscoe (Cambridge, 1992), pp. 53–77, esp. p. 60–1.
[12]  As Maurice Blanchot writes, 'to write is to surrender to the fascination of time's absence', when one approaches 'the essence of solitude', and thus 'to write is to enter into the affirmation of the solitude'. *The Space of Literature*, trans. and intro. Ann Smock (Lincoln, Nebraska, 1982), pp. 30–3.
[13]  Foucault, 'Of Other Spaces', p. 26.

spatial image is part of the First Revelation, and in the Long Text Julian describes it in this way:

> And in this, he shewed a little thing the quantity of an haselnot, lying in the palme of my hand as me semide, and it was a rounde as any balle. I looked theran with the eye of my understanding, and thought: 'What may this be?' And it was answered generally thus: 'It is all that is made.' I marvayled how it might laste, for methought it might sodenly have fallen to nought for littlenes.
>
> (*Revelation*, 5.6–11)

This 'little thing' is most easily comprehended by the human mind as something the size of a nut, a most small and quotidian object, and yet it operates on a boundless scale of metaphor: it is the seed and womb of a single plant or of all creation; it is her own enclosed anchorhold or the entire earth; it is Julian's single soul or that of all Christianity. Any assumptions of spatial reckoning based on reality are inverted in the world of the vision, where Julian is shown in a moment the world's simultaneous magnificence (as God's creation) and insignificance (in relation to God).[14] From this metaphor she learns that all of creation 'lasteth and ever shall, for God loveth it' (*Revelation*, 5.12). While the hazelnut image begins as a lesson in the smallness of the universe and the loving infinity of God, it then turns to challenge the basic premise of relative size itself: 'for till I am substantially oned to him I may never have full reste ne very blisse: that is to say, that I be so fastned to him that ther be right nought that is made betweene my God and me' (*Revelation*, 5.16–18). At this pinnacle of divine union, self and other collapse into each other and scale ceases to exist; space's 'sharp contradictions … are assimilated and destroyed', Julian having 'transcended the contradictions', as the French theorist Gaston Bachelard would explain it.[15] Space is formed and then turned inside-out, because, ultimately, space becomes ineffective as a tool for expressing the mystical relations of self to God within the vision: it is not measurable closeness, but one-ness; not physical enclosure together, but inexpressible unity.

Focused stillness also marks the hazelnut scene and builds this sense of inexpressible unity through both image and rhetoric. The effective conflation of Julian's own fixed viewing with the vision's conception of vastness, both divine and earthly, echoes her own physical stillness while immobile in the sickbed or locked in the anchorhold. Bachelard explains generally how this type of conflation is possible:

> Immensity is within ourselves. It is attached to a sort of expansion of being that life curbs and caution arrests, but which starts again when we are alone. As soon as we become motionless, we are elsewhere; we are dreaming in a world that is immense. Indeed, immensity is the movement of motionless man.[16]

---

14  Later Julian aptly describes this relationship: 'For wele I wot that heven and erth and alle that is made is mekille and large and fair and good. But the cause why it sheweth so litille to my sight was for I saw it in the presence of him that is the maker. For to a soul that seth the maker of all thing, all that is made semeth full litille' (*Revelation*, 8.9–12).

15  Gaston Bachelard, *The Poetics of Space*, trans. Maria Jolas (Boston, 1964), p. 190.

16  Ibid., p. 184.

Julian's motionlessness opens up an apophatic immensity within herself which refuses to be constrained by temporal boundaries – or even the very *thought* of size. As the 'exaltation of space goes beyond all frontiers',[17] so does the exaltation of the soul's union with God. To express this unity, however, Julian again and again returns to approachable spatial metaphors of enclosure and inclusion, metaphors which she ultimately transcends, as demonstrated in this example.

When Julian relates humanity to self and to God in her visionary space, Christ's incarnation becomes the key motif for a correspondence of the wider Church on earth with the divine. The Tenth Revelation is entirely devoted to the sight of the wound of Christ:

> With a glad chere oure good lorde loked into his side and behelde, enjoyenge. And with his swete loking he led forth the understanding of his creature by the same wound into his sid, within. And ther he shwed a fair, delectable place, and large inow for alle mankinde that shalle be saved to rest in pees and in love.
>
> (*Revelation*, 24.1–4)

God-made-man is essentially divinity brought down to earthly proportion, and Julian responds to this with a graceful reversal: Christ's human body now literally incorporates innumerable humanity. His human-scaled wound becomes a perpetual, divinely scaled womb in a way that enables her individual visionary experience to become 'large inow for alle mankinde'.[18] Though Julian is personally led into this divine interior, she willingly shares the space with her 'evencristen'. She is not alone with God; saved mankind accompanies her in both the salvific enclosing space of the vision and in the active reading experience of the text.

Visceral as the open and fleshly wound may be, Christ's humanity provides a place beyond measurement, a place that so challenges physical reality as to compel the reader to understand the theology behind the visualization. This same technique operates in a scene in Julian's Sixteenth Revelation, when Christ again leads her into a new showing:

> And then oure good lorde opened my gostely eye and shewde me my soule in the middes of my harte. I saw the soule so large as it were an endlesse warde, and also as it were a blisseful kingdom, and by the conditions that I saw therein I understoode that it is a wurshipfulle citte. In middes of that citte sitteth oure lorde Jhesu, very God and very man. (*Revelation*, 68.1–5)

In a stunning inversion of the wound's enclosure, now the human soul is infinitely expanded to 'an endlesse warde' and an entire kingdom wherein Christ sits in majesty. The space of the individual soul – just as intimate and personal as the wound in Christ's side – suddenly expands to fathomless dimensions. Not merely 'large', but *endlesse*, so incomprehensible as to enclose the Godhead. Like the hazelnut and the wound in Christ's side, the kingdom of the soul constitutes

---

[17]  Ibid., p. 190.
[18]  On images of pregnancy in Julian, see Maud Burnett McInerney, ' "*In the Meydens Womb*": Julian of Norwich and the Poetics of Enclosure', in *Medieval Mothering*, ed. Bonnie Wheeler and John Carmi Parsons (New York, 1996), pp. 157–82.

one of those 'enclosures in the text [which] paradoxically deliver the reader into a limitless landscape'.[19]

But is Julian's conflation of enclosure and expanse truly as paradoxical as it initially seems? Again, we can turn to Bachelard for an eloquent model of resolution: 'it is through their "immensity" that these two kinds of space – the space of intimacy and world space – blend. When human solitude deepens, then the two immensities touch and become identical'.[20] In Julian's texts, visionary spaces of enclosed intimacy with the divine – the life-sized hazelnut, the wound, the interior of the soul – simultaneously exist as spaces of immense 'world space', embracing all mankind, all her 'evencristen' with herself and the divine. In this way, Bachelard's idea of 'world space', a space that constitutes its own kind of inclusive universe apart from the everyday 'world', helps us to understand the space Julian creates in her visionary encounter. When Julian's solitude deepens, her visionary space is able to bear this astonishing blend of immensities. Intimacy with God does not require privacy of space in the visionary realm, because Julian is afforded a physical reality of privacy with God by means of the anchorhold, and in a related way, the sickbed. As long as the confines of the anchorhold ensure a space of continual intimacy with God, she does not need to retreat into closed-off visionary spaces to achieve this divine intimacy. Julian, focused and immobile in the sickbed or anchorhold, is not forced to struggle against her fellow Christians in order to validate her relationship with God. Instead she is centralized within and nurtured by her surrounding parish while simultaneously afforded a sense of spiritual privacy, a balance which enables humanity to become welcome in her visionary realm. The dynamic spaces of the visionary scenes discussed above exhibit this unusual theological inclusiveness; her movement into the wound in Christ's side, in particular, is depicted 'in such a way as to signify also a movement into the heart of the Church and the discovery of a union with her fellow Christians, effected through the mystical Christ in whom all are to be enclosed'.[21]

Regardless of what life Julian led before her anchoritic enclosure – whether wife, mother, nun or other – she experienced her visions in a fixed setting not unlike the anchorhold she would later inhabit.[22] McAvoy describes the relationship between the two spaces in the following terms:

[T]he sickroom becomes her figurative anchorhold; the inert body which houses her soul echoes its tomb-like walls and the only visible animation is that which emanates from the suspended crucifix before her. Thus, a homogeneity between Julian's worldly suffering in the sickroom and the otherworldly existence she will later embrace within the anchorhold is established even in the early stages of the Short Text.[23]

---

19  Gillespie and Ross, 'The Apophatic Image', p. 60. Much of the preceding analysis complements their consideration of the apophatic image in Julian's visions.
20  Bachelard, *The Poetics of Space*, p. 203.
21  Christopher Abbot, *Julian of Norwich: Autobiography and Theology* (Cambridge, 1999), p. 73.
22  Nonetheless, this essay's approach would also support the security of a cloistered life before anchoritic enclosure; for the latest arguments that Julian had been a nun, see *Writings*, ed. Watson and Jenkins, pp. 4–5.
23  McAvoy, *Authority and the Female Body*, pp. 64–5.

Thus we can perceive some of the similarities and differences between the Short Text and the Long Text: while the visionary enclosures of the hazelnut, the wound and the soul as kingdom originate in *A Vision Showed to a Devout Woman* (and thus outside the anchorhold), their subtle revision in *A Revelation of Love* distinctly reflects the walls of the anchorhold within which they were revised. The Long Text passages which we have just examined contain some significant changes from their Short Text versions. Now based in the security of the anchorhold, Julian's later Long Text rewriting of these representative images adjusts visionary space to infinitely expand around 'alle mankinde that shalle be saved' – a crucial phrase not present in the Short Text – just as the specific description of the soul where Christ sits in majesty as an 'endlesse warde' is only found in the Long Text.[24] After her enclosure in the anchorhold, Julian and her 'evencristen' to whom she so frequently refers can be conflated within the same visionary space because her role as anchoress, physically authorized and contained by the Church, dissolves personal struggle with society. This resolution of the individual will with the communal will was as integral a part of the anchoritic endeavour as the anchoress's embracing of the hardships of withdrawal from that same community. In other words, it was the demanding work of the anchoress to consider enclosure as simultaneously a source of extreme emotionally and physically challenging asceticism and as a catalyst for inner peace.

Besides the three central images of the hazelnut, the wound and the soul as kingdom, the presence of the anchorhold exhibits itself throughout the Long Text by means of several other rhetorical manipulations of space. In *A Revelation*, mutual indwelling becomes the central means of comprehending the Trinity and its relationship to mankind. The extended interpretations in the Long Text of the Fourteenth Revelation include the following description of the Trinity:

> And the depe wisdome of the trinite is our moder, in whom we are all beclosed. And the hye goodnesse of the trinite is our lord, and in him we are beclosed and he in us. We are beclosed in the fader, and we are beclosed in the son, and we are beclosed in the holy gost. And the fader is beclosed in us, the son is beclosed in us, and the holy gost is beclosed in us. (*Revelation*, 54.16–21)

Mother, lord, wisdom, goodness, trinity, father, son, holy ghost, us: with deft twists of *conversio* and *repetitio* Julian relates all of these together by building rhetorical enclosures only to instantly invert and re-enclose them, causing the mind to boggle. And so it should: these divine relationships are necessarily beyond human comprehension, but we can best understand their relation to mankind through comforting enclosures and encapsulating imagery that echo the concept of the womb, that archetypal heterotopic 'system of opening and closing'. Likewise, the knotty theological concept of the Incarnation and human 'sensual soule' receives the same rhetorical treatment, as when Julian details Christ's becoming man: 'for in that same time that God knit him to oure body in the maidens wombe, he toke oure sensual soule. In which taking – he us all

---

[24]  See *Vision*, 13.1–9 and 22.1–9.

having beclosed in him – he oned it to oure substance' (*Revelation*, 57.35–8). Here Julian looks back to the connected interpretations of the First Revelation of the wound in Christ's side and the last revelation of the soul as kingdom with Christ sitting in majesty, when

> plentuously, fully, and swetely was this shewde; and it is spoken of in the furst, wher it saide: 'We be all in him beclosed.' And he is beclosed in us; and that is spoken of in the sixteenth shewing, where he seyth: 'He sitteth in our soule'.
> (*Revelation*, 57.43–6)

Mutual indwelling of the soul and the unmade, unformed Godhead cannot be explained by metaphors bound by the rigidity of earthly space. By constantly layering, inverting and repeating images of enclosure Julian effectively convinces the reader of both the loving presence of an eternally enclosing divinity and the incomprehensibility of that presence.

Enclosure as a concept expands in Julian's remarkably fluid and elastic text to accept a vast range of metaphor: enclosure is the single seed, the hazelnut, the individual human womb, soul, Trinity, Father, Son, Holy Ghost; it is also the anchorhold, the Church, all mankind, all creation. In this stretch, however, enclosure does not break apart or fail as a concept. Instead, enclosure succeeds in suggesting both intimacy and community, both individuality and commonality, within the communion of the Christian faith.

The Long Text also reveals itself syntactically as a product of the anchorhold in its subtle erosion of strict distinctions between Julian as an individual and Christianity as a collective. Rather than project a distanced, exclusive construction of the authorial self, Julian instead uses the text to blend her own identity with that of her fellow Christians. Just as the anchorhold centres her within the community so does Julian centre herself among her 'evencristen' within the vision and presents her revelations as a message for all mankind. She expresses her stance of self-effacing charity by employing the same linguistic structures of enclosure that define the relationship between God and man within this passage from the Long Text (and also present in the Short Text):

> For if I looke singulery to myselfe, I am right nought. But in general I am, I hope, in onehede of cherite with alle my evencristen. For in this onehede stondeth the life of alle mankind that shalle be saved [...] For in man is God, and in God is alle'. (*Revelation*, 9.6–9, 13)

However, this 'onehede of charite', established in the Short Text, is taken to the next level in the Long Text, when Julian later proclaims that the showings themselves demand 'alle mankind' as an audience:

> And this shewing I toke singularly to myselfe. But by alle the gracious comfort that foloweth, as ye shalle see, I was lerned to take it to alle min evencristen, alle in generalle and nothing in specialle [...] *by me alone is understonde alle'*.
> (*Revelation*, 37.3–7; my emphasis)

'By me alone is understonde alle' functions as a kind of commandment to the reader for how to read her words, and the force of this simple phrase reshapes the entire Long Text. We have already seen how Julian prefers to write of 'oure soule' and 'oure good lorde', but in the Long Text this use of the first-person plural gains momentum: she consistently removes the terms 'me', 'mine', 'myselfe' or any such self-designating phrases that would connote a singular identity (thirty-two examples in all are omitted from the Long Text).[25] Even in the passage above she uses 'me' to point the reader towards an understanding of its replacement by the word 'alle'. These minor changes accumulate to form a startling reflection of the empowering effect of anchoritic enclosure. No longer is Julian concerned with clearly defining herself as an individual within the text apart from the wider Christian communion once she is individually secured within the anchorhold by that community. In fact, she goes out of her way to bring society into her authorial and visionary space through deliberate syntactic choices.

Those recurring minor changes do not negate or degrade Julian's presence in the text but primarily serve to positively include saved humanity. That the emendations made in the Long Text actually reflect Julian's more secure sense of self within the anchorhold is confirmed by one of the most significant extractions, a longer passage from Section 6 of the Short Text. She worries that her showings would suggest to the reader that she wrongfully seeks more than woman's share: 'botte God forbede that ye shulde saye or take it that I am a techere. For I meene nought so, no I mente nevere so. For I am a woman, lewed, febille, and freylle' (*Vision*, 6.35–7). Julian's concern, of course, is fully warranted, considering the intolerance she could well have faced in the world, although she seriously questions why that should be so: 'Botte for I am a woman shulde I therfore leve that I shulde nought telle yowe the goodenes of God, since that I sawe in that same time that it is his wille that it be knawen?' (*Vision*, 6.40–2). By taking the vow of an anchoress Julian answers her own question. Embraced by the Church, exalted for her holiness, set above the storm of gendered prejudice, she portrays her textual self as leaving that sinister insecurity and all its cultural baggage at the door. This pivotal omission from the Long Text reveals a mind, as Virginia Woolf would describe it, that has 'consumed all impediments and become incandescent'.[26] In *A Revelation of Love* we discover a polished, self-assured text in which the writer is not preoccupied by any desire 'to make the world the witness of some hardship of grievance' and, as a result, her 'poetry flows from [her] free and unimpeded'.[27] The anchorhold provides Julian with 'a room of her own', a quiet room for devotional intimacy with God, the time and space to contemplate her visions, the reliable support of the community and enough privacy to heal any grievance against society's potential hostility towards her gift.[28] Thus her

---

[25] The new 'synoptic' edition by Watson and Jenkins offers one of the easiest ways of tracking these minor changes.

[26] Virginia Woolf, *A Room of One's Own* (San Diego, 1929; repr. with foreword by Mary Gordon, 1981), p. 59: 'the mind of the artist, in order to achieve the prodigious effort of freeing whole and entire the work that is in him, must be incandescent', p. 56.

[27] Woolf, *A Room of One's Own*, p. 56–7.

[28] We might wonder if Woolf would have reconsidered her famous statement that 'to have a room of her own, let alone a quiet room ... was out of the question, even to the beginning of the nineteenth century' had she been aware of Julian and the medieval anchoritic tradition (*A Room of One's Own*, p. 52).

identity and her body merge with that of the parish church.[29] Although it might not have been possible while active in the world, as a woman dead to the world she becomes spiritually alive to it and a productive part of the union of Christ with humanity. Just as her body was sealed within the physical boundaries of the parish church, so was her own soul inextricably bonded with the unified soul of the mystical Church of her 'evencristen', a particularly incarnational realization, of course. In Julian's fully developed theology she emulates that of St Paul in Ephesians 2:14–17:

> For he is our peace, who hath made both one, and breaking down the middle wall of partition, the enmities in his flesh [...] that he might make the two in himself into one new man, making peace; And might reconcile both to God in one body by the cross, killing the enmities in himself.[30]

The cross, for Julian, is as real as the wood of her anchorhold's door, locking her in the heart of humanity and locking humanity in her heart.

We have seen how Julian's anchoritic enclosure offered a new and privileged proximity to God which enabled her to warmly welcome humanity into her visionary space of 'intimate immensity'. With one foot in the grave, as it were, she is also one step closer to heaven, a blissful expanse that unfolded within her small cell. As Goscelin of St Bertin reminds his anchoress in his *Liber confortatorius*, 'Sed cella mea quam angusta est, dicas. At celi regia amplissima est' ('Yet my cell is so narrow, you may say. But how open is the kingdom of heaven!')[31] Now that God is Julian's sole authority figure, with even the parish priest locked outside in the shadow of the divine, she truly shares in the creative freedom envisioned by Woolf: 'Indeed my aunt's legacy unveiled the sky to me, and substituted for the large and imposing figure of a gentleman, which Milton recommended for my perpetual adoration, a view of the open sky'.[32] Woolf was supported by the reliable income of her aunt's legacy just as Julian was supported by her parish, so that both women could afford to step outside of their usual social obligations and inhabit a new space of productive self-sufficiency: for Woolf, the 'open sky' of writing as a woman, for Julian the 'open sky' of the kingdom of heaven.

The significance of this privileged view shared by Julian and elucidated by Woolf is brought into crisp relief when we turn to the challenging situations of other medieval visionary women such as St Bridget of Sweden and Margery Kempe, two holy women who did not have a room of their own like Julian's anchorhold.[33] If a holy woman dwelled not under the open sky of heaven but in the shadow of society day and night leading the unregulated life of the laity, did she seek enclosed private space with the divine within the interior of the

---

29 Mulder-Bakker, *Lives of the Anchoresses*, describes European anchoresses as 'recluses living in the heart of the community, whose identity all but merged with that of the parish church', p. 12.
30 Abbott also cites this passage in *Autobiography and Theology*, p. 78.
31 Goscelin of St Bertin, *Liber confortatorius*, ed. C. H. Talbot, Analecta monastica: Studia Anselmiana xxxvii (Rome, 1955), p. 77 (my translation).
32 Woolf, *A Room of One's Own*, p. 39.
33 I explore this comparison between St. Bridget and Julian at greater length in my essay 'Creating Intimate Space with God' (see n. 5 above).

vision? How does this inverse connection between domestic space and visionary space displayed in Julian's life and writings exhibit itself in the writings of other visionary women? Margery Kempe embattled society at almost every turn of her busy life in the world. In her visionary realm, she develops an intensely intimate and individual relationship with Christ and the holy family, one that protects her from society with the strength of physical walls; Jesus says to her in a vision, 'Why art thow a-ferd whil I am wyth þe? I am as mythy to kepyn þe her in the felde as in þe strengest chirche in alle þis worlde'.[34] Like Margery, St Bridget of Sweden lived a life of struggle in the world; she, also, denies the wider Christian community a presence in her visionary world, so that in the vision it is only her and God. Christ tells her how her new allegorical 'house' with her bridegroom encloses them together alone, even with a lock that must have 'a kei to vndo it with, þe whilke sall be one hertli desire to be with God', so that they can achieve an intimate mutual indwelling wherein 'þe husband and þe wife – þat menes God and þe saule – alloneli sall have þis kei, þat God may haue fre entre to delite himselfe in þe virtuse of þe saule, and þe saule to com to God when it likes'.[35] Bridget concedes that this divine intimacy is reachable by each individual soul, but her visionary space never expands to accommodate the collective inclusion of 'all mankind that is to be saved' which is so highly developed by Julian.[36]

Julian's inclusive theology departs from the influential twelfth- and thirteenth-century anchoritic guidance texts that she would most likely have read, such as the anonymous *Ancrene Wisse* or Aelred of Rievaulx's *De Institutione Inclusarum*; in these texts humanity is not a spiritual responsibility but rather a distraction outside a window whose curtains should be defensively drawn.[37] Margery Kempe's account of her meeting with Julian, who is depicted as an accessible, kind and patient advisor, more accurately reflects the fourteenth-century shift in anchoritic practice as promoted in Walter Hilton's *Scale of Perfection*, where he urges the anchoress to give audience to her visitors as if 'an angel of hevene wolde come and speke with thee [...], soo redi and so buxom be thou in wille for to speke with thyn even Cristene whanne he cometh to thee.'[38] Ultimately, Julian's ready willingness to speak to her 'evencristen' resulted in this surviving first-hand record of the experience of an anchoress – not via a

---

[34] Margery Kempe, *The Book of Margery Kempe*, ed. Sanford Brown Meech and Hope Emily Allen, EETS o.s. 212 (Oxford, 1940; repr. 1997), ch. 42, p. 101. Virginia Raguin has written a fascinating study on Margery and space: 'Real and Imaged Bodies in Architectural Space: The Setting for Margery Kempe's *Book*', in *Women's Space: Patronage, Place, and Gender in the Medieval Church*, ed. Sarah Stanbury and Virginia Chieffo Raguin (Albany, 2005), pp. 105–40.

[35] Bridget of Sweden, *The Liber Celestis of St Bridget of Sweden*, ed. Roger Ellis. EETS o.s. 291 (London, 1987), p. 189 (26–38).

[36] It is important to remember that this type of analysis of visions in no way subjectively judges them 'good' or 'bad', or more importantly, negates the belief that these visions were sacred revelations sent by God.

[37] See, for example, pp. 20–1 (Part Two) of *Ancrene Wisse: A Corrected Edition of the Text in Cambridge, Corpus Christi College MS 402, with variants from other Manuscripts*, ed. Bella Millett. EETS o.s. 325 (London, 2005); also pp. 4–5 (cap. 4) of *Aelred of Rievaulx's De Institutione Inclusarum*, ed. John Ayto and Alexandra Barratt, EETS o.s. 287 (London 1984).

[38] *The Book of Margery Kempe*, ch. 18, pp. 42–3; Walter Hilton, *The Scale of Perfection*, ed. Thomas H. Bestul (Kalamazoo, 2000), Book 1, ch. 83, p. 124.

male mentor or a passing visitor – and *A Revelation of Love* clearly testifies to the potential for transformative, empowering rewards of a balanced anchoritic enclosure. We should listen to her voice echoing the space of the anchorhold. It might be difficult in today's world to understand the desire to be permanently 'imprisoned' in such a way, but it is helpful to remember that, at least for Julian, in that single cell flourished 'a space that is other, another real space, as perfect, as meticulous, as well-arranged as ours is messy, ill-constructed, and jumbled'.[39] In exchange for Julian's enclosure, the reader in the world is invited to partake of the eternal heterotopia of the visionary text and its perfect, meticulous, loving enclosures with the divine.

---

[39] As Foucault identifies it, a 'heterotopia of compensation': 'Of Other Spaces', p. 27.

# 13

## *'For we be doubel of God's making':*
## Writing, Gender and the Body in Julian of Norwich

LIZ HERBERT McAVOY

In her critique of traditional psychoanalytical discourse pertaining to the threat-ening body of the mother, Luce Irigaray calls for a non-phallic language which, rather than seeking to control this perceived 'threat', will embrace the 'love, desire, language, art, the social, the political, the religious' which she claims the mother brings to the world and which is denied her under patriarchy.[1] For Irigaray, in order for 'woman' to (re)discover her place within her own subjec-tivity and language, she has to cross the chasm back to the place of the mother and reject traditional oedipal configurations which sever her from that primary bond:

> We have to discover a language which does not replace the bodily encounter, as paternal language attempts to do, but which can go along with it, words which do not bar the corporeal, but which speak corporeal.[2]

The oedipal equation which, within Freudian analysis, renders sexual differ-ence primary within human culture, functions, according to Amy Hollywood's appraisal, 'to naturalize the multiple forms of power and oppression on which white, propertied, Christian, European men grounded their supremacy'.[3] In other words, the Freudian configuration of the mother leads to a fetishized, suffering and desubjectivized female body which is dependent upon traditional political and institutional authority for its meaning. I argue that it is just such an alienated and desubjectivized body which Julian herself is in possession of at the moment of her first visionary encounter with the divine 'Other', experienced during her thirty-first year as a woman in 1373. It is also this alienated body which provides the starting point for her attempts to articulate in writing both that encounter and the body which receives it, whether for her own ruminative and exegetical purposes, or with a specific readership in mind. As I shall demon-strate, the bodily nature of Julian's encounter with the divine Other compels her over the course of the next forty or so years of her life to develop a powerfully

[1] Luce Irigaray, 'The Bodily Encounter with the Mother', in *The Irigaray Reader*, ed. Margaret Whitford (Oxford, 1991), pp. 35–46 (43).
[2] Ibid., p. 43.
[3] Amy Hollywood, *Sensible Ecstasy: Mysticism, Sexual Difference, and the Demands of History* (Chicago, 2002), p. 239.

persuasive hermeneutic of the female body which will draw increasingly upon the same semiotics, or sign system, of primary unity (with the mother) as postulated by Julia Kristeva in more recent times.

This is, however, a reading of Julian's hermeneutics which some contemporary commentators have been at pains to reject, in spite of Julian's foregrounding of female and feminine bodies in her writing and the famously innovative representation of God as the universal Mother of humanity. Perhaps most comprehensive in this context was David Aers who, in a 1996 essay, wrote emphatically of Julian: '[Julian] sets aside the "feminine" matrix so extensively illustrated by Bynum ... and she does *not* present herself as a specifically "feminine" subject' (emphasis in the original).[4] For Aers, Julian actively resists aligning herself with the feminine, nor does she exploit any sense of female subjectivity for hermeneutical or authoritative purposes in the way posited by Caroline Walker Bynum in the context of other medieval holy women.[5] As a result, there is for Aers also little feminist psychoanalytical potential within Julian's writing, in spite of the important work undertaken in this area of female mysticism by Simone de Beauvoir and Luce Irigaray, for example:[6]

> There is nothing to direct readers' imaginations in the directions favored by Bynum's medieval subjects, ones that also fascinate those modern scholars who think they find convergences here with Kristeva's celebration of 'abjection'.[7]

Such an appraisal, as I shall demonstrate, tends towards the one-dimensional in its deprioritizing of the conglomeration of female-associated symbols and their multiplicity of meanings which proliferate in Julian's texts. Julian quite clearly, particularly in the early stage of her writing, regarded herself as both female and feminine, as Nicholas Watson has also effectively argued. According to Watson, 'Julian accepts the social models which define proper female activity' but does so in a way which resists 'the passivity and low prestige with which they are traditionally associated'.[8] As I shall also argue, Julian does far more than just 'accept' those social models laid down for her by traditional socio-

4    David Aers, 'The Humanity of Christ: Reflections on Julian of Norwich's *Revelation of Love*', in David Aers and Lynn Staley, *The Powers of the Holy: Religion, Politics, and Gender in Late Medieval English Culture* (Pennsylvania, 1996), pp. 77–104 (92). Aers positions much of his argument in this essay as a counterpoint to an earlier ground-breaking feminist appraisal of Julian's writing, for which see Elizabeth Robertson, 'Medieval Medical Views of Women and Female Spirituality in the *Ancrene Wisse* and Julian of Norwich's *Showings*', in *Feminist Approaches to the Body in Medieval Literature*, ed. Linda Lomperis and Sarah Stanbury (Philadelphia, 1993), pp. 142–67. See also the comments of Nicholas Watson and Jacqueline Jenkins, and Christopher Abbott as noted in my Introduction, p. 11 n. 36.
5    Caroline Walker Bynum, *Holy Feast and Holy Fast: The Religious Significance of Food to Medieval Women* (Los Angeles and London, 1987); and *Fragmentation and Redemption: Essays on Gender and the Human Body in Medieval Religion* (New York, 1991).
6    Simone de Beauvoir included an entire chapter on the subject in her *La Deuxième Sexe* (1948); for which see Simone de Beauvoir, *The Second Sex*, trans. and ed. H. M. Parshley (London, 1988), pp. 679–87. Perhaps even more influential has been the analysis of female mysticism undertaken by Luce Irigaray in her essay 'La Mystèrique', in *Speculum of the Other Woman*, trans. Gillian C. Gill (Ithaca, 1985), pp. 191–202.
7    Aers, 'Humanity of Christ', p. 102.
8    Nicholas Watson, '"Yf women be double naturally": Remaking "Womman" in Julian of Norwich's Revelation of Love', *Exemplaria* 8, 1 (1996), pp. 1–34 (7).

religious ideological stances: she continually ruminates upon them and turns to them in increasingly complex ways in her search for a suitable idiom and hermeneutic with which to express the mystical encounter. Although *per se* the mystical experience is ontologically inexpressible, nevertheless, like Julian's own, it takes place in the 'here and now' of bodily ciphering. Moreover, it is to this 'here and now' to which the mystic must eventually return and from which position she must attempt to both make sense of and articulate her experience. And, of course, the 'here and now' of Julian, as a great many of the other essays included here attest, was rooted in the urban life of late-medieval England, its politico-religious hegemonies, its entrenched gender ideologies and her own deeply gendered body. It is, therefore, precisely this 'doubleness' of the extraordinary nature of the mystic's experience and the ordinariness of her local frames of awareness (what I will identify as her 'inside–outside perceptions') – that is to say, her occupancy of a divinely privileged space within the 'here and now' – which requires a language of 'doubleness' to capture and articulate it. Such a language will attempt to foreground what Hollywood terms the 'ambiguities within bodily existence' and reflect the inescapable fact that mystical transcendence is effected 'only through the body'.[9]

Upon her own early admission in the first of her two texts,[10] *A Vision Shown to a Devout Woman*, as a young woman Julian had actively sought from God the abjection of a 'bodelye syekenes' (*Vision*, 1.2), a wish fully in keeping with accepted late-medieval ascetic practices. By means of this sickness she hoped to gain access to a fuller understanding of Christ's Passion and share with him the three 'woundes' of 'contrition', 'compassion' and 'wilfulle langinge to God' (*Vision*, 1.40–1). Significantly here, Julian also chooses to identify with the figure of Mary Magdalen ('I wolde have bene that time with Mary Maudeleyne': *Vision*, 1.6), whose experience of Christ was ubiquitously represented in the Middle Ages as both bodily and human, one predicated firmly upon her redeemed abjection as former whore.[11] Within contemporary exegetical readings of the Magdalen's relationship with Christ, however, Christ's appearance to her before all others and his instructing of her to take the news of the Resurrection to the disciples[12] also rendered her *apostolorum apostola*: 'apostless to the apostles',[13] essentially a male role but appropriable by Mary Magdalen because of her position as especially chosen messenger of the word of God. Thus, at least on the level of patriarchal discourse, Mary Magdalen was able to transcend the

[9]  Hollywood, *Sensible Ecstasy*, p. 278. My own understanding of the term 'doubleness' in this context rejects the binary normally associated with the term, preferring instead to read it in terms of the endless doublings and multiplicities which we find in Julian's writing.

[10]  All references to Julian's writing will be taken from *The Writings of Julian of Norwich: A Vision Showed to a Devout Woman and A Revelation of Love*, ed. Nicholas Watson and Jacqueline Jenkins (Turnhout, 2006).

[11]  For a detailed examination of the complexity of the Mary Magdalen figure in the Middle Ages, see Susan Haskins, *Mary Magdalen: Myth and Metaphor* (New York, 1993).

[12]  John 20:17.

[13]  On Mary Magdalen's role as apostless see Katherine Ludwig Jansen, 'Maria Magdalena: *Apostolorum Apostola*', in *Women Preachers and Prophets through Two Millennia of Christianity*, ed. Beverley Mayne Kienzle and Pamela J. Walker (Los Angles and London, 1998), pp. 57–96. See also Haskins, *Mary Magdalen*, pp. 55–94.

limitations of her formerly dangerous female body and gain access to the 'traditional' and 'institutional' configurations of power which have always operated
within the realm of the masculine and the intellectual.[14] Julian's early use of
Mary Magdalen in *A Vision*, then, suggests that from the outset of her attempts
to write she is grappling with issues of the female body and acceptable ways of
overcoming its seemingly ontological legacy of cultural problematics. This, of
course, is crucial if she is to substantiate the orthodoxy of her own bodily experiences, justify her necessary incursion upon the 'traditional' and 'institutional'
realms of male religious authority and relay her message to her 'evencristen':
'for I am a woman shulde I therefore leve that I shulde nought telle yowe the
goodenes of God, sine that I sawe in that same time that it is his wille that it be
knawen?' (*Vision*, 6.40–2).

The fact that Julian also draws upon another of the popular female saints early
in the Short Text would seem to corroborate this search for female authority and
expression:

> I harde a man telle of halye kyrke of the storye of Sainte Cecille, in the whilke
> shewinge I understode that she hadde thre woundes with a swerde in the nekke,
> with the whilke she pinede to the dede. (*Vision*, 1.36–8)

Here, the invocation of the virginal Saint Cecelia and her torturous path towards
youthful martyrdom demonstrates clearly Julian's toying with suitable role
models in order to offer a female context for – and justify – the extraordinary
account which is to follow. Like Mary Magdalen, Saint Cecelia also had a specially
configured relationship with Christ which was in no small measure dependent
upon bodily denial and the redirecting of desire from the worldly towards the
spiritual.[15] Cecelia was a particularly popular saint in the later Middle Ages
and, in the eyes of the Church, another appropriate figure for Julian as a young
woman to be identifying with.[16] This invocation of Cecelia therefore alerts her
readers to Julian's orthodoxy, further enhanced by the fact that she had learned
of the saint's life from a 'man [...] of halye kyrke'. Here Julian is most likely to
be alluding to a sermon which she had heard delivered at church and which
had had a marked effect upon her youthful and idealistic imagination. Not only
was Cecelia a young woman living within the world, as Julian quite possibly
had been at that point in her youth,[17] but her life follows the traditional – and,

---

14  Hollywood, *Sensible Ecstasy*, see n. 3 above.
15  For a discussion to the contribution made to the Short Text by the inclusion of Saint Cecelia
see Liz Herbert McAvoy, *Authority and the Female Body in the Writings of Julian of Norwich and
Margery Kempe* (Cambridge, 2005), pp. 147–9. See also Susan K. Hagan, 'St Cecelia and St John
of Beverley: Julian of Norwich's Early Model and Late Affirmation', in *Julian of Norwich: A Book
of Essays*, ed. Sandra J. McEntire (New York and London, 1998), pp. 91–114.
16  Hagan was one of the first commentators to recognise the importance of Julian's identification with Saint Cecelia, commenting, 'Saint Cecelia ... provides Julian with historical affirmation of woman's value as a voice for Christian wisdom in the face of sceptics and nay-sayers'.
'St. Cecelia and St. John of Beverly', p. 108.
17  Not all commentators are convinced about Julian's status as a laywoman prior to her
anchoritic enclosure. For a summary of the debate surrounding her early life, see my introduction, pp. 4–5 above.

on the surface of it, empowering – hagiographic pattern of the young woman's resistance to torture and abjection at the hands of a patriarch whose attempts to subdue her ardour for God fail at every juncture. Whilst rendering her, like Mary Magdalen, 'a powerful preacher, evangelist, and lover of God',[18] nevertheless the hagiographic narrative also constructs Cecelia's young, sealed and virginal body as a deeply physical and fetishized spectacle entirely dependent on the male gaze for its meaning.[19] As such, this body is denied its own female potential as (pro)creative entity, bowing instead to a male-constructed version of itself which is configured to represent an ideal, and *virile* form of piety. Thus, the body of the virgin martyr constitutes the site both of an unnuanced sexualization *and* a discursive sexual erasure which, in Irigarayan terms, is merely the product of an institutionalized attempt to grapple with the Real and harness the power of the female-maternal in service of the male symbolic order.[20] At the same time, however, it offers the male onlooker a glass through which to catch sight of male divinity and in which he himself is reflected. By controlling the meaning of the hagiographic female body in this way, the 'man [...] of halye kyrke' (and thus the Church which he represents) and others like him are also able to control human – and particularly female – access to the divine.

I would argue, therefore, that Julian's early introduction of these popular, mainstream female saints simultaneously allows her to draw on a discourse of male-approved orthodoxy whilst offering a platform to explore the female-focused (pro)creative bodily potential which is denied the female within the male Imaginary but which is central to Julian's mystical insights. Indeed, as Bynum has suggested in the context of other female mystics, 'Women drew from the traditional notion of the female as physical a special emphasis on their own redemption by a Christ who was supremely physical because supremely human'.[21] Thus, the female body, as a complex and multivalent symbol, carries the potential to 'not only reflect and shape reality but also invert, question, reject, and transcend it'.[22] As we shall see, in both texts Julian toys relentlessly with this body as symbol and as hermeneutic and as a place in which the 'complexities of desire and identification play out'.[23] Thus, whilst drawing initially upon the abject hagiographic body of the female saint in what appear to be conventional ways, Julian converts her into a type of smokescreen from behind which she is able to develop an alternative, authoritative, female-focused exegetical frame of reference – an attempt at a female Imaginary even – with that same body, redefined and predicated firmly on her own, located at its core.

In view of Julian's identification with Cecelia then, it comes as no surprise

---

18  *Writings*, ed. Watson and Jenkins, p. 64 n.36.
19  On the fetish of the female saint's body see Hollywood, *Sensible Ecstasy*, pp. 240–1. For Hollywood, the male hagiographer's subtext is a fetishization of the suffering female body as substitute for his own body and his own hopes for immortality. As such, the female is 'susceptible to fixation and reification' in a way which is 'profoundly debilitating' (241).
20  See, for example, Ingaray's 'Any Theory of the "Subject" has always been Appropriated by the "Masculine"', in *Speculum of the Other Woman*, trans. Gillian C. Gill (Ithaca, 1985), pp. 133–46.
21  Caroline Walker Bynum, *Fragmentation and Redemption: Essays on Gender and the Human Body in Medieval Religion* (New York, 1992), p. 146.
22  Hollywood, *Sensible Ecstasy*, p. 217.
23  Ibid., p. 217.

that *A Vision* moves rapidly on to recount a major, life-threatening illness experienced by its author in her thirty-first year. This illness resulted in extreme pain
and bodily abjection and endured, in apt Christic fashion, for three days and
nights, taking Julian to the brink of death:

> Ande when I was thrittye wintere alde and a halfe, God sente me a bodelye
> syekenes in the whilke I laye thre dayes and thre nightes, and on the ferthe night
> I toke alle my rightinges of haly kyrke, and wened nought tille have liffede tille
> daye. And after this I langourede further two dayes and two nightes, and on the
> thirde night I wenede ofte times to hafe passede, and so wened thaye that were
> aboute me. (*Vision*, 2.1–6)

Julian is intent from the onset to stress the severity of her illness, corroborated
also by those who are witnessing it alongside her ('and so wened thaye that
were aboute me'). Moreover, it symptomizes itself as an *intensely* bodily experience ('my sight begane to faile [...] the overe partye of my bodye begane to die
[...] Mine handes felle downe [...] my hede satylde downe on side': *Vision*, 2. 29–
35). In both *A Vision* and the longer *A Revelation* Julian's narration of this pivotal
event relies upon vivid recollection of the bodiliness of her own suffering in its
minute detail and upon seeing it from the perspective of others too, in what
aptly constitutes a type of 'double-vision'. In the Short Text particularly, she
appears to be casting herself – again like Cecelia – as affective spectacle whose
abject body is there to be 'read' by both her onlookers and her readers in full
hagiographic mode in order to prepare them for the extraordinary revelations
which are to follow. By the time she comes to revise this account in her Long
Text version, however, Julian will have no need for this type of hagiographic
smokescreen with its literary performance of the male Imaginary. Excising all
reference to Saint Cecelia from her text, she will turn instead to her own body
for the provision of a primary hermeneutic, allowing that body to speak in ways
more eloquent than those of the ultimately inadequate 'paternal language' of
traditional hagiography.[24]

   Also excised from the Long Text is Julian's representation of her own mother
who, in the Short Text, takes up a prominent position in Julian's sickroom. Here,
Julian establishes her as an archetypical *Mater Dolorosa* figure lamenting the
passing of her child and, in so doing, attaches a powerfully affective discourse
of Marian piety to the narrative of her own sickness:[25] 'My modere, that stode
emanges othere and behelde me, lifted uppe hir hande before me face to lokke
min eyen. For she wened I had bene dede or els I hadde diede' (*Vision*, 10.26–

---

[24] It is highly significant to the argument I will be making that, while erasing Cecelia from the
Long Text narrative, Julian chooses to retain reference to a series of other male saints, including
Peter, Paul and Thomas. She also introduces the lesser-known John of Beverley, whom an
extant Dutch source casts as a reformed murderer, for which see *Writings*, ed. Watson and
Jenkins, p. 236, notes on *Revelation*, 38.13–29. The only female saint whom Julian retains is Mary
Magdalen in her capacity as sexual sinner, thus removing altogether the tortured female body
as configured by male-authored hagiography as a frame of reference for her own experiences
of suffering.
[25] For a protracted analysis of the role played by the Virgin within Western culture see Julia
Kristeva's essay 'Stabat Mater', in *The Kristeva Reader*, ed. Toril Moi (New York, 1986), pp. 160–
85.

8). Read alongside the suffering hagiographic body which Julian has also been constructing in *A Vision*, such an affective moment between mother and child threatens to invoke the same fetishistic appropriation of the (m)other to which I alluded earlier in the context of the virgin martyrologies. Julian is clearly drawing upon internalized cultural discourses of ontological female suffering and ventriloquizing them textually in a less-than-subtle attempt to offer the scene an aura of traditional affective piety. The recognisably affective and specular qualities of this type of account are, however, problematized by the fact that Julian is *not* dead, merely paralysed bodily by illness and transfixed psychologically by the vision of Christ which, unbeknown to her companions and her mother, is unfolding before her own gaze. Indeed, any affect is negated by the complexity of the multiple perspectives offered by Julian at this point: her own, those of Christ, her mother, her readers. The result is a doubling and redoubling which gives rise to a tension both electric and breathlessly articulated. In effect, Julian is leaving her increasingly abject body behind in the sickroom with the onlookers whilst entering a transcendent, visionary realm. She is quite literally there and elsewhere in a way which will eventually offer her an escape route from traditional readings of her own bodily abjection.

Julian's initial articulation of these mystical experiences is both sensory and material ('I [...] sette mine eyen'; 'I sawe the rede blode'; 'I saide'; 'smoke come in [...] with a grete hete and a foule stinke'; 'I harde a bodely jangelinge'; 'I laugh mightelye': *Vision*, 2.26; 3.10; 3.14; 21.26–7; 23.3; 8.43). Paradoxically, however, she represents herself and her body as simultaneously configured by a specular logic from without *and* a transfiguration from within. She is both there and not-there; her body is both abject and transcendent. It is the convoluted doubleness of this inside–outside perception of the body which not only allows for a remarkably nuanced response to her visions but will become fundamental in the Long Text to the forging of a suitable hermeneutic for their articulation and understanding. Moreover, since the scene of its inception is the female-focused and maternalistic space of Julian's sickroom, and the female-focused and (re)productive space of her female body, it is hardly surprising at all that her primary hermeneutic will also be an intensely female and maternal one.[26] Whilst this is in full keeping with Bynum's assessment of women's special relationship with redemption via their own Christ-like physicality,[27] in Julian's hands this treatment moves way beyond mere identification with Christ or Mary: for her, a (re)productive female body can both pave the way to and articulate the redemption of a humanity which is, like its deity, reconfigured along female lines. Throughout her writing there is a sense that Julian is striving to construct a female body which functions as both metatext and semiotic framework and which, in its doubleness, will eventually overlay *and* integrate traditional 'paternal' narratives and interpretations.

If we return to the sickroom narrative of *A Vision*, we can see this fully in action: here, it is the female-focused reciprocity between the bodies of Julian and her mother within the 'here and now' of that room which provides the bridge

---

[26] This is an aspect of Julian's writing for which I have argued at much greater length elsewhere. Again see McAvoy, *Authority and the Female Body*, especially chs 2 and 4.
[27] Bynum, *Fragmentation*, p. 146.

for an articulation of Julian's transition to the mystical space. Not only does her mother's anguish merge with Julian's own physical suffering in a type of *imitatio Maria*, as I have suggested ('Herein I sawe in partye the compassion our oure ladye, Sainte Marye': *Vision*, 10.37), but, in turn, it leads Julian on to a consideration of how 'Criste and sho [Mary] ware so anede in love that the gretnesse of hir love was the cause of the mekillehede of hir paine' (*Vision*, 10.37–40). Typically, Julian's use of the verb 'anede' here is multifaceted: its obvious maternal associations within this particular context serve to deconstruct the hierarchical gender binary of male/female within the text (Christ's humanity is one with his mother's flesh) but the term is also clearly redolent with echoes of primary unity with the mother, of that maternal, pre- or extra-linguistic space identified by Kristeva as the semiotic *chora* – a space which the virgin martyrologies make such concerted effort to deny in their energetic dismembering of the material, female (pro)creative body.[28] Such a space (which Julian will later develop into a full-blown configuration of Christ as 'oure moder [in whom] we profit and encrese': *Revelation*, 58.38) is also identified by Kristeva as the pre-symbolic site of unity which underpins all human existence. As such it is ideally positioned to express the inexpressible which is unfolding before Julian's eyes, since its origins, like that of mystical unity with God, lie before and beyond language. It is also a realm which 'does not reduce the subject to one of understanding, but instead opens up within the subject this other scene of pre-symbolic functions'. It is, therefore, a specifically female space since it draws upon the (unremembered but always latent) lost union with the mother and (again recalling the there-and-not-there of Julian's mystical encounter), 'is no more than the place where the subject is both generated and negated'.[29] Thus, Julian's insight into the primary unity of Mary and Christ, brought about by the compassion of Julian's mother for her own child, invokes both a physical and a theological given which rests firmly upon all humanity's sharing of 'female' flesh. In contemplating her own abjection, she recognises in herself the mystical union of humanity with Christ by means of that same female flesh – which, like Christ, she has taken from *her* mother. Thus, from this early stage of doubling and redoubling in the Short Text, Julian is clearly reading her visionary insights in terms of the feminine and female, plumbing her own experiences of being a woman of the 'vulnerable flesh' and her relationship with her own mother for a suitable hermeneutic with which to articulate these highly complex mystical insights. In drawing on both traditional and affective models of femininity and reconfiguring their scope, Julian destabilizes their hegemony, the end product of which is the gestation of a 'new' language with which to express an intensely embodied experience of mystical unity which incorporates both male and female.

---

[28] Julia Kristeva borrows the term *chora* from Plato's *Timaeus* where it is deployed to denote an 'essentially mobile and extremely provisional articulation'. Kristeva uses it to designate the 'rhythmic' space which precedes language and the entry of the child into the Symbolic. It is where the primary and as yet unbroken bond with the mother is constituted. It therefore underpins, whilst simultaneously being denied by, language and representation. See Julia Kristeva, 'Revolution in Poetic Language', in *A Kristeva Reader*, ed. Toril Moi (Oxford, 1986), pp. 93–8 (94).
[29] Ibid., p. 95.

The Short Text, therefore, offers us the sense that Julian is experimenting with such hermeneutics of the feminine in order to provide an 'intelligible verbal translation'[30] of the ultimately extra-linguistic knowledge of divine unity to which she has been privy. Initially dependent upon the 'paternal language' of male, intellectual rationalism to provide this 'translation', she soon recognises that this language will no longer do. Pressed by her priest upon her recovery to tell him how she is feeling, Julian's answer that she 'hadde raved that daye' (*Vision*, 21.7) is redolent with self-doubt and a struggle to arrive at a logical explanation for seemingly inexplicable experiences. Her attempt to embellish this ('The crosse that stode atte my bedde feete, it bled faste': *Vision*, 21.7–8) leaves Julian so abashed and ashamed at her own inability to trust in God's revelation and articulate it in ways that might make it intelligible, that she is silenced entirely: 'Bot I couth telle it na preste. For I thoght: "Howe shulde a preste leve me? I leved nought oure lorde God"' (*Vision*, 21.13–14). Clearly, she is aware that the normal structures of rationalist language are insufficient as a means of articulating the non-rationalist experiences which she has undergone, even more so in the light of a self-doubt which is clearly predicated on traditional gender hierarchies within the confessor–woman binary and the intellectual distance traditionally posited between a 'lewed, febille, and freylle' woman and God.

Much of the Short Text, therefore, can be read in terms of a quest for a suitable means of expression which will simultaneously move beyond the rational but will also be accessible to it. Such a language of 'doubleness' emerges out of the sickroom-space where Julian herself is most 'doubled', that is to say simultaneously most 'herself' but most negated, where her subjectivity is both generated and denied. In a flash of visionary insight into primary unity with God-the-Mother ('I saw a grete aninge betwyx Criste and us': *Vision*, 10.44) she leads her readers inexorably towards the bursting forth of an inexpressible and reciprocal joy, a type of *jouissance* which is the result of this momentary vision of 'oneness' with Christ:

> And sodaynlye, me behaldande in the same crosse, he chanchede into blisfulle chere. The chaunginge of his chere changed mine, and I was alle gladde and mery as it was possibille. Than brought oure lorde merelye to my minde: 'Whate es any pointe of thy paine or of thy grefe?' And I was fulle merye. (*Vision*, 11.17–20)

This *jouissance* of 'aninge' is one which will again surface many years later in her revised text in which Julian's representation of God as Mother becomes fully formed. For Julian, 'The moders service is nerest, rediest, and sekerest: nerest, for it is most of kind; rediest, for it is most of love; and sekerest, for it is most of trewth' (*Revelation*, 60.12–14). The maternal principle operates intrinsically at all levels: it is fundamental to nature ('nerest'), it is an intrinsic component of love ('rediest') and deeply and intensely metaphysical ('sekerest'). Most pertinently, it leads us back to and towards an inexpressible joy: 'We wit that alle oure moders bere us to paine and to dying. A, what is that? But oure very moder

30  Ibid., p. 97.

Jhesu, he alone bereth us to joye and to endlesse leving – blessed mot he be!' (*Revelation*, 60.15–17). '[A]ninge' with God is thus configured by Julian in terms of a restoration of primary unity with the (m)other in a way that for Julian is again 'doubel':

> For we be doubel of Gods making: that is to sey, substantial and sensual [...] And the seconde person of the trinite is oure moder in kind in oure substantial making, in whom we be grounded and roted, and he is oure moder of mercy in oure sensualite taking. (*Revelation*, 58.32–6)

Julian's construction of a hermeneutics of the feminine able to be read within a Kristevan framework also emerges in other areas of her texts, especially in her visceral representations of Christ's body. Such representations were subject to Elizabeth Robertson's own scrutiny in 1997 in a pivotal essay regarding Julian's ubiquitous use of gynaecentric imagery such as blood flows, wombs and enclosure in both her texts.[31] As Robertson demonstrated, Julian's depiction of a suffering Christic body is much dependent upon these patterns of imagery which are, in turn, closely associated with Julian's development of a hermeneutics of the maternal feminine which I have been examining here. Let us take as one example the Short Text account of the dramatic onset of bleeding which Julian witnesses as her vision of Christ's Passion ensues:

> And in this, sodaynlye I sawe the rede blode trekille downe fro under the garlande alle hate, freshlye, plentefully, and livelye, right as methought that it was in that time that the garlonde of thornes was thrystede on his blessede hede. Right so, both God and man, the same sufferde for me. I conceyvede treulye and mightelye that it was himselfe that shewed it me, withouten any meen. (*Vision*, 3.10–14)

I choose this particular version because it fully exemplifies Julian's experimental yet multifaceted use of the image of Christ's bleeding. Adhering to the traditional affective model which Bynum has established as both feminine and female-focused, Christ's bleeding emanates from an infinitely suffering, infinitely abject, infinitely fleshly body – a body which, as we have seen, is also that of Christ's mother, Mary, and, of course, Julian herself as 'a sinfulle creature lyevande in this wreched fleshe': *Vision*, 3.17). This depiction is immediately followed by Julian's exposition of the hazelnut vision, 'a littille thinge the quantite of a haselle nutte, lygande in the palme of my hande' (*Vision*, 4.7–8) which, 'as rounde as any balle' (*Vision*, 4.8–9), can be read as both a macrocosmic world and a micro-cosmic womb.[32] Julian then explicitly brings the reader's attention back to the newly pregnant Mary as directly inherent to this gynaecentric context she is constructing here: '*In this*, God brought oure ladye to mine understandinge. I sawe hir gasteleye in bodilye lyekenes, a simpille maidene and a meeke, yonge of age, in the stature that sho was when sho conceyvede' (*Vision*, 4.21–3; my emphasis). So, what we have in the Short Text is the following equation: Julian

---

31  See n. 4 above.
32  I have argued this point at greater length in *Authority and the Female Body*, pp. 83–4. See also Liz Herbert McAvoy, 'Feminising the Body in Julian of Norwich's *Revelations of Divine Love*', *Leeds Studies in English* n.s. 33 (2002), pp. 99–113.

→ the flowing of blood → remembering her own fleshliness → vision of the hazelnut/womb → the Annunciate Mary – many of the traditional players upon the affective stage; and the equation remains the same in both texts, in spite of a series of ruminative interpolations which extend the whole account in the Long Text. Whilst one could argue conventionally, as does Aers, that this passage provides 'a vernacular version of a scholastic discourse … reasoning enquiry … [and] spiritual reading',[33] such an interpretation offers only one side of the equation and denies the complexity of the multiple perspectives from which Julian is herself operating. Julian's writing, as we have seen, consciously attempts to deconstruct such rationalist explanation, offering a network of viewpoints from which to articulate her experience for *all* her readers, whether well-versed in scholastic discourse ('them that be wise, for they wit it wele': *Revelation*, 9.2–3) or those who are 'lewed' – that is to say, uneducated and simple. We need only return to the text itself to see that, for Julian, there is no hierarchical opposition between affect and intellect, body and mind. Indeed, her integration of each of these components within her exegeses and analyses, especially in the Long Text, demonstrates quite the contrary. Time after time, she begins her meditations from and within the body as a place she experiences, knows and *can* articulate, leading her readers via that body to an understanding of her mystical insights. She is acutely aware that it is the experience of the body, whether feminine-human or masculine-human, which her readers – her 'evencristen' – will recognise and will also be able to identify with and articulate. This she does in order to pave a way towards an understanding of the very complex theological and mystical issues with which she is dealing and to produce a language ideally crafted to represent the seemingly inexplicable. In other words, wherever we want to look in her writing, Julian starts with what she knows and what she deems her readers or 'evencristen' will know, and leads them gently from the familiar to the deeply unfamiliar, whilst at the same time making it known and recognisable.[34]

This is nowhere more apparent than in the following passage from the Long Text (a passage which has been excised from all but one Long Text manuscript, perhaps by a prurient scribe) in which Julian articulates her perception of the goodness of God again in terms of human abjection:

> For God of his goodnes hath ordained meanes to help us full faire and fele. Of which the chiefe and principal meane is the blessed kinde that he toke of the maiden, with all the meanes that gone before and come after, which belong to our redemption and to our endles salvation […]
>
> Forto the goodnes of God is the highest prayer, and it cometh downe to us, to the lowest party of our need. It quickeneth our soule and bringeth it on life, and maketh it to waxe in grace and in vertu. It is nerest in kinde and rediest in grace. For it is the same grace that the soule seketh and ever shalle, tille we knowe oure God verely, that hath us all in himselfe beclosede. A man goeth upperight, and

---

[33] Aers, 'Humanity of Christ', p. 84.

[34] A useful essay which discusses this aspect of Julian's writing is Nancy Coiner, 'The "homely" and the *heimlich*: The Hidden, Doubled Self in Julian of Norwich's Showings', *Exemplaria* 5, 2 (1993), pp. 305–23.

the soule of his body is sparede as a purse fulle fair. And whan it is time of his nescessery, it is openede and sparede ayen fully honestly. And that it is he that doeth this, it is shewed ther wher he seith: 'H cometh downe to us, to the lowest parte of our nede.' For he hath no dispite of that he made, ne hath no disdaine to serve us at the simpilest office that to oure body longeth in kinde, for love of the soule that he hath made to his awne liknesse. For as the body is clad in the cloth, and the flesh in the skinne, and bones in the flesh, and the harte in the bowke, so are we, soule and body, cladde and enclosedde in the goodnes of God.

*(Revelation, 6.19–37)*

Far from being devoid of the Kristevan abject or the affective, this passage is redolent with both and, as I have argued elsewhere, the body being produced, whilst apparently default male, can also be read as a feminized one, not only in its abjection but also in its (pro)creativity.[35] The flesh which constitutes this body is again the 'blessed kinde that he [Christ] toke of the maiden'. Human flesh is Mary's flesh and Mary's flesh is God's flesh; God's goodness (love) is insepa-rable from it and, by implication, is the full realization of that flesh's procrea-tive potential. In full maternal fashion, it nurtures us in our helpless abjection, that is to say, 'in the lowest part of our need'. And it is a need, of course, that is being configured here by implication in terms of that of the underdeveloped human baby, dependent upon the mother for all bodily things and locked in a fleeting pre-separation and semiotic dependency upon her until its inevitable entry into the Symbolic (and to language) brings about permanent disruption. Here, however, Julian resists such permanent disruption of what Kristeva terms 'pre-*thetic* unity'[36] by recapturing the 'network of traces' and the 'residues of the first symbolizations' which, within poetic language, tend to enter into negotia-tion within the 'symbolic chain'.[37] For Kristeva, such traces of pre-*thetic* unity are released by the type of linguistic slippage characteristic of poetic language and which results in 'the explosion of the semiotic in the symbolic'.[38] As both Ena Jenkins and Vincent Gillespie demonstrate most cogently in their essays included after this one, Julian's texts are saturated with poetic sensibility and language, a poeticity fully in keeping with Bernard McGinn's observation about the nature of 'mystical masterpieces' quoted by Baker earlier in this volume.[39] Thus, if Julian's daring and exposed account of the defecating body is read in the context of the other 'bodily' extracts, this body carries with it the same traces of the semiotic bubbling up by means of the intensely poetic language used to configure it. Not only is the body a purse opening to spare its waste ('soule'), even that waste becomes synonymous with the beauty of the human soul (also 'soule') and, therefore, of God ('the soule that he hath made to his

---

35   See Liz Herbert McAvoy, '"...a purse fulle feyer": Feminising the Body in Julian of Norwich's *A Revelation of Love'*, *Reading Medieval Studies* 34 (2004), pp. 99–113.
36   Kristeva defines *thetic* as 'the signifiable object' which is both a 'denotation' and an 'enuncia-tion': 'Revolution in Poetic Language', p. 106.
37   Ibid., p. 118–19.
38   Ibid., p. 119.
39   'Mystical masterpieces ... are often close to poetry in the ways in which they concentrate and alter language to achieve their ends': Bernard McGinn, *The Foundations of Mysticism*, vol. 1 of *The Presence of God: A History of Western Christian Mysticism* (New York, 1992), p. xiv.

awne liknesse') via Julian's poetic gymnastics. Julian's daring and adept pun on
the word 'soule' here[40] draws an analogy – synonymy even – between the faecal
waste produced by the human body and the transcendent soul and both, therefore, become an expression of an *imago Dei*. For Julian, even the act of defecation
is a vision of God and the very waste matter the body voids itself of (like the
child the mother voids herself of during childbirth) is made, like the soul, in
the likeness of God-our-Mother. This act of human abjection, therefore, offers
the reader a further introit into the complex mystical theology of unity, in effect
another route back to the enclosed realm of the pre-*thetic* semiotic, with which
Julian completes this extract: 'so are we, soule and body, cladde and enclosedde
in the goodnes of God'.

Such a multivalent – and often startling – poeticity within Julian's writing is
far more than a linguistic category: it is integral to the structure and cadence of
her writing, to her use of complex and highly wrought 'webs of metaphor' (as
Jenkins puts it), to her construction of generic pastiche (according to Gillespie)
and to the hermeneutics of the feminine with which I have been dealing here. In
this sense, it is also fully invocative of the rhythm of the semiotic within poetic
language itself, a semiotic which underlies the written and the spoken word
and which can only ever surface in the syntactical and grammatical disruption
which is brought about by and within poetic language and its intricate conno-
tivity. As Kristeva asserts:

> Indifferent to language, enigmatic and feminine, this space underlying the written
> is rhythmic, unfettered, irreducible to its intelligible verbal translation; it is
> musical, anterior to judgement, but restrained by a single guarantee: syntax.[41]

As I have argued, Julian's poetics are firmly dependent upon such semiotics of
the 'female' and the 'feminine': firstly, as articulated overtly and traditionally
within the language and syntax of the male Imaginary; and, secondly, as Julian
develops her own treatment of them.[42] As she becomes more confident in her own
poetics, her strategic use of the female hermeneutic constitutes a veritable haemorrhaging up of the normally unaccommodated semiotic through the multiple
surfaces of her writing in what approximates a 'female Imaginary'. This semiotic
articulation provides, therefore, one of the sites identified by Hollywood as the
place where there can be an extra-Symbolic expression of fully embodied female
practices. For Julian, such 'practices' in their mystical 'doubleness', located both
in and out of symbolically configured time and space, thus render it possible
that 'endless, ceaseless, illimitable desire might be thought and lived outside of

---

[40] Edmund Colledge and James Walsh define Julian's use of the word 'soule' in this extract as
'undigested food' in *A Book of Showings to the Anchoress Julian of Norwich* (Toronto, 1978), p. 306
n. 35. Watson and Jenkins, however, gloss it as a 'meal' or 'food' (*Writings*, ed. Watson and
Jenkins, p. 142, note on ll. 29–31). The latter also concur with my own assertion in ' "…A purse
fulle feyer" ' and in *Authority and the Female Body* that the passage anticipates Julian's portrayal
of God as Mother in chs 55–62 of the Long Text.
[41] Kristeva, 'Revolution in Poetic Language', p. 97.
[42] For Irigaray, syntax is a 'double syntax' because it simultaneously has to contend with the
strictures of masculine ordering whilst dealing with the suppressed syntactical order of the
feminine. Luce Irigaray, 'Questions', in *The Irigaray Reader*, ed. Margaret Whitford (Oxford,
1991; various repr.), pp. 133–9 (134).

a phallic law of [female] impotence'.[43] In the words of Julian herself, and as if echoing these precepts:

> [O]ure lady is oure moder, in whome we be all beclosed and of her borne in Crist. For she that is moder of oure savioure is mother of all that ben saved in our savioure. And oure savioure is oure very moder, in whome we be endlesly borne and never shall come out of him. (*Revelation*, 57.40–3)

The complex conflation of 'lady', 'moder', 'we', 'Crist', 'savioure', 'him' as subjects here points towards the unity of a mystical encounter with God in which the subject is endlessly generated, defined, relinquished and negated, in which all and nothing is possible, a unity which is pre-discursive and extra-linguistic and which, like Julian's God and the earthly mother, is 'the endlesse fulfilling of all true desyers' (*Revelation*, 59.15–16). As such, it cannot be captured in any capacity within a traditionally denotive linguistic register. Indeed, it can only be approximated upon by verisimilitude or a 'connoted mimetic which raises the *chora*, the realm of the pre-*thetic*, to the level of signifier'.[44] And this holds true in both texts: there is a sense in *A Vision* that Julian is experimenting with and prising open language in order to find a suitably expressive connotive register with which to articulate her extraordinary experiences in an all-inclusive way. In the longer *Revelation* she reveals a greater sense of confidence in this new register and its ability to construct an effective hermeneutic to encapsulate the unity of divine love which she has witnessed and experienced. Thus, in the same way as she chose to erase the gendered presences of Saint Cecelia and her own mother from the Long Text account (and therefore the *overt* gendering of the *mise en abîme*),[45] what we find in their place is a feminine which has gone 'underground', as it were, and which has returned to its place of origins in the semiotic. Therefore, just as the defecating body examined above can be read as a default male humanity because of Julian's use of masculine nouns and pronouns to denote it, so also it is connotively feminine in its abjection and productivity. Just as the quick, red, fresh flow of blood which Julian witnesses in her sick-room is denotive of that emanating from a wounded male body, equally it is connotive of specifically female blood flows: the menses, the broken hymen, childbirth. Julian, of course, is characteristically exploiting both denotation and connotation at the same time here in true poetic fashion, another example of the 'doubling' which forms a crucial part of the mystical enterprise and the means of its articulation. For, in Julian's connotive universe, the bridging of binaries and the elision of their differences is ultimately productive of a third category – all

---

43  Hollywood, *Sensible Ecstasy*, p. 278.
44  Kristeva, 'Revolution in Poetic Language', p. 109.
45  The *mise en abîme* is a French critical term without suitable English equivalent which Neil Hertz has defined as 'a casting into the abyss [...] an illusion of infinite regress', a definition which would seem to fit Julian's drawing upon the semiotic well. Such an 'infinite regress' refers to the incorporation within the text or other artistic work of a symbol which replicates in miniature the larger structure, resulting in an 'unending metanymic series'. Neil Hertz, *Textual Strategies: Perspectives in Post-Structuralist Criticism* (Ithaca, 1979). For Cré's understanding of the term in the context of Julian's work, see her essay p. 124 n. 22.

that there is: 'for alle oure life is in thre' (*Revelation*, 58.25). Moreover, this 'thre' is defined by Julian in terms which she has already rendered inherently feminine in her writing: it is 'kinde', 'mercy' and 'grace'; but it is also 'oure fader […] oure moder, and […] oure lorde', which trinitarian equations are subsumed into 'oure moder in kind […] in whom we be grounded and roted' (*Revelation*, 59.34–6).

Such a remarkable and prescient collapsing of gender binaries and disrupting of traditional phallogocentric language in her representation of God as simultaneously man, woman, father, mother, masculine, feminine, bodily, spiritual and spirit, is fully productive of the type of language called for by Irigaray in the extract with which I began this essay. As a language which does not deny the corporeal but which 'goes along with it', in its facilitation of the emergence of semiotic traces within its syntactical idiosyncrasies and rhythmic pulsations, it is both anti-phallic and constructed specifically to approximate upon a vision as closely as is humanly possible. Ultimately it tells of how love, desire, language, writing, the social, the political, the religious, can – and must – 'speak woman' as well as speak man; ultimately it reinstates woman alongside man for a fully coherent expression of full humanity *and* divinity.

# 14

## *Julian's* Revelation of Love: *A Web of Metaphor*

ENA JENKINS

> And all shall be well and
> All manner of thing shall be well
> When the tongues of flame are enfolded
> Into the crowned knot of fire
> And the fire and the rose are one.
>
> T. S. Eliot, 'Little Gidding'

Influenced – perhaps unduly – by an early encounter with Julian in Eliot's *Four Quartets*, I have long read her as a poet, like Dante both a mystical poet and a theological mystic. Hinted at in *A Vision Showed to a Devout Woman*, this becomes a defining characteristic of *A Revelation of Love*[1] and, in looking at both texts as a work in progress, I have perceived both poet and poetic in process of becoming, the growth of a poet's mind as Julian seeks ways of communicating what can be told of the nature of her mystical awakening. To read *A Revelation* as a literary work is to discover a poetic which is both functional and elegant and which is the way in which seeing and seeking proceed.

As Julian makes clear, all is present in the First Revelation, albeit embryonically in *A Vision* and in a developed form in *A Revelation*, in which the full effect of transformation of being is apparent. To recognise Julian as a poet is to see that she has found within herself what Wordsworth would define as 'the feeling intellect'.[2] She writes, 'Oure faith cometh of the kinde love of oure soule, and of the clere lighte of oure reson' (*Revelation*, 55.1–12). Her poetic is one in which 'wonderfully prosaic images'[3] develop organically within a structured context. An aesthetic of the ordinary, originating in *A Vision* in the image of the hazelnut, frees her to articulate a recognition that 'spirituality coinheres in material reality',[4] in everyday life – in her own kitchen, her garden, her family. To read *A Vision*, therefore, is to be drawn into an extraordinary experience; to read *A Revelation* is to enter a vividly realised world, startling in the simplicity

---

[1] *The Writings of Julian of Norwich:* A Vision Showed to a Devout Woman *and* A Revelation of Love, ed. Nicholas Watson and Jacqueline Jenkins (Turnhout, 2006). All quotations are from this edition, identified by section/chapter and line.

[2] William Wordsworth, *The Prelude* (1805), Book XIII, l. 205.

[3] Rowan Williams, *Ponder These Things* (Norwich, 2002), p. xiv.

[4] Glen Cavaliero, *Charles Williams: Poet of Theology* (London, 1983), p. 164.

of images which appear in clusters, form patterns and grow into a complex metaphorical system.

The poetic of *A Revelation* both reflects and reflects on the showings and subsequent contemplative return to them. As a model of the devotional life, this may be compared with other practices – the monastic discipline of *lectio divina*, for example, or the Orthodox custom of visiting the icons. Indeed, the form in which the Crucifixion was exhibited to Julian[5] suggests that these early showings might usefully be described as 'Passion Icons',[6] thus identifying both their iconography and the manner of Julian's devotion. Motivated by an urgent desire to understand and a perceived vocation to communicate, she is enabled to 'make at least something of her experience accessible … using language with the quickening power of the artist'.[7] In finding the way of the poet – close attentiveness, analogy, image, metaphor – she has found an intuition of interrelatedness, a sense that, in the words of Philip Sheldrake, 'all things are interconnected and interconnectedness is the inner reality of things and persons in themselves'.[8] In this sense, Julian's text becomes a rich fabric of metaphor working within structures to open on 'an imaginative universe'.[9]

The series of events with which both texts open – prayers, sickness, healing – forms a prologue. From this point in *A Revelation* a change of tone suggests that careful editing has separated out the showings to give due attention both to the qualities of each and to their interrelatedness, something most evident in the Passion Icons passages. In the course of repeated contemplative return to the whole experience, a three-fold structure has begun to emerge; this, however, will not be finally achieved until the appearance, or recollection, or acceptance, of the revelatory example which becomes Chapter 51, after which it becomes possible to identify three stages in the growth of Julian's understanding. Within the structure, three properties may be discerned. The first, the property of Sight, stated in the priest's instruction and actualised in the Passion Icons, is reinforced in the Third Revelation as Julian is ordered to 'See, I am God. See, I am in all thing […] See, I lede all thing to the end that I ordaine it to' (*Revelation*, 11.42–4). The multiple ways of seeing which lead at last to understanding form a constant in the text and a metaphorical pathway through it. The second property, that of Growth, stated in the hazelnut, is the source of metaphors of birth, development and maturation. Shown as a microcosm of 'all that is made' (*Revelation*, 5.10), in shape it suggests the womb, in function it suggests birth. In its protection of the kernel it is a place of safety and enclosure, as a seed it is a symbol of resurrection. A third property is not as easily identified but may be approached through the word 'homelyhede' which, with its variants, occurs repeatedly, notably in

5   The etymology of the word 'shewing' allows for the sense of 'displaying', for which see the MED, definition 4 (a).
6   Rowan Williams has suggested that 'The point of the icon is to give us a window into an alien world, [it is] sometimes described as a channel for the "energies" of that other form of reference.' See Rowan Williams, *Lost Icons* (Edinburgh, 2002) p. xiv. It is in this sense that I adopt the term in this essay.
7   *A Revelation of Love*, ed. Marion Glasscoe (Exeter, 1996), p. xv.
8   Philip Sheldrake, *Spirituality and Theology: Christian Living and the Doctrine of God* (London, 1998), p. 14.
9   Rowan Williams, *The Wound of Knowledge* (Cambridge, Mass., 1990), p. 151.

the meditative return to the First Revelation in Chapter 7. Here, Julian describes an encounter with a lord who is both 'reverent and dredfulle' and 'homely and curteyse' (*Revelation*, 7.25–6). She confirms this in an 'open example', a 'bodely exsample' (*Revelation*, 7.27, 34) comprising the elusive lord/servant story which points to a God close to his creatures, not 'strange in maner' (*Revelation*, 7.33). The passage, in pre-figuring the parable, anticipates a theological exploration of the Trinity in familial terms as Julian writes of 'this marvelous curtesy and homelyhede of oure fader that is oure maker, in our lorde Jhesu Crist that is oure broder and oure savior' (*Revelation*, 7.42–4) and that of this 'marvelous home-lyhede may no man know in this life, but if he have it by specialle shewing of oure lorde, or of gret plenty of grace inwardly given of the holy gost' (*Revelation*, 7.45–7). Julian is grounded in the homeliness of her early life, the domestic world in which she was formed and the anchorhold in which she came to maturity.[10] All that she has loved and known is enfolded in the word 'kind' which echoes through the text to find its fullest expression in Chapter 53, where she writes:

> whan God shulde make mannes body, he toke the slime of the erth [...] and therof he made mannes body. But to the making of mannes soule he wolde take right nought, but made it. And thus is the kinde made rightfully oned to the maker, which is substantial kinde unmade, that is God. (*Revelation*, 53.35–9)

In the property of Kind, its associations and the metaphors arising from it, Julian affirms a fundamental link between Creator, humankind and the natural world. The three properties are similarly enmeshed: in them all things are seen to be interconnected and from them springs the metaphoricity of the text. As Julian's understanding grows, so she finds 'metaphors of depth rather than surface'[11] or, more accurately, metaphors of depth *and* surface, which state an intention to see a persistent wholeness in a creation which is, to all appearance, flawed and fractured. Moreover, these properties of the work form both a secondary structure and a sub-text.

Disarming images of hazelnut, fish scales and raindrops place Julian firmly in her natural habitat, her 'ownmost' place,[12] and indicate the form which her metaphoricity will take. Such images express a natural delight in the feminine, even the womanly, and, in their ordinariness, modesty and humility. In these reminders of what is most dear to her she is inducted 'with explanation kind',[13] by way of unthreatening epithet and homely illustration, through a joyful accla-

---

10 I am conscious that this assertion, along with similar ones of Julian's origins, is open to contention but an examination of these issues is beyond the remit of this essay. For a persuasive argument for Julian's lay origins see Benedicta Ward, 'Julian the Solitary', *Julian Reconsidered*, ed. Kenneth Leech and Benedicta Ward (Oxford, 1988).
11 Oliver Davies, *A Theology of Compassion* (London, 2001), p. xi.
12 See Paul Ricoeur: 'what is to be interpreted in a text is a proposed world, a world that I might inhabit, and wherein I might project my ownmost possibilities': Paul Ricoeur, 'Philosophy and Religious Language', *Journal of Religions* 54, 1 (1974), pp. 71–85 (41).
13 The manner in which Julian is guided into the Passion Icons finds an echo in Emily Dickinson's poem 1129:
> As Lightning to the Children eased
> With Explanation kind,
> The Truth must dazzle gradually,
> Or every Man be blind.

mation of the Trinity and a glimpse of the young Virgin, into the sequence of four
Passion Icons. In the course of these the tone darkens and the images mutate as
she is made gradually aware of the harrowing nature of the event in which, long
before, she had prayed to participate. So, blood which had flowed freely dries up
to obscure and discolour the face of Christ, only to flow once more, reassuring,
life-affirming – salvific even – as the body is savagely assaulted. In the Fourth
Icon the blood has dried up completely as earthly life ends, leaving an empty
shell. In a parallel metaphor the body is seen in terms of clothing becoming a
'foule, black, dede hame' (*Revelation*, 10.29) which will disintegrate to become
a rag buffeted in a bitter wind. The concept of cloth/clothing as enfolding and
safely enclosing is subverted, undermined and negated as it moves through this
sequence in a text which not only describes, declares and proclaims the showings but analyses them by means of metaphor. It is in Julian's capacity to hold
to the reality both of common life recalled in image and visionary experience
explored in metaphor that she is enabled to 'straddle'[14] the gap, to find an essential unity in her life and the confidence to address her fellow Christians.

The fact and property of Sight also becomes a working metaphor as sight,
insight and perception lead to understanding and form a pathway through
the text. As clothing images are subverted in the Passion Icons, so is sight also
found in its opposite, in blindness which is an obtuse failure, even a refusal to
understand. The metaphor mirrors a developing intellectual awareness of the
challenge presented by the showings as exemplified in a series of questions,
culminating in the plea to which the parable offers an answer. Sight in all its
various meanings is the metaphor by which Julian, transformed, enters the
imaginative universe of the final chapters.

The sickroom in which the visions appear is a kind of enclosure, an envel-
oping darkness, shifting and formless, full of shadows, and it initiates a further
metaphorical sequence. With the approach of death and the dimming of her
sight, Julian becomes confined within her own body and all activity ceases.
What she experiences here is multiple enclosure within a darkness that culminates, contrary to expectation, neither in demonic assault nor in death, but in a
sudden healing. The crucifix becomes 'palpably alive – as if vividly lit in a silent
darkness'.[15] Emerging from the enclosures of sickroom, darkness and fear, Julian
is enabled to focus and to behold. As she has been urged to *see*, so it is indicated
that this may be achieved within enclosure, in a replication of the circumstances
in which the showings first appeared, or so it would seem, in a later bringing
together of the sickroom, which was almost a death bed, and the anchorhold,
which was almost a tomb. Thus, it is enclosure which leads to disclosure in
the spaciousness of the parable and the affirmations of the closing chapters.
Enclosure, too, is linked metaphorically to the knot of images found in the First
Revelation, Julian's offering to Christ of her own feminine, domestic world. Each
of these – the hazelnut, the pellet, the raindrop, the fish scale – has relevance in
shape and function to objects which are seen and structures which enclose. The
nut is emblematic: in shape it is a womb, in function a type of womb, a source

---

14  Christopher Abbott, *Julian of Norwich, Autobiography and Theology* (Cambridge, 1999), p. 44.
15  Marion Glasscoe, *English Medieval Mystics, Games of Faith* (London, 1993), p. 223.

of life. Safely hermetic, it will in due time deliver the potential of new life in the kernel, hinting at the new life of a child. Placed in *A Revelation* between the Virgin of the Annunciation and a perception of God '[who] is oure clotheing' (*Revelation*, 5.3), the nut links metaphors of birth and clothing in a context which allows a passing recollection of swaddling. By association with the hazelnut as creative enclosure and clothing as loving enclosure, an acclamation of the Trinity affirms a God as both loving and familial in the first of a series of what may be described as 'lyric fragments'. Most of these lyric fragments are Trinitarian, exploring and proclaiming the nature of God and recording what Julian has heard as image patterns record what she has seen. The language register of the fragments is elevated, echoing the rhythms of psalm, canticle or liturgical hymn. The interrelatedness of metaphor and the sequence of lyrics together reflect Julian's acceptance of vocation as willing pupil and initially hesitant teacher. Her text forms a web, a woven tapestry, in which she seeks to express the rich complexity revealed in the showings and in her meditative return to them.

The showings begin in contradiction – darkness/light, sickness/healing, death/birth. The first Passion Icon is paradoxically described in images redolent more of Nativity than of Crucifixion: birth memories and images of birth are clearly 'floating' in Julian's mind, of personal moment and initiating a further thread of metaphor. At the simplest and ideal level, childbirth is best experienced in a domestic, a homely setting. Looked at in this way – and there is guidance in the imagery to permit it – there is no difficulty in making an imaginative adjustment to overlay the impression of sickroom/death bed with the expectation of joy in the annunciation motif: Julian's little Virgin is 'a simple maiden and a meeke, yong of age [...] in the stature as she was whan she conceivede' (*Revelation*, 4.25–6). For Rowan Williams, the Orthodox Mother of God of the Sign demonstrates 'one of the most mysterious bits of our belief, for nine months God was incarnate [...] as a foetus growing in Mary's womb'.[16] This is essentially what Julian recalls at a late point in the Long Text:

> he toke the grounde of his werke full lowe and fulle mildely in the maidens wombe. And that shewde he in the furst, wher he broughte that meek maiden before the eye of my understonding [...] in this lowe place he arayed him and dight him all redy in oure poure flesh. (*Revelation*, 60.6–10)

Drawing upon an experience of childbirth, she finds a further strand of metaphor. The flowing blood does not at first alarm her, appearing to recall the blood flow which signals the coming delivery of the child, part of a creative process which also heralds her own rebirth in Christ and redemption made available for all. At no point as the images unfold does the sight of blood appear to distress her: that it was 'so plentuous to my sight that methought [...] it shulde have made the bedde all on bloude' (*Revelation*, 12.6–9) is a vivid recollection, its significance only to be grasped in a perception of the parallel between 'the mother's labour' and Christ's sufferings which 'give birth to human redemption'.[17]

---

16 Williams, *Ponder These Things*, p. 45.
17 Liz Herbert McAvoy, *Authority and the Female Body in the Writings of Julian of Norwich and Margery Kempe* (Cambridge, 2004), p. 81.

Only when blood changes its form, becomes dried up or caked, or when, as in the final Icon, the body is drained of life-blood does she become distraught as:

> the swet body was so discoloured, so drye, so clongen, so dedly, and so pituous as he had bene sennight dead, continually dying. And methought the drying of Cristes flesh was the most paine, and the last, of his passion.
>
> (*Revelation*, 16.22–4)

While the blood flows it is a metaphor of life and of redeemed life, as it 'floweth in all heaven, enjoying the salvation of all mankind' (*Revelation*, 12.24). In a eucharistic reference she writes: 'for ther is no licour that is made that liketh him so wele to geve us' (*Revelation*, 12.11–12).[18] Such positive and life-affirming associations are not to be cancelled by the horror of inflicted pain, not even by the subversion of joy so graphically described in the Eighth Revelation.

Such horror overcome, the metaphors are carried through the text to the parable. Originating in an aesthetic which is peculiarly Julian's own, interlaced and mutually referential metaphors come together to form a web in which she identifies her own complexity, something of 'the God we know as Trinity',[19] and the intrinsic relationship of Kind in which they are linked. Emerging from a period of darkness of mind and in answer to an anguished cry for help, Chapter 51, the parable, may be interpreted as a way-station on pilgrimage, the centre of a labyrinth, a sacred space in which pathways meet and intersect. A sense of spaciousness and Julian's use of a recurrent word – 'endlesse blesse', 'endlesse hevens', 'endlesse life', 'endlesse deth' – together with a renewed confidence revealed in tone and manner, indicate that, for Julian, sight has become understanding; here she sees as God sees. Having been shown in the Passion Icons how redemption was achieved, now she discovers why it became necessary.

The 'example', itself a minimalist allegory of the Fall, opens in an image, iconic in form, of lord and servant. A double portrait, redoubled as each figure is seen in both bodily and spiritual likeness, gives shape to a growing awareness of human complexity in which is refined the intuition of kinship – something first revealed in the simple images of the Passion Icons. Julian will come to recognise in Adam's doubleness a reflection of the complex Being of God, and in Adam's dividedness that reflection occluded but not effaced. Thereafter, the iconic image 'dissolves'[20] into a dramatic narrative as the servant, over-eager to please, falls and 'blindid in his reson and stoned in his minde' (*Revelation*, 51.22–3) turns from his master. His fall, an impulsive act of love which ends in catastrophe, is graphically described to convey a sense of swift and uncontrolled movement. As Julian notes the lord's magnanimity – his readiness to forgive, to share blame, even to 'reward him his frey and his drede' and 'to geve him a gifte' (*Revelation*, 51.43, 43–4) – so a new phase of her spiritual journey begins:

---

[18]  In a similar use of such a metaphor, George Herbert writes in his poem, 'The Agonie':
         Love is that liquor sweet and most divine,
         Which my God feels as bloud, but I as wine.
[19]  Sheldrake, *Spirituality and Theology*, p. xii.
[20]  This cinematic term seems appropriate to the fluid movement of the narrative at this point in the text. For a brief discussion of the cinematic qualities of Julian's writing see Elizabeth Robertson's essay in this volume, pp. 150–1.

'an inwarde gostely shewing of the lordes mening descended into my soule' and her understanding is 'ledde forth [...] to the ende' (*Revelation*, 51.45–6, 53). An intuition that the servant is Adam leads to a pause in which Julian describes herself as standing transfixed 'mekille in unknowinge' – an apophatic moment in which images fall away as she realises that 'every shewing is full of privites (*Revelation*, 51.58–9, 61–2). Julian's state of being, one might suggest, is that known to both mystic and poet[21] – an acceptance of waiting on God or awaiting the one appropriate, essential word or image. For Julian, this timeless moment initiates a return to the 'affirmative way',[22] to the metaphorical pathways which give unity to the whole revelation. The instruction to 'look well'[23] and to 'take hede to alle [...] shewed in the example' (*Revelation*, 51.74–5) prompts a return to the icon of the Fall in order to look again at each figure in terms of clothing and demeanour. A recognition that 'the lord, he is God' leads to the perception that 'in the sighte of God, alle man is one man, and one man is alle man' (*Revelation*, 51.89). Julian dwells lovingly on a Creator deserted by his loved creatures, not simply 'alone in wildernesse' (*Revelation*, 51.104), but homeless. His clothing, she now sees, is appropriately ample, significantly 'blew as asure' (*Revelation*, 51.105). She delights in beauty of face and form and perceptively, with spiritual insight, sees God 'all full of endlesse hevens' (*Revelation*, 51.108). Echoes of the enclosure motif lead to an awareness of the interiority, the 'inscape' of God. Drawn to explore the mystery of the Trinity, Julian 'sees' God looking joyfully at 'his deerwurthy son, which is even with the fader' (*Revelation*, 51.115–16). Images of sight, clothing, enclosure and homeliness are gathered in the intricate web which complements clarity of thought and reasoned argument.

Looking with equal attentiveness at the servant, Julian focuses on discrepancy and incongruity as he stands 'at court' in a workman's clothing which is ill-fitting, grubby, worn, 'unsemely' (*Revelation*, 51.145) and, in a recollection of the Eighth Revelation, 'redy to be ragged and rent' (*Revelation*, 51.144). Reflecting – and in the relaxed mood of interior monologue – she 'sees' him dart suddenly to do whatever he thought would please his lord and it suddenly appears to her that the task may be a quest, a treasure hunt.[24] 'And then', Julian declares, 'I understode that [...] he shuld be a gardener' (*Revelation*, 51.163–4), at which point mind and imagination are alerted. Just as in Chapter 7 images for

---

21  Thomas Merton writes of Julian in a passage which echoes John Keats on 'negative capability': 'This is, for her, the heart of theology: not solving the contradiction, but remaining in the midst of it, in peace, knowing that it is fully solved but that the solution is secret and will never be guessed until it is revealed.' Thomas Merton, *Conjectures of a Guilty Bystander*, ed. Thomas More (New York, 1989), p. 212.

22  Charles Williams, *The Descent of the Dove* (London, 1939), p. 59. Here Williams is discussing the necessarily co-inherent Ways, describing the Affirmative Way of the poet-mystic as 'The one Way which was to affirm all things orderly until the universe throbbed with vitality'.

23  In her discussion of Dante, Helen Luke asserts: 'Dante simply raised his eyes and looked [...] we are to learn an ever deeper looking with the inner eye. Helen Luke, *Dark Wood to White Rose* (New York, 1989), p. 5. I am arguing for Julian's own 'deeper looking with the inner eye' here.

24  The hint of a quest and the reference to 'a tresor in the erthe' recalls the Matthaen parable of a treasure buried in a field for which a man was prepared to give all he had. Matthew: 13:44. An argument develops into an affirmation of Christ's dispossession.

the Passion surfaced, so now Julian is granted a glimpse of Eden in images of garden, gardener and words appropriate to them: 'delve and dike and swinke and swete and turne the erthe up and down [...] and water the plantes' (*Revelation*, 51.164–5). In the pattern which emerges, Creation and Resurrection are interwoven to offer the insight which gives coherence to her Fall story. As, it is implied, the servant waters the earth, so the blood of the Servant redeems mankind – a parallel which becomes almost an identification. The figure of the servant represents Adam but also Christ who chose to 'shadow' him. This is a perception only to be grasped in the timeless moment of the parable and only to be communicated in a hybrid form of discourse in which the analytic and the figurative are intertwined: 'When Adam felle, Godes sonne fell' (*Revelation*, 51.185–6) develops into what can be read in terms of a lyric fragment:

> Adam fell fro life to deth:
> into the slade of this wreched worlde
> and after that into hell.
> Goddes son fell with Adam
> into the slade of the maidens wombe
> which was the fairest doughter of Adam –
> and that for to excuse Adam from blame
> in heven and in erth –
> and mightely he feched him out of hell. (*Revelation*, 51.187–91)

In the opening chapters of the text, as we have seen, the crucifixion story is surprisingly related in images of annunciation, nativity and resurrection. In the ensuing Passion Icons, metaphors of clothing modulate from safe enclosure to torn flesh. In the parable these image patterns are gathered in the figure of Christ transfigured, his clothing now 'of fair semely medolour which is so mervelous that I cannot it discrive, for it is all of very wurshippe' (*Revelation*, 51.263–4). He wears a wedding garment and 'a crowne upon his hed of precious richenes. For it was shewede that "we be his crowne"' (*Revelation*, 51.269–70). The lost treasure 'much desired', the fruit of the garden, is Alman, the prodigal. Julian's reading of the story of Redemption concludes in a majestic, richly allusive psalm. In a measured, credal statement of relationship, the way is opened for further exegesis of the Trinity as the family from which human concepts of family derive. Seeing as God sees, Alman being one man, all times are equally one time. There being once more a necessity to bridge a gap, Julian achieves this in three ways: in concentrating on one aspect of the Fall – there is no Eve and no Serpent, both being contained within the teaching that 'Alman is one man'; in her own comprehensive principle of Kind; and in the hybrid discourse in which analytic and figurative are 'oned', that is to say 'knit' in a metaphorical linearity which places the temporal in the eternal.

In the final chapters of this 'most theological of mystical texts'[25] metaphors are discovered, are gathered, and 'oned' – Julian uses the concept of knit/knot in the sense of healing, mending, restoring. The matter is theological, the mood is

---

[25] Sheldrake, *Spirituality and Theology*, p. 100.

spiritual, and the whole moves towards an affirmation of the centrality of love. In this context, Julian returns to relatedness, the property of Kind which includes home, family, kindred, all that is deemed natural. A way has been opened in father/child terms, which 'float'[26] in her mind and in which she can engage with trinity. Just as she found domestic images, so now she makes a transition, building on earlier Trinitarian statements, to focus on the family. This she does initially in the tentative credal statement 'And thus I saw that God enjoyeth that he is our fader, and God enjoyeth that he is our moder, and God enjoyeth that he is our very spouse' (*Revelation*, 52.1–3). The name by which God is known is Trinity, the dynamic of the Three is familial. Life in the human family, it is implied, to whatever extent it may be modified and twisted out of true within the fallen state, reflects and grows from that dynamic. Delighting in kinship with God, Julian plays her 'game of faith' in variations on the theme of family. She writes, 'I beheld the werking of alle the blessed trinite, in which beholding I saw and understode these three propertes [...] of the faderhed [...], the motherhed [...], the lordhede in one God' (*Revelation*, 58.15–17).[27] Julian celebrates traditional belief while moving within its formal structures, infusing them with a sense of the living God whom she encounters. She perceives that 'alle these have we in kinde and in oure substantial making' (*Revelation*, 58.29–30). 'Kind' is the web of relationships which forms a sacramental bond between God and His creation:

> God is kind in his being: that is to say, that goodnesse that is kind, it is God. He is the grounde, he is the substance [...] And all kindes that he hath made to flowe out of him [...] it shall be restored and brought againe unto him.
> (*Revelation*, 62.10–13)

At no point in *A Revelation* are subtlety of thought and clarity of expression more apparent than in the exegesis of motherhood as a property of Trinity, embraced with confident enthusiasm in Chapter 59. Playing 'the game of faith' with panache, Julian tries out ways of making her thinking plain, beginning with the proviso: 'As verely as God is oure fader, as verely is God oure moder' (*Revelation*, 59.10). There is in the Trinity, she claims, no hierarchy but a dynamic, a dance. Her theological argument develops in another lyric fragment, a canticle notably terse and succinct, its tone strangely at ease with its celebratory mood. Set out experimentally in a form dictated by rhythm and repetition, its place within Julian's poetic becomes evident:

---

26  Caroline Spurgeon, *Shakespeare's Imagery and What it Tells Us* (Cambridge, 1953, new edition, 1975), p. 213.

27  On this, Alexandra Barratt comments: 'The later medieval good lord was, in the most literal sense of the word a 'paraclete' – an advocate to stand at one's side in court and therefore a suitable metaphor for the Holy Spirit.' See Alexandra Barratt, 'Lordship, Service and Worship in Julian of Norwich', in *The Medieval Mystical Tradition: Exeter Symposium VII*, ed. E. A. Jones (Cambridge, 2004), pp. 177–37. I would also suggest, however, that within the context of Julian's 'family of the Trinity' this may be extended to include the concept of a fatherly or godfatherly figure, one standing or standing up for another.

I it am,
the might and goodnes of faderhode,
I it am,
the wisdom and the kindnes of moderhode,
I it am,
the light and the grace that is all blessed love.
I it am
the trinite.
I it am
the unite.
I it am
the hye sovereyn goodnesse of all manner thing.
I it am that maketh the to love.
I it am that makith the to long.
I it am,
the endlesse fulfilling of all true desyers. (*Revelation*, 59.11–16)

The lyric states the essence of Julian's theology, expressing both intellectual grasp and emotional response: that is to say, the 'feeling intellect'. It celebrates an unequivocal affirmation of fatherhood, motherhood and 'sovereyn goodnes' within the Trinity: the Archetypes co-exist in a pattern of loving relationship.

Nevertheless, the focus in Chapters 59–63 is on the motherhood of Christ: 'And thus is Jhesu our very moder in kinde of our furst making, and he is our very moder in grace by taking of our kind made' (*Revelation*, 59.32). Concentration on Christ our Mother leads into a meditation: 'we ware made by the moderhed of kind love [...] the service and the office of moderhode in alle thing' (*Revelation*, 60.3–11). Julian returns to her own experience to bring human mother and Christ our Mother together in a comparison which is more than analogy, more than metaphor, only to be understood as a reaffirmation of the sacramental bond of kind which links Creator and created.

Central to Julian's Trinitarian theology is the realisation that substance and sensuality are not conflicting aspects of human being but that, in an intended wholeness, they may rightly be called 'oure soule, and that is by the oning that it hath in God' (*Revelation*, 56.18–19). This leads to a perception of

That wurshipful citte that oure lorde Jhesu sitteth in, it is our sensualite in which he is enclosed. And our kindly substance is beclosed in Jhesu.
(*Revelation*, 56.19–21)

It is an image which recurs in the last showing of 'the soule [...] as it were an endlesse warde [...], a blisseful kingdom [...], a wurshipfulle citte' and, in an echo of Julian's 'own most place', that of Christ: 'For in mannes soule is his very wonning' (*Revelation*, 68.2–4, 27). Thus, she returns to the dominant images of the Passion Icons, having discovered that, whether in sickroom, kitchen or anchorhold, domestic interior or sacred space, she and her God are mutually 'inclosyd'. This most intricate enfolding, as of the child in the mother's womb, confirms for her the orthodoxy of her trinitarian belief. So, in reaffirming Christ as God in whom our substance is 'inclosyd', and Christ as the Incarnate who, in

choosing the enclosing garment of flesh was the agent of redemption, she stands
on firm ground, confirming her earlier statement:

> And fertheremore I saw that the seconde person, which is oure moder substan-
> tially, the same derewurthy person is now become oure moder sensual. For we be
> doubel of Gods making. (*Revelation*, 58.30–2)

Julian's argument finds its conclusion in a restatement of the concept of mutual
enclosure. Deeply involved and concentrated on the bond of love exemplified
in motherhood, she loses herself in a reminiscence of nurture, of a mother 'that
woot and knoweth the neede of her childe [and] kepeth it full tenderly, as the
kinde and condition of moderhed will' (*Revelation*, 60.45–6). Understanding the
dynamic of love which is the Trinity, she perceives in it the interconnectedness
of a family. Motherhood, though it may be experienced as particular to Christ,
is not exclusively of Christ. The divine attributes are shared, are interchangeable
within the dance of the Trinity; the Three

> are not separated by their power nor by their place, they are divided not by their
> energy nor by their will, keeping inseparable their grounding and interpenetra-
> tion one with another.[28]

The world of *A Revelation*, so essentially Julian's ownmost place, is made available for others, for those who, blind and unwise, in the sinful condition which
all share, are yet bonded in kind. The form of the invitation to enter is not only
in what is written but in the manner of the writing – its poetic of close attentiveness, of metaphorical patterns, of the familiar made strange by association, by
the interweaving of generic forms: anecdote, narrative, lyric, praise, proclama-
tion. These are the ways in which a poet's evocation of a world both realistic and
imaginative works; and this may well be one reason for the widespread interest
the text continues to arouse – in searchers for spiritual truth, in academics in
related fields, in poets and writers of fiction. To conclude that Julian's poeticity
governs the form of her text is not to suggest that she was aware of herself as
a poet or as a theologian. She clearly did not wish to be aware of herself at all,
except in so far as self-examination enabled her to follow the vocation entrusted
to her. So, in her creative imagination, what might have appeared incongruous
is 'knitt and onyd' as the extraordinary experience of a mystic is mediated to
her fellow Christians through her delight in the familiar and the ordinary, in the
images of kitchen and garden, family and childhood, and in the web of metaphorical patterns which grow from them.

---

[28]  I owe this quotation from John Damascene to Dr John Herbert, offered during a conversation on the word *perichoresis* (the mutual in-dwelling which constitutes the relationship between
the components of the Trinity). See Johannes Damascenus, *Contra Jacobitas* 78, PG 94, 1476 B.

# 15

## '[S]he do the police in different voices': Pastiche, Ventriloquism and Parody in Julian of Norwich[1]

### VINCENT GILLESPIE

'Catholicism was language itself, a complete set of images, and such a rich one, with which to live and name the world.'
Michèle Roberts in *Walking on the Water: Women Talk About Spirituality*, ed. Jo Garcia and Sara Maitland (London, 1983), p. 59.

Many scholars and readers of Julian have puzzled over the strangeness of her text's structure and the curiously recursive and apparently involuted way that she expounds her showings. Right from the outset, she challenges standard interpretative strategies with her claim in the first chapter of the Long Text that the showing of the Crown of Thorns both 'comprehended and specified the blessed Trinity' in which 'all the shewinges that foloweth be groundide and oned'.[2] This is typical of her dizzying changes of visual and intellectual perspective: both comprehensive and specific; effortlessly moving from image (crown) to abstraction (Trinity); grounding and unifying all that follows in a single metaphor. The linear analytical approach – schematizing, programming, spotting theological sources and rhetorical conventions – struggles to respond to this kind of discourse. Her text seems actively to resist this kind of scholastic

1 This paper is deeply indebted to work undertaken collaboratively with Maggie Ross, especially our joint articles 'The Apophatic Image: The Poetics of Effacement in Julian of Norwich', in *The Medieval Mystical Tradition in England: Exeter Symposium V*, ed. Marion Glasscoe (Cambridge, 1992), pp. 53–77, and '"With mekeness aske perseverantly …": On Reading Julian of Norwich', *Mystics Quarterly* 30 (2004), pp. 125–40. See also Vincent Gillespie, 'Strange Images of Death: The Passion in Later Medieval English Devotional and Mystical Writing', *Analecta Cartusiana* 117 (1987), pp. 110–59; Vincent Gillespie, 'Postcards from the Edge: Interpreting the Ineffable in the Middle English Mystics', in *Interpretation Medieval and Modern: The J. A. W. Bennett Memorial Lectures: Perugia 1992*, ed. Piero Boitani and Anna Torti (Cambridge, 1993), pp. 137–65.
2 All citations of Julian's text will normally be from *The Writings of Julian of Norwich: A Vision Shewed to a Devout Woman and A Revelation of Love*, ed. Nicholas Watson and Jacqueline Jenkins (Turnhout, 2006), this quotation on p. 123. This edition, like that of Colledge and Walsh, is based on Paris, Bibl. Nat. MS fonds Anglais 40, written by an English hand in the third quarter of the sixteenth century. Citations from the slightly later London, British Library MS Sloane 2499 will be from *Julian of Norwich: A Revelation of Love*, ed. Marion Glasscoe (Exeter, 1993). In some of the detailed discussions that follow, I prefer Sloane to Paris. For an assessment of the textual problems, see Marion Glasscoe, 'Visions and Revisions: A Further Look at the Manuscripts of Julian of Norwich', *Studies in Bibliography* 42 (1989), pp. 103–20.

reading. Instead Julian's dominant imagery speaks of enfolding, embracing and enclosing, invoking an all-encompassing three-dimensional aesthetic: 'He is oure clothing that for love wrappeth us, and windeth us, halseth us and all becloseth us, hangeth about us for tender love' (*Revelation*, 5.3–4).

This does not mean that the linearity of the standard critical method is totally excluded, but the range of textual voices she uses, and her subtle and strategically shifting nuances of style and register, demand a different way of listening. More profitable is a version of an ancient monastic form of dialogue with the text derived from *lectio divina* (divine reading) of Scripture, traditionally described as rumination or meditation.[3] Just as monastic reading generates what Jean Leclercq calls the 'literature of reminiscence', so we must become sensitized to the nuances and verbal play of Julian's text, so that key ideas and concepts (such as 'enclosing' or 'beholding') begin to resonate together.[4]

The showings seem to have required from Julian an acutely attentive stillness (she calls this paradoxical state 'willful abiding') and the suspension of her hermeneutic preconceptions. Julian's text demands from its readers these same qualities. Her re-enactment in the opening of the first revelation (Chapter 4) of Mary's yielding of control and self-will in the Annunciation is the key to her own openness to the showings, and her willingness to 'conceive' of their truth (the gynaecological pun is Julian's).[5] Readers of her text need to aspire to the same condition, which Julian calls 'meekness' or 'reverent dread': 'Lo me, Gods handmayd' (Sloane, ed. Glasscoe, p. 6). This necessary and radical openness to the theological and rhetorical strategies of the text rests on a profound participation in a kenotic process.[6] In modern terms, this translates into a willingness to listen to the text without a pre-formed interpretative agenda. Julian is repeatedly told in her showings to stop seeking for easy answers to hard questions. Similarly, modern readers have to be attentive to the complexity and sophistication not only of Julian's ideas but also of the strategies that she uses to explore and communicate them. Indeed, readers may at times become aware that they are no longer the agent of reading but are themselves textual constructs which are being read and challenged, just as Julian has the sense at the end of the third showing that the soul has been closely 'examined' by God in the course of the revelation.

---

3    For the suggestion that Julian was engaged in a process of *lectio divina* on her showings, see *A Book of Showings to the Anchoress Julian of Norwich*, ed. Edmund Colledge and James Walsh (Toronto, 1978), pp. 131–2.
4    J. Leclercq, *The Love of Learning and the Desire for God*, trans. C. Misrahi (2nd edn, New York, 1974), pp. 90–1. See also the interesting discussion in Brad Peters, 'A Genre Approach to Julian of Norwich's Epistemology', in *Julian of Norwich: A Book of Essays*, ed. Sandra J. McEntire (New York, 1998), pp. 115–52.
5    Gillespie and Ross, 'The Apophatic Image', p. 62; Tarjei Park, 'Reflecting Christ: The Role of the Flesh in Walter Hilton and Julian of Norwich', in *The Medieval Mystical Tradition in England: Exeter Symposium V*, ed. Marion Glasscoe (Cambridge, 1992), pp. 17–37, esp. pp. 33–4.
6    For analysis of *kenosis* in Julian's text, see Gillespie and Ross, 'The Apophatic Image', pp. 59–60, and bibliography cited there; 'Postcards from the Edge', *passim*; and, more broadly, Nicholas Watson, 'Conceptions of the Word: The Mother Tongue and the Incarnation of God', in *New Medieval Literatures* 1, ed. Wendy Scase, Rita Copeland and David Lawton (Oxford, 1997), pp. 85–124. For recent general discussion of the theological concept, see *Letting Go: Rethinking Kenosis*, ed. Onno Zijlstra (Bern, 2002); *Exploring Kenotic Christology: The Self-Emptying of God*, ed. C. Stephen Evans (Oxford, 2006).

Julian's closing gesture here typically encodes what she sees as the appropriate response to this testing examination: 'Thus mightily, wisely, and lovingly was the soule examined in this vision. Than saw I sothly that me behoved nedes to assent with great reverence, enjoying in God' (*Revelation*, 11.46–8). The text requires us to give up the illusion of our activity and initiative, our only activity being that of intensely attentive receptivity which Julian calls 'beholding'.

'Beholding' emerges as a transactional state in which God constantly beholds and comprehends us and we struggle fitfully to behold him, but fail to comprehend him in this life:

> The continual seking of the soule pleseth God ful mekille. For it may do no more than seke, suffer and trust. And this is wrought in every soule that hath it by the holy gost [...] The seking with faith, hope, and charity pleseth oure lord, and the finding pleseth the soule, and fulfilleth it with joy. (*Revelation*, 10.57–63)

Julian states that the skills necessary for seeking into this 'beholding' will be taught by God: that is, they go beyond normal human modes of inquiry and analysis: 'It is God wille that we seke him [the Paris manuscript reads: in] to the beholdyng of him [...] And how a soule shall have him in his beholdyng he shal teche himselfe' (Sloane, ed. Glasscoe, p. 16). This process does *not* demand the 'sacrifice' of reason in the sense of its denial. Rather, in accordance with medieval models of contemplation, reason has first to be exercized to the utmost, and then we are asked to pass beyond it to be open to a higher reason.[7] It is incorporated and transfigured into a new way of knowing, understanding, 'wurking, thanking, trusting, enjoyeng' (*Revelation*, 86.3), all of which, Julian would say, are '*Goddes* wurking' (my emphasis), not man's. Seeking into 'beholding' is the core work of Julian's response to her showings. It is also a viable critical methodology for reading Julian's account of that work. As always, Julian shows us how to do it: 'I beheld the shewing with all my diligence. For in this blessed shewing I behelde it as one in Gods mening' (*Revelation*, 9.22–3). Her beholding allows her to see the totality of the showings from God's perspective (as one who shared God's meaning); her beholding allows her to see the irreducible unity of the showing (I beheld it all in one, by means of God's showing); and she beholds it as one who has herself become a means of showing, a signifier for those who, she expects, will follow her as performers of her text: 'And that I say of me, I mene in the person of alle my evencristen, for I am lerned in the gostely shewing of our lord God that he meneth so' (*Revelation*, 8.31–2). This classic word-knot

---

7   See, for example, A. J. Minnis, 'The Sources of *The Cloud of Unknowing*: A Reconsideration', in *The Medieval Mystical Tradition in England: Exeter Symposium I*, ed. Marion Glasscoe (Exeter, 1982), pp. 63–75; A. J. Minnis, 'Affection and Imagination in "The Cloud of Unknowing" and Hilton's "Scale of Perfection"', *Traditio* 39 (1983), pp. 323–66. For the theological background, see M. D. Chenu, *La Théologie comme Science au XIIIe Siècle*, 3rd edn, Bibliothèque Thomiste 33 (Paris, 1957), pp. 33–57, 93–100; Ulrich Köpf, *Die Anfänge der theologischer Wissenschaftstheorie im 13. Jahrundert*, Beitrage zur historischen Theologie 49 (Tübingen, 1974), pp. 107–12 and 266–7; Andrew Louth, *The Origins of the Christian Mystical Tradition* (Oxford, 1981), pp. 132–58, esp. pp. 153–4.

or semantic cluster on 'menen' is how God 'meneth' or speaks, and how Julian and the readers of her text become the word spoken by God.[8]

But that speech is usually not straightforward or clear. There are problems in transcribing the ineffable Word into the fallen language of men and expressing its totality in the one-dimensional linearity of its written manifestation.[9] Julian works hard to address these problems, but knows they can never be overcome. In her text, language is always viewed as slippery, imperfect and provisional. It is only a means to the end of beholding God. Julian's Long Text always requires us to attend deeply and suspiciously to the texture of the writing, and in doing so the reader soon becomes aware of Julian's skilful command of different linguistic moods and registers, narrative voices and rhetorical levels of style.

Julian is the mistress of multiple vernacular discourses, capable of alluding to and pastiching various contemporary styles of religious and philosophical writing, without ever allowing any of them to become dominant or specifying. Her text is a vast echo chamber of allusion and imitation, but there are relatively few occasions when it is possible to identify her source unequivocally once it has been through the crucible of her imagination. This is one of the key ways in which her text subverts normal critical (and perhaps theological) reading. It is essential to her strategy of truth-telling that she is able to float above the discourses that predominated in her contemporary textual environment, promiscuously bathing herself in them as and when her argument requires them, but never being possessed or controlled by them. Annie Sutherland has shown how in the Long Text most of her biblical allusions are woven into and subsumed within the warp and weft of her argument rather than being consciously and deliberately deployed as *auctoritates* or proof texts.[10] Likewise, in Julian's relations to other religious discourses she stands aloof, preferring to reforge her own discourse, to write her own performative utterance using dominant religious discourses tactically and often parodically. Julian is aware that her text 'functions in the heart of a cluster of social determinations', as Paul Zumthor puts it.[11] Her deference to the historically determined *magisterium* of Holy Church shows this vividly. But, aware as she is of devotional conventions and interpretative norms, especially in relation to prayer, and other 'means' of worship developed by the Church in time, she is also aware of the need to be true to her own distinctive vision of Love. For Julian, the necessary narrative honesty required of her as the intermediary of that vision of Love prevents her from allowing her understanding to be articulated exclusively or even mainly in the worn and threadbare discourses prevalent in her lifetime. To do so would risk making God in the image and

---

8    For more on this word, see Gillespie and Ross, 'The Apophatic Image', p. 69.
9    On ineffability in the Middle English tradition, see my 'Postcards from the Edge', *passim*. More generally, see Kevin Hart, *The Trespass of the Sign: Deconstruction, Theology and Philosophy* (Cambridge, 1992); *Mysticism and Language*, ed. Steven Katz (Oxford, 1992); Michael Sells, *Mystical Languages of Unsaying* (Chicago, 1994); *Mystics: Presence and Aporia*, ed. Michael Kessler and Christian Sheppard (Chicago, 2003).
10    Annie Sutherland, '"Our feyth is groundyd in goddes worde": Julian of Norwich and the Bible', in *The Medieval Mystical Tradition in England: Exeter Symposium VII*, ed. E. A. Jones (Cambridge, 2004), pp. 1–20. See also her chapter in this volume.
11    Paul Zumthor, *Speaking of the Middle Ages*, trans. Sarah White (Lincoln, Nebraska, 1986), p. 58.

likeness of man's fallen language. There is here an important general issue about self-textualisation and cultural coding. If visionary experience is written down in the popular registers and codes of theology and devotional writing, it runs the risk of losing its specificity and uniqueness.[12] Julian is not only aware of this, but within her text she actually dramatizes and deconstructs her own instinctive tendency to process her showings in this way.

This is not just an issue of ineffability (though that is always part of her own horizon of expectation as a 'reader' of her own showings and a writer of her texts). It is rather an issue of communicability: how can Julian ensure that, however the reader or hearer 'takes' her text, they do so in a way that preserves the freshness of her showings and immediacy of her understanding of them (even when that immediacy has taken twenty years to achieve). In the Short Text, Julian asks for three gifts that are traditional and almost predictable in their devotional and affective reach: mind of Christ's Passion; bodily sickness to share in the suffering of Christ; and three metaphorical wounds of contrition, compassion and wilful longing to God (*Vision*, 1.40–1). But their delivery in her showings blasts through the banality of the requests and transports them onto an altogether more abstract and theologically ambitious plane. The Short Text is stylistically much more austere and affective than the Long Text, is notably more schematic with its lists and numberings of observations and implications, and generally has the feel of a theologically cautious, perhaps even defensive, stocktaking exercise.[13] If, as I believe, the Short Text is a *probatio* text, produced in connection with the enquiries surrounding her entry into the enclosed life of an anchoress, then it may date from much later than 1373, but rather from her eventual decision to enter religion (a decision perhaps even triggered or otherwise marked by the second vision of 1388).[14] The Short Text already shows signs

---

[12]  For useful discussion of this important and contentious issue, see Anna Maria Reynolds, 'Some Literary Influences in the *Revelations* of Julian of Norwich', *Leeds University Studies in Language and Literature* 7–8 (1952), pp. 18–28; Lynn Staley Johnson, 'The Trope of the Scribe and the Question of Literary Authority in the Works of Julian of Norwich and Margery Kempe', *Speculum* 66 (1991), pp. 820–38; Denise Nowakowski Baker, *Julian of Norwich's Showings: From Vision to Book* (Princeton, 1994); Felicity Riddy, '"Women Talking about the Things of God": a Late-Medieval Sub-Culture', in *Women and Literature in Britain 1150–1500*, ed. Carol M. Meale, 2nd edn (Cambridge, 1996), pp. 104–27; Felicity Riddy, 'Julian of Norwich and Self-Textualization', in *Editing Women*, ed. Ann M. Hutchison (Cardiff, 1998), pp. 101–24; Christopher Abbott, *Julian of Norwich: Autobiography and Theology* (Cambridge, 1999), pp. 47–60.
[13]  On this difference, see Simon Tugwell, *Ways of Imperfection: An Exploration of Christian Spirituality* (London, 1984), pp. 187–207; B. A. Windeatt, 'Julian of Norwich and Her Audience', *Review of English Studies*, n.s. 28 (1977), pp. 1–17.
[14]  Nicholas Watson, 'The Composition of Julian of Norwich's *Revelations of Love*', *Speculum* 68 (1993), pp. 637–83, pp. 670–2. On the *probatio vitae* necessary before a bishop would sanction enclosure, see Ann K Warren, *Anchorites and their Patrons in Medieval England* (Berkeley, 1985), pp. 53–91, esp. pp. 71: 'In all known instances probation was ordered for women who were proceeding to the anchorite life without having been nuns'; E. A. Jones, 'A New Look into the *Speculum Inclusorum*', in *The Medieval Mystical Tradition in England, Ireland and Wales: Exeter Symposium VI*, ed. Marion Glasscoe (Cambridge, 1999), pp. 123–45. My hypothesis about the genesis of the Short Text may be significant for the question of Julian's life before enclosure and whether she was already a nun when she received her showings. My view is that she was not. See Benedicta Ward, 'Julian the Solitary', in *Julian Reconsidered*, ed. Kenneth Leech and Benedicta Ward (Oxford, 1988), pp. 11–35. For revelations to an anchoress subsequently (and very rapidly) submitted in letter form to a spiritual 'fadyr' and other clerical authorities, see *A Revelation of Purgatory*, ed. Marta Powell Harley, Studies in Women and Religion 18 (Lewiston NY, 1985).

of rewriting, with the false peroration after the long and gloomy meditation on sin (*Vision*, 23.29–31) being modified and somewhat diluted by the more positive and upbeat theology of its final pages. A decision to abandon the Short Text in favour of a wholesale and much more radical rewrite is perhaps reflected by the headnote to Chapter 86 of the Long Text in Sloane, in a passage that suggests that the Short and Long versions were to perform different functions and needed very different textual and rhetorical strategies: 'The good lord shewid this booke shuld be otherwise performid than at the first writing' (Sloane, ed. Glasscoe, p. 134).

In discussions of Julian's sources and influences she can sometimes emerge as the grateful beneficiary of antecedent (largely male and largely clerical) Latin writers who provide her with the interpretative matrix and visionary vocabulary to process her own experiences.[15] Her compositional process, and her quizzical relationship with other religious texts, is messier, more radical and ultimately far more artistically controlled. Zumthor argues that 'the historical development of cultures … rarely proceeds by linear sequences, formalizable in a closed discourse, but generally by a multidimensional expansion'.[16] Julian strives for just such a multidimensional expansion in her Long Text, in response to the authority of a God of paradoxically complex simplicity, whose revelations never go in straight lines. Again and again, she demonstrates the ability to deploy contemporary religious and philosophical discourses in tightly controlled tactical ways without ever putting her faith or reliance on any of them to describe or account for the essence of her showings. Instead, she uses the local velocity of those discourses and registers to project her own text into new and surprising directions. These provisional discourses, codes and registers are only 'means' to be discarded on the journey to the promised end revealed by Christ who is the 'soverayne techare' (*Vision*, 6.38). Julian rejects the shell/kernel model of hermeneutics beloved of medieval (and many modern) commentators. Her interpretative strategies rest on a complex and subtle manipulation of the local textual experience of her audience.

Part of that experience is the constant sense of having our textual competencies challenged, manipulated, denied and overpassed. The texture of her discourse is always unsettled, provisional and protean. Her writing has many of the dialogic characteristics of Bakhtinian 'heteroglossia', eager to exploit 'whatever force is at work within a given literary system to reveal the artificial constraints of that system' and using 'parodic stylisations of canonized genres and styles'.[17]

---

Mary C. Erler, ' "A Revelation of Purgatory" (1422); Reform and the Politics of Female Visions', *Viator* 38 (2007), pp. 321–47, notes (p. 325) that at the onset of her revelations Birgitta of Sweden was instructed that she 'suld obei to one master of diuinite, and shewe hime hir reuelacions þat were shewed vnto hir': Bridget of Sweden, *The Liber Celestis of St Bridget of Sweden*, vol. 1, ed. Roger Ellis, EETS o.s. 291 (1987), p. 3.

15   On the issue of Julian's probable knowledge of some Latin grammatical constructions at the time of the composition of the Short Text, see the thoughtful analysis of Colledge and Walsh's claims that she was *literata* by Michael J. Wright: 'Julian of Norwich's Early Knowledge of Latin', *Neuphilologische Mitteilungen* 94 (1993), pp. 37–45.

16   Zumthor, *Speaking of the Middle Ages*, p. 72.

17   M. Bakhtin, *Problems of Dostoevsky's Poetics* (Ann Arbor, Michigan, 1973), pp. 153–65; Mikhail Bakhtin, *The Dialogic Imagination* (Austin, Texas, 1992), pp. xxxi, 6.

Warily resistant to the reductive, the schematic and the programmatic, her text
is full of surprises, textual aporias that suddenly (such an important word in
Julian's textual universe) open up beneath our feet. Just as we make ends meet,
Julian moves the ends. This happens in big and small ways. In Revelation 3,
for example, Julian embarks on a conventional simile to describe the strange
beauty of Christ's bleeding head: 'the fairehede and the livelyhede is like …'.
As if recognizing that the simile creates a centrifugal force in the text, drawing
attention away from the core image and setting off a chain reaction of linked
signifiers, in effect subordinating her showing to the very linguistic *means* from
which Christ has liberated it and her, the analogy is overthrown in the Sloane
text with an enigmatic assertion of ineffable irreduceability: 'the fairehede and
the livelyhede is like nothing but the same' (Sloane, ed. Glasscoe, p. 10).[18] Similarly, in Revelation 8, when watching the dying Christ, her expectations of the
imminent death of Christ are overthrown:

> And I loked after the departing with al my mightes and wende to have seen the
> body alle dead. But I saw him not so. And right in the same time that methought
> by seming that the life might no lenger last, and the shewing of the ende behoved
> nedes to be nye – sodenly, I beholding in the same crosse, he changed in his
> blisseful chere (*Revelation*, 21.5–9).

Physiological necessity and narrative expectation (and probably the conventions
of numerous contemporary Passion narratives) have led her to attempt to extrapolate the 'shewing of the ende'. But the divine logic proves to be unpredictable
and unreadable. The script is torn up. The programmatic affective response of
grief is rendered inappropriate. The *sudden* change of cheer changes hers: 'and I
was as glad and mery as it was possible' (*Revelation*, 21. 9–10).

Already in the Short Text (and in some ways more explicitly there, as her
ventriloquial artistry has yet to fully develop), we can see her pointing to the
provisionality of her borrowed discourse, in a passage that prefigures (or may
be an early response to) the great 1388 showing of Trinitarian Love:

> And of this knawinge er we moste blinde. For many men and women leves that
> God is allemighty and may do alle, and that he is alle wisdome and can do alle.
> Botte that he is alle love and wille do alle, thar thay stinte. (*Vision*, 24.16–19)

This serves to signal her familiarity with the common discourse and lexis
describing the powers of the Trinity, and her awareness that, like her, many
Christians find the final leap of faith and trust hard to take.[19] Compare, for
example, this passage from William Flete's popular and influential *Remedies
against tribulation*:

---

[18] The apophatic force of this manoeuvre is entirely suppressed in the Paris Manuscript, which
reads 'Nevertheles the fairehede and the livelyhede continued in the same bewty and livelines'
(*Revelation*, 7.15–16). This looks like a particularly cloth-eared ('livelyhede … livelines') and
literal-minded attempt to make sense of something like Sloane's reading. There is nothing
comparable in the Short Text at this point.
[19] In the comparable passage in the Long Text (*Revelation*, 73.24), the reference to 'many men
and women' has been replaced by the courteously inclusive 'some of us'.

And therefore thenk weel that his myght may do alle thinge and his wisdom kan and his goodnesse wole, and trusteth fully therto he wole saue ӡou and brynge ӡou to his euere lastynge joye, quan he seeth beste tyme for ӡou.[20]

The teaching is the same in both, as is the play on tenses. But Julian folds into her version an awareness of its limitations and of the human difficulties in accepting it. Indeed this same passage from Flete's text, which overall has many resonances with Julian's Trinitarian teachings, contains another parallel with Julian. Flete encourages his readers (who, like the inscribed (and later excized) audience of Julian's Short Text, are aspiring to contemplative life) to:

Beleve, seyd oure lord Jesu, that god the fader is al myghtful, as who seyth, ther is no thing impossible to god, but alle is possible to hym that alle synnes may for ӡeue and alle wronges redresse and brynge soules to his blisse.

Julian, in querying God's assertion that all shall be well, receives (in the Long Text only) the response: ' "That that is unpossible to the is not unpossible to me. I shalle save my worde in alle thing and I shalle make althing wele" ' (*Revelation*, 32.41–3). Although both these passages may derive independently from Scripture, Flete's introduction of his gloss on God's words ('as who seyth') is reminiscent of Julian's most common markers of ventriloquial intervention into her text ('as if he had said'/'as thus').[21] Both writers are groping towards expressing the apophatic and ineffable, just as Plotinus typically marked his textual approach to the apophatic by 'hoion' ('as it were').[22]

Julian's dialogue, with the conventions and techniques of affective piety, extends to a virtuosic manipulation of linguistic register. Shifts between registers and moods often signal themselves with verbal punctuation ('as if'; 'as thus'; 'as if he had said').[23] The opening of the Fourth Revelation (Chapter 12) returns to the linear narrative of the Passion meditations, subjecting another episode to her intense and unwavering attention: 'And after this I saw, beholding, the body plentuously bleeding in seming of the scorging' (*Revelation*, 12.1–2).[24] Still in the non-discursive mode of 'beholding', she sees the bleeding body not in

---

[20]  William Flete, '*Remedies against Temptations*': *The Third English Version of William Flete*, ed. E. Colledge and N. Chadwick, Archivio Italiano per la Storia della Pieta V (Rome, 1967), p. 227. The Latin *De remediis contra temptationes* was written by William Flete probably between 1352 and 1358. The text had considerable circulation in Latin and English, undergoing at least three recensions and elaborations of the vernacular text along the way. For discussion, see M. B. Hackett, 'William Flete and the *De Remediis contra Temptaciones*', in *Medieval Studies presented to Aubrey Gwynn S. J.*, ed. J. A. Watt, J. B. Morrall and F. X. Martin (Dublin, 1961), pp. 330–48; Benedict Hackett, Edmund Colledge, and N. Chadwick, 'William Flete's 'De Remediis contra Temptaciones' in its Latin and English Recensions: The Growth of a Text', *Mediaeval Studies* 26 (1964), pp. 210–30.

[21]  Colledge and Walsh (p. 426) suggest Luke 18.26–7 and 1.37.

[22]  On this apophatic *topos* in Plotinus, see Sells, *Mystical Languages of Unsaying*, pp. 16–17.

[23]  Introductory verbal punctuation of this sort occurs throughout the text but is most densely found in the showings before the 'misty' example of the Lord and the Servant. See, for example, Chapters 12, 15, 19, 24, 25, 36, 40, 42, 43, 70.

[24]  Colledge and Walsh (p. 342) point out that the Short Text reading 'in the semes' (Section 8) might refer to long incised wounds, such as might be caused at the scourging. The Long Text's more ambiguous 'in seming', therefore, puns on both the physicality of the suffering and its analogical function as a figure or likeness of something else.

the context of the historical or temporal narrative of the Passion. 'In seming' alludes to the context of the scourging, but its referentiality gestures elsewhere. Julian recognizes this in the way she grounds her description in the discourse of affective meditation, but she signals that this grounding is tactical rather than definitive by drawing attention to the consciously heightened language and the provisionality of the register, in a passage added in to the Long Text: 'as thus: the fair skinne was broken full depe into the tender flesh with sharpe smitinges all about the sweete body' (*Revelation*, 12.2–3).

There is something artfully contrived here: the onomatopoeic rhythm; the alliteration on f and s; the mechanically regular alternation of adjectives and adverbs; the conventionalized epithets. Most significant is the way the introductory 'as thus' keeps the language at arm's length and marks it as pastiche. Julian is employing this emotionally coded discourse as a tactical springboard, an affective trigger.[25]

She moves on from this to play with another affective phrase: 'the dereworthy blode', which is repeated anaphorically three times as part of her exploration of the theological force of its 'precious plenty'. It is 'the precious plenty of his dereworthy blode' that acts out the Harrowing of Hell and the triumphant Ascension into heaven in this schematized version of the salvific act. This episode, where the key player in the drama of salvation is metonymically replaced by his own saving blood, is surprisingly introduced by 'Beholde and see', a phrase Julian elsewhere uses to signal expository locutions spun out from Christ's gnomic utterances (cf. Chapters 24 and 42).[26] Julian is setting up a tension between the narrative and visual elements of the Harrowing and Ascension as they are usually portrayed in words or in pictures, and the abstract but empowering placement of the key concept of the precious plenty of Christ's 'dereworthy blode'. The scene is thus rendered, in an almost Langlandian fashion, as both familiar and deeply strange.[27] Julian contrives the passage to gather imaginative and narrative velocity from the language she deploys while at the same time typically stretching it to the limits of its referentiality. To 'behold and see' the story she tells here requires real effort and a dizzying sense of dislocation. For, having played with the affective lexis of Passion meditations, Julian moves almost immediately to begin the process of effacing the familiar linearity and materiality of the description of the suffering Christ and of our response to it. Returning to the key concept of plenitude, she now uses the blood to create an

---

[25] Colledge and Walsh (p. 342) and Watson and Jenkins (p. 166) note the parallel with the language of *The Privity of the Passion*, edited in *Yorkshire Writers: Richard Rolle of Hampole and his Followers*, ed. C. Horstman (London, 1895), 1, pp. 198–218, esp. pp. 200–9. But the same lexical set is also found in other Passion meditations, lyrics, and popular prayers such as *The Fifteen Oes*.

[26] The phrase 'Beholde and see' is also used in *The Privity of the Passion*, ed. Horstman, *Yorkshire Writers*, 1, p. 201. It is also common in addresses direct to the audience in medieval drama, and in hymns and religious lyrics. But the centrality of 'beholding' in Julian's contemplative *praxis* gives particular force to her use of the imperative.

[27] Christ's wounds and his blood perform similar functions in *The Prickynge of Love*, ed. Harold Kane, Salzburg Studies in English Literature: Elizabethan and Renaissance Studies 92:10 (Salzburg, 1983), 1, pp. 16–17. *The Pricking* may well be one of the vernacular texts that Julian is tactically pastiching.

apophatic surface that effaces its own physicality and the linear narrative expectations of the Passion story: 'so plentuously the hote blode ran oute that there was neither sene skynne ne wound, but as it were al blode' (Sloane, ed. Glasscoe, p. 19; Paris changes the word order).

Denying us the affective means of a conventional response, she provides us with a gathering image on which to still the imagination. Only the surface of hot blood is allowed to remain, emphasizing the immediacy of the encounter and the eternal present tense in which her beholding unfolds. In other respects the blood denies its materiality:

> And whan it come wher it should a fallen downe, than [Paris: ther] it vanyshid […] And this was so plenteous to my sigt that methowte, if it had be so in kind and in substance for that tyme, it should have made the bed al on blode and a passid over aboute. (Sloane, ed. Glasscoe, p. 19)

This effacement of the material and frustration of the linear and the temporal draws us deeper into the showing by creating an appetite for the apophatic from her (and our) curiosity about what happens to the blood. The bleeding continues until, seeing non-naturalistically but 'with avisement' (a deeply abstract mode of perception already explored in Chapter 11), she is able to penetrate the surface 'seemings' of the image. Instead of the blood passing over the bed, Julian's perception passes over into a meditation on the precious plenty of God's love, transforming the image of physical excess into a metaphor for overpassing generosity and self-emptying:

> it is oure kinde and alblissfully beflowyth us be the vertue of his pretious love […]. The pretious plenty of his dereworthy blode overflowith al erth and is redye to wash al creaturs of synne. (Sloane, ed. Glasscoe, pp. 19–20)

'As thus' is also used by Julian to introduce Christ's words that form a 'special understanding and teching' of miracles:

> 'It is knowen that I have done miracles here before, many and fele, high and mervelous, wurshipfulle and gret. And so as I have done I do now continually and shall do in coming of time.' (*Revelation*, 36.50–2)

Putting words into Christ's mouth is one of Julian's most audacious innovations in her text, and her textual construction of his linguistic register is interesting. Julian contrives a series of high style doublets ('many and fele … worshipfulle and gret'), reflecting the dignity of her speaker. At the same time, she characteristically makes Christ inhabit past, present and future tenses in his 'working'. This enacts and invokes a divine perspective that is simultaneously out of time and manifested in all times.

The marker phrase 'as if he had said' is regularly used by Julian to signal her ventriloquial expositions of the enigmatic locutions revealed to her in her showings. Increasingly as the Long Text progresses, her showings deal with the exposition of words rather than images. Christ speaks to her in cryptic, laconic utterances which Julian, as the intermediary or 'mean', provisionally translates into contemporary discourse:

> And with this our gode lord seyd ful blisfully 'Lo how that I lovid the', as if he
> had seid: 'My derling, behold and se thy lord, thy God, that is thy maker and thyn
> endles ioy. Se what likyng and bliss I have in thy salvation, and for my love enioy
> now with me.' (Sloane, ed. Glasscoe p. 35)

She places herself at the meeting place of the ineffable and the discursive. She
then tentatively transcribes into language – 'as it may be seid, that is to mene'
– her own developing understanding of these liminal sayings: 'This is the understondyng simply as I can sey of this blissid word: "Lo how I lovid the". This
shewid our gode lord for to make us glad and mery' (Sloane, ed. Glasscoe,
p. 35). In fact, her understanding of the enigmatic 'Lo how that I lovid the' has
changed between the Short Text and the Long Text. Whereas in Sloane's Long
Text Christ speaks to Julian in the tender language of bridal mysticism (darling,
joy, liking, bliss, enjoy), in the Short Text her early attempt to put words into
Christ's mouth produces a much more predictable and affective speech:

> 'Lo how I loved the', as if he hadde saide: 'My childe, if thow kan nought loke
> in my godhede, see here howe I lette open my side and my herte be clovene in
> twa, and lette oute blude and watere all that was tharein. And this likes me, and
> so wille I that it do the.' (*Vision*, 13.2–5)

The infantilising address of clerical Passion meditations in the Short Text has
been replaced by the more abstract bridal imagery of the Long Text.[28] Moreover,
the explanation that Julian extrapolates from the utterance in the Short Text
there risks being pulled back into the linear narrative of the Crucifixion or being
focused on the affective stereotype of the wounded sacred heart of Jesus. That
motif is central to the Long Text but only in a much more apophatically abstract
version than a facile devotion to the humanity of Christ (the kind of 'dalliance
of the manhood' which Margery Kempe was encouraged to transcend). Julian's
ventriloquism of Christ becomes more subtle and more challenging in the transition from Short to Long Text, where Julian is keen to empower her reader to
obey Christ's invitation to 'loke in my Godhede'.

The phrase 'as if he said' is sometimes used to signal her transposition into
words of a more abstract understanding of an event. So the 'great deed' that
will be performed by God is glossed: 'Than meneth our good lorde thus, as
if he saide: "Beholde and se. Here hast thou matter of mekenesse, here hast
thou matter of love"' (*Revelation*, 36.33–4). Here Julian gives no fewer than three
lexical signals that she is appropriating and expounding the 'meaning' of the
words of God. The 'thus' formula, linked to 'as if he saide', leads into a locution
that begins with 'Behold and se' to mark the need for special attentiveness on
the part of the listener or reader. This showing is then further explained as something that God delivers deep into man's understanding at a level that affects all

---

[28] At the opening of the second sentence here, Paris retains the conventional address to 'My
childe' found in the Short Text, so it may be that the Sloane scribe is guilty of eyeskip in this
passage. But the tenor of the passage is generally more sophisticated and abstract in the move
from Short to Long Text.

the spiritual senses in a profound synthesis of comprehension that transcends human affections:

> tenderly our lord God toucht us and blissfully clepyth us, seyand in our soule: 'Lete by al thi love my dereworthy child. Entend to me, I am enow to the, and enioye in thi saviour and in thi salvation.' (Sloane, ed. Glasscoe, p. 50; Paris reads 'Let me alone' which makes much less sense in context)

Such strategies aspire to the very multi-modality that Julian seems to have felt as fundamental to her own visionary experience.

This is not to say that Julian escapes the textual constructedness of her discourses that is an inescapable function of reading and hearing, writing and living in a particular time and space.[29] But it is to say that she manipulates that constructedness with unusual deftness and tactical skill. And that deftness and skill is not only manifested at the micro-textual level of almost subliminal lexical signals. At the macro-textual level of chapters, or indeed whole revelations, Julian displays equal skill at 'borrowing' textual velocity and narrative texture from familiar genres of religious writing. Julian may have conceived of the Short Text and Long Text as inhabiting different genres and displaying different generic and linguistic markers. The many expansions in the Long Text certainly broaden the generic range of Julian's writing to encompass iconographical, theological and philosophical discourses not represented in the Short Text. Julian is an hospitable but highly controlled writer, allowing these discourses to discharge their narrative potential in carefully constructed tactical deployments, without ever letting any one of those guest discourses or genres swamp the *ordinatio* or *modus agendi* of her own metanarrative.

Julian displays unusual sensitivity to her own textual construction by being alert to the way that her conscious mind naturally slides into the registers and narrative conventions of dominant contemporary genres. In Chapter 6 of the Long Text, for example, Julian introduces a long excursus on prayer. Arguing that good prayer is a naked cleaving to the goodness of God in its most abstract form, Julian ruminates on the ways that mechanical and liturgical prayer can occlude this abstract goodness with its emphasis on 'means'. She then transcribes her own immediate thoughts on the subject, which 'came to my minde in the same time', and the texture of the writing immediately shifts to reflect the devotional clichés of her time (and perhaps of her own earlier life):

> For this, as I shall say, came to my minde in the same time: we pray to God for his holy flesh and for his pretious blode, his holy Passion, his deareworthy death and wounds [...] and we pray him for his sweete moder love that him bare [...] and we pray by his holy cross that he dyed on. (Sloane, ed. Glasscoe, p. 8)

---

[29] On the 'orality' of Julian's textual construction, see Felicity Riddy, ' "Women Talking about the things of God" ', pp. 113–14. For women as readers of religious texts, see the extensive bibliography in Jocelyn Wogan-Browne, 'Analytical Survey 5: "Reading is Good Prayer": Recent Research on Female Reading Communities', in *New Medieval Literatures* 5, ed. Wendy Scase, Rita Copeland and David Lawton (Oxford, 2002), pp. 229–97; Rebecca Krug, *Reading Families: Women's Literate Practice in Late Medieval England* (Ithaca, 2002); Mary C. Erler, *Women, Reading and Piety in Late Medieval England* (Cambridge, 2002).

'This' discrete semantic unit is being presented as Julian's subconscious, conditioned and therefore almost instinctive linguistic response to the subject of prayer. The results are not impressive: the usual suspects of contemporary prayers and meditations are lined up for inspection in this sentence, each noun clinging pathetically onto its clichéd adjective.[30] Against this array of predictable and rather jaded religious language, Julian simply reiterates her understanding of the true nature of prayer with the mantra-like repetition of the bare clause 'it is of his godeness'. More matter and less art.[31]

In Revelation 14, Chapter 46, of the Long Text, Julian plays with the register and lexis of contemporary philosophical writings (and perhaps particularly of penitential and homiletic texts) to discuss the moral blindness and lack of self-knowledge that mortals display. There is a low-grade Boethianism in much of this, but nothing that could not have been acquired by osmosis from many proverbial, penitential or homiletic writings. Indeed, the whole chapter follows the moral trajectory of a good many penitential lyrics.[32] She starts from a stress on the need for self knowledge in a transient world: 'But our passand lif that we have here in our sensualite knowith not what ourself is' (Sloane, ed. Glasscoe, p. 64). The striving for self knowledge, however, will never be fully realised until after death: 'But we may never fulle know oureselfe into the last point, in which pointe this passing life and alle manner of wo and paine shall have ane ende' (Revelation, 46.8–9). We should not, therefore, strive or dispute, but as obedient children of the church, should suffer patiently and abide: 'And therwith I am wele apaide, abiding our lords wille in this hye marveyle. And now I yelde me to my moder holy church, as a simpil childe oweth' (Revelation, 46.40–1). So far, so conventional.[33] But Julian is content to inhabit this conventional narrative form only because by this stage in her showings she has already devized ways of complicating and finessing it. The teaching on the deferral of full self knowledge until death, for example, is conventional enough. But many of the conventional terms ('pointe', 'passing', 'paine', 'wo') have already been charged with resonance and accumulated meaning by her exploration of them in her earlier ruminations on the Passion of Christ. Moreover, she makes it clear that this conventional register is being used to a double purpose:

[30] Compare the lexis of these phrases with the commonplace vernacular prayers such as *The Fifteen Oes*, or those collected by R. H. Robbins: 'Private Prayers in Middle English Verse', *Studies in Philology* 36 (1939), pp. 466–75; 'Popular Prayers in Middle English verse', *Modern Philology* 36 (1939), pp. 337–50; 'Five Middle English Verse Prayers from Lambeth MS. 541', *Neophilologus* 38 (1954), pp. 36–41. I am indebted to Alex da Costa for this suggestion, and for her perceptive comments on Julian's attitudes to private prayer.
[31] Her more developed teachings on prayer, drawing on the abstract language of contemplative prayer treatises, are found in Revelation 14, Chapters 41–43.
[32] See, for instance, some of the lyrics in the Vernon manuscript, e.g. nos 95, 100, 102, 105, 106, 107, 114 in *Religious Lyrics of the XIVth Century*, ed. C. Brown, 2nd edn rev. by G. V. Smithers (Oxford, 1952); *Twenty-Six Political and Other Poems*, ed. J. Kail, EETS o.s. 124 (1904), nos 1, 7, 22. Also worth comparison are the Middle English versions of the *Penitential Psalms*.
[33] For an homiletic comparison, *Fasciculus Morum: A Fourteenth-Century Preacher's Handbook*, ed. and trans. Siegfried Wenzel (London, 1989) offers a compendium of contemporary preaching clichés on penance, tribulation and the need for grace and obedience to Mother Church.

And yet in al this tyme, from the begynnyng to the end, I had ii manner of beholdyng: that one was endless continuant love with sekirnes of kepyng and blisful
salvation, for of this was al the shewing; the other was the common techyng of
holy church in which I was aforn enformyd and growndid, and wilfully haveing
in use and understondyng. (Sloane, ed. Glasscoe, pp. 64–5)

Julian contrasts the enfolding and overarching salvific shape of her own showings with the historically contextualized teachings of the Church and her own
devotional practices. But she does not merely assert her obedience to those
teachings. She also enacts that obedience by demonstrating in her choice of
vocabulary how deeply she is 'enformyd and growndid' in it. The whole chapter
becomes a display of her 'wilfully haveing in use' the penitential teachings of
the Church on self-knowledge, transience, obedience and the need for mercy
and grace. The chapter is both radical and orthodox at the same time, and her
skill lies in showing both facets simultaneously.

But she may have had mixed feelings about the language in which these
teachings were usually couched. Later on, in Revelation 16, Chapter 76, Julian
redeploys this same self-castigating penitential register, but this time puts it in
the mouth of the devil as part of his temptation to the soul to wallow in self
hatred and despair:

for the chongeabilitie that we arn in in ourselfe we fallen often into synne. Than
we have this be the stering of our enemy, be our owne foly and blyndhede; for
they seien thus: 'Thou wittest wele thou art a wretch, a synner, and also ontrew;
for thou kepist not the command [Paris: covenant]; thou behotist oftentymes our
lord that thou shalt don better, and anon after, thou fallist agen in the same,
namely in slauth, in lesyng of tyme'; for that is the begynning of synne, as to my
syghte. (Sloane, ed. Glasscoe, p. 123)

In Julian's eyes, such words lead to sin, because they deny the mercy and love
of her 'curteyse Lorde'.[34]

Similarly in Revelation 13, Chapter 28 (a chapter which Sloane heads with
the generic subheading 'a remedye agayn tribulation', significantly recalling
William Flete's popular treatise) she confronts the Church's dominant discourse
of tribulation, sin and punishment and weaves into it her own by now well-
established emphasis on Christ's compassion and love:

Ya, so ferforth I saw that our lord ioyth of the tribulations of his servants with
reuth and compassion, to ech person that he lovyth to his bliss for to bringen,
he levyth upon them something that is no lak in hys syte, wherby thei are lakid
and dispisyd in thys world, scorned, rapyd and outcasten; and this he doith for

---

[34]  Colledge and Walsh's suggested analogue from Book II Chapter 12 of Hilton's *Scale of Perfection* (p. 687) is unpersuasive. But see the description of the death of an evil man, accompanied by the 'voyce of creatures clamerynge and criynge' in the *Speculum Christiani*, ed. Gustaf
Holmstedt, EETS o.s. 182 (London, 1933 for 1929), pp. 50–2. Similar play of voices is found in
the Middle English version of the pseudo-Augustine (Paulinus of Aquilea) *Epistola ad Julianum
vel Henricum Comitem* (*Liber exhortationis*), in *The Wycliffe Bible*, II: *The Origin of the First Revision
as presented in* De Salutaribus Documentis, ed. S. L. Fristedt, Stockholm Studies in English 21
(Stockholm, 1969).

to lettyn the harme that thei shuld take of the pompe and the veyn glory of this wrechid lif, and mak ther way redy to come to hevyn, and heynen them in his bliss without end lestyng; for he seith: 'I shal al tobreke you for your veyn affections and your vicious pryde; and after that I shal togeder gader you and make you mylde and meke, clene and holy, by onyng to me.' And than I saw that ech kynde compassion that man hath on his even cristen with charite, it is Criste in him. (Sloane, ed. Glasscoe, pp. 39–40)

The register and lexis here are immediately recognizable from contemporary penitential texts, and in particular from exhortations on the uses of tribulation (scorn, pomp, vainglory, wretched life).[35] Moreover, she daringly places the awesome and terrifying teachings of the Church in the mouth of Christ: 'I shal al tobreke you for your veyn affections and your vicious pryde; and after that I shal togeder gader you and make you mylde and meke, clene and holy, by onyng to me'. But this does not sound like Julian's loving Christ: the clichés are too abrupt and blunt (vain affections, vicious pride) and the results are too cloyingly predictable (mild and meek, clean and holy). Only the final reference to 'onyng' and to the displayed love to 'even cristen' as a manifestation of Christ's saving love for mankind suggest that Julian is once again seeking to explore and understand how the paternalistic *magisterium* of the Church relates to the milder context of her faith in the tirelessly enfolding (and maternalistic) love of Christ.[36] In her dialogue with the teachings of the Church, Julian emerges as both intelligently forthright in her questioning and thoughtfully obedient (but by no means cowed) in her responses to ecclesiastical authority. Julian responds to the fears that are commonly brought to religion, and the fears that institutional religion often engenders in order to control its members. But she ultimately sidesteps them, as she sidesteps much of the paraphernalia of institutional religion, as 'means' that may become a hindrance to the end of knowing, loving and, above all, beholding God.

Julian is not merely being polite when she says her text is for her fellow Christians. Indeed, it was considered to be a particular responsibility of an anchoress to 'schew takynyngs [tokenings] of luf' to 'thi eeuencristene'.[37] But her showings require a particular set of interpretative skills from their readers. Reflecting on her own struggles to understand and articulate the meaning of her showings, Julian is careful to inscribe into her work clear guidance for her readers, and to leave for them clear signs of the provisionality of her own understandings and

35 Watson and Jenkins (p. 212) and Colledge and Walsh (p. 37) suggest as an analogue *The Chastising of God's Children and the Treatise of Perfection of the Sons of God*, ed. Joyce Bazire and Eric Colledge (Oxford, 1957). The s.xv copy in Cambridge, Trinity College MS B. 14. 19 survives as part of a compilation, perhaps of Norfolk provenance, which also contains *The Pricking of Love*, Richard Lavenham's *Litel tretys* on the deadly sins, an expanded copy of the so-called *Lay Folk's Catechism*, and an interestingly pertinent treatise on discerning the voices of the world, the flesh and the devil from that of God. The range of texts in this compilation is suggestive of the kinds of vernacular materials that Julian is ventriloquising and pastiching.
36 For a similar, but more schematic and formulaic, linkage between penitential and tribulation themes, see *Memoriale Credencium: A Late Middle English Manual of Theology for Lay People*, ed. J. H. L. Kengen (Nijmegen, 1979).
37 See *How ane ankares sal haf hir to þaim þat comes to hir*, in *Yorkshire Writers*, ed. Horstman, 1, pp. 106–7. The passage derives from Book I, Chapter 83 of Walter Hilton's *Scale of Perfection*.

of the language in which they are expressed. In Chapter 51, emerging from the interpretative maelstrom of the Lord and the Servant, she sums up her own experience of working with her showings:

> For twenty yere after the time of the shewing, save thre monthes, I had teching inwardly, as I shall sey: 'It longeth to the to take hede to all the propertes and the condetions that were shewed in the example, though the thinke that it ben misty and indefferent to thy sight'. (*Revelation*, 51.73–6)

Extrapolating from her own practice of tactically using but never resting on a range of dominant religious discourses, the coda to Chapter 86, found only in the Sloane manuscript, and possibly a scribal addition, is generous and permissive in the invitation it extends to other readers to perform Julian's text in their own voices and from their own conditions and experiences of life:

> But take everything with other and trewly vndertsonden all is according to holy scripture and growndid in the same, and that Ihesus our very love, light and truth shall shew to all clen soules that with mekenes aske perseverantly this wisdom of hym. (Chapter 86, coda: Sloane, ed. Glasscoe, p. 135)

Julian's ideal reader must be 'meke' (in the kenotic sense of being in a state of 'wilful abiding', open to 'beholding' what God shows) but above all 'perseverant'. They must learn to take heed of all the 'propertes and condetions' of her writing, and in particular to be carefully attentive to the ventriloquial voices that play tactically throughout her text. Her stylistic originality lies in her construction of a challenging new textual synthesis that works as much by juxtaposition and contrast as by exposition and exemplification. Her book is 'begunne […] but it is not yet performid', precisely because it refuses to allow itself to be safely inscribed into the canons of conventional religious discourse. That is her challenge, but it is also the source of her shocking and surprising stylistic and theological richness.

# 16

## *Julian's Afterlives**

### SARAH SALIH

Julian of Norwich has never been completely forgotten. Alexandra Barratt's textual history of *A Revelation* shows that:

> Julian's texts have had a more robustly continuous life than those of any other Middle English mystic. Their history – in manuscript and print, in editions more or less approximating Middle English and in translations more or less approaching Modern English – is virtually unbroken since the fifteenth century.[1]

Academic interest in her has increased rapidly since the mid twentieth century, and she is now a fixture in the academic canons of the Middle English mystics, of medieval women writers and of vernacular theologians. However, and almost alone amongst such figures, she has a present-day public profile beyond the academy of professional medievalists and theologians. Julian, in fact, currently enjoys what medievalists will recognise as a cult. Like a medieval cult, it adapts and supplements its core materials, in this case *A Revelation*, in order to construct a figure who can address changing circumstances. Julian has a cult centre at the reconstructed cell in St Julian's Church, Norwich; she is the patron of the monastic Order of Julian of Norwich, based in Wisconsin; she is iconographically identifiable as a wimpled figure with a cat or hazelnut. Devotional objects and souvenirs, the modern-day equivalents of pilgrim badges, can be bought in worship centres, Christian bookshops and, increasingly, online. The word is spread by a proliferation of texts: as well as numerous editions, translations, abbreviations and selections of the *Revelation*, there are devotional commentaries, meditations and plays.[2] Her words have been set to music and inserted into liturgies.[3] Beyond committed Christian circles, she is known as a minor tourist attraction in her home town of Norwich, and via her presence, sometimes in disguise, in novels, poems and at least one film. Though almost all accounts of Julian are

* Versions of this material were delivered at the Uses of the Past Conference, Norwich, July 2006, the New Chaucer Society Congress, New York, July 2006 and the Gender and Medieval Studies Group Conference, Norwich, January 2007: thanks to the organisers and to all who attended.

1 Alexandra Barratt, 'How Many Children Had Julian of Norwich? Editions, Translations and Versions of her Revelations', in *Vox Mystica: Essays on Medieval Mysticism in Honour of Professor Valerie M. Lagorio*, ed. Anne Clark Bartlett (Cambridge, 1995), pp. 27–39 (27).

2 The British Library catalogue lists twenty-five versions of Julian's text, and Amazon.co.uk has twenty-nine.

3 Alan Wilson, *Our Faith is a Light: For Soprano Solo, S.A.T.B. Choir and Organ* (London, 1985).

constructed from the basic elements of her texts, her anchoritism and something of the late medieval urban environment, the emphases vary, producing, amongst others, feminist Julians, conservative Julians and eco-Julians.

Most are grounded, however, in a consensual selection of the major points of interest in Julian's writing. Almost all depictions cite her envisioning of all creation in a 'little thing the quantity of an heselnot, lying in the palme of my hand' (*Vision*, 5.7–8),[4] and her assertion that 'Jhesu Crist, that doth good against evil, is oure very moder' (*Revelation*, 59.7). The most widely quoted passages are those which show her confidence in God's love and in ultimate salvation: 'love was his mening' (*Revelation*, 86.14); 'Thou shalt not be overcome' (*Revelation*, 68.54) and, in the phrase which has come to stand for the totality of her thought, 'alle shalle be wele' (*Revelation*, 27.10).

The impact of the hazelnut vision has been greatly intensified since the mid twentieth century by its likeness to the quintessentially modern image of the world seen from space.[5] It thus apparently testifies to the timeless truth of Julian's vision and to the validity of ecological concerns. Kenneth Leech uses the image to call for an earth-based 'hazelnut theology'.[6] In imaginative responses to Julian's text, the hazelnut's ecological resonance contributes to its function as a synecdoche – and something of a reification – of mysticism itself. Denise Levertov, who said that she was drawn to Julian by her images, found in those images the extra-temporal moment of the visionary:

> God for a moment in our history
> placed in that five-fingered
> human nest
> the macrocosmic egg, sublime paradox
> brown hazelnut of All that Is –
> made, and belov'd, and preserved.
> As still, waking each day within
> our microcosm, we find it, and ourselves.[7]

As Nicholas Watson and Jacqueline Jenkins note, writers' responses to the hazelnut often take the form of an identification with the visionary.[8] Levertov's dialogue with Julian imitates Julian's dialogue with Christ; her text encloses Julian's by incorporating italicized quotations from *A Revelation*. The conflation of egg and nut, here representing moments of Julian's childhood and her maturity, make the image encompass all time, in the lifecycle contracted to an egg, as well as all matter. Levertov's egg/nut also recalls Hildegard of Bingen's vision of the cosmos as 'a vast instrument, round and shadowed, in the shape of an

---

4   All references to Julian's writing will be taken from *The Writings of Julian of Norwich: A Vision Showed to a Devout Woman and A Revelation of Love*, ed. Nicholas Watson and Jacqueline Jenkins (Turnhout, 2006) and will be cited by section/chapter and line.

5   Sheila Upjohn, *Why Julian Now? A Voyage of Discovery* (London, 1997), p. 131.

6   Kenneth Leech, 'Hazelnut Theology: Its Potential and Perils', in Kenneth Leech and Benedicta Ward, *Julian Reconsidered*, (Oxford, 1988), pp. 1–9 (5).

7   Ed Block, 'Interview with Denise Levertov', *Renascence* 50, 1–2 (1997), pp. 4–15 (7); Denise Levertov, 'The Showings: Lady Julian of Norwich, 1342–1416', in *Breathing the Water* (New York, 1987), pp. 75–82, section 4.

8   *Writings*, ed. Watson and Jenkins, p. 20.

egg', the modern image constructing a thread of feminist-eco-mysticism to link
these otherwise quite dissimilar medieval visionaries.[9] In the poems of Sarah
Law, a former administrator of the Julian Centre in Norwich, the hazelnut is
imagined as both the content and the mechanism of another communication
across time, space and cultures, between Julian and the Sufi mystic Rumi.[10] Iris
Murdoch recalls and deliberately twists the scene in her novel, *Nuns and Soldiers*,
in which Christ appears to Anne Cavidge, a former nun who sees herself as
a 'secret anchoress'.[11] Though Anne, who has doubtless read Julian, expects a
hazelnut, he shows instead a pebble, but its import is the same, and within the
novel's reality the vision is both useful and true:

> Still holding hard to the edge of the table, Anne stared at the stone. Then she said
> slowly, 'Is it so small?'
> 'Yes, Anne.'
> 'Everything that is, so little?'
> 'Yes.'[12]

The hazelnut's ability to signify spiritual knowledge survives the translation of the image into narratives which are otherwise explicitly resistant to its
ground in medieval Christian thought. The film *Anchoress* bases its protagonist
on another fourteenth-century English anchoress, Christine Carpenter of Shere,
Surrey.[13] The historical Christine's enclosure, unauthorized departure from the
anchorhold and re-enclosure are documented, but there is no evidence for her
inner life or the form of her piety.[14] The film fills this blank space with Julian.
In a recurrent shot of Christine holding a round object in the palm of her hand,
the film quotes the vision of the hazelnut to signify the authentic, interior spirituality of the young anchoress, contrasted to a Church imagined as repressive,
dogmatic and misogynist. The film thus appropriates Julian for an anti-ecclesias-
tical position, and in doing so produces a reification of mysticism as an unmedi-
ated expression of inner spirituality, independent of the devotional practices of
its historical moment.

As Frodo Okulam writes, Julian's exploration of the motherhood of Jesus

---

[9]  Hildegard of Bingen, *Scivias*, trans. Columba Hart and Jane Bishop (New York, 1990),
p. 93.
[10]  Sarah Law, 'Two Mystical Poems', in *The Lady Chapel* (Exeter, 2003), pp. 40–1.
[11]  Iris Murdoch, *Nuns and Soldiers* (London, 1980), p. 62.
[12]  Ibid., p. 292.
[13]  *Anchoress*, dir. Chris Newby (1993). Thanks to Jacqueline Jenkins whose paper, 'Styling
History: Aesthetics and Authority in *The Anchoress* and *The Navigator*', at The Middle Ages
on Film conference, St Andrews, July 2005, alerted me to this connection and to Liz Herbert
McAvoy for the gift of a copy of the film.
[14]  Copies and translations of the documents of her enclosure and re-enclosure are displayed
in St James's Church, Shere, Surrey, for an analysis of which see Liz Herbert McAvoy, 'Gender,
Rhetoric and Space in the *Speculum Inclusorum*, *Letter to a Bury Recluse* and the Strange Case
of Christina Carpenter', in *Rhetoric of the Anchorhold: Place, Space and Body in the Discourses of
Enclosure*, ed. Liz Herbert McAvoy (Cardiff, 2008 forthcoming), pp. 111–26. See also Miri Rubin,
'An English Anchoress: The Making, Unmaking and Remaking of Christine Carpenter', in *Prag-
matic Utopias: Ideals and Communities 1200–1630*, ed. Rosemary Horrox and Sarah Rees Jones
(Cambridge, 2001), pp. 204–17 for further detail on the historical record and the film.

answers a contemporary desire for 'positive female images of the divine'.[15] The topos has acquired a politics which it did not have in Julian's day. In the author's note to *Mother Julian and the Gentle Vampire*, Jack Pantaleo claims Julian as 'the world's first recorded feminist', and though this novel rehearses various minority responses to Julian, there is indeed a strong feminist element in her present-day fame.[16] As Karen Armstrong shows, supporters of women's ordination cite Julian 'to prove that the transcendent and ineffable reality of the divine can just as easily be represented by feminine as well as masculine imagery' and hence that women can perform priestly functions.[17] On her controversial election in June 2006 as the first woman leader of the US Episcopal Church, Bishop Katherine Jefferts Schori preached a homily which included the passage:

> That bloody cross brings new life into this world. Colossians calls Jesus the first-born of all creation, the firstborn from the dead. That sweaty, bloody, tear-stained labor of the cross bears new life. Our mother Jesus gives birth to a new creation – and you and I are His children.[18]

This is a clear echo of Julian's meditation on a bleeding crucifix and her subsequent articulation of the motherhood of Christ:

> oure very moder Jhesu, he alone bereth us to joye and to endlesse leving – blessed mot he be! Thus he sustaineth us within him in love, and traveyled into the full time that he wolde suffer the sharpest throwes. (*Revelation*, 60.16–18)

Schori's allusion to Julian is an economical reminder that neither female participation nor feminine images of the divine are new to the Christian churches. That Julian should be cited in preference to the various Christian men who have written on God's motherhood indicates that she functions as female role model as well as theological authority. However, Christian interest in Julian's conception of divine maternity does not necessarily translate into support for women's ordination, or indeed for any other feminist positions. Sheila Upjohn insists that 'Julian never implies that Christ is female' in order to allay the 'alarming thought' that 'the militant feminists' might be right to think of God as a woman.[19]

Many general readers must first have encountered Julian in the words woven into the meditation of time, timelessness and truth of T. S. Eliot's 'Little Gidding':

> And all shall be well and
> All manner of thing shall be well
> When the tongues of flame are in-folded
> Into the crowned knot of fire
> And the fire and the rose are one.[20]

15   Frodo Okulam, *The Julian Mystique: Her Life and Teachings* (Ottawa, 1998), p. 1.
16   Jack Pantaleo, *Mother Julian and the Gentle Vampire* (Roseville, 1999), p. 4. Thanks to Sarah Law for telling me about this book.
17   Karen Armstrong, *The End of Silence: Women and the Priesthood* (London, 1993), p. 139.
18   http://www.ecusa.anglican.org/75383_76300_ENG_HTM.htm.
19   Sheila Upjohn, *In Search of Julian of Norwich* (London, 1989), pp. 53, 51.
20   T. S. Eliot, *Collected Poems 1909–1962* (London, 1974), p. 223.

As I suggested earlier in this chapter, 'All shall be well' is the essential phrase which has come to signify 'Julian of Norwich'. It captions images of Julian such as the modern window between the reconstructed cell and St Julian's Church; is regularly highlighted in devotional booklets; appears on prayer cards, bookmarks, mugs and fridge magnets. Quotation of an isolated phrase, however, necessarily obscures the way in which the *Revelation* tests and worries at the implications of the statement. Christ's words, 'Sinne is behovely, but alle shalle be wele, and alle shalle be wele, and alle maner of thinge shalle be wel' (*Revelation*, 27.9–11) do not go unchallenged: the questioning Julian persists 'how might alle be wele?', 'methought it was unpossible that alle maner of thing shuld be wele' (*Revelation*, 29.2–3; 32.39). Finally accepting the reassurance 'That that is unpossible to the is not unpossible to me. I shalle save my worde in alle thing, and I shalle make althing wele' (*Revelation*, 32.41–2), she nevertheless notes that it is not an answer. It is instead a formula which enables her to accept that the reconciliation of her vision to the teaching of the Church is possible somewhere outside of human understanding. Most sympathetic readers of Julian are at pains to emphasize that the optimism of her salvation theology is hard-won and complex; that it is not, as C. S. Lewis feared it might be, 'mere drivel'.[21] When it is printed in a decorative font on a household object, 'all shall be well' tends instead to function as a simpler and less provisional statement: Leech worries that such items mislead readers into 'pseudo-optimism'.[22] Removed from its dialogic context, 'all shall be well' seems to be an answer, even the answer, a truth which transcends the historical and textual locations of its articulation. Certainly the phrase has become a cliché, and quotations of 'all shall be well' in secular contexts often treat it sceptically or comically. Murdoch, whose fiction is deeply engaged with Julian-like questions about lived ethics, quotes the phrase itself with darkest irony. 'All shall be well, and all shall be well, as Julian remarked', says the protagonist of *The Black Prince*, with utterly unwarranted optimism, for all turns out, for him, very badly indeed.[23]

Julian the author has been resurrected from her text. Her persona and biography are constructed out of the handful of autobiographical details in *A Vision*, fewer in *A Revelation*, her appearance in *The Book of Margery Kempe*, contextual evidence and a good dose of supposition. The emphasis of this construction tends strongly towards making Julian seem more familiar and contemporary, in line with the often explicitly anti-historicist tenor of her cult: as Michael McLean, then the rector of St Julian's, put it: 'We believe that Julian is a woman of our day; that in some mysterious providence of God her wisdom has been "saved up" for our generation.'[24]

Several writers provide Julian with a history of personal relationships suitable

[21] C. S. Lewis, *Collected Letters vol. II: Books, Broadcasts and War 1931–1949*, ed. Walter Hooper (London, 2004), p. 369.
[22] Leech, 'Hazelnut Theology', p. 7.
[23] Iris Murdoch, *The Black Prince* (London, 1999), p. 221. The butt of a baroque Murdochian plot, he dies while wrongfully imprisoned for the murder of a rival writer, having been framed by the victim's vengeful wife, jealous of his love for her daughter, Julian.
[24] Michael McLean, 'Introduction', in *Julian: Woman of our Day*, ed. Robert Llewelyn (London, 1985), pp. 1–10 (2).

for a woman of our day, using Benedicta Ward's reconstruction of her biography. Ward argued that the showings occur in a secular household, not a nunnery, and that Julian was therefore more likely to have been, aged thirty, a 'young widow living in her own household' than a nun of Carrow priory.[25] She tentatively suggests that Julian might have borne and lost at least one child, for which, as she acknowledges, there is no direct evidence. This last hypothesis relies on a circular argument: Julian wrote about motherhood, so we suppose her to have been a mother, which supposition then brings emotional intensity to our reading of her maternal imagery. This narrative appeals intuitively to many commentators: Upjohn, for example, felt Ward's argument 'had the ring of truth'.[26] Dana Bagshaw's play *Cell Talk* and Anya Seton's novel *Katherine*, amongst others, take the opportunity of fictionalisation to insert a bereavement into Julian's biography.[27] Ralph Milton's novel *Julian's Cell* develops the theme at perhaps the greatest length to construct a Julian who is distinguished from her contemporaries by her guilt-free enjoyment of marital sexuality.[28] Here Julian overcomes her mother's alarming pre-wedding advice 'You must lie down on your back and let him do whatever he wants. It will hurt at first. But it is necessary', to find 'gentle joy' in her marriage bed, and rebukes Margery Kempe for her rejection of her husband.[29] Milton imagines Julian's theory of the motherhood of Jesus to be a straightforward transcription of her own experience of mothering:

> her reverie sometimes brought a sense of closeness, of a holy presence, and many times she thought God's nurturing love must be like the mothering love she felt as she fed the child with herself. In those moments she could not imagine anger at the tiny helpless infant in her arms, or imagine how a God who created such a wondrous child could feel anger toward it.[30]

Julian's anchoritism provokes a certain unease: a life of virginity, silence and enclosure potentially seems self-indulgent, quietist or just too medieval. As Beelzebub says in Upjohn's play *Mind out of Time*, 'It's ridiculously easy to discredit a woman, particularly one who probably never married and who spent all her life after the age of thirty in one room.'[31] To have been married, then, and preferably a mother too, bolsters a woman's credibility by establishing her successful achievement of heterosexuality. To suppose Julian to have been a life-long virgin invites further questions as to whether she was asexual, whether she struggled with sexual temptation, or whether she was lesbian, possibilities which do not recommend themselves to the generally conservative sexual politics of writers on Julian. Upjohn acknowledges that the appeal of the widow-

25  Benedicta Ward, 'Julian the Solitary', in Leech and Ward, *Julian Reconsidered*, pp. 11–35 (23). The argument had been made previously, but Ward's version has circulated most widely.
26  Upjohn, *Why Julian Now?* p. 118.
27  Dana Bagshaw, *Cell Talk*, performed by Cameo Theatre Company, St Julian's, Norwich, 11 September 2005; Anya Seton, *Katherine* (London, 1954), p. 514.
28  Ralph Milton, *Julian's Cell: An Earthly Story of Julian of Norwich* (Kelowna, 2002). I am grateful to Daniel Pinti for letting me know of this text.
29  Milton, *Julian's Cell*, pp. 27, 30, 199.
30  Milton, *Julian's Cell*, p. 34.
31  Sheila Upjohn, *Mind out of Time* (Norwich, 1979), p. 15.

hood hypothesis is that it enables her to reject R. H. Thouless's vulgar-Freudian attribution of 'suppressed primitive sexual desires' to Julian.[32] The significant exception is *Mother Julian and the Gentle Vampire*, a novel featuring a reverse-vampire heroine named, unsubtly, Lesbianna, and in which Julian is chastely 'oned' with her maid/companion, Lucy.[33]

Fictive and non-fictive treatments of Julian also accommodate her to modern tastes by reimagining the anchoress as counsellor. Although *Ancrene Wisse* discourages anchoresses from instructing or showing their learning to their visitors, the *Book of Margery Kempe* proves that Julian advised at least one person, or at the very least that contemporaries thought it credible that she might have done so.[34] The *Book* also shows, however, that Julian's reputation was, specifically, for expertise in the discernment of spirits. Margery describes her visions and devotions 'to wetyn yf þer wer any deceyte in hem, for þe ankres was expert in swech thyngys & gowde cownsel cowd ʒeuyn', and Julian's lengthy answer directly addresses her concerns and does not stray from that topic.[35] The passage has the dual effect of showing that the orthodoxy of Margery's visions was confirmed by a qualified specialist and that Julian limited her teaching to one acknowledged area of expertise. Modern retellings, however, often expand Julian's role into that of a general counsellor or even therapist. Robert Llewelyn suggests that recluses performed the functions of 'social workers, marriage counsellors, Samaritans, psychiatrists'.[36] Brian Thorne calls Julian a 'radical psychotherapist' and refers to her 'work as a counsellor'.[37] Thorne's version of the meeting with Margery articulates his own therapeutic ideal, while departing in many respects from the scene in the *Book*:

> The Julian who listened patiently to the garrulous Margery Kempe who reports the experience in her own writings had no desire to intervene with gratuitous and pious platitudes. She knew that letting Margery talk about herself was a sure way to bring her back to trust in herself and in God as long as she was not impeded by adverse judgements or condemnatory looks.[38]

This account omits any reference to the established doctrine and practice of *discretio spirituum* or to the *Book*'s use of the scene to place both women securely within orthodoxy. The concern of the *Book* was not Margery's sense of self but the nature of her visionary experiences, and Julian could hardly have gained

[32] Upjohn, *Why Julian Now?* p. 86.
[33] Pantaleo, *Mother Julian*, p. 88.
[34] *Ancrene Wisse*, trans. Hugh White (Harmondsworth, 1993), p. 35.
[35] *The Book of Margery Kempe*, ed. Sanford Brown Meech and Hope Emily Allen, EETS o.s. 212 (London, 1940), p. 42; see Nancy Caciola, *Discerning Spirits: Divine and Demonic Possession in the Middle Ages* (Ithaca, NY, 2003) for the intense anxiety raised by this problem and Naöe Kukita Yoshikawa, *Margery Kempe's Meditations: The Context of Medieval Devotional Literature, Liturgy and Iconography* (Cardiff, 2007), pp. 62–7 for a discussion of the issue in the *Book*. I am grateful to Naöe for prepublication access to her work.
[36] Robert Llewelyn, *With Pity not Blame: The Spirituality of Julian of Norwich and* The Cloud of Unknowing (London, 1982), p. 6.
[37] Brian Thorne, *Mother Julian, Radical Psychotherapist*, Annual Julian Lecture 1993 (Norwich, undated), p. 7.
[38] Brian Thorne, *Julian of Norwich: Counsellor for our Age* (London, 1999), p. 17.

a reputation for discernment unless an adverse judgement were a real possibility. Such historically specific concerns, however, would be irrelevant or even counter-productive to the reconstruction of Julian into a figure who meets a more modern need for a patron saint of therapy.

The meeting of Margery and Julian is the main topic of Bagshaw's play *Cell Talk*, which elaborates the single recorded encounter into a long-standing relationship of mutual support; of Law's poem 'Margery's Harbour'; and of an icon-painting by Brother Leon of Walsingham, of which postcard reproductions can be bought at the Julian Centre.[39] All of these depart from Thorne's – and indeed the *Book*'s – model of wise counsellor and humble client by constructing a mutually respectful relation between women whose differences are complementary, rather than oppositional. Law's poem is particularly noticeable for allowing Margery's voice, to which she allots a richly concrete string of images of cloth, sea and ships, to tell the meeting. Milton, however, uses the encounter to contrast Julian's spirituality with Margery's thoroughly medieval – that is, incoherent, anti-sexual, self-dramatising and guilt-ridden – religiosity, and follows through this conception of a non-meeting of minds to the unconventional conclusion that Julian's counsel failed because 'Margery didn't really hear what she had to say.'[40]

However, the most widely circulated scene of Julian as counsellor was published in 1954, when *The Book of Margery Kempe* was known only to a handful of academic medievalists. In Anya Seton's still-popular bodice-ripper *Katherine*, Julian's advice saves the heroine, Katherine Swynford, from despair. Seton's Julian represents an interiorized, indeed proto-Protestant, piety. She discourages physical penance and the 'shining mist' of her face is contrasted with the 'bland, wooden, indifferent' face of the statue of the Virgin at Walsingham, represented in traditional anti-Catholic fashion as an imposition on the credulous.[41] The imaginative task Seton sets herself is that of putting Julian in dialogue with a historically attested contemporary whose career and concerns would seem on the face of it quite alien to her. Seton shares the perception of John Swanson that Julian's thought constitutes an effective pastoral theology.[42] Katherine begins the episode sceptical that Julian's spiritual knowledge has any relevance to her personal troubles, but Seton constructs a dialogue in which passages from *A Revelation* are adapted as Julian's response to Katherine's depression:

'Lady', whispered Katherine, 'it must be these visions were vouchsafed to you because you knew naught of sin – not sins like mine – lady, what would *you* know of – of adultery – of murder –'
Julian rose quickly and placed her hand on Katherine's shoulder. At the touch, a soft rose flame enveloped her, and she could not go on.
'I have known all manner of sin', said Julian quietly. 'Sin is the sharpest scourge. ... Yet listen to what I was shown ... He turned on me His face of lovely pity and

39  Law, *Lady Chapel*, pp. 37–9.
40  Milton, *Julian's Cell*, p. 200.
41  Seton, *Katherine*, p. 511, p. 502.
42  John Swanson, 'Guide for the Inexpert Mystic', in *Julian: Woman of our Day*, ed. Llewelyn (London, 1985), pp. 75–88 (87).

Plate 2. 'Pantheon: Julian of Norwich', a cartoon by Martin Rowson, *Independent on Sunday*, 8 March 1998, by kind permission of the artist.

he said: *it is truth that sin is the cause of all this pain: sin is behovable – none the less all shall be well.*'[43]

The ensuing conversation, continuing this juxtaposition of romantic narrative with direct quotation, is occasionally awkward, but it is the product of a synthetic historical imagination.

The identification of a recluse as a counsellor helps modern readers to familiarize anchoritism. It counters arguments that the anchoritic life is solipsistic or quietist without either endorsing the very concrete late-medieval attitude to prayer-treasuries or having recourse to functionalist anthropological explanations, such as those which see the recluse as a communal safety-valve, enacting

43 Seton, *Katherine*, p. 511

the virtues which a mercantile society cannot afford to practise for itself. Leech imagines Julian counselling John Ball, in order to argue that 'Her life of solitude was not a selfish, egotistical withdrawal … but a life of love, warmth and care towards her "even-Christians".'[44] The counselling scene also appeals to feminist commentators as an exercise in practical sisterhood, which shows Julian able to bond with a woman of a different style of piety, such as Margery Kempe, or a secular woman, such as Katherine Swynford.

It is presumably this incarnation of Julian as supreme agony aunt which accounts for her presence on the back cover of Donna Freitas's *Becoming a Goddess of Inner Poise*: 'With *InStyle* magazine on one nightstand, and Julian of Norwich on the other, author Donna Freitas has her finger on the pulse of a new generation of women and understands the spiritual issues that most concern them.' This is particularly telling because Freitas in fact does not synthesize or adapt Julian's thought to present-day concerns, but invokes her only to reject her as irredeemably medieval:

> How does Chick Lit stand up spiritually to the likes of *Showings*, by Julian of Norwich – nun-extraordinaire from the fourteenth century (as Julian was not doing a lot of shagging, nor hitting the bottle, except perhaps at church and then in v. limited quantities, I assume). … Can the likes of *Bridget Jones's Diary* and *Confessions of a Shopaholic* prove to be sacred stories?[45]

Julian is entirely irrelevant to Freitas's pursuit of the spiritual message of chick-lit, and is invoked only to be superseded. The blurb-writer, however, evidently assumed that it is obligatory to cite Julian in any Christian text directed at women.

Such perfunctory invocations of Julian construct an object ripe for satire. Reductive constructions of Julian as counsellor, nurturer and optimist are ridiculed in Martin Rowson's 'Pantheon' cartoon (Plate 2), in which the anchorhold is modernized into the secular feminine confessional enclosure of the hairdressing salon. Julian, often feminized to 'Juliana', or to 'Dame', 'Lady' or 'Mother' Julian, is here an androgynous figure seen dimly through the glass.[46] 'All shall be well' becomes phatic soothing, emptied of content.

A final example of the modernisation of Julian is the invention of Julian's cat. This animal originates in *Ancrene Wisse*'s permission for anchoresses to keep a cat and appears in several images, including the very high-profile window in St Saviour's chapel, Norwich Cathedral, as a visual signifier of anchoritism.[47] This symbolic image is then read as evidence of the historical existence of an actual cat. The cat has made its way from iconography to narrative fiction and has even become the protagonist of a children's book, *Julian's Cat*.[48] Pantaleo takes

---

44  Kenneth Leech, 'Contemplative and Radical: Julian meets John Ball', in *Julian: Woman of our Day*, ed. Llewelyn (London, 1985), pp. 89–101 (90).
45  Donna Freitas, *Becoming a Goddess of Inner Poise: Spirituality for the Bridget Jones in All of Us* (San Francisco, 2005), p. 9. Thanks to Anke Bernau for telling me of this book.
46  'Dame Ielyan', is used in *The Book of Margery Kempe*, but there is no contemporary attestation for the other titles; *Book of Margery Kempe*, p. 42.
47  *Ancrene Wisse*, p. 192.
48  Mary E. Little, *Julian's Cat: The Imaginary History of a Cat of Destiny* (Wilton, 1989).

the cat as a given, and weaves it into the plot with the detail that it could sense Julian's impending visions.[49] The cat rounds off the construction of a domesticated persona of Julian as an altogether cosier kind of single woman than the enclosed career-virgin and learned theologian which she was.

The comparison of Julian with her contemporary, Margery Kempe, is irresistible and instructive, for Margery has also been reimagined as our contemporary, but by an entirely different constituency. Margery, though predicted a local cult in her *Book*, has not acquired a significant devotional following. Julian's words have been frequently excerpted, with the first and most popular pocket-book of quotations, *Enfolded in Love*, selling around 100,000 copies.[50] I know of only one devotional booklet of quotations from Margery, and even that introduces her with the qualification that she was 'not a teacher' but a 'housewife'.[51] The leaflet sold at Margery's parish church, St Margaret's, King's Lynn, describes her as 'more than just a pilgrim', but stops well short of endorsing her as saint or mystic.[52] Margery's current constituency is instead dominated by academics, to some of whom she is a figure of more than historical interest. She has recently become one of the key exhibits of the branch of postmodern literary theory which Jeffrey Jerome Cohen calls 'critical temporal studies', and which disrupts the concept of time as moving at uniform speed in a single linear direction.[53] Carolyn Dinshaw considers Margery as an exemplar of queerness, arguing that her misfit with her contemporaries makes her 'an anachronism even in her own (temporally heterogeneous) time' and recommends reading her in a simultaneously historicized and dehistoricized fashion, as a figure who 'lives in a multitemporal, heterogenous *now*' and can be 'a life possibility for the present'.[54] The non-academic public for Julian, however, has for years been operating under the assumption that Julian offers a life possibility for the present, and indeed that she belongs more properly to the present than to the Middle Ages in which she happened to live and write.

[49] Pantaleo, *Mother Julian*, p. 262.
[50] *Enfolded in Love: Daily Readings with Julian of Norwich*, ed. Robert Llewelyn (London, 1980); Robert Llewelyn, *Memories and Reflections* (London, 1998), p. 183.
[51] *The Mirror of Love: Daily Readings with Margery Kempe*, ed. Gillian Hawker (London, 1988), p. vii.
[52] Elizabeth James, *The St Margaret's of Margery Kempe*, pamphlet.
[53] Jeffrey Jerome Cohen, *Medieval Identity Machines* (Minneapolis, 2003), p. 9.
[54] Carolyn Dinshaw, 'Margery Kempe', in *The Cambridge Companion to Medieval Women's Writing*, ed. Caroline Dinshaw and David Wallace (Cambridge, 2003), pp. 222–39 (236, 237).

# Select Bibliography

## Manuscripts

*Julian of Norwich*
London, British Library MS Additional 37790
London, British Library MS Sloane 2499
London, British Library MS Sloane 3705
London, Westminster, Cathedral Treasury MS 4
MS St Joseph's College, Upholland
Paris, Bibliotèque Nationale MS Fonds Anglais 40

*Other*
Cambridge, Trinity College MS B. 14. 19
Hertford, Hertfordshire Archives and Local Studies, 1AR
London, British Library, MS Cotton Nero D 7
London, British Library, MS Harley 2162
London, National Archives: Public Record Office, PROB 11/6
Norwich, Norfolk Record Office, NCC Aleyn
Norwich, Norfolk Record Office, NCC Wylbey
Oxford, Bodleian Library, MS Ashmole 59

## Primary sources

*Julian of Norwich*
*A Book of Showings to the Anchoress Julian of Norwich*, ed. Edmund Colledge and James Walsh, 2 vols (Toronto: Pontifical Institute for Mediaeval Studies, 1978)
*Enfolded in Love: Daily Readings with Julian of Norwich*, ed. Robert Llewelyn (London: Darton, Longman and Todd, 1980)
*Julian of Norwich: A Revelation of Love*, ed. Marian Glasscoe (Exeter: Exeter University Press, 1976; various repr.).
*Julian of Norwich: Showing of Love: Extant Texts and Translation*, ed. Sr Anna Maria Reynolds and Julia Bolton Holloway (Florence: Sismel, 2001)
*Julian of Norwich's Revelation of Love*, ed. and trans. Elisabeth Dutton (International Sacred Literature Trust, Plymouth: Rowman and Littlefield Press, 2008)
*Julian of Norwich's Revelations of Divine Love: The Shorter Version ed. from BL Add. MS 37790*, ed. Frances Beer (Heidelberg: Winter 1978)
Kempster, H., 'The Westminster Text of *A Revelation of Love*', *Mystics Quarterly* 23 (1997), pp. 177–245
*Revelations of Divine Love Recorded by Julian of Norwich*, ed. Grace Warrack (London: Methuen and Co., 1901)

*The Shewings of Julian of Norwich*, ed. Georgia Ronan Crampton, TEAMS (Kalamazoo: Western Michigan University Press, 1994)

*The Writings of Julian of Norwich:* A Vision Showed to a Devout Woman *and* A Revelation of Love, ed. Nicholas Watson and Jacqueline Jenkins (Turnhout: Brepols, 2006)

*Other primary sources*

Aelred of Rievaulx, *Aelred of Rievaulx's De Institutione Inclusarum*, ed. John Ayto and Alexandra Barratt, EETS o.s. 287 (London: Oxford University Press, 1984)

——, *De Institutione Inclusorum* in *Opera Omnia* 1, ed. A. Hoste and C. H. Talbot, CCCM, 1 (Turnhout: Brepols, 1971)

——, 'Rule of Life for a Recluse', in *Treatises, the Pastoral Prayer*, ed. David Knowles (Kalamazoo: Cistencian Publications Inc., 1971), pp. 43–102

*Anchoress*, dir. Chris Newby (1993)

*Anchoritic Spirituality: 'Ancrene Wisse' and Associated Works*, ed. Anne Savage and Nicholas Watson (New York: Paulist Press, 1991).

*Ancrene Wisse, A Corrected Edition of the Text in Cambridge, Corpus Christi College MS 402, with Variants from other Manuscripts*, ed. Bella Millett, EETS o.s. 325 (Oxford: Oxford University Press, 2005)

*A Revelation of Purgatory by an Unknown Fifteenth-Century Woman Visionary: Introduction, Critical Text and Translation*, ed. Marta Powell Harley, Studies in Women and Religion 18 (Lewiston, NY: E. Mellen Press, 1985)

*A Talkyng of þe Loue of God*, ed. Sr Dr D. W. Westra (The Hague: Martinus Nijhoff, 1950)

Augustine, *Confessions*, ed. James O'Donnell, 3 vols (Oxford: Clarendon Press, 1992)

——, *Confessions*, trans. R. S. Pine-Coffin (Harmondsworth: Penguin, 1961)

Baker, Augustine, *Secretum*, ed. John Clark (Salzburg: Institut für Anglistik und Amerikanistik, Universität Salzburg, 1997)

Barratt, Alexandra (ed.), *Women's Writing in Middle English* (London: Longman, 1992)

Bridget of Sweden, *The Liber Celestis of St Bridget of Sweden*, vol. 1, ed. Roger Ellis, EETS o.s. 291 (London: Oxford University Press, 1987)

Clark, Andrew (ed.), *Lincoln Diocese Documents, 1450–1544*, EETS o.s. 149 (London: Oxford University Press, 1914)

Dinnis, Enid, *The Anchorhold: A Divine Comedy* (London: Sands and Company, 1934)

*Dives and Pauper*, ed. P. H. Barnum, EETS o.s. 275 (London: Oxford University Press, 1976)

Ducange, Charles, *Glossarium Mediae et Infimae Latinitatis*, vol. 5 (Paris, 1842)

Duncan, Leland L. (ed.), *Testamenta Cantiana*, Archaeologia Cantiana (London, 1906)

Dunstan, G. R. (ed.), *The Register of Edmund Lacy, Bishop of Exeter, 1420–1455: Registrum Commune*, vol. 4, Devon and Cornwall Record Society n.s. 16 (Torquay: Canterbury and York Society, 1971)

Eliot, T. S., *Collected Poems 1909–1962* (London: Faber and Faber, 1974)

*An Exposition of Qui habitat and Bonum est in English*, ed. Björn Wallner, Lund Studies in English XXIII (Lund, 1954)

*Fasciculus Morum: A Fourteenth-Century Preacher's Handbook*, ed. and trans. Siegfried Wenzel (London and University Park, PA: Pennsylvania State University Press, 1989)

Flete, William, *'Remedies against Temptations': The Third English Version of William Flete*, ed. E. Colledge and N. Chadwick, Archivio Italiano per la Storia della Pieta V (Rome, 1967)

*Foedera Conventiones, Literae, et Cujuscunque Generis Acta Publica etc.*, ed. Thomas Rymer, 20 vols (London, 1704–32)

Gervase of Tilbury, *Otia Imperialia*, ed. and trans. S. E. Banks and J. W. Binns (Oxford: Oxford University Press, 2002)

Gibbons, A. (ed.), *Early Lincoln Wills*, Lincoln Record Society 1 (Lincoln, 1888)

Goscelin of St Bertin, *Goscelin of St. Bertin: The Book of Encouragement and Consolation [Liber Confortatorius] – The Letter of Goscelin to the Recluse Eva*, ed. Monika Otter (Cambridge: D. S. Brewer, 2004)

——, *Liber confortatorius*, ed. C. H. Talbot, Analecta Monastica: Studia Anselmiana xxxvii (Rome: Herder, 1955)

Hildegard of Bingen, *Scivias*, trans. Columba Hart and Jane Bishop (New York, 1990)

Hilton, Walter, *The Scale of Perfection*, ed. Thomas H. Bestul, TEAMS (Kalamazoo: Western Michigan University Press, 2000)

*Horae Beatae Mariae Virginis or Sarum and York Primers with Kindred Books and Primers of the Reformed Roman Use*, ed. E. Hoskins (London, 1901)

*How ane ankares sal haf hir to þaim þat comes to hir*, in *Yorkshire Writers – Richard Rolle of Hampole and His Followers*, ed. C. Horstman, new edition with preface by A. C. Barlett (Cambridge: D. S. Brewer, 1999)

*Inventory of Church Goods temp. Edward III* (Archdeaconry of Norwich), transcribed by Dom Aelred Watkin, 2 vols (Norfolk: Norfolk Record Society, 1947 and 1948)

Kempe, Margery, *The Book of Margery Kempe*, ed. Barry Windeatt (Cambridge: D. S. Brewer, 2004)

——, *The Book of Margery Kempe*, ed. Sanford Brown Meech and Hope Emily Allen, EETS o.s. 212 (London: Oxford University Press, 1940; repr. 1997)

Law, Sarah, 'Two Mystical Poems', in *The Lady Chapel* (Exeter: Stride Publications, 2003), pp. 40–1

Levertov, Denise, 'The Showings: Lady Julian of Norwich, 1342–1416', in *Breathing the Water* (New York: Norton, 1987), pp. 75–82

Lewis, C. S., *Collected Letters vol. II: Books, Broadcasts and War 1931–1949*, ed. Walter Hooper (London: HarperCollins, 2004)

Little, Mary E., *Julian's Cat: The Imaginary History of a Cat of Destiny* (Wilton: Morehouse Publications, 1989)

*Memoriale Credencium: A Late Middle English Manual of Theology for Lay People*, ed. J. H. L. Kengen (Nijmegen, 1979)

Milton, Ralph, *Julian's Cell: An Earthly Story of Julian of Norwich* (Kelowna: Northstone Publishing, 2002)

*Missale ad Usum Insignis Ecclesium Eboracensis*, ed. W. G. Henderson, Surtees Society 59–60 (Durham, 1874)

Murdoch, Iris, *Nuns and Soldiers* (London: Vintage, 1980)

——, *The Black Prince* (London: Vintage, 1999)

*Myrour of Recluses: A Middle English Translation of* Speculum Inclusorum, ed. Marta Powell Harley (Madison and London: Fairleigh Dickinson, 1995)

*Nova Legenda Anglie*, ed. Carl. Horstman, 2 vols (Oxford: Clarendon, 1901)

*Of the Knowledge of Ourselves and of God: A Fifteenth-Century Spiritual Florilegium*, ed. James Walsh and Eric Colledge (London: Mowbray, 1961)

Pantaleo, Jack, *Mother Julian and the Gentle Vampire* (Roseville, 1999)

*Paston Letters and Papers of the Fifteenth Century*, ed. Norman Davis, 2 vols (Oxford: Clarendon, 1971–6)

*The Paston Women: Selected Letters*, ed. Diane Watt (Cambridge: D.S. Brewer, 2004)

Pecock, Reginald, *The Repressor of Over Much Blaming of the Clergy*, ed. Churchill Babington, Chronicles and Memorials of Great Britain (Kraus Reprint, 1966)

Pseudo-Augustine (Paulinus of Aquilea), *Epistola ad Julianum vel Henricum Comitem (Liber exhortationis)*, in *The Wycliffe Bible*, II: *The Origin of the First Revision as presented in* De Salutaribus Documentis, ed. S. L. Fristedt, Stockholm Studies in English 21 (Stockholm: Almquvist and Wiksells, 1969)

*Religious Lyrics of the XIV*th *Century*, ed. C. Brown, 2nd edn rev. by G. V. Smithers (Oxford: Clarendon, 1952)

Robbins, R. H., 'Popular Prayers in Middle English verse', *Modern Philology* 36 (1939), pp. 337–50

——, 'Private Prayers in Middle English Verse', *Studies in Philology* 36 (1939), pp. 466–75

——, 'Five Middle English Verse Prayers from Lambeth MS. 541', *Neophilologus* 38 (1954), pp. 36–41

Rolle, Richard, *Richard Rolle: Prose and Verse*, ed. S. Ogilvie-Thomson, EETS 293 (London: Oxford University Press, 1988)

*Speculum Christiani*, ed. Gustaf Holmstedt, EETS o.s 182 (London: Oxford University Press, 1933 for 1929)

*Speculum Inclusorum auctore anonymo anglico saeculi xiv*, ed. Livarius Oliger, Lateranum n.s. 4/1 (Rome, 1938)

Seton, Anya, *Katherine* (London: Reprint Society, 1954; various repr.)

Tanner, Norman P. (ed.), *Heresy Trials in the Diocese of Norwich, 1428–31*, Camden Society 4th Series 20 (London: Royal Historical Society, 1977)

*The Beauchamp Pageant*, ed. Alexandra Sinclair (Donington: The Richard III and Yorkist History Trust, 2003)

*The Chastising of God's Children and the Treatise of Perfection of the Sons of God*, ed. Joyce Bazire and Eric Colledge (Oxford: Blackwell, 1957)

*The Cloud of Unknowing and Related Treatises on Contemplative Prayer*, ed. Phyllis Hodgson, *Analecta Cartusiana* 3 (Exeter: University of Exeter Press, 1982)

*Þe Holy Boke Gratia Dei*, in *Richard Rolle and þe holy Boke Gratia Dei*, ed. Sister Mary Luke Arntz (Salzburg: Universität Salzburg, 1981)

*The Hours of Catherine of Cleves*, introduction and commentaries by John Plummer (London: George Braziller, 1966)

*The Lay Folks Mass Book*, ed. T. F. Simmons, EETS o.s. 71 (London: Oxford University Press, 1879)

*The Life of Christina of Markyate: A Twelfth Century Recluse*, ed. and trans. C. H. Talbot (Oxford: Oxford University Press, 1959; reprinted Toronto: Toronto University Press, 1998)

*The Mirror of Love: Daily Readings with Margery Kempe*, ed. Gillian Hawker (London: Moorhouse Publishing, 1988)

*Theodori Mopsuesteni Expositionis in Psalmos*, ed. Lucas de Coninck, Corpus Christianorum Series Latina 88A (Turnholt: Brepols, 1977)

*The Prickynge of Love*, ed. Harold Kane, Salzburg Studies in English Literature: Elizabethan and Renaissance Studies 92:10 (Salzburg: Institut für Anglistik und Amerikanistik, Universität Salzburg 1983)

*The Privity of the Passion*, in *Cultures of Piety: Medieval Devotional Literature in Translation*, ed. A. C. Bartlett and T. H. Bestul (New York: Cornell University Press, 1999)

*The Prymer or Lay-Folks Prayer Book*, ed. H. Littlehales, EETS o.s. 105 and 109 (London: Oxford University Press, 1895–7)

*The Rous Roll: With an Historical Introduction on John Rous and the Warwick Roll*, ed. Charles Ross (repr., Gloucester, 1980)

*The Sarum Missal edited from Three Early Manuscripts*, ed. J. Wickham Legg (Oxford: Oxford University Press, 1916)

Wilson, Alan, *Our Faith is a Light: For Soprano Solo, S.A.T.B. Choir and Organ* (London, 1985)

*Yorkshire Writers – Richard Rolle of Hampole and His Followers*, ed. C. Horstman, new edition with preface by A. C. Barlett (Cambridge: D. S. Brewer, 1999)


*Secondary sources*


*On Julian*

Abbott, Christopher, *Julian of Norwich: Autobiography and Theology* (Cambridge: D. S. Brewer, 1999)

Aers, David, 'The Humanity of Christ: Reflections on Julian of Norwich's *Revelation of Love*', in David Aers and Lynn Staley, *The Powers of the Holy: Religion, Politics, and Gender in Late Medieval English Culture* (Philadelphia: Pennsylvania State University Press, 1996), pp. 77–104

Baker, Denise N., 'Julian of Norwich and Anchoritic Literature', *Mystics Quarterly* 19 (1993), 148–60

——, *Julian of Norwich's* Showings: *From Vision to Book* (Princeton: Princeton University Press, 1994)

——, 'The Image of God: Contrasting Configurations in Julian's *Showings* and Walter Hilton's *Scale of Perfection*', in *Julian of Norwich: A Book of Essays*, ed. Sandra J. McEntire (New York and London: Garland, 1998), pp. 35–60

Barratt, Alexandra, 'How Many Children Had Julian of Norwich? Editions, Translations and Versions of her Revelations', in *Vox Mystica: Essays on Medieval Mysticism in Honour of Professor Valerie M. Lagorio*, ed. Anne Clark Bartlett (Cambridge: D. S. Brewer, 1995), pp. 27–39

——, ' "In the Lowest Part of Our Need": Julian and Medieval Gynecological Writing', in *Julian of Norwich: A Book of Essays*, ed. Sandra J. McEntire (New York and London: Garland, 1998), pp. 239–56

——, 'Julian of Norwich and the Holy Spirit, "Our Good Lord" ', *Mystics Quarterly* 28 (2002), pp. 78–84

——, 'Lordship, Service and Worship in Julian of Norwich', in *The Medieval Mystical Tradition in England: Exeter Symposium VII*, ed. E. A. Jones (Cambridge: D. S. Brewer, 2004), pp. 177–88

Bartlett, Anne Clark, *Male Authors, Female Readers: Representation and Subjectivity in Middle English Devotional Literature* (Ithaca: Cornell University Press, 1995)

Clark, J. P. H., 'Fiducia in Julian of Norwich', *Downside Review* 99 (1981), pp. 97–108

——, 'Nature, Grace and Trinity in Julian of Norwich', *Downside Review* 100 (1982), pp. 203–20

——, 'Predestination in Christ according to Julian of Norwich', *Downside Review* 100 (1982), pp. 79–81

——, 'Time and Eternity in Julian of Norwich', *Downside Review* 109 (1991), pp. 259–76

Coiner, Nancy, 'The "homely" and the *heimlich*: The Hidden, Doubled Self in Julian of Norwich's Showings', *Exemplaria* 5, 2 (1993), pp. 305–23

Colledge, Edmund and James Walsh, 'Editing Julian of Norwich's *Revelations*: A Progress Report', *Medieval Studies* 39 (1976), pp. 404–27

Cré, M., 'Westminster Cathedral Treasury MS 4: A Fifteenth-Century Spiritual Compilation' (unpublished MPhil diss., University of Glasgow, 1997)

——, 'Authority and the Compiler in Westminster Cathedral Treasury MS 4: Writing a Text in Someone Else's Words', in *Authority and Community in the Middle Ages*, ed. Donald Mowbray, Rhiannon Purdie and Ian P. Wei (Stroud: Sutton Publishing Ltd, 1999), pp. 153–76

——, *Vernacular Mysticism in the Charterhouse: A Study of London, British Library, MS Additional 37790*, The Medieval Translator 9 (Turnhout: Brepols, 2006)

Dutton, Elisabeth, 'Augustine Baker and Two Manuscripts of Julian of Norwich's *Revelation of Love*,' *Notes and Queries* 250, 3 (2005) pp. 329–37

——, *Julian of Norwich and Late-Medieval Devotional Texts* (Cambridge: D. S. Brewer, 2008)

Flood, Robert H., A *Description of St Julian's Church, Norwich and an Account of Dame Julian's Connection with It* (Norwich, 1936)

Gillespie, Vincent, 'Strange Images of Death: The Passion in Later Medieval English Devotional and Mystical Writing', *Analecta Cartusiana* 117 (1987), pp. 110–59

——, 'Postcards from the Edge: Interpreting the Ineffable in the Middle English Mystics', in *Interpretation Medieval and Modern: The J. A. W. Bennett Memorial Lectures: Perugia 1992*, ed. Piero Boitani and Anna Torti (Cambridge: D. S. Brewer, 1993), pp.137–65

——, and Maggie Ross, 'The Apophatic Image: The Poetics of Effacement in Julian of Norwich', in *The Medieval Mystical Tradition in England: Exeter Symposium V*, ed. Marion Glasscoe (Cambridge: D. S. Brewer, 1992), pp. 53–77

——, and Maggie Ross, ' "With mekeness aske perseverantly …": On Reading Julian of Norwich', *Mystics Quarterly* 30 (2004), pp. 125–40

Glasscoe, Marion, 'Means of Showing: An Approach to Reading Julian of Norwich', *Analecta Cartusiana* 106, 1 (1983), pp. 155–77

——, 'Visions and Revisions: A Further Look at the Manuscripts of Julian of Norwich', *Studies in Bibliography* 42 (1989), pp. 103–20

——, *English Medieval Mystics: Games of Faith* (London: Longman, 1993)

Greeson, Hoyt S., 'Glossary to the British Library Sloane 2499 Manuscript', in *Julian of Norwich, Showing of Love: Extant Texts and Translation*, ed. Sister Anna Maria Reynolds and Julia Bolton Holloway (Florence: Sismel, 2001), pp. 627–82

Hagan, Susan K., 'St Cecelia and St John of Beverly: Julian of Norwich's Early Model and Late Affirmation', in *Juluan of Norwich: A Book of Essays*, ed. Sandra J. McEntire (New York and London: Garland, 1998), pp. 90–114

Inge, William Ralph, *Studies of English Mystics: St Margaret's Lectures 1905* (London: John Murray, 1906)

Jantzen, Grace M., *Julian of Norwich: Mystic and Theologian* (London and New York: Paulist Press, 1987)

Johnson, Lynn Staley, 'The Trope of the Scribe and the Question of Literary Authority in the Works of Julian of Norwich and Margery Kempe', *Speculum* 66 (1991), pp. 820–38

Jones, E. A., 'A Mystic by Any Other Name: Julian (?) of Norwich', *Mystics Quarterly* 33, 3–4 (2007), pp. 1–17

Kempster, H., 'A Question of Audience: The Westminster Text and Fifteenth-Century Reception of Julian of Norwich', in *Julian of Norwich: A Book of Essays*, ed. Sandra J. McEntire (New York and London, 1998), pp. 257–89

Llewelyn, Robert, *With Pity not Blame: The Spirituality of Julian of Norwich and* The Cloud of Unknowing (London: Darton, Longman and Todd, 1982)

——, *Memories and Reflections* (London: Darton, Longman and Todd, 1998)

——, (ed.), *Julian: Woman of our Day* (London: Twenty-Third Publications, 1985)

McAvoy, Liz Herbert, *Authority and the Female Body in the Writings of Julian of Norwich and Margery Kempe* (Cambridge: D. S. Brewer, 2004)

——, ' "… a purse fulle feyer": Feminising the Body in Julian of Norwich's *A Revelation of Love*', Leeds Studies in English n.s. 33 (2002), pp. 99–113

——, ' "And Thou, to Whom This Booke Shall Come": Julian of Norwich and Her Audience, Past, Present and Future', in *Approaching Medieval English Anchoritic and Mystical Texts*, ed. Dee Dyas, Valerie Edden and Roger Ellis, Christianity and Culture: Issues in Teaching and Research 2 (Cambridge: D. S. Brewer, 2005), pp. 101–13

McEntire, Sandra J. (ed.), *Julian of Norwich: A Book of Essays* (New York and London: Garland, 1998)

McInerney, Maud Burnett, ' "In the Meydens Womb": Julian of Norwich and the Poetics of Enclosure', in *Medieval Mothering*, ed. Bonnie Wheeler and John Carmi Parsons (New York: Routledge, 1996), pp. 157–82

McLean, Michael, 'Introduction', in *Julian: Woman of our Day*, ed. Robert Llewelyn (London: Twenty-Third Publications, 1985), pp. 1–10

Maissoneuve, Roland, 'The Visionary Universe of Julian of Norwich: Problems and Methods', in *The Medieval Mystical Tradition in England: Exeter Symposium I*, ed. Marion Glasscoe (Exeter: University of Exeter Press, 1980), pp. 86–98

——, *L'univers visionnaire de Julian of Norwich* (Paris: OEIL, 1987)

Masson, Cynthia, 'The Point of Coincidence: Rhetoric and the Apophatic in Julian of Norwich's *Showings*', in *Julian of Norwich: A Book of Essays*, ed. Sandra J. McEntire (New York and London: Garland, 1998), pp. 153–81

Miles, Laura Saetveit, 'Julian of Norwich and St Bridget of Sweden: Creating Intimate Space with God', in *The Rhetoric of the Anchorhold: Place, Space and Body within the Discourses of Enclosure*, ed. Liz Herbert McAvoy (Cardiff: University of Wales Press, 2008)

Nuth, Joan M., *Wisdom's Daughter: The Theology of Julian of Norwich* (New York: Crossroad Publishing, 1991)

Okulam, Frodo, *The Julian Mystique: Her Life and Teachings* (Ottawa: Twenty-Third Publications, 1998)

Park, Tarjei, 'Reflecting Christ: The Role of the Flesh in Walter Hilton and Julian of Norwich', in *The Medieval Mystical Tradition in England: Exeter Symposium V*, ed. Marion Glasscoe (Cambridge: D. S. Brewer, 1992), pp. 17–37

Pelphrey, Brant, *Love Was His Meaning: The Theology and Mysticism of Julian of Norwich*, Salzburg Studies in English Literature 92, 4 (Salzburg: Institut Für Anglistik Und Americanistik Universität Salzburg 1982)

Peters, Brad, 'A Genre Approach to Julian of Norwich's Epistemology', in *Julian of Norwich: A Book of Essays*, ed. Sandra J. McEntire (New York and London: Garland, 1998), pp. 115–52

Reynolds, Anna Maria, 'Some Literary Influences in the *Revelations* of Julian of Norwich', *Leeds University Studies in Language and Literature* 7–8 (1952), pp. 18–28

Riddy, Felicity, ' "Women Talking about the Things of God": A Late Medieval Sub-Culture', in *Women and Literature in Britain, 1150–1500*, ed. Carol M. Meale (Cambridge: Cambridge University Press, 1993), pp.104–27

——, 'Julian of Norwich and Self-Textualization', in *Editing Women*, ed. Ann M. Hutchison (Cardiff: University of Wales Press, 1998), pp. 101–24

——, '"Publication" before print: the case of Julian of Norwich', in *The Uses of Script and Print, 1300–1700*, ed. Julia Crick and Alexandra Walsham (Cambridge: Cambridge University Press, 2004) pp. 29–49

Robertson, Elizabeth, 'Medieval Medical Views of Women and Female Spirituality in the *Ancrene Wisse* and Julian of Norwich's *Showings*', in *Feminist Approaches to the Body in Medieval Literature*, ed. Linda Lomperis and Sarah Stanbury (Philadelphia: University of Pennsylvania Press, 1993), pp. 142–67

Staley, Lynn, 'Julian of Norwich and the Crisis of Authority', in David Aers and Lynn Staley, *The Powers of the Holy: Religion and Gender in Late Medieval English Culture* (Philadelphia: Pennsylvania State University Press, 1996), pp. 107–78

Sutherland, Annie, '"Our feyth is groundyd in goddes worde": Julian of Norwich and the Bible', in *The Medieval Mystical Tradition in England: Exeter Symposium VII*, ed. E. A. Jones (Cambridge: D. S. Brewer, 2004), pp. 1–20

Swanson, John, 'Guide for the Inexpert Mystic', in *Julian: Woman of our Day*, ed. Robert Llewelyn (London: Twenty-Third Publications, 1985), pp. 75–88

Thorne, Brian, *Mother Julian, Radical Psychotherapist*, Annual Julian Lecture 1993 (Norwich, undated)

——, *Julian of Norwich: Counsellor for our Age* (London: Guild of Pastoral Psychology, 1999)

Tugwell, Simon, 'Julian of Norwich as a Speculative Theologian', *Fourteenth-Century English Mystics Newsletter* 9 (1983), pp. 199–209

——, *Ways of Imperfection: An Exploration of Christian Spirituality* (London: Darton, Longman and Todd, 1984)

Upjohn, Sheila, *Mind out of Time* (Norwich, 1979)

——, *In Search of Julian of Norwich* (London: Darton, Longman and Todd, 1989)

——, *Why Julian Now? A Voyage of Discovery* (London: Eerdman's, 1997)

Ward, Benedicta, 'Julian the Solitary', in Kenneth Leech and Benedicta Ward, *Julian Reconsidered*, (Oxford: SLG Press, 1988), pp. 11–35

Watson, Nicholas, 'The Composition of Julian of Norwich's *Revelation of Love*', *Speculum* 68 (1993), pp. 637–83

——, '"Yf women be double naturally": Remaking "Womman" in Julian of Norwich's *Revelation of Love*', *Exemplaria* 8, 1 (1996), pp. 1–34

——, 'Visions of Inclusion: Universal Salvation and Vernacular Theology in Pre-Reformation England', *Journal of Medieval and Early Modern Studies* 27 (1997), pp.145–87

——, 'The Trinitarian Hermeneutic in Julian of Norwich's Revelations of Love', in *Julian of Norwich: A Book of Essays*, ed. Sandra J. McEntire (New York and London: Garland, 1998), pp. 61–90

——, 'The Middle English Mystics', in *The Cambridge History of Medieval English Literature*, ed. David Wallace (Cambridge: Cambridge University Press, 1999), pp. 539–65

——, 'Julian of Norwich', in *The Cambridge Companion to Medieval Women's Writing*, ed. Carolyn Dinshaw and David Wallace (Cambridge: Cambridge University Press, 2003), pp. 210–21

Watt, Diane, *Medieval Women's Writing: Works By and For Women in England, 1100–1500* (Cambridge: Polity Press, 2007)

Windeatt, Barry, 'Julian of Norwich and her Audience', *The Review of English Studies*, n.s. 28 (1977), pp. 1–17

——, 'The Art of Mystical Loving: Julian of Norwich', in *The Medieval Mystical Tradition in England: Exeter Symposium I*, ed. Marion Glasscoe (Exeter: University of Exeter Press, 1980), pp. 55–71

——, '"Pryvytes to us": Knowing and Re-vision in Julian of Norwich', in *Chaucer to Shakespeare: Essays in Honour of S. Ando*, ed. Toshiyuki Takamiya and Richard Beadle (Cambridge: D. S. Brewer, 1992), pp. 87–98

——, 'Julian of Norwich', in *A Companion to Middle English Prose*, ed. A. S. G. Edwards (Cambridge: D. S. Brewer, 2004), pp. 67–81

Wright, Michael J., 'Julian of Norwich's Early Knowledge of Latin', *Neuphilologische Mitteilungen* 94 (1993), pp. 37–45

Wright, Robert E., 'The "Boke Performyd": Affective Technique and Reader Response in the *Showings* of Julian of Norwich', *Christianity and Literature* 36, 4 (1987), pp. 13–32


*Background and context*

Ackerman, R.W., 'The Liturgical Day in *Ancrene Riwle*', *Speculum* 53 (1978), pp. 734–44

Alexander, Jonathan and Paul Binski (eds), *Age of Chivalry: Art in Plantagenet England 1200–1400*, Royal Academy of Arts (London: Orion Publishing Co. Ltd, 1987)

Alford, John, 'Biblical *Imitatio* in the Writings of Richard Rolle,' *ELH* 40 (1973), pp.1–23

Anderson, M. D., *The Imagery of British Churches* (London: John Murray, 1955)

Armstrong, Karen, *The End of Silence: Women and the Priesthood* (London: Fourth Estate, 1993)

Aston, Margaret, *Faith and Fire: Popular and Unpopular Religion, 1350–1600* (London: Hambledon Press, 1993)

——, 'Lollards and the Cross', in *Lollards and their Influence in Late Medieval England*, ed. Fiona Somerset, Jill C. Havens and Derrick G. Pitard (Cambridge: D. S. Brewer, 2003), pp. 99–113

Atherton, Ian, Eric Fernie, Christopher Harper-Bill and Hassell Smith (eds), *Norwich Cathedral; Church, City and Diocese 1096–1996* (London: Hambledon Continuum, 1996)

Auerbach, Eric, 'The Brown Stocking', in *Mimesis: The Representation of Reality in Western Literature* (Princeton: Princeton University Press, 1953)

Bachelard, Gaston, *The Poetics of Space*, trans. Maria Jolas (Boston: Beacon Press, 1964)

Bakhtin, M., *Problems of Dostoevsky's Poetics* (Ann Arbor: Ardis, 1973)

——, *Dialogic Imagination* (Austin, Texas and London: University of Texas Press, 1992)

Barratt, Alexandra, 'The Prymer and English Passion Lyrics', *Medium Aevum* 44 (1975), pp. 264–79

——, 'Anchoritic Aspects of *Ancrene Wisse*', *Medium Aevum* 49 (1980), pp. 32–56

de Beauvoir, Simone, *The Second Sex*, ed. and trans. H. M. Parshley (London: Picador, 1988)

Bell, D., *What Nuns Read: Books and Libraries in Medieval English Nunneries* (Kalamazoo: Western Michigan University Press, 1995)

Bennett, Judith M., 'Patriarchal Equilibrium', in Judith M. Bennett, *History Matters: Patriarchy and the Challenges of Feminism* (Philadelphia: University of Pennsylvania Press, 2006)

Bestul, T. H., *Texts of the Passion: Latin Devotional Literature and Medieval Society* (Philadelphia: University of Pennsylvania Press, 1996)

Bhattacharji, S., 'Medieval Contemplation and Mystical Experience', in *Approaching*

*Medieval English Anchoritic and Mystical Texts*, ed. Dee Dyas, Valerie Edden and Roger Ellis, Christianity and Culture: Issues in Teaching and Research 2 (Cambridge: D. S. Brewer, 2005), pp. 51–62

Biernoff, Suzannah, *Sight and Embodiment in the Middle Ages* (New York: Palgrave, 2002)

Binski, Paul, *Medieval Death: Ritual and Representation* (London: Yale University Press, 1996; repr. 2001)

——, *Becket's Crown: Art and Imagination in Gothic England 1170–1300* (New Haven: Yale University Press, 2004)

Blanchot, Maurice, *The Space of Literature*, trans. and intro. Ann Smock (Lincoln, Nebraska: University of Nebraska Press, 1982)

Block, Ed, 'Interview with Denise Levertov', *Renascence* 50, 1–2 (1997), pp. 4–15

Blomefield, Francis, continued by Charles Parkin, *An Essay Towards a Topographical History of the County of Norfolk*, 5 vols (Norwich, 1739–75)

Bœspflug, François, *La Trinité dans l'Art d'Occident (1400–1460): Sept Chefs-d'œuvre de la Peinture* (Strasbourg: PUS, 2000)

Brigg, W. (ed.), *The Herts Genealogist and Antiquary* (Harpenden, 1895–99)

Broadie, Alexander, review of Katherine H. Tachau's *Vision and Certitude in the Age of Ockham: Optics, Epistemology and the Foundations of Semantics, 1250–1345*, *Speculum* 65, 4 (1990), pp. 1061–3

Brown, Carleton and Russell Hope Robbins (eds), *Index of Middle English Verse* (New York, 1943)

Brundage, James A. and Elizabeth Makowski, 'Enclosure of Nuns: The Decretal *Periculoso* and its Commentators', *Journal of Medieval History* 20 (1994), pp. 143–55

Burrow, J. A., 'Fantasy and Language in *The Cloud of Unknowing*', in *Essays on Medieval Literature* (Oxford: Oxford University Press, 1984), pp. 132–47

Bynum, Caroline Walker, *Holy Feast and Holy Fast: The Religious Significance of Food to Medieval Women* (Los Angeles and London: University of California Press, 1987)

——, *Fragmentation and Redemption: Essays on Gender and the Body in Medieval Religion* (New York: Zone Books, 1991)

Caciola, Nancy, *Discerning Spirits: Divine and Demonic Possession in the Middle Ages* (Ithaca, NY: Cornell University Press, 2003)

Camille, Michael, 'The Language of Images in Medieval England, 1200–1400', in *Age of Chivalry: Art in Plantagenet England 1200–1400*, ed. Jonathan Alexander and Paul Binski (London: Orion Publishing Co. Ltd, 1987), pp. 33–40

Cannon, Christopher, 'Enclosure,' *The Cambridge Companion to Medieval Women's Writing*, ed. Carolyn Dinshaw and David Wallace (Cambridge: Cambridge University Press, 2003), pp. 109–23

Carruthers, Mary, *The Book of Memory: A Study of Memory in Medieval Culture*, Cambridge Studies in Medieval Literature 10 (Cambridge: Cambridge University Press, 1990)

——, 'Sweetness', *Speculum* 81 (2006), pp. 999–1013

Cavaliero Glen, *Charles Williams: Poet of Theology* (London: Macmillan Press, 1983)

Chazelle, Celia M., 'Pictures, Books and the Illiterate: Pope Gregory I's letters to Serenus of Marseilles', *Word and Image* 6 (1990), pp. 138–53

Cheetham, Francis, *English Medieval Alabasters* (Oxford: Phaidon, 1984; repr. The Boydell Press, 2005)

Chenu, M. D., *La Théologie comme Science au XIIIe Siècle*, 3rd edn, Bibliothèque Thomiste 33 (Paris, 1957)

Clark, John P. H., *The Cloud of Unknowing: An Introduction*, Analecta Cartusiana 119, 4 (Salzburg: Institut für Anglistik und Amerikanistik, Universität Salzburg 1995)

Clay, Rotha Mary, *The Hermits and Anchorites of England* (London: Methuen, 1914)

Cockerell, S. C. and M. R. James, *Two East Anglian Psalters at the Bodleian Library* (Oxford: Printed for the Roxburghe Club by J. Johnson, 1926)

Cohen, Jeffrey Jerome, *Medieval Identity Machines* (Minneapolis: University of Minnesota Press, 2003)

Connell, R. W., *Masculinities* (Berkeley: University of California Press, 1995)

Constable, Giles, 'Ælred of Rievaulx and the Nun of Watton: An Episode in the Early History of the Gilbertine Order', in *Medieval Women*, ed. Derek Baker (Oxford: Blackwell, 1978), pp. 205–26

Cotton, Simon, 'Mediaeval Roodscreens in Norfolk: Their Construction and Painting Dates', *Norfolk Archaeology* 40, pp. 44–54

Davies, Oliver, *A Theology of Compassion* (London: SCM Press, 2001)

Denton, Jeffrey, 'Image and History', in *Age of Chivalry: Art in Plantagenet England 1200–1400*, ed. Jonathan Alexander and Paul Binski (London: Orion Publishing Co. Ltd, 1987), pp. 20–5

Dinshaw, Carolyn, 'Margery Kempe', in *The Cambridge Companion to Medieval Women's Writing*, ed. Caroline Dinshaw and David Wallace (Cambridge: Cambridge University Press, 2003), pp. 222–39

Dodwell, Barbara, 'The Monastic Community', in *Norwich Cathedral; Church, City and Diocese 1096–1996*, ed. Ian Atherton, Eric Fernie, Christopher Harper-Bill and Hassell Smith (London: Hambledon Continuum, 1996), pp. 231–54

Dronzek, Anna, 'Gender Roles and the Marriage Market in Fifteenth-Century England: Ideals and Practices', in *Love, Marriage and Family Ties in the Later Middle Ages*, ed. Isabel Davis, Miriam Müller and Sarah Rees Jones (Turnhout: Brepols, 2003), pp. 63–76

Duffy, Eamon, 'Holy Maydens, Holy Wyfes: The Cult of Women Saints in Fifteenth- and Sixteenth-Century England', in *Women in the Church*, ed. W. J. Sheils and Diana Wood (Oxford: Blackwell, 1990), pp. 175–96

——, *The Stripping of the Altars: Traditional Religion in England c.1400–1580* (New Haven: Yale University Press, 1992)

Duggan, Lawrence G., 'Was art really the "book of the illiterate"?' *Word and Image* 5 (1989), pp. 227–51

Duncan, Thomas G. (ed.), *A Companion to the Middle English Lyric* (Cambridge: D. S. Brewer, 2005)

Elkins, Sharon, *Holy Women of Twelfth Century England* (Chapel Hill, NC: University of North Carolina Press, 1988)

Erickson, Carolly, *The Medieval Vision: Essays in History and Perception* (New York: Oxford University Press, 1976)

Erler, Mary C., 'English Vowed Women at the End of the Middle Ages', *Mediaeval Studies* 57 (1995), pp. 155–205

——, *Women, Reading and Piety in Late Medieval England*, Cambridge Studies in Medieval Literature (Cambridge: Cambridge University Press, 2002)

——, '"A Revelation of Purgatory" (1422); Reform and the Politics of Female Visions', *Viator* 38 (2007), pp. 321–47

Evans, C. Stephen (ed.), *Exploring Kenotic Christology: The Self-Emptying of God* (Oxford: Oxford University Press, 2006)

Finch, Jonathan, 'The Churches', in *Medieval Norwich*, ed. Carole Rawcliffe and Richard Wilson (London: Hambledon Continuum, 2004), pp. 49–72

Foucault, Michel, 'Of Other Spaces', trans. Jay Miskowiec, *Diacritics* 16, 1 (1986), pp. 22–7

Freitas, Donna, *Becoming a Goddess of Inner Poise: Spirituality for the Bridget Jones in All of Us* (San Francisco: Jossey Bass Wiley, 2005)

Fuss, Diana, *The Sense of an Interior: Four Writers and the Rooms that Shaped Them* (London: Routledge, 2004)

Gibson, Gail McMurray, *The Theater of Devotion: East Anglian Drama and Society in the Late Middle Ages* (Chicago: University of Chicago Press, 1989)

Gilchrist, Roberta, *Contemplation and Action: The Other Monasticism*, The Archaeology of Medieval Britain (London: Pinter, 1995)

——, *Norwich Cathedral Close: The Evolution of the English Cathedral Landscape* (Woodbridge: The Boydell Press, 2005)

——, and M. Oliva, *Religious Women in Medieval East Anglia: History and Archaeology c.1100–1540*, Studies in East Anglian History 1 (Norwich: University of East Anglia, 1993)

Greatrex, Joan, 'Monk Students from Norwich Cathedral Priory at Oxford and Cambridge, c.1300 to 1530', *English Historical Review* 106 (1991), pp. 555–83

——, *Biographical Register of the English Cathedral Priories of the Province of Canterbury c.1066 to 1540* (Oxford: Oxford University Press, 1997)

Gregory, Candace, 'Raising the Good Wife: Mothers and Daughters in Fifteenth-Century England', in *Reputation and Representation in Fifteenth-Century Europe*, ed. Douglas L. Biggs, Sharon D. Michalove and A. Compton Reeves (Leiden: Brill, 2004), pp. 145–67

Grise, A., 'Women's Devotional Reading in Late-Medieval England and the Gendered Reader', *Medium Aevum* 71 (2002), pp. 209–55

Gunn, Cate, *Ancrene Wisse: From Pastoral Literature to Vernacular Spirituality* (Cardiff: University of Wales Press, 2008)

Hackett, Benedict, 'William Flete's 'De Remediis contra Temptaciones' in its Latin and English Recensions: The Growth of a Text', *Mediaeval Studies* 26 (1964), pp. 210–30

——, Edmund Colledge and N. Chadwick, 'William Flete and the *De Remediis contra Temptaciones*', in *Medieval Studies presented to Aubrey Gwynn S. J.*, ed. J. A. Watt, J. B. Morrall and F. X. Martin (Dublin: Colm O. Lochlainn, 1961), pp. 330–48

Hamburger, Jeffrey F., 'The Place of Theology in Medieval Art History: Problems, Positions, Possibilities', in Jeffrey F. Hamburger and Anne-Marie Bouché, *The Mind's Eye: Art and Theological Argument in the Middle Ages* (Princeton: Princeton University Press, 2006), pp. 11–31

Hanna, Ralph, 'Some Norfolk Women and their Books, ca. 1390–1440', in *The Cultural Patronage of Medieval Women*, ed. J. Hall McCash (Athens: University of Georgia Press, 1996), pp. 288–305

——, 'John Dygon, Fifth Recluse of Sheen: His Career, Books and Acquaintance', in *Imagining the Book*, ed. Stephen Kelly and John J. Thompson (Turnhout: Brepols, 2006), pp.127–41

Harper-Bill, Christopher and Carole Rawcliffe, 'The Religious Houses', in *Medieval Norwich*, ed. Carole Rawcliffe and Richard Wilson (London: Hambledon Continuum, 2004), pp. 73–90

Hart, Kevin, *The Trespass of the Sign: Deconstruction, Theology and Philosophy* (Cambridge: Cambridge University Press, 1992)

Haskell, Ann S., 'The Paston Women on Marriage in Fifteenth-Century England', *Viator* 4 (1973), pp. 459–71

Haskins, Susan, *Mary Magdalen: Myth and Metaphor* (New York: Riverhead Books, 1993)

Hassall, A. G. and Dr W. O. Hassall, *Treasures of the Bodleian Library* (London: Gordon Fraser, 1976)

Heffernan, T. J. and E. A. Matter (eds), *The Liturgy of the Medieval Church* (Kalamazoo: Western Michigan University Press, 2001)

Hertz, Neil, *Textual Strategies: Perspectives in Post-Structuralist Criticism* (Ithaca: Cornell University Press, 1979)

Hollywood, Amy, *Sensible Ecstasy: Mysticism, Sexual Difference, and the Demands of History* (Chicago: University of Chicago Press, 2002)

Hussey, S. S., 'The Text of *The Scale of Perfection*: Book II', *Neuphilologische Mitteilungen* 65 (1964), pp. 75–92

Irigaray, Luce, 'Any Theory of the "Subject" has always been Appropriated by the "Masculine"', in *Speculum of the Other Woman*, trans. Gillian C. Gill (Ithaca: Cornell University Press, 1985), pp. 133–46

——, 'La Mystèrique', in *Speculum of the Other Woman*, trans. Gillian C. Gill (Ithaca: Cornell University Press, 1985), pp. 191–202

——, 'The Bodily Encounter with the Mother', in *The Irigaray Reader*, ed. Margaret Whitford (Oxford: Blackwell, 1991; various repr.), pp. 35–46

——, 'Questions', in *The Irigaray Reader*, ed. Margaret Whitford (Oxford: Blackwell, 1991; various repr.), pp. 133–9

James, Elizabeth, *The St Margaret's of Margery Kempe*, pamphlet

Jansen, Katherine Ludwig, 'Maria Magdalena: *Apostolorum Apostola*', in *Women Preachers and Prophets through Two Millennia of Christianity*, ed. Beverley Mayne Kienzle and Pamela J. Walker (Los Angles and London: University of California Press, 1998), pp. 57–96

Jones, E. A., 'A New Look into the *Speculum Inclusorum*', in *The Medieval Mystical Tradition in England, Ireland and Wales: Exeter Symposium VI*, ed. Marion Glasscoe (Cambridge, 1999), pp. 123–45

——, 'Christina of Markyate and the *Hermits and Anchorites of England*', in *Christina of Markyate: A Twelfth-Century Holy Woman*, ed. Samuel Fanous and Henrietta Leyser (London: Routledge, 2004), pp. 229–53

——, 'Hermits and Anchorites in Historical Context', in *Approaching Medieval English Anchoritic and Mystical Texts*, ed. Dee Dyas, Valerie Edden and Roger Ellis, Christianity and Culture: Issues in Teaching and Research 2 (Cambridge: D. S. Brewer, 2005), pp. 3–18

Kandiyoti, Deniz, 'Bargaining with Patriarchy', *Gender and Society* 2, 3 (1988), pp. 274–90

Katz, Steven (ed.), *Mysticism and Language* (Oxford: Oxford University Press, 1992)

Ker, N. R., 'Medieval Manuscripts from Norwich Cathedral Priory', *Transactions of the Cambridge Bibliographical Society* 1 (1949), pp. 1–28

——, *Medieval Libraries of Great Britain: A List of Surviving Books*, 2nd edn (London: Royal Historical Society, 1964)

Kessler, Michael and Christian Sheppard (eds), *Mystics: Presence and Aporia* (Chicago: University of Chicago Press, 2003)

Kirby, Joan W., 'Women in the Plumpton Correspondence: Fiction and Reality', in *Church and Chronicle in the Middle Ages: Essays Presented to John Taylor*, ed. Ian Wood and G. A. Loud (London: Hambleton Continuum, 1991), pp. 219–32

Knowles, John A., *Essays in the History of the York School of Glass-painting* (London and New York: SPCK, 1936)

Köpf, Ulrich, *Die Anfänge der theologischer Wissenschaftstheorie im 13. Jahrundert*, Beitrage zur historischen Theologie 49 (Tübingen: Mohr, 1974)

Kristeva, Julia, 'Revolution in Poetic Language', in *A Kristeva Reader*, ed. Toril Moi (Oxford: Blackwell, 1986), pp. 93–8

——, 'Stabat Mater', in *The Kristeva Reader*, ed. Toril Moi (New York: Columbia University Press, 1986), pp. 160–85

Kroesen, Justin E.A. and Regnerus Steensma, *The Interior of the Medieval Village Church* (Louvain: Peeters Publishers, 2004)

Krug, Rebecca, *Reading Families: Women's Literate Practice in Late Medieval England* (Ithaca: Cornell University Press, 2002)

Lawes, Richard, 'Can Modern Psychology Help Us Understand Baker's *Secretum Sive Mysticum?*', in *That Mysterious Man: Essays on Augustine Baker OSB 1575–1641*, ed. Michael Woodward (Abergavenny: Three Peaks Press, 2001) pp. 245–59

Leclercq, J., *The Love of Learning and the Desire for God*, trans. C. Mishrai (2nd edn, New York: Fordham University Press, 1974)

Leech, Kenneth, 'Contemplative and Radical: Julian meets John Ball', in *Julian: Woman of our Day*, ed. Robert Llewelyn (London: Twenty-Third Publications, 1985), pp. 89–101

Leyser, Henrietta, 'Hermits and Anchorites in Historical Context', in *Approaching Medieval English Anchoritic and Mystical Texts*, ed. Dee Dyas, Valerie Edden and Roger Ellis, Christianity and Culture: Issues in Teaching and Research 2 (Cambridge: D. S. Brewer, 2005), pp. 3–18

Lindley, Philip, *Image and Idol: Medieval Sculpture* (London: Tate Publishing, 2001)

Louth, Andrew, *The Origins of the Christian Mystical Tradition* (Oxford: Oxford University Press)

Luke, Helen, *Dark Wood to White Rose* (New York: Parabola Books, 1989)

McAvoy, Liz Herbert (ed.), and Mari Hughes-Edwards (eds), *Anchorites, Wombs and Tombs: Intersections of Gender and Enclosure in the Middle Ages* (Cardiff: University of Wales Press, 2005)

——, *Rhetoric of the Anchorhold: Place, Space and Body within the Discourses of Enclosure* (Cardiff: University of Wales Press, 2008)

——, 'Gender, Rhetoric and Space in the *Speculum Inclusorum, Letter to a Bury Recluse* and the Strange Case of Christina Carpenter', in *Rhetoric of the Anchorhold: Place, Space and Body in the Discourses of Enclosure*, ed. Liz Herbert McAvoy (Cardiff: University of Wales Press, 2008 forthcoming), pp. 111–26

McGinn, Bernard, 'Love, Knowledge and Unio Mystica in the Western Christian Tradition', in *Mystical Union and Monotheistic Faith: An Ecumenical Dialogue*, ed. Moshe Idel and Bernard McGinn (New York: Continuum International Publishing Group, 1989), pp. 59–86

——, *The Foundations of Mysticism*, vol. 1 of *The Presence of God: A History of Western Christian Mysticism* (New York, 1992)

——, *The Flowering of Mysticism: Men and Women in the New Mysticism, 1200–1350*, vol. 3 of *The Presence of God: A History of Western Christian Mysticism* (New York: Crossroad Publishing Company, 1998)

——, 'Theologians as Trinitarian Iconographers', in *The Mind's Eye: Art and Theological Argument in the Middle Ages*, ed. Jeffrey F. Hamburger and Anne-Marie Bouché (Princeton: Princeton University Press, 2006), pp. 186–207

McSheffrey, Shannon, *Gender and Heresy: Women and Men in Lollard Communities, 1414–1520* (Philadelphia: University of Pennsylvania Press, 1995)

Maddern, Philippa, 'A Woman and Her Letters: The Documentary World of Elizabeth Clere,' in *Maitresse of My Wit: Medieval Women, Modern Scholars*, ed. Louise D'Arcens and Juanita Feros Ruys (Turnhout: Brepols, 2004), pp. 29–45

——, 'Gentility', in *Gentry Culture in Late Medieval England*, ed. Raluca Radulescu and Alison Truelove (Manchester: Manchester University Press, 2005), pp. 18–34

Marks, Richard, *Image and Devotion in Late Medieval England* (Stroud: Sutton Publishing Ltd, 2004)

Marrow, James H., *Passion Iconography in Northern European Art of the Late Middle Ages and Early Renaissance: A Study of the Transformation of Sacred Metaphor into Descriptive Narrative* (Kortrijk: Ghemmert, 1979)

Marsh, Thomas, *The Triune God: A Biblical, Historical and Theological Study* (Dublin: Columba Press, 1994)

Martin, Roger, 'The State of Melford Church and our Ladie's Chappel at the East End, as I did know it', in David Dymond and Clive Paine, *The Spoil of Long Melford Church: The Reformation in a Suffolk Parish* (Ipswich: Salient Press, 1992)

Mary Philomena, Sister, 'St Edmund of Abingdon's Meditations before the Canonical Hours', *Ephemerides Liturgicae* 78 (1964), pp. 33–57

Matter, E. Ann, *The Voice of My Beloved: The Song of Songs in Western Medieval Christianity*, Middle Ages Series (Philadelphia: University of Pennsylvania Press, 1990)

Merton, Thomas, *Conjectures of a Guilty Bystander*, ed. Thomas More (New York: Doubleday, 1989)

Millett, Bella, '*Ancrene Wisse* and the Book of Hours', in *Writing Religious Women: Female Spiritual and Textual Practices in Late Medieval England*, ed. Denis Renevey and Christiania Whitehead (Cardiff: University of Wales Press, 2000), pp. 21–40

Mills, David, '"Look at me when I'm speaking to you": The "Behold and See" Convention in Medieval Drama', *Medieval English Theatre* 7, 1 (1985), pp. 4–12

Minnis, A. J., 'Literary Theory in Discussions of *Formae Tractandi* by Medieval Theologians', *New Literary History* 11 (1979–80), pp. 133–45

——, 'The Sources of *The Cloud of Unknowing*: A Reconsideration', in *The Medieval Mystical Tradition in England: Exeter Symposium I*, ed. Marion Glasscoe (Exeter: University of Exeter Press, 1982), pp. 63–75

——, 'Affection and Imagination in and *The Cloud of Unknowing* and Hilton's *Scale of Perfection*', *Traditio* 39 (1983), pp. 323–66

——, 'Affection and Imagination in "The Cloud of Unknowing" and Hilton's "Scale of Perfection"', *Traditio* 39 (1983), pp. 323–66

——, *Medieval Theory of Authorship: Scholastic Literary Attitudes in the Later Middle Ages* (London: Scolar Press, 1984)

Moreton, C. E., *The Townshends and their World: Gentry, Law, and Land in Norfolk c.1450–1551* (Oxford: Oxford University Press, 1992)

Morgan, Nigel, 'The Coronation of the Virgin by the Trinity and Other Texts and Images of the Glorification of Mary in Fifteenth-Century England', in *England in the Fifteenth Century*, ed. Nicholas Rogers, Proceedings of the 1992 Harlaxton Symposium (Stamford: Paul Watkins, 1994), pp. 223–41

Morris, Colin, *The Sepulchre of Christ and the Medieval West: From the Beginning to 1600* (Oxford: Oxford University Press, 2005)

Mulder-Bakker, Anneke B., *Lives of the Anchoresses: The Rise of the Urban Recluse in Medieval Europe* (Philadelphia: University of Pennsylvania Press, 2005)

Newman, Barbara, *God and the Goddesses: Vision, Poetry and Belief in the Middle Ages* (Philadelphia: University of Pennsylvania Press, 2005)

Oliva, Marilyn, 'Aristocracy or Meritocracy? Office-Holding Patterns in Late Medieval English Nunneries', in *Women in the Church*, ed. W. J. Sheils and Diana Wood (Cambridge: D. S. Brewer, 1991), pp. 197–208

——, *The Convent and the Community in Late Medieval England: Female Monasteries in the Diocese of Norwich, 1350–1540* (Woodbridge: The Boydell Press, 1998)

Olson, Linda, and Kathryn Kerby-Fulton (eds), *Voices in Dialogue: Reading Women in the Middle Ages* (Notre Dame: University of Notre Dame Press, 2005)

Pächt, Otto and J. J. G. Alexander, *Illuminated Manuscripts in the Bodleian Library, Oxford, Vol. 3: British, Irish and Icelandic Schools* (Oxford: Oxford University Press, 1973)

Page, William (ed.), *Victoria History of the County of Norfolk* (University of London Institute of Historical Research, Folkestone: Dawson, 1975)

Parker, Patricia, *Literary Fat Ladies: Rhetoric, Gender, Property* (London and New York: Methuen, 1987)

Parkes, M. B. 'The Literacy of the Laity', in *Literature and Western Civilisation*, The Mediaeval World vol. 2, ed. D. Daiches and A. Thorlby (London: Aldus Books, 1973), pp. 555–78

Phillips, Kim M., *Medieval Maidens: Young Women and Gender in England, 1270–1540* (Manchester: Manchester University Press, 2003)

Pritchard, Gillian, 'Religion and the Paston Family', in *Daily Life in the Late Middle Ages*, ed. Richard Britnell (Stroud: Sutton Publishing Ltd, 1998), pp. 65–82

Raguin,Virginia Chieffo, 'Real and Imaged Bodies in Architectural Space: The Setting for Margery Kempe's *Book*', in *Women's Space: Patronage, Place, and Gender in the Medieval Church*, ed. Sarah Stanbury and Virginia Chieffo Raguin (Albany: State University of New York Press, 2005)

Raw, B., 'The Prayers and Devotions in the Ancrene Riwle', in *Chaucer and Middle English Studies in Honour of Rossell Hope Robbins*, ed. B. Rowland (London: Allen and Unwin, 1974), pp. 260–71

Rawcliffe, Carole and Richard Wilson (eds), *Medieval Norwich* (London: Hambledon Continuum, 2004)

Renevey, Denis, *Language, Self and Love: Hermeneutics in the Writings of Richard Rolle and the Commentaries on the Song of Songs* (Cardiff: University of Wales Press, 2001)

——, and Christiania Whitehead (eds), *Writing Medieval Women: Female Spiritual and Textual Practices in Late Medieval England* (Cardiff: University of Wales Press, 2000)

Richmond, Colin, *John Hopton: A Fifteenth-Century Suffolk Gentleman* (Cambridge: Cambridge University Press, 1981)

——, 'The Pastons Revisited: Marriage and the Family in Fifteenth-Century England', *Bulletin of the Institute of Historical Research* 58 (1985), pp. 25–36

——, 'Elizabeth Clere, Friend of the Pastons', in *Medieval Women: Texts and Contexts in Late Medieval Britain: Essays for Felicity Riddy*, ed. Jocelyn Wogan-Browne, Rosalynn Voaden, Arlyn Diamond *et al.* (Turnhout: Brepols, 2000), pp. 251–73

Ricoeur, Paul, 'Philosophy and Religious Language', *Journal of Religions* 54, 1 (1974), pp. 71–85

Riddy, Felicity, *Regionalism in Late Medieval Manuscripts and Texts* (Cambridge: D. S. Brewer, 1991)

——, ' "Women talking about the things of God": A Late-Medieval Sub-Culture', in *Women and Literature in Britain 1150–1500*, ed. Carol M. Meale, 2nd edn (Cambridge: Cambridge University Press, 1996), pp. 104–27

Riehle, Wolfgang, *The Middle English Mystics*, trans. Bernard Standring (London: Routledge and Kegan Paul, 1981)

Roberts, Michèle, *Walking on the Water: Women Talk About Spirituality*, ed. Jo Garcia and Sara Martland (London: Virago, 1983)

Rosenthal, Joel T., 'Local Girls do it Better: Women and Religion in Late Medieval East Anglia,' in *Traditions and Transformations in Late Medieval England*, ed. Douglas

Biggs, Sharon D. Michalove and A. Compton Reeves (Leiden: Brill, 2002), pp. 1–20

Ross, Charles, 'The Estates and Finances of Richard Beauchamp Earl of Warwick', Dugdale Society Occasional Papers 12 (1956), pp. 1–22

Rubin, Miri, *Corpus Christi: The Eucharist in Late Medieval Culture* (Cambridge: Cambridge University Press, 1991)

——, 'An English Anchoress: The Making, Unmaking and Remaking of Christine Carpenter', in *Pragmatic Utopias: Ideals and Communities 1200–1630*, ed. Rosemary Horrox and Sarah Rees Jones (Cambridge: Cambridge University Press, 2001), pp. 204–17

Rudy, Gordon, *Mystical Language of Sensation in the Later Middle Ages*, Studies in Medieval History and Culture (New York and London, 2002)

Rushforth, G. McN., *Medieval Christian Imagery* (Oxford: Clarendon, 1936)

Sandler, Lucy Freeman, *The Peterborough Psalter in Brussels and Other Fenland Manuscripts* (London: Harvey Miller, 1974)

Schiller, Gertrud, *Iconography of Christian Art*, trans. Janet Seligman, 2 vols; vol. 2 *The Passion of Jesus Christ* (London: Lund Humphries, 1972)

Scott, Kathleen *et al.* (eds), *An Index of Images in English Manuscripts: From the Time of Chaucer to Henry VIII c.1380–c.1509*, 3 vols (Turnhout: Brepols, 2002)

Sells, Michael, *Mystical Languages of Unsaying* (Chicago: University of Chicago Press, 1994)

Sheingorn, Pamela, 'The Bosom of Abraham Trinity: A Late Medieval All Saints Image', in *England in the Fifteenth Century: Proceedings of the 1986 Halaxton Symposium*, ed. Daniel Williams (Woodbridge: The Boydell Press, 1987), pp. 273–95

Sheldrake, Philip, *Spirituality and Theology: Christian Living and the Doctrine of God* (London: Darton, Longman and Todd, 1998)

Shinners, John R., 'The Veneration of Saints at Norwich Cathedral in the Fourteenth Century', *Norwich Archaeology* 40 (1988), pp. 133–44

Simpson, James, *The Oxford English Literary History Volume 2: 1350–1547: Reform and Cultural Revolution* (Oxford: Oxford University Press, 2002)

Sitwell, G., 'Private Devotions in the *Ancrene Riwle*', in *The Ancrene Riwle*, ed. and trans. M. B. Salu (Exeter: University of Exeter Press, 1990), pp. 193–6

*Spiritus: A Journal of Christian Spirituality* 5, 1 (2005)

Spurgeon, Caroline, *Shakespeare's Imagery and What it Tells Us* (Cambridge: Cambridge University Press, 1975)

Stanbury, Sarah, 'Visualizing', in *A Companion to Chaucer*, ed. Peter Brown (Malden, Massachusetts: Blackwell Publishers Ltd, 2000), pp. 459–79

Sutherland, Annie, 'The Dating and Authorship of the *Cloud* Corpus: A Reassessment of the Evidence', *Medium Aevum* 71 (2002), pp. 81–100

——, 'Biblical Text and Spiritual Experience in the English Epistles of Richard Rolle', *Review of English Studies* n.s. 56 (2005), pp. 697–711

——, 'Religious Practice', in *Medieval Norwich*, ed. Carole Rawcliffe and Richard Wilson (London: Hambleton Continuum, 2004), pp. 137–55

Tanner, Norman, *The Church in Late Medieval Norwich 1370–1532* (Toronto: Pontifical Institute of Medieval Studies, 1984)

——, 'The Cathedral and the City', in *Norwich Cathedral: Church, City and Diocese 1096–1996*, ed. Ian Atherton, Eric Fernie, Christopher Harper-Bill and Hassell Smith (London: Hambledon Continuum, 1996), pp. 255–80

Tillotson, John, 'Visitation and Reform of the Yorkshire Nunneries in the Fourteenth Century', *Northern History* 30 (1994), pp. 1–21

Truelove, Alison, 'Literacy', in *Gentry Culture in Late Medieval England*, ed. Raluca

Radulescu and Alison Truelove (Manchester: Manchester University Press, 2005), pp. 84–99

Turner, Denys, *The Darkness of God: Negativity in Christian Mysticism* (Cambridge: Cambridge University Press, 1995)

Virgoe, Roger, 'The Divorce of Sir Thomas Tuddenham', *Norfolk Archaeology* 34 (1969), pp. 406–18

——, 'The Ravishment of Joan Boys', in *East Anglian Studies: Essays Presented to J. C. Barringer on his Retirement*, ed. Adam Longcroft and Richard Joby (Norwich: Marwood, 1995), pp. 276–81

Voaden, Rosalynn, *God's Words, Women's Voices: The Discernment of Spirits in the Writing of Later-Medieval Women Visionaries* (York: York Medieval Press, 1999)

Warren, Ann K., *Anchorites and their Patrons in Medieval England* (Berkeley: University of California Press, 1985)

Warren, Nancy Bradley, *Spiritual Economies: Female Monasticism in Later Medieval England* (Philadelphia: University of Pennsylvania Press, 2001)

Watson, Nicholas, 'Conceptions of the Word: The Mother Tongue and the Incarnation of God', in *New Medieval Literatures* 1, ed. Wendy Scase, Rita Copeland and David Lawton (Oxford: Clarendon, 1997), pp. 85–124

——, 'The Middle English Mystics', in *The Cambridge History of Medieval English Literature*, ed. David Wallace (Cambridge: Cambridge University Press, 1999), pp. 539–65

Watt, Diane, *Secretaries of God: Women Prophets in Late Medieval and Early Modern England* (Cambridge: D. S. Brewer, 1997)

Whitaker, Elaine E., 'Reading the Paston Letters Medically', *English Language Notes* 31 (1993), pp. 19–27

Williams, Charles, *The Descent of the Dove* (London: Faber and Faber, 1939)

Williams, Rowan, *The Wound of Knowledge* (Cambridge, Mass.: Cowley Publications, 1990)

——, *Lost Icons* (Edinburgh: T. and T. Clark, 2002)

——, *Ponder These Things* (Norwich: Canterbury Press, 2002)

Withycombe, Elizabeth Gidley (ed.), *Oxford Dictionary of English Christian Names*, 2nd edn (London: Clarendon Press, 1950)

Wogan-Browne, Jocelyn, 'Analytical Survey 5: "Reading is Good Prayer": Recent Research on Female Reading Communities', in *New Medieval Literatures* 5, ed. Wendy Scase, Rita Copeland and David Lawton (Oxford: Oxford University Press, 2002), pp. 229–97

Woolf, Virginia, *A Room of One's Own* (San Diego: Harcourt Press, 1981)

Yoshikawa, Naoë Kukita, *Margery Kempe's Meditations: The Context of Medieval Devotional Literatures, Liturgy and Iconography* (Cardiff: University of Wales Press, 2007)

Zijlstra, Onno (ed.), *Letting Go: Rethinking Kenosis* (Bern: Peter Lang, 2002)

Zimmerman, B., 'The White Friars at Ipswich', *Proceedings of the Suffolk Institute of Archaeology* 10 (1891–1900), pp. 196–20

Zumthor, Paul, *Speaking of the Middle Ages* (Lincoln, Nebraska: University of Nebraska Press, 1986)

Websites
http://www.ecusa.anglican.org/75383_76300_ENG_HTM.htm
http://www.norfolkchurches.co.uk

# Index

(Page numbers in **bold** type refer to illustrations and their captions)